Community Recreation
and People with Disabilities

Community Recreation and People with Disabilities
Strategies for Inclusion
Second Edition

◆ ◆ ◆ ◆

Stuart J. Schleien, Ph.D., CTRS, CLP
University of Minnesota
Minneapolis, Minnesota

M. Tipton Ray, M.Ed., CTRS
Inclusive and Therapeutic Recreation
St. Paul, Minnesota

Frederick P. Green, Ph.D., CTRS
University of Southern Mississippi
Hattiesburg, Mississippi

·P·A·U·L·H·
BROOKES
PUBLISHING Cº

Baltimore • London • Toronto • Sydney

Paul H. Brookes Publishing Co.
Post Office Box 10624
Baltimore, Maryland 21285-0624

Typeset by Brushwood Graphics Inc., Baltimore, Maryland.
Manufactured in the United States of America by
The Maple Press Company, York, Pennsylvania.

Library of Congress Cataloging-in-Publication Data
Schleien, Stuart J.
   Community recreation and people with disabilities : strategies for
   inclusion / by Stuart J. Schleien, M. Tipton Ray, Frederick P.
   Green.
      p.   cm.
   Rev. ed. of : Community recreation and persons with disabilities. 1988.
   Includes bibliographical references (p.   ) and index.
   ISBN 1-55766-259-2
   1. Handicapped—Recreation—United States. 2.   Handicapped—Services for—United
States. 3.   Recreation centers—United States. 4.   Recreational surveys—United States.
I.   Ray, M. Tipton. II.   Green, Frederick P. III.   Schleien, Stuart J. Community recreation
and persons with disabilities. IV.   Title.
GV183.5.S35   1997   96-7795
790.1'96'0973—dc20   CIP

British Library Cataloguing-in-Publication data are available from the British Library.

Contents

◆ ◆ ◆ ◆ ◆

List of Tables and Figures

◆ ◆ ◆ ◆ ◆

About the Authors

◆ ◆ ◆ ◆ ◆

Stuart J. Schleien, Ph.D., CTRS, CLP, School of Kinesiology and Leisure Studies, University of Minnesota, 224 Cooke Hall, 1900 University Avenue, S.E., Minneapolis, MN 55455

Dr. Schleien is Professor and Division Head in Recreation, Park, and Leisure Studies, with a joint appointment in Special Education, at the University of Minnesota. Internationally recognized for his service and scholarly contributions in the fields of therapeutic recreation and special education, Dr. Schleien was the recipient of the Theodore and Franklin Roosevelt Award for Excellence in Recreation and Park Research in 1996 by the National Recreation and Park Association, the Researcher of the Year Award in 1990 by the Minnesota Recreation and Park Association, and the Educator of the Year Award in 1987 by Arc Minnesota. He is the author of nearly 100 journal articles, research monographs, and book chapters, and has written seven books in the areas of inclusive community recreation and outdoor education, lifelong leisure and friendship skills development, and therapeutic recreation. He has presented his work throughout the United States and Canada and in Australia, England, Germany, Israel, and Sweden.

M. Tipton Ray, M.Ed., CTRS, 807 Fairmount Avenue, St. Paul, MN 55105

Mr. Ray is a consultant in private practice with a focus on inclusive and therapeutic recreation. Mr. Ray's professional recreation career spans 20 years and includes strong practitioner experiences as a therapeutic recreation specialist for a nursing home and ICF/MR; a leisure advocate/integration coordinator for a county Arc; a co-ordinator of local, state, and federal recreation-related grant initiatives; an ADA consultant; and a wilderness/outdoor recreation instructor/trip leader for mixed ability groups. He has worked extensively with Scouts, summer camp staff, group home care providers, parent groups, educators, and other key players. Mr. Ray has authored several journal articles, curricula, and guidebooks related to inclusive community recreation, leisure education and school transition, and self-determination in outdoor recreation settings and has presented at many national workshops and conferences on these topics.

Frederick P. Green, Ph.D., CTRS, School of Human Performance and Recreation, University of Southern Mississippi, Box 5142, Hattiesburg, MS 39406

Dr. Green is Assistant Professor of Therapeutic Recreation at the University of Southern Mississippi. He has been serving people with disabilities in community and outdoor settings since the mid-1970s. He has extensive outdoor and camp experience with individuals with severe disabilities, with service ranging from camp counselor to camp director. As Coordinator of the Recreational Sports–Disabled Student Recreation Program at Southern Illinois University, he created and developed innovative programs for including students with disabilities in recreational sports programs. He is focusing his research on the social inclusion of individuals with cognitive disabilities.

About the Contributors

◆ ◆ ◆ ◆ ◆

Maurice K. Fahnestock, M.Ed., CTRS, Division of Recreation, Park, and Leisure Studies, University of Minnesota, 204-B Cooke Hall, 1900 University Avenue, S.E., Minneapolis, MN 55455

Mr. Fahnestock has worked since the early 1980s with children and adults with disabilities and their families in community, park and recreation, school, community education, group home, and institutional settings. He is a doctoral candidate, graduate research assistant, and an instructor at the University of Minnesota.

Linda A. Heyne, Ph.D., CTRS, University of Minnesota, 109 Norris Hall, 172 Pillsbury Drive, S.E., Minneapolis, MN 55455

Dr. Heyne is Research Associate at the Rehabilitation Research and Training Center, Institute on Community Integration, and Associate Graduate Faculty with the School of Kinesiology and Leisure Studies. She coordinates the Intergenerational Inclusive Preschool Project at the Jewish Community Center of the Greater St. Paul Area. Since the mid-1980s, her research and professional efforts have been directed toward including people with disabilities in community recreation, working with families, intergenerational programming, and using qualitative research methods.

Jennifer B. Mactavish, Ph.D., Health, Leisure and Human Performance Research Institute, Physical Education and Recreation Studies, University of Manitoba, 310 Max Bell Centre, Winnipeg, Manitoba, R3T 2N2 Canada

Dr. Mactavish is Assistant Professor and Research Associate whose past professional experiences and current research interests focus on people with developmental disabilities and their families and issues specific to enhancing life quality through community therapeutic recreation, physical activity, and sport.

Leo H. McAvoy, Ph.D., CLP, Division of Recreation, Park, and Leisure Studies, University of Minnesota, 209 Cooke Hall, 1900 University Avenue, S.E., Minneapolis, MN 55455

Dr. McAvoy is Professor at the University of Minnesota. His research involves educational techniques for visitors to park areas and outdoor education resources, high-risk outdoor adventure, personal and social benefits of wilderness, and management of outdoor adventure programs. He has published the results of his research in numerous journals, books, and symposium proceedings. He has presented his work at national and international professional conferences and symposia on interpretation, outdoor education, integrated wilderness programs, outdoor leadership, and the environmental management of park lands. He has chaired the Leisure Research Symposium at the National Recreation and Park Association Annual Congress and is a member of the Academy of Leisure Sciences.

John E. Rynders, Ph.D., Department of Educational Psychology, University of Minnesota, 255 Burton Hall, Minneapolis, MN 55455

Dr. Rynders is Professor in Special Education Programs at the University of Minnesota where he specializes in mental retardation and early education/special education. He is experienced as a teacher of people with disabilities of all ages, as a school principal, and as a researcher on topics such as early intervention/family support and inclusive programming. Dr. Rynders has published numerous articles and was awarded the Theodore Tjossem Outstanding Research Award by the National Down Syndrome Congress for his work with people who have Down syndrome and their family members. He has just completed a book, *Down Syndrome, Birth to Adulthood: Giving Families an EDGE* (Love Publishing Co., 1996).

Foreword to the First Edition

◆ ◆ ◆ ◆ ◆

Community Recreation and Persons with Disabilities: Strategies for Integration is the first text that provides both the conceptual framework and the specifics of application relative to integrated leisure lifestyles for persons with disabilities. As such, it responds to an issue that will become an increasingly important social priority as the 21st century approaches.

The conceptual foundation for this text rests on the interrelated aspects of the least restrictive environment and environmental or ecological models for active participation in recreation. Given this foundation, concepts discussed in the text may be readily applied to the challenge of developing programs that are meaningful and accessible for all people—not just individuals with disabilities.

The least restrictive environmental approach to program development requires an identification of the functional strengths of the potential participant and the provision of an environment, modified only to the minimal degree necessary, that corresponds to the abilities of the participant. Nondisabled persons, for example, utilize least restrictive environments by skiing on beginner ski slopes, or by scoring handicaps at the golf course or at the bowling alley. Integration of the person with a disability into the lifestyle of the community involves a process that differs only minimally from the generic social integration process utilized by society as a whole.

The environmental or ecological model for program development addresses the milieu of activity involvement instead of the prevailing pattern of myopic attention to the activity. Again, the issues are common to society as a whole, and are not unique to individuals with disabilities. Transportation, fees and charges, the skill demands of an activity (as determined by activity analyses), dress codes, levels of competition, and so on are as exclusionary to activity participation for the "normal" population as for persons with disabilities.

Based upon this conceptual foundation, authors Stuart J. Schleien and M. Tipton Ray have provided a clear and valid application of the process approach to the integration of persons with disabilities within the spectrum of community leisure services. Following a thorough presentation of the planning process, the authors address the innovative issues of environmental assessment and modification, behavioral analysis and functional growth, and the evaluation process, with specific attention to the cognitive, affective, and psychomotor domains. A key strength of

---

This foreword, written by Dr. Fred Humphrey for the first edition of this book, has been reprinted here in the second edition as a special tribute to this great leader and pioneer in therapeutic recreation and inclusive recreation services. This writing remains timeless, as have most of his thoughts and ideas, as he continues to guide our efforts.

the text is the closing chapter, which provides a series of case studies that clearly illustrate the application of concepts and approaches in a community setting.

The excellent balance achieved by the authors between conceptual issues and the application process is a testament to the expertise of Schleien and Ray in the development of integrated community-based programs. Dr. Schleien's professional career has been heavily focused, both as a practitioner and as an educator, in the area of community integration of persons with disabilities. The texts and journal articles authored by Dr. Schleien have made significant contributions to the fields of therapeutic recreation and special education. Similarly, Mr. M. Tipton Ray, who is in the final stages of his doctoral program at the University of Minnesota, has a sound, unique, and varied background of practitioner experiences that contributes substantially to the conceptual–application balance in the text.

Human services face a multitude of challenges as the 21st century approaches. In this excellent textbook, Schleien and Ray have provided a framework for service delivery that has not only generic application to all populations but also has basic relevance to all human services providers—whether they are social workers, special educators, doctors, nurses, therapeutic recreators, or parents.

Fred Humphrey, Ph.D., CTRS, CLP
University of Maryland
1922–1994

Preface

◆ ◆ ◆ ◆ ◆

L ife, Liberty, and the Pursuit of Happiness. These are the inalienable rights of
citizens of the United States. This does not imply that only those citizens "of
sound mind and body" are protected by our country's constitution. *All* American citizens have these rights, and, therefore, every citizen should have access to all of the
programs and services available in the community—medical, religious, educational, and recreational. The purpose of this second edition is to provide a practical
and philosophical basis for including children and adults with disabilities in community leisure services and to examine the planning, design, implementation, and
evaluation of inclusive community recreation programs.

We have learned a great deal about accommodating individuals of varying abilities in inclusive programs and settings. In fact, we no longer are satisfied with the
mere physical integration of individuals; our only goal is for individuals with disabilities to become socially included in programs and services. This goal is reflected
in the change in the book's title to *Community Recreation and People with Disabilities: Strategies for **Inclusion*** (formerly *Integration*).

This book represents the culmination of almost 20 years of work involving the
inclusion of children and adults with disabilities in community environments. Its
major focus is on modifying existing services so that they can accommodate all
people who want to participate versus merely developing or providing additional
segregated services. The authors understand and accept the place for separate,
"handicapped-only," recreation programs within the continuum of leisure service
delivery. For people with disabilities, however, these segregated programs must be
considered only as second-priority alternatives.

The nine chapters in this book grew out of the relative dearth of specific information on designing, implementing, and evaluating inclusive community leisure
services. Efforts have been made to provide information and guidelines on the following issues and topics most commonly sought by therapeutic recreation specialists, community recreation professionals, parents, care providers, and teachers:

- Why should community leisure services be accessible to everyone?
- What are the roles and responsibilities of recreation professionals, families,
  teachers, and other key players in the recreation inclusion process?
- How does one implement inclusive recreation programs that meet the needs of
  participants both with and without disabilities?
- How do we facilitate friendships and other social relationships within the con-
  text of inclusive recreation?
- How are these program participants and programs evaluated?

- Do exemplary programs exist that could be replicated in other community recreation settings?

Chapter 1 establishes the rationale and philosophical basis for providing community leisure services and for including people with disabilities in these programs. This chapter includes a definition and brief historical overview of community leisure services and special populations. Much of the discussion focuses on segregated versus inclusive services and on the impact of mandatory legislation such as the Individuals with Disabilities Education Act (IDEA) of 1990 and the Americans with Disabilities Act (ADA) of 1990 on the educational and leisure services provided to people with disabilities. The many advantages of inclusive leisure services to all citizens, including individuals without disabilities, are examined.

In Chapter 2, a program planning process is presented that systematically produces guidelines for planning inclusive community leisure services. The planning of the ideal program—the truly accessible and inclusive program—is delineated as the final component of the continuum of service model. A process of inclusive leisure services designating the tasks to be accomplished by community recreation professionals is discussed in detail. Also, an inclusive community leisure services planning and implementation model is presented that defines the roles and responsibilities of professionals, parents, care providers, and other "key players." In order to conduct a "shared responsibility delivery system" of leisure services, a networking matrix displaying these players' collaboration in the system is examined. Other general strategies that could be employed by a municipality to promote inclusive leisure services are outlined. These strategies include conducting architectural accessibility surveys of community facilities, establishing community leisure advisory boards, and providing in-service training to existing staff at these sites.

Chapter 3 is a response to the many studies and reports that detail common obstacles to inclusive recreation. Perceived and real barriers to inclusive recreation are identified and systematically addressed. Specific programmatic and administrative solutions to common barriers are suggested, including a state-of-the-art and replicable architectural accessibility survey.

Chapter 4, authored by Dr. Jennifer B. Mactavish, is a new chapter for this second edition. This chapter offers a broad perspective on the nature of, benefits of, and constraints to family recreation. Through our programming efforts, we have come to realize how necessary it is to include family members and other care providers in every aspect of the program, from the identification of needs to the final evaluation, and everything in between. The chapter's most important element is its presentation of strategies to help families build bridges with community professionals.

The Recreation Inventory for Inclusive Participation is presented in Chapter 5; this provides a systematic approach for studying environments and for overcoming obstacles to participating in community recreation programs. This inventory is used as an initial screening device for future participation and as a means of identifying necessary skills for participating in the environment or activity. This fundamental tool assists the program planner in identifying modifications and strategies to enhance participation by people with disabilities and to promote friendship among the participants.

Chapter 6 is another new chapter for this second edition. Written by Dr. John E. Rynders and Maurice K. Fahnestock, it introduces and illustrates five specific strategies for enhancing the social inclusion of participants with disabilities. In addition, it summarizes the status of opportunities for inclusive recreation, offers a set of recommended professional practices, and provides a case study describing the efforts of a municipal park and recreation department that has been implementing inclusive recreation services since the 1970s.

Chapter 7 is the third new chapter for the book. Written with Dr. Linda A. Heyne, the authors take a critical view of the development of friendships and other relationships within the context of inclusive recreation. Intrinsic strategies (e.g., social skills development) and extrinsic strategies (e.g., preparing environments for friendly encounters) are described in detail. A friendship evaluation procedure concludes the chapter.

Chapter 8 contains vital information on participant and program evaluation. This chapter presents instrumentation and easily followed step-by-step procedures on conducting evaluations in the recreation agency. An added feature of this section is the inclusion of all forms necessary for the evaluation process, which are presented in completed fashion in the chapter and as blank forms in Appendix F for easy reproduction.

The final chapter of this edition, Chapter 9, provides the reader with a wealth of information regarding seven exemplary programs from around the United States and from Israel. These exemplary programs illustrate the types of viable intervention strategies that may be implemented in a variety of recreation environments. The reader may discover a situation in one of these programs that closely parallels his or her own setting and may perhaps glean some specific suggestions from the information contained in this chapter. These exemplary programs are presented clearly and comprehensively so that they are replicable by other agencies. One might argue that successful major systems changes are unique to the municipality and that any attempt to disseminate strategies for change (e.g., segregated to inclusive programs) is difficult and useless. We believe that by disseminating these model programs, other agencies could make any necessary modifications to their services and could anticipate similar obstacles in future program endeavors.

Appendices of references and resources, including blank forms for use by the reader, are provided. These detailed appendices should prove to be a valuable resource for therapeutic recreation specialists, community recreation professionals, parents, care providers, and teachers who are attempting to create inclusive recreation programs. A complete annotated bibliography containing 30 annotations of the most current and relevant literature concerning community leisure services and people with disabilities is provided.

This book represents the efforts of a group of parents and professionals in community recreation, therapeutic recreation, special education, adapted physical education, and psychology. These individuals represent the administrative, programmatic, and familial perspectives that are necessary to promote inclusive community leisure services, and they have taken a proactive approach to ensuring that existing leisure services become accessible to children and adults with and without disabilities. No longer can society afford to exclude people from programs based on their special needs or challenges. Regardless of the type of disability, each member of the community has the right to full participation in community recreation. Professionals and families must continue to work toward total accessibility and social inclusion and consequent full participation through the structuring and restructuring (i.e., engineering) of recreational environments and activities.

The time has come to adopt a new way of thinking, founded on the premise that the community belongs to everyone, and everyone belongs in the community.

The authors propose that the following four principles be incorporated in every model guiding the development of inclusive recreation services:

- Programs designed for people must be age suitable and based on personal interest, not on diagnosis or label.
- Programs preparing people for inclusive recreation participation must occur within their home communities, not in restrictive, contrived, and irrelevant environments.
- Communication and coordination among participants, family members, and practitioners must occur if inclusive services are to be initiated and are to thrive over time.
- Participants with and without disabilities, family members, and recreation practitioners must take a shared responsibility approach to help ensure that every community member's needs and interests are met, including the recreation and social needs of entire families.

By including people with disabilities in typical recreation programs, the authors strongly believe that the entire community benefits. Through exposure to and ongoing interaction with people with disabilities, individuals without disabilities gain knowledge about and become more sensitive to individual differences, develop more accepting attitudes, and broaden their own opportunities for friendship.

It is our intent to share what we have learned over 20 years about community recreation services and people with disabilities in order to reach these goals. The ultimate goal was expressed eloquently by then-President George Bush in 1990: *"With today's signing of the landmark Americans with Disabilities Act, every man, woman, and child with a disability can now pass through once-closed doors into a bright new era of equality, independence, and freedom."* We wish you much success in your endeavors. Please feel free to communicate with us about your successes and needs.

Acknowledgments

◆ ◆ ◆ ◆ ◆

We are honored to present this second edition to the professional, lay, and academic communities, and we wish to express our appreciation to those who have played a significant role in its conceptualization and development. We are grateful for their creative efforts, generous cooperation, and personal and professional example.

We are excited to add to this revised edition important and timely contributions crucial to any inclusion effort. We are pleased to include recent work of Dr. Jennifer B. Mactavish, Assistant Professor, Recreation Studies Degree Program, University of Manitoba; and Dr. Linda A. Heyne, Research Associate and Coordinator, Inclusive Recreation Project, Institute on Community Integration, University of Minnesota, both of whom are quickly developing an international reputation for their efforts to enlighten and educate recreation professionals about the critical roles that families play in the inclusive leisure experience and the powerful relationship between leisure and friendship, respectively. Their efforts are helping professionals to provide leisure experiences that are truly more inclusive. Maurice (Mo) K. Fahnestock, Teaching Assistant and Doctoral Candidate, Division of Recreation, Park, and Leisure Studies, University of Minnesota, is a welcome addition as he has much to offer the recreation professional. Mo has been a consummate leader in the inclusive leisure movement during and since his position as supervisor of adaptive recreation for a large suburban park and recreation department. Finally, we are particularly excited to include Dr. John E. Rynders, Professor, Special Education Programs, University of Minnesota, as one of our chapter authors. Dr. Rynders is nationally known for his efforts to successfully include individuals with disabilities in recreational and educational programs, and we feel fortunate to have him share his expertise here.

We wish to formally express our appreciation to the people who authored the stories in Chapter 9, which so aptly illustrate for readers that inclusion is possible and that it is happening in ways that benefit everyone involved. We strongly encourage readers to contact these people to talk with them further about their efforts and ways that their inclusion approaches may be replicated in the readers' home communities. There are many examples of inclusive community recreation programs throughout the United States. We attempted to find a few that exemplified our aims in this edition and that had relevance to our readers. There are many, many more examples we would have liked to share. These efforts legitimize our efforts. We hope that these efforts are receiving the recognition and support that they justly deserve. In particular, we want to thank the following colleagues whose practical solutions and professional vision bolstered our writing of this edition: Dale Abell, Director, Technical Assistance Services/Accessibility Consulting Group, the Ability Center of Greater Toledo, Sylvania, Ohio; the Institute on Community Integration, University of Minnesota; Cynthia Burkhour, Inclusive Recreation Consultant, Jenison, Michigan; Jill McLaughlin and Jennifer Bowerman, formerly of the Extended Services Department, Rockford, Illinois, Park District; South Suburban Adaptive Recreation (Bloomington, Richfield, Edina, Eden Prairie) Minnesota; The Arc Ramsey County; and members of the Leisure/Recreation Committee, The Association for Persons with Severe Handicaps (TASH).

Students striving to appreciate the inclusion movement know that the philosophical impetus for our efforts has roots in the international community. We are pleased, therefore, to include among our exemplary programs an example from Israel. We are grateful to the timely efforts of Dr. Shlomo Katz, Professor, Psychology Department, and Dr. Chaya Schwartz, Associate Professor, School of Social Work, both at Bar-Ilan University, Tel Aviv, Israel, to share their story with readers; we know that inclusion efforts, whether state or local, national or international, have relevance and importance to our increasingly global community.

Special thanks are extended to Christa Horan, Production Editor for Paul H. Brookes Publishing Co., for her conscientious editing of the manuscript.

We also would like to thank Kay Lowinske and Joni Strozyk for their diligent efforts in word processing multiple drafts of this text. It is not always an easy task interpreting margin notes from multiple authors, but they have done so capably. We are especially delighted that Kay was available to assist with both the first and the second edition of this book.

Most important, we wish to express our sincere appreciation to all of the key players who desire to be active participants in the inclusion movement. We are especially impressed by the many people within our home communities who, through their shared values and beliefs, sheer determination, advocacy, hard work, and cooperation, demonstrate by example that communities belong to and should be shared by *everyone*. This inspires us to excel in our efforts to make communities inclusive. These communities continue to be the proving grounds for the inclusion strategies included in this text. However, there is still much to be done. We are grateful that they have allowed us the opportunity to be their partners in the critical venture we call *Inclusion*.

We wish to dedicate this book to
Dana, Jenna, and Alexa.
Evan, my EBGB and recreation inspiration.
Mary, Paul, and Robert.

In memory of Dr. Fred Humphrey
(1922–1994)

Community Recreation
and People with Disabilities

Community Recreation and People with Disabilities

◆ ◆ ◆ ◆ ◆

To become the basis of daily thought and action, inclusion, like any value, must be personal and relevant for each individual. Instead of providing a definition of inclusion, we must now ask people to define inclusion for themselves. . . . Through this dialogue, a more personal connection and understanding is made about what inclusion really means and, hopefully, how essential it is for all of us.

J. York, 1993, p. 2

Participating in recreation activities is an important aspect of life in U.S. society. Active, vital, and socially connected individuals participate in a wide range of activities and settings during their lifetime. This active leisure lifestyle includes participating in individual and team games, athletic programs in schools, recreational sports on college campuses, team and individual activities sponsored by places of employment, outdoor education activities, and family recreation. Many people recognize the immense value of quality recreation programs and facilities. Intramural recreational sport programs, for example, are the most regularly attended activities, with the exception of academic classes, by students on college campuses (Bohlig, 1991). Recreation activities that meet the needs of individuals in community and social settings promote physical health and conditioning and provide participants with opportunities for developing social relationships and new skills. They also help individuals find a desirable balance between recreation and work. Families that recreate together typically are happier and more cohesive as a unit (Mactavish, 1994, 1995).

Unfortunately, recreation programming has had relatively low priority in programs for people with disabilities. This neglect is unfortunate because participating in recreation activities has been found to be an important factor in successful community adjustment (Hayden, Lakin, Hill, Bruininks, & Copher, 1992; Hill &

Bruininks, 1981; Schleien, Meyer, Heyne, & Brandt, 1995). In recognition of the need for such programs, specific recreation and leisure skill educational techniques (Schleien, Kiernan, & Wehman, 1981; Voeltz, Wuerch, & Wilcox, 1982) and leisure education curricula (Bender & Valletutti, 1976; Dattilo, 1991; Ray, 1994; Rynders & Schleien, 1991; Schleien, Meyer, et al., 1995; Wehman & Schleien, 1981; Wessel, 1976; Wetherald & Peters, 1986) have been developed since the 1970s for people with disabilities. Participating in recreation activities is associated not only with developing collateral skills (Newcomer & Morrison, 1974; Schleien, Heyne, & Dattilo, 1995; Schleien et al., 1981; Strain, Cooke, & Apolloni, 1976) but also with reducing maladaptive behaviors (Adkins & Matson, 1980; Flavell, 1973; Schleien et al., 1981; Voeltz & Wuerch, 1981).

Although the short- and long-term benefits of recreation programs for people with disabilities continue to be recognized, the quality of available services still needs improvement. Specific recreation and leisure skill instruction in home and school environments is needed to enable people with disabilities to participate maximally in community recreation activities, and communities must make specific efforts to accommodate such programs.

The rationale for developing recreation opportunities in community settings for people with disabilities is well established from both theoretical (e.g., social value) and practical (e.g., deinstitutionalization) perspectives. Recreation participation in community settings offers the person with a disability the opportunity to develop a positive self-concept through successful experiences and satisfying relationships with peers. Channels for self-expression, opportunities to interact with the environment, and establishing a more personally fulfilling way of life are other positive results of participating in inclusive community recreation.

Federal legislation supports children and adults with disabilities by prohibiting discrimination against people with disabilities by architectural as well as programmatic constraints. It has facilitated the movement of large numbers of people with disabilities into community living situations, which places the responsibility for recreation and other programming upon community agencies. In short, the laws have paved the way for people with disabilities to live, learn, work, and recreate in settings alongside peers without disabilities.

Providing inclusive services, however, requires a great deal of preparation— acquiring fundamental skills, for example—by recreation professionals, care providers, and the participants themselves. At the same time, the concerns of the professionals and family members must be anticipated to facilitate programs that meet the leisure and social needs of all of the residents of a community. The recreation service delivery system that successfully accommodates individuals with and without disabilities in community settings, therefore, must be carefully designed by several key players in a collaborative and comprehensive manner. ("Key players" are defined and discussed in Chapter 2.)

HISTORICAL OVERVIEW

But what then am I? A thing which thinks. What is a thing which thinks? It is a thing which doubts, understands, conceives, affirms, denies, wills, refuses, which also imagines and feels.

R. Descartes, 1964, p. 31

To borrow from Descartes, "But what then is a person with a disability?" Too often, such an individual is considered to be one who does not think, feel, or imagine and exists at the will of society. She or he is thought of as living in a condition of perpetual dependency on others, a condition generally regarded as disgraceful and, often, despicable. Individuals with disabilities generally have been ignored by society. Indeed, society has considered individuals with disabilities to be unworthy of equal membership (Repp, 1983).

Historically, people with disabilities have been treated poorly, even cruelly. Evidence of cruelty to individuals with disabilities can be found as far back as the Spartans of ancient Greece, who eliminated people with disabilities because they were considered "imperfect." In Rome, people with disabilities survived as fools or court jesters and, later, in France and Germany, as neighborhood and court buffoons. As centuries passed, individuals with disabilities occasionally were provided with food, clothing, and shelter but not with treatment; nor did they enjoy the rights and protections that existed for citizens without disabilities. During the Middle Ages (about A.D. 400 to A.D. 1500), some individuals with disabilities were regarded with superstitious reverence, while others were subjected to crude cranial surgery, purgation, and rituals of exorcism to "drive out the devil." In the mid-17th century, homeless, outcast, and bodily and mentally infirm people were placed in asylums. Once institutionalized, they received no treatment, rehabilitation, or education; only minimal custodial care was provided.

Some isolated advances in the treatment of individuals with disabilities appeared in the 18th century, harbingers of things to come. In 1785, Valentine Haüy founded a school in Paris for educating blind people, and, at about the same time, work was begun in both Germany and France to educate people with hearing impairments. In 1794, Phillipe Pinel went into an asylum and abolished the whips, chains, and stocks then used to control inmates and replaced them with kindness and gentleness, which proved to be much more effective.

The actual beginnings of therapeutic treatment, however, occurred during the early 1800s when drives for education and political reform became widespread in the Western world. Between 1800 and 1950, some humanitarians and educators became concerned with the problem of educating people with disabilities. Systematic programs of sensorimotor training were developed, the first compulsory school laws to provide educational services were enacted, and institutional care for some was initiated. The first successful public residential institutions for people with disabilities were established in France, Germany, and the United States. By 1898, a total of 24 state schools were in operation in 19 of the United States. Also, laboratories were developed to prepare teachers to work with people with disabilities. But inclusion was still the dream of the future; institutions still kept people out of community life and perpetuated the belief that people with disabilities were "different."

The late 19th century saw the rise of professional organizations for teachers and other personnel who worked with individuals with disabilities. Since 1950, more interest has been taken on behalf of individuals with disabilities than at any other period in history. Opportunities to participate actively in community life have been extended to people with disabilities through various legislative acts at the local, state, and federal levels. The tortuous path to inclusion followed by people with disabilities parallels the one followed by ethnic and other minority groups.

FEDERAL LEGISLATION AND ITS
EFFECTS ON RECREATION PROGRAMMING

Since 1920, many of the problems confronting people with disabilities have been addressed in legislation and in programs initiated at the federal level. For example, the Social Security Act of 1935 (PL 74-271) provided federal grants-in-aid to states for maternal and child health and welfare and for services to children with physical disabilities.

In the 1950s, congressional action increased the funding for various research, educational, and vocational training projects to address the needs of individuals with disabilities. In the Cooperative Research in Education Act of 1954 (PL 83-531), for instance, Congress provided financial support for research concerning the education of children with disabilities. In the following year, PL 85-926 was enacted. It provided aid through grants to universities and colleges and to state educational agencies to prepare teachers and other professionals to work in the field of mental retardation. The Mental Retardation Facilities and Community Mental Health Centers Construction Act of 1963 (PL 88-164) extended PL 85-926 to include the training of professionals to work with children with all types of disabilities. The Elementary and Secondary Education Act of 1965 (PL 89-10) expanded the definition of "disadvantaged" to include school-age people living in state residential institutions or state-supported private schools (Repp, 1983).

The philosophical shift from segregated to inclusive recreation programs has been fueled primarily by landmark federal legislation that encourages advocates to support people with disabilities. Pertinent legislation and how each act has influenced recreation services are listed in Table 1.1. It should be noted that, at the time of this printing, several of these laws are up for renewal. For example, the Individuals with Disabilities Education Act (IDEA) of 1990 is being considered for reauthorization in both the House of Representatives and the Senate. The proposals contain amendments that may weaken the rights of people with disabilities. Some groups are proposing to eliminate the requirement for related services such as physical and occupational therapy and therapeutic recreation.

The Architectural Barriers Act of 1968 (PL 90-480) requires that all buildings and facilities designed, constructed, altered, or leased with federal funds be made accessible and usable by individuals with physical disabilities. Recreational facilities built with federal contributions are included.

The Rehabilitation Act of 1973 was the first law to address rehabilitative services for people with disabilities. It authorized more than $1 billion for training and placing people with intellectual and physical disabilities in employment. Section 504, "Nondiscrimination under Federal Grants," or the "Civil Rights Act for Persons with Handicaps," prohibits discrimination solely on the basis of disability. This act has served as the legal basis for many civil rights lawsuits involving discrimination against people with disabilities.

The Education for All Handicapped Children Act of 1975 mandated "free and appropriate public education and related services" for all children with disabilities in the "least restrictive environment." Every local school district is required to formulate an individualized education program (IEP) for each child covered by the act; the IEP must be based on each child's unique needs. Recreation is included in "related services." The implication is that parents who choose to have their child receive instruction in recreation activities can insist that goals and objectives for the activities be included in the child's IEP.

Table 1.1.　Federal legislation relating to recreation services for people with disabilities

Year	Law	Influences on recreation
1968	Architectural Barriers Act (PL 90-480)	Requires recreation facilities to be made accessible
1973	Rehabilitation Act (PL 93-112)	Prohibits discrimination in recreation programs on the basis of disability
1975	Education for All Handicapped Children Act (PL 94-142)	Identifies recreation as a "related service" in public education
1986	Education of the Handicapped Act Amendments (PL 99-457)	Mandates early intervention programs, including recreational services
1990	Individuals with Disabilities Education Act (IDEA) (PL 101-476)	Identifies therapeutic recreation as a related or support service as part of transition plans
1990	Americans with Disabilities Act (PL 101-336)	Expands civil rights in the areas of employment, public accommodations, public services, transportation, and telecommunications
1994	Elementary and Secondary Education Act (PL 103-382)	Supports families in their promotion of inclusive services

In 1986, amendments (PL 99-457) were enacted to strengthen the Education for All Handicapped Children Act by mandating preschool programs for 3- to 5-year-olds with disabilities as well as early intervention program plans for infants and toddlers (from birth to 3 years) with disabilities and their families.

The Individuals with Disabilities Education Act (IDEA) of 1990 reauthorized PL 94-142 once again. This law not only guarantees public education and related services for all children with disabilities but also requires that transition plans be included in secondary-age students' IEPs. IDEA mandates identifying necessary transition services, which include independent living and community participation, among others. Therapeutic recreation is identified as a related or support service that can be requested as part of the IEP requirement.

The Americans with Disabilities Act of 1990 comprehensively eliminated discrimination against people with disabilities in the areas of employment, transportation, public accommodations, public services, and telecommunications. Potential employers are forbidden to discriminate against qualified individuals with disabilities and are required to provide reasonable accommodations at worksites for people with disabilities. All new public transportation and demand–response service vehicles are required to be made accessible. All areas of public accommodation, including recreational areas, must be made accessible, and nondiscriminatory practices must be implemented. In addition, telephone companies are required to provide relay services to individuals with hearing and speech impairments.

One final law that works in favor of the inclusive community recreation movement is PL 103-382, the Elementary and Secondary Education Act of 1994, which was reauthorized by the U.S. Senate. It enables family members to become increasingly involved in and more assertive about decisions concerning the quality of their children's lives, whether the children live in or out of the family home. Section 315 contains the Families of Children with Disabilities Support Act of 1994. This family advocacy legislation includes support for families that try to promote the inclusion of their children with disabilities in all aspects of community life. In addition, it promotes the use of existing social networks, strengthens natural sources of support, and promotes the building of connections to existing community resources and services.

Because of these landmark policy changes and their effects on services for people with disabilities, parents, therapeutic recreation specialists, and skilled recreation professionals (i.e., those skilled workers who have not received traditional training in services for people with disabilities) have actively sought ways to ensure equal access in inclusive recreation environments. Despite the many segregated programs that continue to be offered, the trend is toward new, inclusive alternatives that provide options for individuals with disabilities who want to have typical leisure lifestyles like those of their peers without disabilities.

Agencies throughout the world have responded by working toward the social and participatory inclusion of individuals with disabilities in existing programs. The mission statements that are being written by such inclusive agencies contain strong and direct language to meet both the recreation and the social needs of people who traditionally have not been served. The following sample mission statements reflect the values that are espoused throughout this book.

The Jewish Community Center of the Greater St. Paul Area is a social work agency created by and primarily for the benefit of the Jewish community. The agency purposes are to enhance the Jewish educational effectiveness of all its programs; to enhance the physical, emotional, social, and intellectual growth and development of people of all ages; to strengthen the family; and to develop positive identification with one's Jewish background and heritage. The JCC is a family agency. The whole family is given the opportunity to participate in a wide variety of activities, in addition to the programs available to your child with a special need. While JCC membership is required, no one will be denied participation in programs due to an inability to pay. Confidential fee adjustments can be arranged if a family is unable to afford full membership and program costs. The Center is open to everyone regardless of race, religion, national origin, disability, age, gender, sexual orientation, or ability to pay.

South Suburban Adaptive Recreation (SSAR) enhances opportunities for residents who have disabilities to actively participate in recreational programs. SSAR provides these opportunities in either integrated or segregated settings, depending upon the individual's desire. The purpose of this program is to provide community education, recreation/leisure programs, and related services designed for residents who have disabilities within the four suburban areas of Bloomington, Richfield, Edina, and Eden Prairie, Minnesota. Integration allows individuals who have disabilities the opportunity to participate in recreation programs with nondisabled peers. We will make every reasonable effort to help residents with disabilities participate in the programs. To ensure a safe, positive integrative experience, staff will talk with each participant and their parents to get to know the participant's desires, abilities, and needs prior to the beginning of the program.

Parents, practitioners, and researchers should continue to examine and reexamine effective ways to promote inclusive recreation programming. Topics of particular interest may include developing friendships and other relationships between people who do and do not have disabilities, increasing consumer and family support and involvement, overcoming architectural and attitudinal barriers, making neighborhoods and entire communities more inclusive, serving children with emotional and behavioral disorders and attention-deficit/hyperactivity disorder in inclusive programs, and changing systems to provide more inclusive and enduring services.

NEEDS ASSESSMENT: AN EVALUATIVE TOOL

Austin, Peterson, Peccarelli, Binkley, and Laker (1977) distributed questionnaires to municipal park and recreation departments and the health care and correctional facilities in Indiana to determine the status of therapeutic recreation services. Of the 50 responding parks and recreation departments, 80% expressed the belief that their agencies should provide recreation services to people with disabilities. Although 76% of these departments offered some form of therapeutic recreation service, in only 5% was the person in charge a therapeutic recreation specialist. For 92% of the departments, the presence of a specially trained staff member was cited as essential to establishing an accommodative program. These data revealed that 1) the existing programs were not extensively developed, 2) a majority of the community recreation departments were not adequately serving individuals with disabilities, and 3) correctional facilities offered even fewer therapeutic recreation services to inmates.

Schleien, Porter, and Wehman (1979) addressed the topic of community recreation services in a survey of community agencies and programs in the state of Virginia. The purpose of their investigation was to assess the roles of the various agencies in providing for the leisure needs of people with developmental disabilities. The sample included county and regional parks and recreation departments, special education coordinators of public school systems, community mental health and mental retardation service boards, state hospitals serving people with mental illness and mental retardation, and other programs funded by the Virginia Developmental Disabilities Unit of the Virginia Department of Mental Health and Mental Retardation.

Some form of recreation service was offered to people with developmental disabilities by 69% of the agencies; 31% offered no recreation services at all. This finding indicated a need for more ongoing (rather than sporadic) recreation services in the state. Some responding agencies admitted providing inadequate recreation; of them, 66% reported that they could generate improvements if professional expertise and appropriate instructional materials were made available, and 58% specified the need for a relevant leisure skills curriculum on which to base programs.

To determine the quantity and quality of recreation programs and services in Minnesota, Schleien and Werder (1985) conducted a needs assessment inventory of park and recreation departments, community education agencies, and schools. Returns were received from 73% of the units. The collected data enabled the investigators to 1) identify perceived responsibilities and the degree of coordination among agencies, 2) determine the scope and nature of special recreation services offered, and 3) determine the extent of inclusion of participants with and without disabilities. The study also revealed several weaknesses and needs in recreation services throughout the state as well as ideal opportunities for future growth in service provision.

In a more recent survey, Schleien, Germ, and McAvoy (in press) asked 484 community leisure service agencies in Minnesota to identify the professional practices that they used and the barriers that they encountered to include people with disabilities. The more ubiquitous inclusionary practices included increased financial assistance to serve individuals with disabilities; more outreach to families, care providers, and program users; and greater use of program adaptations. Constraints included perceived staff skill deficiencies and participant-to-staff ratio inadequacies. On the whole, it appears that many more individuals with disabilities are being included in community recreation activities in the mid-1990s than in years past.

Based on careful analysis of the various obstacles to developing recreation skills and community access found in Minnesota, five recommendations, which may be applicable to programs in many states, follow (Schleien et al., in press; Schleien & Werder, 1985):

1. Establish distinct networks of communication across agencies to reduce duplicating effort and to complement resources.
2. Expand the range of recreation activity offerings.
3. Encourage and establish more inclusive community recreation programs.
4. Increase the number of specially trained personnel, and support them across agencies.
5. Generally improve access to and availability of community recreation programs.

Using a national sample of 336 adults with mental retardation who lived in foster and small group homes, Hayden et al. (1992) found that the lifestyles of these individuals were less than that expected or considered desirable. The investigators highlighted that a large proportion of residents reported to have "practically never" participated in leisure activities that are considered customary in our culture: engaging in hobbies, visiting friends, attending a sporting event, going to meetings and clubs, and participating in community center activities. A high proportion of the residents of the foster and group homes regularly engaged in passive activities, such as watching television, taking car rides, and listening to the radio or records.

In earlier studies conducted throughout the United States to evaluate the status of recreation services that are available to individuals with disabilities, Edginton, Compton, Ritchie, and Vederman (1975) and Lancaster (1976) identified the major factors inhibiting the widespread provision of inclusive services: 1) lack of funding, 2) poorly trained professional personnel, and 3) lack of awareness of the need for community recreation services for individuals with disabilities. These findings are similar to the constraints identified by Schleien et al. (in press).

The finding that few inclusive recreation service delivery models have been developed at the community level is not confined to any one state. Furthermore, few of the existing validated community leisure service delivery systems address the total lifestyle and leisure needs of people with disabilities and their families who live in communities with larger populations of people without disabilities; that is, they may live in the communities, but they are not part of the communities. Thus, although the delivery of therapeutic recreation services is legally mandated and although many communities have at least verbalized their acceptance of the responsibility to provide inclusive services, the necessary personnel, methods, and procedures to implement the mandates and draw people with disabilities into the mainstream of the community have not been adequately developed.

NORMALIZATION AND INCLUSIVE COMMUNITY LEISURE SERVICES

Therapeutic recreation preference has shifted from providing specialized and separate services to including people with disabilities in general recreation programs. This shift in philosophy is the result of a series of national trends propelled by the deinstitutionalization movement and the concepts of normalization and what Wolfensberger (1972, 1983, 1995) labeled "social role valorization."

Normalization is a Scandinavian concept that has served as a guiding principle for all services to people with disabilities. According to Lakin and Bruininks (1985), the intent of using normalization as a guiding principle is not to make people with disabilities "normal" but to set a standard by which all services to people with disabilities can be measured. Accordingly, services to people with disabilities and the manner in which the services are delivered should be as close to the cultural norm as possible (Nirje, 1969). This means that community recreation services and activities for people with disabilities should not be different, nor should they be separated from the services received by peers without disabilities, just because the individual has a disability.

Deinstitutionalization is a social policy change that is partially a reflection of adherence to the least restrictive environment, which is the environment in which the needs of the individual can best be met while simultaneously affording the individual the greatest opportunity to interact with peers without disabilities. Deinstitutionalization refers to changing the residential service system so that people with disabilities are less likely to live in institutional settings and more likely to live in community (or normalized) settings. The impact of the deinstitutionalization movement is that people with disabilities are more likely to be living in the community and thus are more likely to be asking for community-based recreation services. As a result, community recreation personnel should soon expect that a natural proportion (or approximately 10%) of participants in community recreation programs will have a disability. Reynolds (1981) summarized the major premise and corollaries of the normalization principle. After listing the common misconceptions that hinder the implementation of the principle, he went on to discuss normalization as it relates to recreation programming. He predicted (*in 1981*) a substantial shift in the roles and orientations of therapeutic recreation specialists and educators and then discussed the five trends that follow. These trends illustrated several new service functions and challenges:

1. Large group diversional activities and coordinated special events will be decreased in favor of *individualized* leisure and educational programming (emphasis added).
2. The medical model will be replaced by programming that is oriented toward leisure services.
3. Individuals will be taught appropriate behaviors using behavioral techniques, as applied behavior analysis methodologies will be reconciled with the principle of normalization.
4. Therapeutic recreation and special education personnel will adopt roles as advocates and as liaisons with communities to ensure respect for the rights of people with disabilities to participate in community leisure opportunities.
5. The problem of transfer of training and generalization will be addressed by teachers of leisure skills.

As applied to recreation programs, a normalization goal offers people with disabilities opportunities for physical access to settings with peers without disabilities as a means to learning social, leisure, and sports skills. A normalization process offers inclusive programming that promotes the total leisure lifestyles of people with disabilities. In short, the concept of normalization means that recreation providers look beyond individual techniques and programs to the broader scope of leisure delivery systems and how they influence social inclusion within community recreation settings for people with varying abilities.

Wolfensberger (1983) coined the term "social role valorization" to broaden the meaning of normalization: "The most explicit and highest goal of normalization must be the creation, support, and defense of valued social roles for people who are at risk of social devaluation" (p. 234).

Social role value, in other words, means bringing roles and conditions that are valued by the majority community to the lives of typically devalued people. Two paths can be followed to reach this goal: 1) develop the competencies of a culturally devalued individual, and 2) enhance the individual's social image or value in the perceptions of other members of society.

The concept of normalized and socially valued recreation services gained momentum throughout the 1970s and 1980s, and inclusive community recreation programming began to emerge. This period saw the beginning of empirical research to develop instructional strategies to promote the facilitation of recreation services. With the development of new instructional technologies, innovative research was demonstrating that people with disabilities could acquire age-appropriate (age-suitable) leisure and social skills in inclusive environments. Leisure skill instruction in inclusive settings has been found to promote social interaction between participants with and without disabilities, develop positive attitudes toward people with disabilities by participants without disabilities, and develop friendships among people of varying abilities (Green & Schleien, 1991; Heyne, Schleien, & McAvoy, 1993; Kennedy, Smith, & Austin, 1991; Schleien, Meyer, et al., 1995).

Although the normalization principle and social value concept have been guiding forces behind efforts to include people with disabilities, adherence to this philosophy by human services professionals does not guarantee that people with disabilities who live in the community will be less socially isolated than if they were living in large public institutions. Providing opportunities for people with disabilities to live in neighborhoods alongside residents without disabilities, to work, or to go to neighborhood schools is consistent with normalization, but such opportunities alone do not ensure that social inclusion will occur. All too often, people with disabilities who reside in communities have minimal contact with people without disabilities in their neighborhoods (Hayden et al., 1992). In addition, people with disabilities generally spend little time working and living in community environments (Crapps, Langone, & Swaim, 1985) and may actually decrease their involvement in community activities over time (Birenbaum & Re, 1979; Hayden et al., 1992). The extent of social inclusion in a community may be measured by how people with disabilities are viewed by their peers who do not have disabilities, how much of the environment they share, and how much they participate in the same kinds of social interactions as their peers without disabilities (Green, Schleien, Mactavish, & Benepe, 1995; Kunstler, 1985; Meyer & Kishi, 1985). Green and Schleien (1991) suggested that true social inclusion is achieved when regular and friendly interactions take place between community residents with and without disabilities.

Social role value and its accompanying social inclusion support accommodating individuals with disabilities in community recreation programs. The scarcity of segregated programs may suggest that inclusion thus far has been successful. Nevertheless, the fact that any segregated programs are still offered leads to the question of what is keeping them alive in the face of the growing belief that such programs are not consistent with social role value.

Evolution of Segregated Programs

In years past, segregated services often were initiated by parents whose children had disabilities. Indeed, voluntary parent associations were established initially to provide support services for such children (Ross, 1983). The absence of programs—or the reluctance of general program providers to accept children with disabilities—led parent associations (e.g., The Arc) to develop segregated recreation services. Meyer and Kishi (1985) studied the concerns expressed by parents regarding the quality, benefits, and safety of inclusive services and concluded that these concerns were best understood in the context of previous experiences with agencies. For example, parents who invested great amounts of time, money, and energy in providing needed services for children with disabilities understandably were hesitant to turn these children over to the very agencies that once were unwilling to provide for them.

Social attitudes also have been cited as a reason for the existence and proliferation of segregated programs. Wilkenson (1984) interviewed the personnel of various agencies that serve people with disabilities. Respondents reported that some parents whose children had disabilities feared that if the children participated in general programs with their peers without disabilities, they would suffer physical harm and isolation. At the same time, barriers to inclusion were erected by the attitudes and misconceptions of parents whose children did not have disabilities; these parents feared that their children would "catch" a disability or have a less valuable recreation experience in inclusive programs. Hence, these parents withdrew their children from inclusive programs.

In an exploratory study that addressed the nature and benefits of and constraints on recreation for families that included children with disabilities, Mactavish (1994) reported a number of useful suggestions by parents to facilitate the organization of inclusive recreation services. Mactavish also elicited several reasons for the continued failure of inclusive programs to accommodate individuals with disabilities and for the continued existence of segregated programs. The parents interviewed in this study craved better information and direct consideration in the marketing of inclusive community leisure services. Specifically, they appeared to interpret marketing deficiencies as subliminal messages: The services were either not prepared or not willing to accommodate children with disabilities. One of the more prevalent parental suggestions addressed the need for more family-oriented, or family-centered, programming. Such programs may be in great demand, but they are in short supply.

Perceived Responsibilities

Community recreation agencies also are responsible for the continued existence of segregated programs. It is possible that these departments continue to offer such programs because segregated services have been the accepted models for serving people with disabilities and, thus, are viewed as the norm (Schleien et al., in press; Schleien & Green, 1992).

In a survey of community agencies, Wilkenson (1984) found that some respondents believed that it was the responsibility of special associations or organizations to deal with and serve people with disabilities; others attributed the failure to offer inclusive services to a scarcity of requests for such programs by consumers with disabilities and their families; and for still others, another barrier to developing and implementing inclusive programs was the inefficiency of agency staff members who have had little experience in working with people with disabilities. Schleien et al. (in press) support these findings.

McGill (1984) and Schleien and Werder (1985) suggested that the reluctance of recreation program staffs to share responsibility for integrating general programming can be understood in terms of the reliance placed on trained specialists to serve people with disabilities. Rynders and Schleien (1991) and Schleien, Green, and Heyne (1993) have recommended, subsequently, that therapeutic recreation specialists and special educators try to erase the mystique surrounding people with disabilities by deemphasizing their need for special programs and facilities and encouraging the use of general services and general service providers.

The responsibility for failing to fully integrate community leisure services, however, also must be shared by people with disabilities and their families or care providers. Several studies have shown that people with disabilities generally do not choose to use community programs. The professional literature lists a variety of issues that hinder the inclusion of people with disabilities in community leisure services (see Table 1.2).

A sample of adults with visual impairments who were surveyed by Sherrill, Rainbolt, and Ervin (1984) reported that they wanted to be accepted into community recreation and neighborhood athletic programs. Nevertheless, only 10% actually participated in community recreation programs; 47% did not even know what programs their communities offered. Despite the expressed desire to become involved in inclusive community activities, several respondents were instrumental in starting segregated activities such as beep baseball or bowling leagues for people with visual impairments and blindness.

Residents of a large community facility serving adults with mental retardation who had previously resided in state institutions (Birenbaum & Re, 1979) also expressed a desire for more independence and more community involvement. Yet 83% of these adults were found to spend much of their leisure time in passive residential activities (Hayden et al., 1992). Furthermore, although the community activities led by staff members declined over the 4-year longitudinal study, respondents did not venture into the community alone or with friends or family members. The investigators speculated that this decline in community involvement may have been a result of the residents' lack of necessary skills for engaging in community activi-

Table 1.2. Why inclusive programs are not offered

1. Voluntary service organizations that provide separate and segregated programs may be hesitant to relinquish their participants to agencies that previously had ignored them lest the agency programs be inadequate or inferior.
2. Parents of children without disabilities may oppose inclusive programs.
3. People with disabilities and their parents or care providers do not express their desires for general programs to the right people.
4. People with disabilities may fail to participate in general programs for a variety of reasons.
5. General recreation service providers who previously had been led to believe that they did not possess the expertise to work effectively with people with disabilities may question their abilities to conduct inclusive programs.

ties or, possibly, of their reluctance to travel in what they considered to be a "dangerous community."

Residents with mental retardation in a group home were found by Crapps et al. (1985) to spend the majority of their free time in their homes and to rely almost completely on their supervisors for field trips. The investigators differentiated between passive integration (i.e., a person with a disability participates in a community activity that is planned and implemented by a supervising adult) and active integration (i.e., a person with a disability selects an environment and/or activity). Lack of skills may limit an individual's involvement in the community to passive integrative experiences unless the individual receives training in specific skills related to the use of community recreation environments. Schleien, Meyer, et al. (1995) noted that when an individual lacks the skills to participate in leisure options, the range of those options becomes meaningless in light of the individual's limitations.

INHIBITORS AND FACILITATORS OF RECREATION PARTICIPATION

Environmental barriers, long a concern of practitioners who work with individuals with disabilities, have been brought to the attention of the general public by legislation and consumer advocates. Successful functioning in our society requires the ability to understand, interpret, and react appropriately to signs, symbols, and messages in the environment. Successful functioning also requires the ability to move about with minimal difficulty, to assimilate and learn from previous experiences, and to have access to resources.

Children and adults with disabilities may be greatly hampered in their daily activities by subtle emotional obstacles as well as obvious physical barriers. Often, people with disabilities do not recognize the causes of their frustration or the reasons for their limited participation in typical activities; it may take a degree of awareness of their own leisure lifestyles and exposure to community activities and settings with their peers without disabilities for them to realize that they are missing experiences that others have. Availability of transportation and access into and mobility within recreation areas and facilities are features that must be present in a program in order for recreation participation by people with disabilities to be successful. Lack of knowledge and education in using recreational services, inaccessibility of services because of physical or geographic impediments, and the presence of architectural barriers will inhibit travelers who have disabilities. When these individuals are prevented from traveling around the community independently, they may suffer from boredom and, subsequently, may turn to an inappropriate use of free time that minimizes community participation.

Children and adults with disabilities often are excluded from many recreation options because of the limitations imposed on them by their physical impairments. In general, community recreation programs do not provide the types of modifications necessary to accommodate such individuals. For example, special equipment and materials, adequate activity space and facilities, the scheduling of activities, suitable rules and regulations, and the employment of special instructors all are required for programs aiming to overcome the many barriers to participation. Thus, it is important to ascertain what individuals with disabilities *perceive* as obstacles to participating in typical recreation programs and to determine how these obstacles can be removed or overcome.

Federal legislation has played a critical role in removing environmental barriers. The 1968 Architectural Barriers Act, for example, requires that any structure built or renovated with public funds be physically accessible to individuals with disabilities. For the law to be effective, however, strict enforcement of the act is essential. In addition, architects, urban planners, and transportation engineers should be made aware of the needs of people with disabilities. Medical technology and engineering also can contribute to increasing the participation of people with disabilities in activities by providing safe and effective appliances that facilitate mobility and help people overcome physical impairments.

Kennedy et al. (1991) identified three major obstacles to delivering cultural arts opportunities to the community for people with disabilities: 1) lack of trained personnel to serve participants with disabilities, 2) architectural barriers, and 3) attitudinal barriers. These obstacles also prevent access to various public and private recreation services in the community. Yet consumers who have disabilities, like their peers without disabilities, have the right to expect certain levels of service from recreation providers. Such levels have been identified by Austin and Powell (1981), for instance, as economic feasibility, clearly stated user fees and charges, and an accessible environment. Wolfensberger (1972) recommended that at least one half of any governing or advisory board consist of consumers representing the special group(s) to be served.

Several inhibitors to successful recreation and social participation have been identified on the basis of family interviews by Heyne et al. (1993):

1. Children's communication problems and short attention spans
2. Lack of social acceptance as equal partners by others
3. Logistics of meeting transportation, feeding, and toileting needs

Mactavish (1994) reported that parents discouraged their children with mental retardation from participating in segregated activities. Instead, parents preferred that their children with disabilities receive "normative" experiences through inclusive recreation. Likewise, parents who themselves had disabilities and who had children with disabilities identified a preference for inclusive recreation programs (Mactavish, 1994).

Of a sample of 30 adults with visual impairments who were interviewed by Sherrill et al. (1984), 72% reported negative experiences relating to acceptance and inclusion in their communities during adolescence; nevertheless, as adults, they desired acceptance into activities in their home communities.

When individuals with disabilities move into public residential facilities, they still should be provided with recreation services in the community where, it can be anticipated, they will eventually return. The reason is that frequently, individuals who are deinstitutionalized are left stranded between institutionalized recreation programs and community agencies without the proper preparation and education to make the necessary adjustments (Forest, 1987; Hayden et al., 1992).

GUIDELINES FOR INCLUSIVE COMMUNITY LEISURE SERVICES

Valuing social roles demands inclusion instead of segregation. The salient issue for people who have disabilities is not simply gaining full access to community resources; the actual issue is becoming a full participant in community life (Schleien,

Meyer, et al., 1995). A segregated program, even if it is offered by a community, does not provide participants with the benefits of social inclusion, the only means to social valuing. Segregated programs have been defended as a preparation for engaging in community programs, and they are preferable to isolation (Schleien & Green, 1992); however, rather than maximize the skills of each individual with a disability, they tend to focus on the lowest common denominator—the skill common to all participants, no matter how elementary. Furthermore, segregated program activities tend to enroll large numbers of participants. For example, it is not uncommon to find large numbers of individuals with mental retardation participating at a track and field event conducted by a local chapter of Special Olympics. Programs such as these are not at all typical of the more solitary adult leisure pursuits of individuals without disabilities. Large groupings also tend to discourage interactions with people without disabilities who may be using the community facility concurrently (Green & Schleien, 1991).

All too often, people with disabilities are kept in segregated programs because they are judged not to be ready to participate in general activities. The segregated program, intended as a "steppingstone" to participating in typical activities, becomes, instead, the only kind of program that many people with disabilities ever experience. The alternative to special programming is individual skill instruction within the context of inclusive recreation programs. In this manner, the individual with a disability learns to participate in the targeted activity in its natural context, having to respond appropriately to the activity's recreational and social demands. Instruction in the activity may be provided apart from the group activity at a different time or place or, preferably, while the activity is occurring. Individualized skill instruction, rather than large-group instruction occurring in a segregated group, is the preferred way to promote social inclusion.

In 1981, Reynolds identified five normalization trends in community recreation service delivery. Table 1.3 lists these trends and offers new perspectives on where community recreation service delivery may be heading.

BENEFITS OF INCLUSION FOR PEOPLE WITH DISABILITIES

Including people with disabilities in community recreation programs can be beneficial to all participants. The opportunity to learn from and socialize with peers without disabilities has been cited as a significant benefit for participants with disabilities. For example, teens who had mental retardation requiring limited supports increased their frequencies of appropriate social interactions with teenagers without disabilities who volunteered to teach them playground skills and decreased their inappropriate playground behavior (Donder & Nietupski, 1981). A second benefit was observed by Fletcher (1990) and McGill (1984): Inclusive play opportunities are stimulating and highly motivating for children with disabilities, offering them opportunities to imitate the play behavior of peers without disabilities. Heyne et al. (1993) and Stainback and Stainback (1985) supported the notion that students without disabilities serve as models of age-appropriate dress, language, gestures, and leisure behavior for students with disabilities. The presence of peers without disabilities also may provide more opportunities for social interaction.

Brinker (1985) compared the social interactions of individuals with mental retardation requiring extensive supports in segregated and inclusive settings. The in-

Table 1.3. Trends in providing leisure services for people with developmental disabilities

Away from	Toward
Isolated, random activities	Developmental programs
Segregated environments	Inclusive community-based programs
Intervention in isolation of other disciplines	Interdisciplinary approaches in partnership with family
Little accountability for assessing individual and program progress	High degree of internal and external accountability
Little concern for advocacy issues	Greater concern for larger environmental barriers that prevent individuals and families from being accepted

vestigator concluded that inclusive groupings promoted more social behavior than did segregated groupings. Brinker's findings were supported by the observations of Rynders et al. (1993) that individuals with mental retardation requiring extensive supports interacted more often with their peers without disabilities in inclusive settings than with their peers with mental retardation in either inclusive or segregated settings. Although these findings should not be extended to all people with disabilities, they support the belief that inclusive activities are more beneficial for people with disabilities than are segregated activities (Green & Schleien, 1991; Hutchison & McGill, 1992). The findings also suggest that many individuals with disabilities prefer inclusive activities and therefore, at the very least, deserve choices in their pursuit of leisure experiences (Dattilo, 1994; Hawkins, 1993).

BENEFITS OF INCLUSION FOR PEOPLE WITHOUT DISABILITIES

Eliminating many previously perceived and real constraints to inclusive programs, such as intrinsic (e.g., skill limitations of learners with disabilities) and extrinsic (e.g., architectural, transportation) barriers, has been achieved. A substantial hurdle that people with disabilities and their advocates still must overcome, however, remains: the negative attitudes among teachers and practitioners, administrators, and parents and their children without disabilities. They continue to be major constraints to successful inclusive programs (Rynders & Schleien, 1991; Sapon-Shevin, 1992). However, more and more administrators, board members, teachers, parents, recreation professionals, outdoor educators, and other members of education and recreation communities increasingly are asking one question: What will be the impact on the learning processes of peers without disabilities of including students with disabilities in general recreation programs, general education classes, and general environmental/outdoor education environments (Vandercook, York, & MacDonald, 1991)?

Many social psychologists and other researchers fear that the presence of a child with a disability in a program will disrupt or put at risk the learning processes for those children who do not have disabilities, and that the children without disabilities will not learn as much because the entire group will be held back. A look at theory and past research, however, may give a better sense and understanding of the potential effects of a child or children with disabilities on the learning of other children.

Behavior, according to Lewin's (1935) social psychology theory, is a function of the individual and the environment. Deutsch (1949, 1962), who derived his social interdependence theory from Lewin's work, held that each individual's outcomes are affected by the actions of others in the group. Bandura (1977) expanded Lewin's theory and developed a social learning theory in which learning is closely tied to the environment created by others in the learning group. Thus, theory may be considered to suggest that members of an educational group may influence one another.

But what does actual research indicate about the effects of children with disabilities on educational groups? Rosenbaum (1980) cited evidence from several sources, including extensive literature reviews, that indicates that positive, mixed, and negative effects on academic achievement can be shown by ability level. Rynders et al. (1993) reviewed the literature from a number of sources indicating that mixed-ability groups have no positive or negative differential effect on pupil achievement. Johnson and Johnson (1989) cited a number of their studies of classrooms using cooperative learning strategies that demonstrate many positive educational outcomes for all children in heterogeneous groups. Furthermore, research in developmental psychology has shown that in mixed educational settings that require social interaction, cognitively immature children make substantial gains in cognitive growth at no cost to the cognitive status of advanced children (Murray, 1982).

The most widely endorsed disadvantage of mixed-ability groups is reduction in the motivation and achievement of individuals with greater abilities (Reid, Clunies-Ross, Goacher, & Vile, 1981). Other investigators, however, have found that typically developing children who attend inclusive education and recreation programs make expected progress in language, cognitive, motor, perceptual, and social development (Bates & Renzaglia, 1982). Nevertheless, the controversy continues. Many teachers and administrators continue to espouse that children with disabilities disrupt and cause problems for children without disabilities in mixed-ability inclusive environments although there is no evidence—no conclusive research findings—to support this opinion (Dattilo, 1994; Schleien, Hornfeldt, & McAvoy, 1994).

Attitudes of children without disabilities toward their peers with disabilities in inclusive settings have been studied extensively in recent years. Heyne et al. (1993) found that children without disabilities expressed overwhelmingly positive attitudes, both before and after play sessions with playmates who had developmental disabilities, and showed a more accurate conception of developmental disability after contact.

Voeltz (1982) surveyed elementary school students to measure their attitudes toward peers with significant disabilities. More positive attitudes were expressed by students in schools that included children with significant disabilities than by students who attended schools in which no students with disabilities were present. Moreover, in a school that sponsored a peer-interaction program for children with mixed ability, students expressed the most positive attitudes of all groups studied. Sixth graders involved in a program tutoring peers who had mental retardation requiring limited to extensive supports showed an increase in positive attitudes toward these classmates (Fenrick & Petersen, 1984). High school students without disabilities, who gave instruction to their peers with severe disabilities in several activities including recreation, reported substantial benefits in the areas of self-concept, social cognition, reduced fear of human differences, increased tolerance, and new friendships, to name a few (Peck, Donaldson, & Pezzoli, 1990). In fact, research indicates that peer tutors without disabilities benefit a great deal and in various ways from their interactions with their peers with disabilities across many age groups and settings (Hall, 1994; McEvoy et al., 1988; Snell, 1993). Inclusive activities, in fact, were found to be very enjoyable to children without disabilities (Donder & Nietupski, 1981). Anecdotal data were collected by investigators from a study in which teenagers without disabilities volunteered to teach playground skills to peers who had mental retardation requiring limited support. The teens without disabilities commented that they enjoyed their recess periods and playground activities more when they were acting as peer tutors than they had prior to becoming tutors.

Schleien et al. (1994) assessed the amount of environmental information acquired by 88 second and third graders without disabilities who participated in a 1-day inclusive outdoor education experience with children who had severe developmental disabilities. Learning gains of the participants without disabilities in the inclusive classes were assessed using a pretest, posttest, and retest design. The results indicated that 1) all the children without disabilities showed statistically significant gains in learning environmental education concepts, and 2) the presence of learners with developmental disabilities in the inclusive classes did not have a detrimental effect on the learning gains of those without disabilities. Studies such as this one help dispel the notion that participants without disabilities "lose out" when programs include individuals with disabilities. The evidence showing that activities can be informative, beneficial, and enjoyable for participants without disabilities in classes with peers who have developmental disabilities provides strong support for inclusive programs. Participating in inclusive recreation programs can make life-changing differences for children and youth with disabilities; as studies suggest, it is not only people with disabilities who benefit from such programs—ultimately, the community benefits as well.

The evidence of positive experiences in inclusive activities encourages practitioners at community recreation agencies to expand the inclusive options for their constituents. Expanding such options makes good sense not only to the designers and consumers of such programs but also to the parents of children with and without disabilities and their advocates. Recreation practitioners are learning that, with careful attention to design, inclusion works to everyone's benefit. Just as important is the unquestionable transfer of positive attitudes from recreation programs to other community affairs.

Communities benefit as recreation professionals continue to grow more accepting and more accommodating of all people with disabilities and extend this attitude to other areas in communities. On attitude assessments, practitioners have indicated that inclusive services have taught them not to be afraid of people who have different abilities and that individuals with disabilities are disabled only to the extent that they are so perceived.

Including people with disabilities in community recreation programs is an essential element in completing the process of social role valorization—valuing people socially. Successful social inclusion requires key players who are involved in service delivery to adopt a philosophy and value system that is consistent with this process. Of central importance in this philosophy is the recognition that people with disabilities are valuable individuals; hence, they have the right to participate in the same programs as their peers. Agencies must articulate and practice a policy of making existing programs inclusive rather than providing only special segregated programs. Recognizing that creating and providing segregated programs is exclusionary and results in alienating and removing people with disabilities from the rest of society is a vital component of this philosophy. Making a commitment to inclusion also requires agencies to actively recruit participants with disabilities and their families to share facilities and programs with people without disabilities.

PREPARING PERSONNEL

Lord's (1983) advice to personnel involved in inclusive recreation efforts denotes an attitude that is essential to inclusive activities. Instead of asking, "Is this person ready for inclusion?" one should ask, "What support does this person need to be involved and to participate in this program?"

The question may well be the critical factor in the training of personnel by community recreation agencies. Administrators of public recreation agencies are accountable for ensuring that their personnel are prepared to share the responsibilities of accommodating participants with disabilities. Effective inclusion depends on general program staff members and therapeutic recreation specialists working together to achieve the common goal: social inclusion. The emphasis, therefore, should be on generalists rather than on specialists. Only ongoing, on-site technical assistance and consultation should be provided by specialists to the agency practitioner once the program has been implemented. The specialists serve best by providing support to agency personnel for furthering inclusion and deemphasizing an individual's ongoing need for specially trained staff and special programs.

SUMMARY

Lord's (1983) advice makes a good guiding principle in all efforts to support people with disabilities in community recreation programs. Accepting social role valorization—valuing the individual for her- or himself—means trying to include individuals with disabilities in all aspects of society. It is not enough merely to open programs to people with disabilities; the professionals in charge of the programs must go further and actively recruit and encourage the participation of people with disabilities and provide them with successful and ongoing mechanisms of support.

The rationale that segregated programs are preparation for future inclusion denotes a false attitude. Social inclusion is based on an all-or-nothing principle: If one is not in, one is out! Unless an individual with a disability is embraced as a valued person within all aspects of society, her or his inborn rights will continue to be denied.

Admittedly, not all leisure experiences in least restrictive environments are successful. The privilege of achieving or failing, however, is part of a learning process that, for far too long, has been denied individuals with disabilities. In the final analysis, it is up to consumers, parents, therapeutic recreation specialists, and community recreation administrators and practitioners to ensure that people with disabilities are guaranteed their right to engage in the learning process. Consequently, inclusive programs must be continuously available to all members of a community for lifelong experimentation of participation in least restrictive environments. Opening additional opportunities for participating in inclusive programs increases the probability that the lives of individuals with disabilities will be as meaningful as possible.

The authors of this book propose that the following four principles be incorporated in every model guiding the development of inclusive recreation services:

- Programs designed for people with disabilities must be age suitable and based on personal interest, not on diagnosis or label.
- Programs preparing people for inclusive recreation participation must occur within their home communities, not in restrictive, contrived, and irrelevant environments.
- Communication and coordination among participants, family members, and practitioners must occur if inclusive services are to be initiated and are to thrive over time.
- Participants with and without disabilities, family members, and recreation practitioners must take a shared responsibility approach to help ensure that every community member's needs and interests are met, including the recreation and social needs of entire families.

By including people with disabilities in typical recreation programs, the authors strongly believe that the entire community benefits. Through exposure to and ongoing interaction with people with disabilities, individuals without disabilities gain knowledge about and become more sensitive to individual differences, develop more accepting attitudes, and broaden their own opportunities for friendship.

Creating Opportunities for Inclusive Recreation

2

Preparing People and Environments

◆ ◆ ◆ ◆ ◆

The organized movement for public park and recreation services has a distinctive and widely documented history (Chubb & Chubb, 1981; Meyer & Brightbill, 1964). Much of the organization of public recreation services centers on providing leisure services that reflect broad neighborhood or community interests. Developing organized and publicly funded recreational services has been a way for local governments to address the health and well-being of their constituencies in a manner that is consistent with the prevailing belief that recreation participation contributes to the quality of life (Kelly, 1982; Sessoms, 1984; Spangler & O'Sullivan, 1995). As one of the larger components of the community's leisure service delivery system, park and recreation agencies hold as a predominant concern the public interest. As Kelly (1982) stated so succinctly, "Public recreation, then, is . . . based on a social ethic of common responsibility for the 'life, liberty, and the pursuit of happiness' of *all members* of the community" (emphasis added; p. 380).

Public parks and recreation services have become, in essence, a mandate of the community. These services are expected to mirror the leisure and recreational needs, desires, and expectations of a constituency whose tax dollars they require. With increased pressure from private and commercial recreation concerns with whom they compete, parks and recreation agencies must make an objective and comprehensive appraisal of their niche in the community leisure service delivery system, along with the management and planning systems they employ (Rossman, 1995; Russell, 1982; Whyte, 1992). An appropriate beginning to this appraisal is to gain a perspective on community leisure service options available to people with disabilities and to identify a process model that provides the recreation professional with a systematic approach to delivering inclusive community leisure services. Finally, the recreation professional must be apprised of several general, yet critical, strategies to "setting the stage" for inclusive community leisure services. Strategies include networking with "key players," establishing a community leisure advisory board, conducting architectural accessibility audits, and providing staff training. This chapter provides information on creating opportunities to ensure inclusion of citizens with disabilities in general recreation environments.

LEISURE SERVICE OPTIONS AVAILABLE TO PEOPLE WITH DISABILITIES

Change is a constant in society, the effects of which continuously challenge decision makers in both public and private organizations, especially park and recreation professionals (Cummings & Busser, 1994; Hultsman & Colley, 1995; Humphrey, 1986; Whyte, 1992). Professionals attempt to predict and interpret the effects of change in order to forecast and weigh constituent and community needs against available resources and supports. Mission statements and organizational objectives must be critiqued and revised, as necessary, to address new and changing priorities within organizations and communities and their constituencies (Rossman, 1995; Sessoms, 1984). Passing the Americans with Disabilities Act (ADA) of 1990 is a good example of how decision makers have examined agency priorities and responded to the challenges of changing or expanding constituencies (e.g., children and adults with disabilities) who have the desire and the right to have access to public services (e.g., parks and recreation) that historically have been provided by other people (e.g., parents, care providers, volunteers) and organizations (e.g., advocacy agencies, social services, therapeutic recreation).

Family members, care providers, schools, therapeutic recreation specialists, and advocacy agencies historically have been the primary leisure service providers for people with disabilities (e.g., The Arc). Each will continue to play a very important role in the leisure education and leisure lifestyle development of children and adults with disabilities (LIFE Project Staff, 1991; Ray, 1991, 1994; Ray, Schleien, Larson, Rutten, & Slick, 1986; Schleien, Meyer, Heyne, & Brandt, 1995; Schleien, Rynders, Heyne, & Tabourne, 1995). As a result of the misconception that others have taken primary responsibility for providing leisure services, public recreation agencies may assume that the leisure needs of people with disabilities are being met and, therefore, may concentrate efforts on meeting the leisure needs of the majority population (i.e., people without disabilities), giving less attention, if any, to the leisure needs and desires of community members with disabilities.

The ADA, as well as related state and local legal mandates, should assure people with disabilities that their leisure needs are a priority and can and will be addressed at the community level. However, the potential for excluding people with disabilities from community leisure experiences offered by public parks and recreation agencies will continue as long as planning and programming priorities are considered "for the majority" and as attitudes are maintained that "others" carry a greater burden or higher responsibility for implementing leisure opportunities than do public recreation employees.

In all fairness to park and recreation agencies and their professional employees, it is quite doubtful that excluding citizens with disabilities from program and facility planning decisions is a deliberate discriminatory practice. In fact, the obstacles that prevent or inhibit people with disabilities from receiving community leisure services are more often a result of administrative oversight, lack of systematic program planning, or other barriers rather than of discrimination. These obstacles and specific suggestions on how to overcome them are comprehensively addressed in Chapter 3. Whatever the cause, people with disabilities have not, as a whole, been receiving adequate or appropriate communitywide leisure services.

Figure 2.1 illustrates a continuum of community recreation options for people with disabilities present in many communities throughout the country. This continuum ranges from *noninvolvement* (noninclusion of individuals with disabilities in the leisure lifestyle of the community) through *segregated* (separation of individuals into "handicapped only" groups), *integrated* (involvement in "mixed ability" groupings with use of systematically planned and implemented supports), and *inclusive* (full involvement in and access to community recreation opportunities). Each is described, and specific examples are given to highlight each aspect of this continuum. It is the authors' belief (and the purpose of this text to illustrate) that inclusive leisure options should become the norm in communities, as the other options may only serve to further exclude or limit people with disabilities from achieving complete acceptance and full inclusion in their communities. The authors recognize, however, that some communities may need to offer a range of leisure services for citizens with disabilities to adequately address the leisure needs and desires of all constituents (Bullock, Mahon, & Welch, 1992).

Noninvolvement

When a society fails to provide for the needs of individuals with disabilities, *barriers of omission* result (Kennedy, Smith, & Austin, 1991; Smith, 1985). If only family members, care providers, special educators, therapists, and others intimately familiar to the person with a disability are capable of facilitating and implementing leisure experiences for this person, then there is little chance for that person to

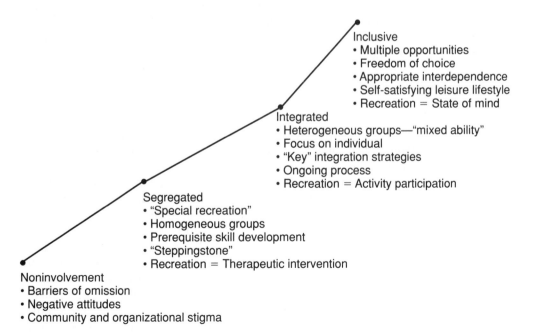

Figure 2.1.   A continuum of leisure service options for people with disabilities.

achieve full, unequivocal inclusion in the community. Barriers of omission occur within a leisure service agency when it fails to adequately assess and/or address the leisure needs and interests of citizens with disabilities. A major responsibility of the community recreation professional is to adequately assess the needs, interests, and preferences of potential recreation participants prior to selecting and implementing specific programs and services. Failure to do so may hinder the opportunity for all citizens living in the community to have satisfying leisure experiences within community recreation environments. As members of the community, people with disabilities have a right to be included in the process and outcomes of community leisure service delivery.

Barriers of omission also result when recreation professionals fail to acquire the necessary skills, through staff training and development, to make recreation programs inclusive. Without these necessary skills, recreation professionals must depend on others (e.g., advocacy groups, care providers, family members) to provide meaningful leisure experiences for people with disabilities. As a result, recreational programs and facilities continue to cater to the needs, interests, and abilities of a majority constituency, which is largely without disabilities.

Although the *intent* of legal mandates such as the ADA is to require physical and programmatic access to leisure settings and services, the *spirit* of the law (i.e., ensuring equal access and opportunities because people with disabilities are recognized as valued members of the community, too) may be omitted. An example of this type of barrier of omission occurs when a leisure service agency fails to involve people with disabilities, their families, and advocates in planning, designing, and constructing a new community-built playground for children and young adolescents. Wheelchair accessibility is provided, but only in the children's area, thereby omitting the needs and interests of young adolescents with disabilities who want to be near their classmates without disabilities. Barriers of omission, related to negative attitudes and various community and organizational stigma, threaten to keep people with disabilities in the "basement of noninvolvement" unless recreation professionals and other key individuals cooperate to facilitate moving people with disabilities into higher and more valued levels of leisure involvement. Approaches that recreation professionals can take to overcome barriers related to negative attitudes and stigma are further highlighted in Chapter 3.

Segregated Options

One must initially assume that barriers of omission have been overcome sufficiently to allow people with disabilities to use community leisure environments. The next option likely to be encountered on the continuum is segregated, "handicapped only," programs. People participating in these programs typically are assigned special staff services, equipment, and environments in which to receive a leisure experience. Specialized staff such as therapeutic recreation specialists, care providers, or special education teachers are employed because they often have a knowledge and understanding of the participants' skills, abilities, and behaviors. They can provide specialized services through interventions, such as speech interpretation or behavior management, to help ensure that the programs are conducted smoothly and that participants interact appropriately. Special adaptive equipment, such as therapy balls or positioning cushions, and facilities, such as therapeutic swimming pools in hospitals or activity rooms in institutional settings, can be scheduled to accommodate participants with disabilities. People who use segregated programs may prefer to associate with peers with similar disabilities (in such activities as wheelchair basketball or Friday night dances for people with mental retardation), may have been "placed" there by parents or care providers, or may not have opportunities to associate with peers without disabilities because any number of obstacles impede their ability to take advantage of integrated or inclusive recreation programs.

Specialized or segregated programs typically are developed by individuals (e.g., therapeutic recreation specialists, allied health professionals, parent groups) who believe that service provision is most effective when people with disabilities are grouped together. Special recreation programs can become extensions of therapeutic recreation programs and may border on being prescriptive and interventionist in approach. The goal of such programs is to habilitate or rehabilitate the participant with disabilities in order to prepare him or her for more normalized settings. A potential problem with this approach is that decisions about program content and process are left solely up to professionals who may believe that they alone know what is best for their "client." The result is that people with disabilities often are not involved in program planning and implementation because others are determining what is needed in terms of more "therapeutic recreation." This overreliance on professionals reinforces the stereotype that people with disabilities do not know what is best for them. Overreliance also breeds dependency on professionals, who, without input from the participant or the participant's family, may not always know what is best for the participant.

Although the main purpose of this text is to promote equal access and inclusion for people with disabilities in community leisure service settings, the authors would be remiss if the more positive implications of special recreation services were not mentioned. If activities are age appropriate and functional and are offered in least restrictive or general settings (i.e., settings also used by people without disabilities), then segregated programs may provide individuals with disabilities with a safe, structured, and secure leisure experience. The participant must feel comfortable in new leisure environments if future inclusion efforts are to be successful. With the concentrated attention of staff and the use of intervention strategies designed for each individual, participants with disabilities could acquire substantial recreation and social skills within the context of an enjoyable leisure activity. Special or segregated recreation programs, therefore, can serve as steppingstones to more inclusive environments and experiences (Reynolds, 1981; Schleien & Green, 1992; Wilhite & Kleiber, 1992). It is critical, however, that specific "exit" criteria be delineated to ensure that participants in these programs can move through the continuum to less restrictive, integrated, and inclusive programs. Exit criteria include behavioral changes in the participant (e.g., leisure and/or social skill acquisition, appropriate play behaviors), as well as a fixed amount of time for program implementation (e.g., an 8-week period). The latter criterion typically is determined by recreation professionals and activity leaders. Progress described in other qualitative ways is jointly determined by recreation staff, care providers, and participants with disabilities through specific evaluative methods such as those described in Chapter 8. This does not imply that all supports for the participant with a disability are immediately withdrawn. Rather, the participant will have the opportunity to experience enjoyment and, possibly, disappointment in the same recreational contexts as his or her peers without disabilities. Participants with disabilities no longer will be insulated from the community by overprotective care providers and professionals. Participants will be able to apply the skills that they have acquired in the segregated recreation programs to the multitude of leisure experiences available in the community.

There are many good community models illustrating special recreation services throughout the United States. For a detailed discussion of these types of services and exemplary programs, consult additional texts (e.g., Kennedy et al., 1991).

Integrated Options

The integrated leisure service option provides people with disabilities the opportunity to be involved in general community recreation programs and to participate alongside participants without disabilities. Although specialized staff and services may still be used, little or no assumption is made beforehand that these considerations are appropriate or even necessary. Integrated services provide the recreation professional with a systematic and coordinated approach to facilitating participation for individuals with disabilities.

Whereas segregated programs comprise, by definition, more homogeneous "handicapped only" groupings, integrated programs are more heterogeneous in nature and bring together people with "mixed abilities." The rationale for integrated programming is that participants bring into the recreation program intact skills and abilities, thus further contributing to the diversity typically found in such programs. Such richness of experience creates a positive dynamic in the group that permits participants to learn from each other. If the primary mission of the public recreation agency is to contribute to the social, physical, educational, and cultural growth of the individual, what better forum is there than an integrated program with participants of mixed abilities?

Because integrated recreation programs are viewed as a way for individuals to participate in and enjoy their preferred leisure activities, the program focus moves away from planning and implementing special recreation services for members of special populations to looking at the unique characteristics of individual participants. Recreation professionals in such programs will raise such questions as "Why did this individual register for this program?" "What are this person's expectations?" "What skills or experiences does this individual bring to the program?" "How will this person interact with the other participants?" "How can I, as the recreation programmer, meet this individual's needs?" These questions require answers from the individual participant registering for the program. Because assumptions often are based on the characteristics of disability, these questions should be applied to any participant, regardless of whether the person has a disabling condition. Depending on the answers to these and other pertinent questions, community recreation professionals can consider any combination of key strategies that will facilitate the physical and social integration of the participant with disabilities in the recreation program. In fact, this text is a response to expressed needs to assist recreation professionals in understanding, appreciating, and employing integration strategies in day-to-day program planning and delivery.

Another approach to integrated services is described as "reverse mainstreaming" (Schleien & Green, 1992). This approach modifies programs traditionally designed as segregated for people with disabilities to attract and include participants without disabilities. This assumes that current segregated programs, with concomitant supports, satisfactorily address most of the needs of participants. However, social integration often is lacking. Therefore, some modification of programs and instruction often is necessary to entice participants without disabilities to join these programs in order to enhance the possibility of positive relationships being formed. There are, however, disadvantages to such integration efforts: 1) participants without disabilities often do not remain in programs over the long term; 2) natural proportions of people with to people without disabilities is not achieved; 3) participants with disabilities may not gain skills that allow them to successfully gain access to nonsegregated programs; and 4) the extent of socialization is limited to peers who desire to be in these programs, thereby reducing the opportunity to be exposed to more diverse groups.

Inclusive Options

Inclusive leisure service options should be the ultimate goal of all recreation personnel and programs. Participants with disabilities should come to understand that access to community leisure settings and programs is possible and can be achieved without difficulty and with the full support of leisure providers and the community as a whole. People with disabilities should be considered "participants," not "the handicapped." Therefore, they are entitled to the same respect and attention afforded any other member of the community when recreation programming is being planned, designed, and implemented.

Inclusive leisure options are so named to suggest that multiple leisure opportunities exist throughout the community. The individual who has a disability is able to select and gain access to preferred recreation programs without exerting more effort than would a person without disabilities. Using appropriate levels of interdependence, the person with disabilities is able to call upon any number of necessary support systems for assistance in taking advantage of these recreation programs. The participant is able to realize the ultimate goal of achieving a satisfying leisure lifestyle free of any significant intrinsic (e.g., skill limitations, characteristics of disability) and extrinsic (e.g., transportation, barriers of omission) constraints. Although this may be an idealized or utopian view of leisure and recreation for the individual with a disability, most people who use community recreation facilities are exercising their leisure needs in this very way. People without disabilities have come to expect and demand such variety and accessibility from public park and recreation systems.

Also referred to as the "zero exclusion approach" (Schleien & Green, 1992), inclusive leisure options rely on the following program components to be successful:

1. New programs to meet the changing needs of consumers with and without disabilities
2. Productive, collaborative relationships based on mutual respect between professionals in therapeutic recreation and general community recreation
3. Aggressive recruitment of participants with and without disabilities to programs through user-friendly, nondiscriminatory advertisements
4. Accurate assessment of the needs, skills, and interests of all potential participants within the community
5. Commitment by the agency to make inclusive programs the rule rather than the exception so that people with and without disabilities are given a variety of options for recreation participation
6. Commitment by the community to socially integrate and include all community members and to segregate individuals based on (dis)ability levels

In summary, there may be some justification for requiring programs at each of the leisure services options—segregated, integrated, and inclusive—on the continuum. Many people with disabilities may need the specialized training offered through segregated programs in order to participate in community leisure services. However, those people with disabilities who have the potential to participate alongside peers without disabilities within integrated programs or who have the skills or desire to independently choose and attend an inclusive leisure setting should be given sufficient opportunities and support to do so. Segregated programs, therefore, become a means to an end: a steppingstone, at best, to equal access to and participation in community leisure settings. Decisions concerning at which level to start this process should be based on a collective assessment of the skills and abilities of the potential consumer with disabilities. As noted previously, the continuum of leisure service options for people with disabilities is represented in Figure 2.1. Key issues, such as freedom of choice and barriers of omission, are listed under each option.

IDENTIFYING A PROCESS FOR INCLUSIVE LEISURE SERVICES

If community recreation agencies and staff accept the continuum model of leisure service provision, then using this approach will be a positive step in meeting the individual leisure and recreation needs of people with disabilities. It can be anticipated that greater numbers of individuals with disabilities will utilize the community leisure service system. The model proposes a strategy whereby these individuals will be given maximum opportunities to move through the full range of available leisure services, choosing from a vast menu of leisure possibilities. Regular participation in integrated and inclusive programs will become the norm for individuals who had heretofore been relegated to special, segregated recreation programs or to the "basement of noninvolvement": unseen, unwanted, and largely ignored.

For the continuum concept to work, however, community leisure service providers must closely examine their systems of service delivery. This would include making an objective appraisal of the mission or philosophical foundation of the agency and of the agency's procedures for selecting, implementing, and evaluating programs and management practices. If agency personnel do not have a clear understanding of their purpose or methods of service delivery, there is the possibility that negative attitudes, organizational stigma, and other barriers of omission will continue to prevent or inhibit people with disabilities from taking advantage of leisure services.

Much of the effectiveness of service delivery for people with disabilities is the result, therefore, of the ability of community leisure service professionals, parents, care providers, and advocacy groups to react appropriately if and when specific barriers arise. Such responsiveness is important because if parents, care providers, and individuals with disabilities perceive that a service system does not welcome them, then they will stay away (West, 1984). If past attempts to utilize leisure service systems have failed because of any number of extrinsic or intrinsic barriers (see Chapter 3), then people with disabilities, or those significant others facilitating decisions on behalf of these individuals, will shy away from further attempts to use these systems. They may even create various segregated systems to meet the "special" needs of people with disabilities, as was the case with advocacy groups such as

The Arc, which formed recreation programs for children, youths, and adults with developmental disabilities because communities failed to address their leisure needs. Therefore, it is essential that leisure service organizations, especially public parks and recreation agencies, have in place a systems planning process with a strong and unequivocal mission in support of inclusion.

In order to identify and address the needs of its community, a park and recreation organization often develops a model of service delivery based on general social planning theories and processes (Edginton, Compton, & Hanson, 1980; Herchmer, 1994; Rossman, 1988, 1995) such as the model depicted in Figure 2.2. Models of this type help personnel to organize services around a central, philosophical mission. A simply expressed mission reflecting the policies noted previously might read: "To provide leisure opportunities that contribute to the social, physical, educational, cultural, and general well-being of the community and its people" (Sessoms, 1984, p. 19). (See Chapter 1 for more elaborate inclusive mission statements.) The program plan, its implementation, and subsequent evaluation are considered within the overall mission of the agency. This model assumes interaction between all components (i.e., tasks I–VI), representing a process that is dynamic.

Studies have focused on the perceived or actual barriers encountered by recreation professionals and/or participants with disabilities that limit the latter's access to more general and inclusive community leisure environments. The most salient of these efforts is highlighted throughout Chapter 1 and will not be reiterated here. The authors of these studies have sought to identify both social and architectural barriers and to suggest ways to overcome them. However, the studies appear to include a prior assumption that the barriers themselves prevent access to leisure services. The studies suggest that if a specific barrier is eliminated, then services will automatically be considered accessible. This assumption is fallacious because it does not address the broader issues related to the ongoing physical and

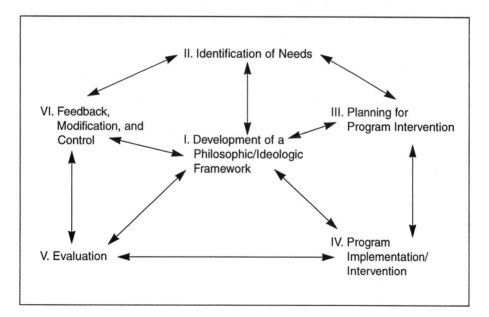

Figure 2.2. A general social planning process model. (Adapted from Edginton, Compton, and Hanson, 1980.)

social inclusion of people with disabilities into diverse leisure environments. Granted, overcoming isolated barriers may provide the participant with *temporary* access to services. Unfortunately, the entire system of leisure service delivery is geared to an able-bodied population that is more adaptive or flexible in its ability to accept system inadequacies. If a service system fails to meet the needs of individuals without disabilities, for example, then the individuals can either compromise standards and expectations, thus settling for less, or go somewhere else to meet their leisure and recreation needs. More specific, if potential participants without disabilities do not care for the services offered in a particular setting because the programs are not interesting or because the program leadership is inadequate or incompetent, for example, then they can choose to take advantage of a variety of alternative commercial or quasi-public leisure service settings such as fraternal organizations, the YMCA/YWCA, or other private recreation centers. For many people with disabilities, public recreation programs may be the only affordable alternatives available for developing and practicing leisure skills and behaviors. If the leisure service systems are inadequate or poorly administered, then people with disabilities may not have the necessary comprehension, ability, or financial means to make appropriate choices. It is an accepted tenet of professionals that successful programs largely are a result of providers' understanding the needs, desires, and motivations of potential consumers prior to program planning and design (Busser, 1993; Little, 1993). However, these tenets should apply equally to potential consumers who have disabilities.

The model depicted in Figure 2.2, although useful for a general analysis of social systems, may be too vague for the community recreation professional. This individual might need a more specific picture of the leisure service delivery system in which she or he is expected to operate, not some idealized flow model. It is likely that many park and recreation departments already have adapted various model processes and strategies for meeting the leisure needs of their constituents, including people with disabilities. However, some of these models may not provide the recreation professional with a reliable, comprehensive, or logical approach to total community leisure service delivery, including serving citizens with disabilities in public parks and recreation programs.

The quality of a community's leisure program for its citizens depends on the leisure service model process it implements. A comprehensive process, for example, representing professionally acceptable community recreation program planning methods (Rossman, 1995; Russell, 1982) would include the following 10 components:

1. Gathering information
2. Identifying needs
3. Selecting programs
4. Publicizing programs and conducting recruitment
5. Conducting registration
6. Implementing programs
7. Evaluating programs
8. Summarizing findings and reporting
9. Providing appropriate feedback
10. Determining future efforts

Progressing through each of these steps is a logical approach to ensuring that a comprehensive and inclusive community recreation program is designed and implemented. It is likely, however, that community recreation departments will diverge from this model, thereby affecting the quality of services and, ultimately, their inclusiveness.

One example concerns a segregated or special recreation program model in which the agency assumes the chief decision-making role with little or no regard for input from potential participants. Many of these activities are planned without considering individuals' needs, preferences, skills, or abilities, particularly in relation to functional, community-based skills development, including social inclusion with peers without disabilities. Inattention to the needs of potential consumers with disabilities, coupled with the fact that most decisions are made on behalf of consumers by the recreation professional, distinguishes this segregated service from the more inclusive leisure service process highlighted previously. Special population groups may be recruited by contacting advocacy agencies or special education classrooms, but they may be provided activities that are stereotypical of such groups (e.g., Friday night dances for young adults with mental retardation, Sunday morning playground groups for children with autism, Special Olympics, therapeutic swimming programs for people with physical disabilities). Programs often are terminated with essentially no evaluation or follow-up. Individuals with disabilities must "wait" until recreation staff members suggest a new program. The following dysfunctional model, greatly distinguishable from sound and typical program planning practices, often characterizes a process for providing segregated leisure services:

Step 1. Agency selects activities.
Step 2. Potential consumers are recruited through special education classrooms, advocacy agencies, and promotional brochures that advertise these "handicapped" programs.
Step 3. Programs are implemented.
Step 4. Programs either are terminated with no formal evaluation or follow-up or continue indefinitely with little to no opportunity to use the program as a steppingstone to more inclusive experiences.
Step 5. Participants await future programs.

Other agencies may practice many of the steps of the inclusive leisure service process, but they diverge in several critical ways. The areas in which such programs typically do not measure up include the following: inadequate information gathering by the agency regarding the community and people in the community who have disabilities, insufficient publicity and recruitment activities to inform these people that community recreation programs and services are available and inclusive, and minimal opportunities to evaluate and obtain feedback on current programs and to plan to improve future program offerings. Another divergence may be found in recreation programs administered by unskilled recreation specialists. These specialists may be willing to include people with disabilities in recreation activities, but they may not understand how to do so effectively. Through systematic planning, staff training, and collaborative networks (described more fully later in this chapter), these programs can reach their full potential to be inclusive of all community members. Until that time, these less-than-perfect programs continue to limit the full access of people with disabilities to recreation and leisure services. The following example illustrates these points.

The program coordinator of a municipal park and recreation agency in a suburban community is aware that two of the more popular activities organized by the agency have been swimming at the community swimming pool and participating in the softball league. In response, the program coordinator increases staffing at the swimming pool and establishes a softball league. Participants purchase season passes to the pool and register teams and players for the league. The few people with disabilities and their families who want to participate are either denied access to the pool by the program coordinator because policy prohibits flotation devices (a needed adaptation for the individual with a disability to use the pool) or are referred to the local Special Olympics coordinator because the softball league is deemed too competitive. By the Labor Day weekend, the program coordinator counts the number of participants and the amount of summer revenues and announces to her director that the summer recreation program has been a huge success. The director and the program coordinator decide to repeat the programs the following year.

What the program coordinator has failed to consider are the needs of the many community residents who are not participating in her program. Examples of such residents are the local teenagers who hang out at the shopping mall all day, nursing facility residents who sit on their porches and play cards or just watch the world go by, and residents of large public facilities who have significant multiple disabilities and who stay indoors almost all of the time. What do these people do all summer? They are not being served by the local recreation program. Also, evaluation is based on quantitative data (e.g., numbers of participants) without regard for more qualitative outcomes (e.g., skills development, leisure lifestyle enhancement, socialization). Community recreation departments run an extreme risk of creating barriers of omission when they design and implement programs based on past practices only and the types and numbers of facilities they operate. This model of service delivery is unacceptable to the consumers, both with and without disabilities, who could and should be served within this community.

The 10 program planning steps highlighted previously must serve as the community leisure agency's systems planning process if full inclusion is to be achieved. Appendix A outlines this comprehensive and inclusive leisure service process and task analyzes the appropriate and relevant steps that recreation agencies can take to organize services to be inclusive—from mission development to program evaluation and future planning. The following section describes each component of the process and explains and defines each more thoroughly. Recreation professionals can expand this process by identifying additional tasks and responsibilities to make services even more inclusive within their respective communities.

A PROCESS ANALYSIS OF INCLUSIVE COMMUNITY LEISURE SERVICES: GUIDELINES FOR DECISION MAKING

Prior to developing any plan to implement community leisure services, recreation personnel must be well-grounded in the philosophy of the municipal park and recreation agency and knowledgeable about potential customers. This knowledge gives the recreation professional guidelines with which to make program planning decisions and to practice his or her profession (Hultsman & Colley, 1995). It is the municipal park and recreation agency that typically develops this philosophical mission around which individual community recreation professionals may design and implement programs. Specifically, the municipal park and recreation agency has the public interest at the core of its service philosophy. This philosophical mission is concerned with improving the quality of life in areas such as health, well-being, self-concept, and happiness and with the affirmation that recreation and leisure experiences are important in achieving this improved quality of life, however it may be defined. Thus, a sound program philosophy is composed of a successful blending of personal, professional, and community beliefs and values into clear operational methods.

Before starting, recreation professionals should bear in mind several key tenets that may guide them in providing community leisure services:

1. People have a right to recreation that is personally satisfying.
2. The essence of leisure is freedom: freedom to choose among a variety of leisure options and experiences.
3. The leisure experience differs among individuals; therefore, programs should be designed to address various needs, interests, and abilities.
4. People have a right to have access to quality leisure environments.
5. People have a right to participate in preferred leisure experiences in the most inclusive settings.
6. Leisure opportunities should be provided in a consistent manner to all potential participants without regard to sex, religion, age, socioeconomic status, sexual orientation, or physical or mental ability.

When considering the responsibility to provide accessible leisure services for people with disabilities, the community recreation professional first must ensure that the philosophical position of the agency is nondiscriminatory in practice, policy, and attitude. Second, the professional should make certain that programs and services are physically accessible, chronologically age appropriate, and flexible enough to allow participants to enter the continuum of leisure service options at the most appropriate, least restrictive, most inclusive level. Finally, programs and services should adequately address the personal needs and preferences of potential participants with disabilities and should be affordable and conveniently reached by participants. Following is a list of steps for implementing community leisure services.

A. Gather Information An absolute necessity for effectively providing recreation services is a comprehensive knowledge of neighborhood residents, the potential users of community leisure services. The community recreation professional must have a sense of the diverse leisure attitudes and preferences of the residents. Knowledge of community demography also has been demonstrated to be critical when considering the "variety, emphasis, and type of recreation activities enjoyed by people" (Russell, 1982, p. 70). Demographic factors that influence such preferences include ethnic heritage, residence, age, educational level, occupation, social status, family lifestyles, and religious affiliation. Metropolitan and regional planning agencies, as well as a variety of social service organizations, generally can provide recreation staff with this information and are easily approached via telephone, fax, or electronic mail.

Knowledge of available resources helps to avoid costly duplication of services. It also helps to maximize coordination of resources to ensure efficient and effective programming (Howe, 1993; McLean, 1993; Whyte, 1992). The authors certainly are aware of and support the many levels of collaboration and resource sharing already occurring in communities among parks and recreation departments, schools, community education, sports associations, scouting, and the like. Resources of interest to recreation staff include facilities, settings, materials and equipment, staff, budget, neighborhood support, and alternative leisure service systems (e.g., voluntary/youth serving, private, commercial).

A final component concerns the leisure behavior of neighborhood constituencies. Information regarding community participation patterns and motivations gives the recreation planner additional bases for making decisions. However, recreation staff must not assume that past recreation behavior is a sole predictor of future preferences and needs (Howe, 1993). Instead, recreation planners must rely on preference assessments described next.

B. *Identify Needs* Closely related to the fact-finding process highlighted in step A is identifying individual needs and preferences of potential participants. The most effective way to determine such preferences is to describe activities in "plain English" rather than in therapeutic terms. For example, potential participants may express interest in health and fitness through aerobic dancing rather than by saying they have a "desire for enhanced socialization," "improved cognitive ability," or "increased gross motor coordination." Community recreation professionals, program leaders, and other recreation professionals most likely are aware of these types of therapeutic activity goals. Recognizing that individuals relate differently to activities and experiences, the recreation professional surveying the community usually begins by developing a list of diverse activities and asking community residents to rank them according to preference or interest (see Appendix B for an example). The recreation professional also might take a less formal approach and simply ask people in the community about the types of activities that they would like to see offered at the community recreation site. The community recreation professional can then begin to identify programs and activities based on these expressed preferences and to construct a program that will more effectively meet individual needs within preferred activities.

The recreation professional utilizes similar techniques for determining the activity preferences of people with disabilities. Parents, care providers, teachers, and therapeutic recreation specialists may assist with assessing preferences. These people can offer the community recreation professional information concerning the lifestyles, interests, and leisure behaviors of people with disabilities. An additional means of gaining knowledge about the leisure needs and preferences of people with disabilities is to contact advocacy agencies. These agencies typically have a sense of the general needs of people with a particular disability type. For example, the local chapter of The Arc might recommend that the community recreation professional offer teens with mental retardation more opportunities to socialize with peers without disabilities. The recreation professional could then suggest programs that are social and inclusive in nature, such as teen dances, team athletics, and cooperative art projects.

C. *Select Programs* The community recreation professional must use the demographic information and the recreation preferences indicated in steps A and B to develop a number of program alternatives. The challenge for the professional is addressing as many of these diverse community preferences as possible, bearing in mind the available resources and anticipated rate of participation. It is not surprising that preferred programs have a greater chance of being attended than do those that were developed based on the preferences of the community recreation professional. Also, the recreation professional should offer a range of programs that permit participants to choose between active (e.g., athletic) or passive (e.g., crafts) activities. In addition, the recreation professional can expect participants to have a varying range of abilities, skills, and familiarity with any given activity. Programs must be designed to allow participants opportunities for personal growth and socialization, as well as for having fun in a stimulating yet comfortable environment. Instructors can maximize participants' potential for meeting these needs by empathizing with participants, clearly articulating program objectives, maintaining nonjudgmental attitudes, and recognizing individual potential. Of course, programs should be offered for every age group represented in the community and should be prepared to expand should the need arise. For example, if a greater percentage of participants are adults rather than children, then more adult programs should be offered.

Community recreation professionals should demonstrate extreme caution when identifying specialized programs for people with disabilities. Using nomenclature such as "handicapped programs" or "special needs programs" has a tendency to stigmatize people with disabilities and could send a clear message that people with disabilities are not welcome in general programs. Characterizing people with disabilities as "handicapped" denies them their right to be people first and to participate in programs developed for people without disabilities in the same age group. The community recreation professional must make it clear that programs and services are inclusive for everyone. Many communities, in accordance with ADA mandates, are making clear statements of inclusiveness on printed matter (e.g., program brochures, catalogs), which can help to prevent misunderstandings. If special recreation programs are offered, then consumers should be made aware that these programs are designed for people with disabilities as steppingstones to more inclusive experiences and that people with disabilities are invited to participate in nonsegregated offerings, if preferred.

D. *Publicize Programs and Conduct Recruitment* It is essential that the community recreation professional consider various means to effectively communicate program offerings. As Russell (1982) advised, "Turning potential users into actual ones . . . entails communication, persuasion, and timing" (p. 247). Communication initially occurs in the information-gathering and needs-identification stages. If the message between the community recreation professional and the constituency is clear, then appropriate leisure programs and services can be identified. It is critical, therefore, that recreation organizations develop a comprehensive and effective information program (Bright, 1994).

A variety of print media (e.g., fliers, brochures, newspapers, posters) typically is used for this purpose. However, the professional must consider the audience to whom leisure services are to be marketed and sold and, therefore, may want to consider audio, video, electronic mail, or other media as appropriate. Having determined what type of media will be used, a marketing plan must be devised by the recreation professional to address issues related to user recruitment. A comprehensive marketing plan considers all known resources. Included in this plan is a knowledge of individuals and agencies that provide all types of social and health services to people with disabilities (e.g., advocacy groups, allied health professionals), as well as a list of the names and addresses of potential consumers, including people with disabilities. The community recreation professional collaborates with others (see Figure 2.3 on p. 41) to implement this marketing plan.

The recreation professional attempts to persuade potential users to register for and be active participants in proposed programs. When considering potential users who have cognitive or sensory impairments, the recreation professional must communicate with parents, other care providers, teachers, or advocacy agency personnel. As the recreation professional discusses the individual merits or benefits of participating in community leisure programs, he or she may need to explain how modifying and adapting programs and settings to suit the individual needs of the participant will take place (see Chapter 6). The recreation professional, when in the persuasion phase, may need to refer to step B for further support. Finally, the promotional effort must take place early enough to ensure that potential participants are informed about programs prior to the registration period. For example, general and special education teachers and classrooms may have separate mailboxes; brochures about general program offerings meant to be distributed to students through teachers will not necessarily find their way into both mailboxes. Therefore, the competent professional will ensure that distribution is complete. As noted by Russell (1982), "Ideal timing takes experimentation with local media deadlines, the scope of the program [i.e., duration, frequency], and the lifestyle of the constituency" (p. 248).

A common method of advertising programs is through a published program brochure that identifies the program, meeting time, dates and duration, restrictions (e.g., fees, age, personal equipment needs), locations, and instructor. Also essential and mandated by the ADA is a statement of nondiscrimination that openly invites the active participation of people with special needs, particularly people with disabilities. The following are sample nondiscrimination statements:

> The Westland Department of Parks and Recreation actively seeks and supports participation by all people with a variety of interests and abilities in recreational programs and services. Please call us so that we will know how to serve you better.
>
> (Westland, MI)

> ARLE is for all! ARLE (Adaptive Recreation/Learning Exchange) does not discriminate on the basis of disability in the admission or access to, or treatment or employment in, its services, programs, and activities. All programs are compliant with the Minnesota Human Rights Act and the Americans with Disabilities Act.
>
> (Bloomington, Richfield, Edina, Eden Prairie, MN)

Community recreation professionals should avoid using general nondiscrimination statements that sound like "legalese." In the authors' opinion from working with various parent groups, it is necessary for brochure statements to sound friendly, sensitive, and inviting in order to make a person feel welcomed to the leisure setting.

E. Conduct Registration If program offerings have been identified and designed according to the preferences and needs of potential users, and if the community recreation professional has implemented a successful publicity campaign, then the result should be programs that are filled to capacity. Programs cannot be implemented, however, until specific characteristics of the participants are identified. The program instructor will want to know facts about the participants, such as age, gender, past experiences in similar activities, how participants learned of the program, their motivations for registering, their personal goals or expectations, and so forth. A comprehensive registration process will ensure that this information is obtained.

It is at this stage of the inclusive community leisure service process that special considerations are identified. These special considerations may include but are not limited to extent and level of physical and/or mental disability, presence of adaptive behaviors (i.e., ability to understand and participate in recreation experiences with minimal assistance), past experiences in integrated/inclusive environments, medical concerns, behavioral approaches, and so forth. The Recreation Inventory for Inclusive Participation (RIIP) (Chapter 5) provides the community recreation specialist with a format to explore specific individual and program considerations. Once these special considerations are identified, the community recreation professional can determine whether and what program modifications must be made to successfully accommodate the participant with disabilities. Recreation personnel are cautioned not to assume that people with disabilities should be placed in available special recreation program offerings. Such actions are contrary to ADA mandates, which allow potential participants to choose more inclusive programs if desired. Other decision rules governing program modification and strategies to achieve the goals of integration and inclusion are highlighted in later chapters of this text.

F. Implement Programs The program implementation phase of the inclusive community leisure service process translates preparation and planning into action. The participant may or may not understand the comprehensive organization conducted prior to participating in the program. Staff ideally will have received the necessary training to apply specialized as well as general strategies for successfully including and involving all participants in programs. However, depending on how the program is implemented and the positive or negative reactions of other participants, the community recreation professional should be able to ascertain the efficacy of the chosen program planning approach. The entire purpose of moving systematically through this process is to avoid potential pitfalls (e.g., program objectives not being met) that may affect future program efforts. Specifically, one objective of particular importance to participants with disabilities is overcoming barriers to successfully gaining access to and participating in community leisure programs.

It is also at this step when recreation professionals implement the various accommodations identified on the RIIP forms (see Chapter 5). The ADA requires recreation agencies to make its "services, programs, and activities readily accessible to and usable by individuals with disabilities" (U.S. Department of Justice, 28 CFR Part 35, Subpart D, 35.150 [b][1]). Agencies can accomplish this by making adaptations and modifications in their programs, policies, practices, facilities, and equipment. Subsequent chapters in this text identify many ways that recreation professionals can make program adaptations and modifications. Further guidelines for making these decisions are in Chapter 6.

Recreation professionals should keep abreast of the contributions that assistive technology is making in enabling people with disabilities to achieve more access, independence, and levels of participation in community environments such as leisure settings ("Finding funding for assistive technology," 1993; Levin & Enselein, 1990; Moon, Hart, Komissar, & Friedlander, 1995). The Technology-Related Assistance for Individuals with Disabilities Act of 1988 (PL 100-407) and its amendments of 1994 (PL 103-218) specifically address means by which individuals with disabilities and their families and other consumers can receive information and financial assistance to gain access to assistive technology products and services. Simple assistive technology can be effectively and inexpensively incorporated to make leisure environments more accessible and inclusive. Examples include communication devices for people with sensory impairments (e.g., telecommunication devices for the deaf [TDD]; braille, large print, audio publications/signage; FM loop systems for amphitheaters and interpretive programs), universal design concepts (e.g., lever handles, Velcro, clear pathways, ramps, other architectural features that benefit people both with and without disabilities), pressure switches for battery-powered toys and electrical appliances (e.g., popcorn machines), and support people (e.g., volunteer advocates, mainstreaming companions, sighted guides, sign-language interpreters). See Appendix E for names and addresses of assistive technology–related organizations (e.g., AbleData, Ablenet, Inc.).

G. Evaluate Programs Evaluation in itself is a process. The community recreation professional will use this process to determine the efficiency and effectiveness of programs (Howe, 1993). Program evaluation also may yield information concerning utilization of resources, needs assessment, program identification and planning, program implementation, and whether the programs meet the leisure and social skill needs of individual participants. Evaluation aids in program and administrative accountability from individual, organizational, and community perspectives. Recreation staff and activity instructors demonstrate accountability to participants at specific recreation centers and programs by ensuring that programs and facilities are open to everyone and that reasonable accommodations can be made for those participants who need them. In addition, the municipal park and recreation agency demonstrates its commitment to providing comprehensive and accessible leisure service as mandated by its service mission and the law. In short, information gleaned from evaluation efforts assists the recreation professional in improving the overall delivery of community leisure services. (See Chapter 8 for a more detailed explanation of the evaluation process and methods of evaluating programs.)

H. Summarize Findings and Report Without a concise analysis of the evaluation data and a clear mechanism for reporting these data, appropriate modifications to improve implementation of the inclusive community leisure service process cannot be made. Conducting such an analysis permits the recreation professional to identify and act on program or administrative strengths and weaknesses prior to planning and implementing new programs. The evaluation findings must be succinctly written in narrative form and in language easily understood by administrative personnel within the municipal park and recreation or local government agencies, parents, care providers, and other stakeholders. These findings, when reported to key individuals, or "key players," can be useful to recreation personnel and to people with disabilities who are current or potential customers. Presenting findings (particularly regarding successful programs!) also is useful to recreation planners for public relations and for marketing and promoting future programs. Such presentations demonstrate to the public that programs are becoming more inclusive; that successful community integration is possible; and that the municipal park and recreation agency has the personnel, organization, and motivation to ensure that community leisure services will be open and accessible to all community members.

I. Provide Appropriate Feedback Criticism is valuable, particularly when it is constructive. Recreation personnel are likely to share criticisms and suggestions for program modification throughout the leisure service process. Further support for changes in the process should come from individuals and agencies that are involved with community leisure services. Soliciting feedback from others is an essential link to successfully implementing this process. It also strengthens the bond developed by individuals and agencies through networking. This, in turn, provides continued support for providing inclusive leisure services by the community recreation professional. Community leisure advisory boards (discussed later in this chapter), as well as other neighborhood or district planning councils, are ideal forums for exchanging information and providing feedback on the efficacy of inclusive recreation programming. As the process is refined and reworked, inclusive community leisure services will become less of a novelty. Planning and implementing recreation programs and leisure services for people with disabilities will be common occurrences with broad community acceptance and support.

J. Determine Future Efforts Implementing this part of the inclusive community leisure service process is critical to providing year-round inclusive community leisure services and to ensuring that recreation professionals are responsive to ever-changing needs, demands, resources, and values of the community (Cummings & Busser, 1994). The entire process should be scrutinized by community recreation personnel and by the community as a whole. The philosophy and mission of the municipal park and recreation agency may be modified during this time to reflect improved approaches to delivering leisure services based on evaluative findings and feedback from colleagues and participants. Through their efforts to improve service provision, community recreation professionals and the agencies that they represent assume an advocacy role. Their position should be proactive, not reactive (Herchmer, 1994). These professionals will continue to employ systematic organizational tactics and appropriate service methodology to bring about inclusive community leisure services.

SETTING THE STAGE FOR INCLUSIVE RECREATION: GENERAL PROGRAM STRATEGIES

Identifying a specific process to systematically plan for inclusion in community leisure services by people with disabilities is both appropriate and necessary. However, community recreation professionals must generate momentum to set the community leisure service process in motion. Implementing this process may be a difficult task for personnel who lack the training, motivation, or skills to do so. This chapter presents various strategies that are essential for achieving inclusive community leisure services. These strategies include identifying and developing networks or communication linkages among people and agencies concerned about community leisure services, auditing architectural accessibility of leisure service settings, and providing comprehensive training for current and potential recreation professionals. All of these steps are precursors to the systematic inclusion of people with disabilities in leisure activities or settings. Obstacles formerly thought to be insurmountable by parents, consumers, and the community recreation professional, among others, will be dissipated as information is obtained about community support systems and the accessibility of current facilities and programs. Additional strategies for meeting individual participants' unique needs are covered in depth in subsequent chapters.

A. Building Bridges to Inclusion Through Networking Although it is expected that the community recreation professional has the requisite skills and knowledge to plan and implement appropriate recreation programs and services for the neighborhood constituency, seldom does she or he operate alone in this process. The key to successfully including people with disabilities in community leisure service settings depends greatly on the amount and quality of networking that is done. Many professionals, as well as advocates for people with disabilities, agree that inclusion is a community issue (Amado, Conklin, & Wells, 1990; Arsenault, 1990; Gold & McGill, 1988; Kappel, Nagel, & Wieck, 1990). Mobley and Toalson (1992), in their review of the issues, trends, and challenges to be faced by park and recreation professionals in the 21st century, noted that leisure services are an "integral part of the total community" (Toalson & Mobley, 1993, p. 57) and, as such, "it is important for the profession to involve the community in establishing coalitions through which it can move toward accomplishing its mission" (Toalson & Mobley, 1993, p. 59). Hutchison and Lord (1979), in particular, succinctly made a case for networking and collaboration when they stated

> Since serious barriers to involvement exist in our services and communities, any community which hopes to significantly alter the quality of life for its citizens who have disabilities needs individuals and groups of people who are dedicated to developing alternatives. (p. 37)

Effective networking initially involves making connections with professionals from various disciplines, with families and people with disabilities, and with other community members—all of whom share common interests and concerns regarding leisure opportunities in the community for people with disabilities. Networking is a process. As such, it involves establishing ongoing and collaborative working relationships between the recreation professional and a variety of key players. Networking can be initiated through a contact passed along by a colleague, through an introduction and business card exchanged at a meeting, by "browsing" the Internet, and through a telephone conversation or personal meeting. The astute recreation professional will determine the strengths of these social contacts and will solicit the assistance of others in planning and delivering community leisure services. Furthermore, a good professional will recognize that information and resources needed to successfully implement community recreation offerings will have to come from a variety of sources. Networking is an excellent method of identifying these sources.

An effective way to identify significant and worthwhile contacts is to develop a "Networking Matrix" (Figure 2.3). This matrix lists key players who can aid in designing and delivering community leisure services. The predominant key players will be potential consumers who have disabilities, their family members (in particular, parents) and care providers, and others who provide advocacy support or service (e.g., The Arc, MS Society) to these consumers. Collaborating with these individuals is critical to any successful effort to achieve ongoing inclusion in recreation settings and activities. However, the recreation professional should make additional efforts to contact and solicit support from other key players, as necessary.

The networking matrix identifies key players in the community and their specific roles and responsibilities within this process (Appendix C). This matrix and the responsibilities involved may vary from community to community. The community recreation professional is encouraged to use the matrix as a guide and to adapt it to his or her agency's and community's needs. The matrix may be further personalized by identifying specific individuals and agencies within each category according to contact person, agency or category affiliation, address, and telephone num-

Inclusive community leisure service process	Community rec. professionals	Parents and care providers	Consumers	Advocacy groups	School/day program personnel	Allied health professionals	Private rec. services	Quasi-public rec. services	Professional/educational resources
1. Gather information	X	X	X	X	X	X	X	X	X
2. Identify needs	X	X	X	X	X	X		X	X
3. Select programs	X	X	X	X	X		X	X	X
4. Publicize programs and recruit	X	X	X	X	X	X	X	X	X
5. Conduct registration	X	X	X		X	X			
6. Implement inclusion strategies	X	X	X	X	X	X	X	X	X
7. Implement programs	X				X		X	X	
8. Evaluate programs	X						X	X	X
9. Summarize findings and report	X								X
10. Provide appropriate feedback	X	X	X	X	X	X	X	X	X
11. Determine future efforts	X	X	X	X	X	X	X	X	X

Figure 2.3. Networking matrix for identifying responsibilities of "key players" in the inclusive community leisure service process. (Circumstances related to community, participants, and/or agency may require additions, deletions, or other changes in these recommendations.)

ber. A sample form called the Networking Referral List appears in Appendix C. This list provides a ready reference of key players for the individual who is planning or administering services.

The networking matrix process is a simple one. Assume, for example, that the community recreation planner is beginning to plan the agency's programs for the summer, the busiest season of the year. The planner would first ensure that all information regarding potential participants and available resources is obtained and evaluated. Then the planner would consider the initial steps of an inclusive community leisure service process to identify the steps necessary to achieve these objectives. Next, the planner would identify those key players who could assist in each step of the process. The community recreation planner could refer to others on or add others to the Networking Referral List of key players. The recreation planner can then contact individuals and agencies by telephone, through standard or electronic mail, or face-to-face in order to solicit such information as special needs considerations, referrals of potential participants, and leisure preferences. Proceeding through each step of the process and working collaboratively with the various key players identified within the matrix, the recreation planner not only will plan and implement the summer season programs more efficiently but also will likely increase participation rates, thus fostering full inclusion. Furthermore, consumers with disabilities and their parents, care providers, and advocates will be satisfied by these efforts.

As a final note, the recreation professional must be comfortable with what may well be a new "working" (i.e., collaborative) relationship with people not usually involved in planning, implementing, and evaluating the leisure service delivery process. These new collaborative relationships must be built on trust, respect, mutuality, and a sense of common purpose—the full inclusion of people with disabilities in the life of the community, including leisure experiences. This networking process affirms that the cooperation of the various individuals and agencies concerned with the needs of people with disabilities is critical to the success of inclusive community leisure services. Networking is a proactive approach that assures the community that tax dollars are being spent wisely and that capable recreation professionals are administering these programs for the benefit of all community members.

B. *Establishing a Community Leisure Advisory Board* The rationale for including people with disabilities in the leisure lifestyle of the community is based on an understanding and appreciation of the empirical, philosophical, and demonstrated practical considerations for ensuring inclusion. However, concern continues about who is responsible for taking the lead and implementing actions that lead to inclusion in community recreation programs and settings. Public laws such as the ADA clearly place responsibility on public and private providers of leisure services to ensure access and inclusion. In practice, recreation providers, whether following the mandates of laws such as the ADA, continue to have difficulties implementing inclusion in their programs and will rely on parents, care providers, service agencies, and/or specialists (e.g., allied health professionals, teachers) to create, provide, and lead leisure programs for consumers with disabilities. Although this text and the many specific and proven strategies illustrated in it can instill within the recreation professional more confidence in taking the lead for inclusive services, an avenue may be required whereby interested people (i.e., key players) may gather in common purpose, on an ongoing basis, to address issues and obstacles that arise. Establishing a community leisure advisory board is a natural extension of the networking initiative, which will enable key players to continue their mutual efforts to ensure inclusion of people with disabilities in the community, particularly as it relates to leisure.

This advisory board could be made up of a number of representatives from each category of key players. Members should have a personal and professional commitment to people with disabilities and their rights, as citizens of the community, to full access to and inclusion in leisure experiences typically enjoyed by community members who do not have disabilities. The community recreation agency seems to be in the best position to establish the advisory board, as it represents the agency responsible for meeting the recreation and leisure needs of all citizens of a given locale. Establishing a leisure advisory board also affirms that inclusion in leisure programs and settings is a community issue and can best be ensured through a cooperative, collaborative mechanism, such as an advisory board. From a practical standpoint, the recreation provider stands to gain much valuable input and support from this voluntary and representative group. Many communities already have in place community or neighborhood advisory councils that deliberate on a variety of issues. A community leisure advisory board may stand alone or be an adjunct or subcommittee of these and other already-established councils (e.g., Special Education Advisory Councils, Community Transition Interagency Committees, Community Education Associations).

To ensure that the board's decisions truly represent the wishes of the people that the advisory committee has been founded to serve, 30%–50% of its members should be people with disabilities and their family members (Wolfensberger, 1972). In addition, recreation departments must involve staff who provide services to consumers without disabilities to ensure that true and long-lasting systems change occurs. That is, if the advisory committee is made up only of staff whose role is to provide recreation programs only to people with disabilities, then there is a greater risk that community recreation administrators will not gain sensitivity to or hear arguments for full inclusion, thereby delaying the inclusion process. In fact, the objectives of the advisory board would best be served if administrators or other decision makers and policy makers from the community leisure agency were actively involved on this board.

The community leisure advisory board has the potential to be an effective "change agent" within a community. Thus, it should pay particular attention to these 10 primary functions (Ray, 1991):

1. *Formulate and state a common vision of inclusion in leisure settings.* Board members should arrive at a common definition of inclusion and what it means from an agency standpoint, as well as from a family and community perspective. It may be helpful to formulate a mission or position statement as a guide.

2. *Connect with existing planning groups to coordinate interagency efforts and resources.* Other school and community groups already may be addressing these issues. To be most efficient and effective, groups should collaborate.

3. *Establish clear agendas and action plans.* Be focused and assure each member that his or her time is well spent. Set goals and objectives that contribute to real versus perceived change in service delivery.

4. *Incorporate strengths of key players.* Be sure that the board represents stakeholders and other key players who can make discernable contributions to systems changes. All members should agree to make contributions while serving on the board.

5. *Represent and advocate for the needs and rights of people with disabilities.* Board members should advocate for the rights of citizens with disabilities to have full access to the same options and opportunities enjoyed by citizens without disabilities.

6. *Monitor and evaluate services.* Provide feedback to recreation administrators, design and administer customer satisfaction surveys, and set up focus groups to discuss services.

7. *Meet regularly to discuss threats to and opportunities for full inclusion.* Meetings should be regularly scheduled and convenient for members. Identify issues and plans for removing of obstacles or for implementing unique strategies.

8. *Develop and disseminate resources and reports.* The board should keep minutes and, when applicable, copies of survey data findings; position papers; ac-

cessibility audits; collections of articles or other written, audio, and video reports that can then be made available to interested people or agencies.

9. *Design and test strategies to promote positive systems change that ensures full inclusion.* For example, the board can advise agencies receiving funds to improve services, assisting with decisions on allocating funds and resources. Training curricula may be designed with board members as presenters.

10. *Create an atmosphere of change and risk taking.* The board should be self-reinforcing. Members should feel comfortable expressing themselves and their viewpoints and ideas, knowing that there is mutual respect and consideration for one another. Visioning exercises and brainstorming should be incorporated into agendas to allow for creativity and appreciation of a team effort in addressing potentially devisive issues.

Meetings should be formal enough to address the issues and tasks at hand but casual enough to allow for dialogue and friendly conversation among members. This openness and sharing creates feelings of trust, belonging, awareness, empathy, shared commitment, and accountability—all enhancing the prospects for full community leisure inclusion. Monthly or bimonthly meetings are best, 1–2 hours in length. Decisions are reached by consensus, but differences of opinion may necessitate some compromise, on occasion. Remember, inclusion is a process, and there may be more than one approach to achieving it. The community leisure advisory board then serves to demonstrate, by example, that inclusive communities are possible when people with similar concerns and a common vision come together to share mutual support, resources, and commitment to community members who happen to have disabilities.

   C.   *Conducting an Architectural Accessibility Audit*   Citizens with disabilities in all communities are in need of facilities and programs that allow them to meet the basic needs that contribute to their personal welfare and growth (Cangemi, Williams, & Gaskell, 1992). These needs include recreation and leisure. Many people with disabilities have unique requirements, based on their individual disability characteristics, that must be met for them to participate in recreation activities in community environments. It is the recreation professional's responsibility to reasonably accommodate these individuals, including making programs and settings accessible to people with mobility and sensory impairments. For example, specific adaptations may need to be made in order to eliminate architectural barriers in parks and recreation facilities. Common adaptations include ramps, wider doorways, and brailled signage. One way to analyze what specific adaptations or modifications may be needed is by conducting a comprehensive accessibility audit, or on-site survey, using the Americans with Disabilities Act Accessibility Guidelines (ADAAG; 36 CFR Part 1191) (Architectural and Transportation Barriers Compliance Board, 1992) as the minimum standard of compliance.

   The National Policy for a Barrier-Free Environment has estimated that 1 in 10 people in the United States has limited mobility as a result of a temporary or permanent physical disability. The number of these individuals will continue to increase as improved medical techniques make mobility possible for more and more people. Also, as the overall population ages, an ever-increasing number of older people, many with mobility and sensory problems, will make up much of the constituency served by community leisure organizations.

Although the federal government and individual states have provided legislation to make facilities accessible for people with disabilities—Section 502 of the Rehabilitation Act of 1973, for example, established the Architectural and Transportation Barriers Compliance Board to enforce the Architectural Barriers Act of 1968 (PL 90-480), ensuring that new construction and alterations covered by the ADA are "readily accessible to and usable by individuals with disabilities" (ATBCB, 1992)—the physical environment of our communities continues to be designed to accommodate people without disabilities. Feigned ignorance of the laws, lack of enforcement, and the preponderance of waiver claims combine to restrain full accessibility of public and private parks and recreation settings. Recreation administrators, architects, and site planners, in the "spirit" of the ADA, must recognize the inherent rights of all citizens, regardless of their disability, and mobilize their planning resources to design and create recreational places that will successfully include people with disabilities in barrier-free environments (Bedini & McCann, 1992).

A necessary first step toward achieving barrier-free facilities is conducting an accessibility study. This comprehensive analysis provides a review of the architectural and environmental barriers that could limit the participation of individuals with disabilities in community recreation programs and activities. It also might give planners useful information about standards and criteria for designing and modifying facilities that can be used by all citizens of a given locale.

ADAAG provides scoping provisions and technical specifications for designing the following features (partial listing) in both public and private recreation settings (outdoor recreation settings included):

- Accessible routes of travel
- Surfaces
- Space allowance and reach ranges
- Ramps, stairs, elevators, lifts
- Doors, entrances
- Bathrooms, showers
- Alarms, detectable warnings
- Signage

Copies of the ADAAG may be obtained by contacting the ATBCB in Washington, D.C.; and several publishers, including the National Recreation and Park Association (NRPA) and other private firms (Driskell & Wohlford, 1993), are making the guidelines available in a form that makes them usable by the recreation professional. In Appendix D is a complete copy of a building access survey developed by a state agency and based on the ADAAG published at the time that the survey was developed. These surveys are presented as a workbook for personnel and may be reproduced for use in the reader's community.[1]

Community recreation professionals or facility planning staff within the leisure service agency should take primary responsibility for surveying all relevant community or neighborhood recreation settings. Trained volunteers may be utilized

---

[1]At the time that this edition went to press, the ATBCB was considering rule proposals for making specific recreation facilities and outdoor developed areas readily accessible to and usable by people with disabilities, including sports facilities, places of amusement, playgrounds, golf courses, and boating and fishing facilities. Contact the ATBCB for current guidelines (see Appendix E).

to assist and could come from universities (e.g., recreation facilities planning class, future therapeutic recreation specialists, architecture students) or be recruited through the community leisure advisory board. Coordinating and conducting these audits might, in fact, be an appropriate responsibility of this board, working collaboratively with the leisure service agency. It is important that the survey team be interdisciplinary and include members with disabilities, as their perspectives will ensure that both the spirit and the intent of the ADA are considered (Cangemi et al., 1992).

The authors have successfully utilized university recreation students to assist with data collection. Students received preservice training on how to conduct surveys of 42 recreation centers within a major Midwest metropolitan area, using a survey workbook similar to the one in Appendix D. This training consisted of the following:

1. Philosophical and legislative rationale for architectural accessibility of community leisure settings
2. Purpose of the survey, including intended outcomes, current status of facility accessibility, and utilization of the findings by the leisure service agency recreation staff
3. Methods to conduct the survey, deadline for completing the survey and for reporting the data

Recreation sites were divided among pairs of students working together to analyze each category within the survey instrument. Tape measures or yardsticks and one survey instrument per recreation center were provided to each student dyad. To enhance communication and understanding among the investigators, recreation staff, and student surveyors, a memorandum describing the proposed accessibility audit and listing survey procedures was sent to each recreation center director prior to data collection. (An informational meeting at a central location could also be scheduled, if necessary.) Students were then given a standard "telephone protocol" for initial contact; this served as a means of introduction and allowed students and recreation center staff to arrange a time to conduct the audit. The recreation center director was given the option to participate in the audit; it was anticipated that the survey would take 90 minutes or less to complete. The investigators continued to facilitate implementation of the audit and to serve as a resource to the student surveyors during data collection. (Smaller communities with fewer park and recreation facilities may not need as many volunteers.)

After the surveyors completed the audits and returned the data accumulated about each recreation center, the investigators recorded on a simple matrix the name of the center and the total number of code violations per category. This matrix listed the municipal park and recreation facilities surveyed and the features of each (e.g., parking, bathrooms). Areas of noncompliance, including total violations within that area, were noted. This summary information was then submitted to the recreation agency for further analysis by personnel in the recreation and planning divisions. Recommendations for eliminating specific architectural barriers cited in the audits could then be examined by municipal park and recreation administrators, planners, and recreation program and facility staff.

Upon receipt of the data, the recreation agency followed the following procedures to aid in interpreting the data. Aspects of this particular system of analysis are generalizable to other recreation agencies.

1. The data were entered into the agency computer corresponding with the agency's five geographic districts.
2. Spreadsheets were created to allow survey questions and data to be correlated with each recreation center within that district.
3. All noncompliance information was identified for correction.
4. Information from the audit was disseminated to recreation staff and agency administrative personnel.
5. Staff reviewed the data and verified or updated information. New data were entered into the computer.
6. Correction activities were cataloged under one of two major headings: maintenance or capital improvement.
   a. Maintenance catalog activities could include replacing or adding grab bars at the correct height and distance, placing strips and signs in parking stalls to permit handicapped accessibility, and placing tactile identification on doors.
   b. Capital improvement catalog activities could include doorway enlargement, restroom remodeling, and major building renovations.
7. Recreation, planning, and maintenance staff members reviewed the catalog and established a method of merging requests for maintenance with identified access deficiencies.
8. Center personnel request use of maintenance catalog.
9. Repairs and changes would be made in accordance with the survey requirements or recommendations under state and federal statutes.

Accessibility issues, once raised, must be approached jointly with other personnel within the municipal park and recreation agency. Certainly, funding priorities must be considered when anticipating changes or renovations to bring facilities "up to code" and in compliance with the ADA. More important, one should become aware of the capacity of recreation settings to become accessible for people with disabilities. If accessibility features are known, then one can make informed decisions during program planning and implementation to ensure accessibility. For example, instead of denying access to a person with a physical disability because the facility is not wheelchair accessible, the community recreation planner could develop a reciprocal agreement with another organization such as a church, synagogue, school, community center, or rehabilitation hospital to use their facilities if these are more accessible than the recreation agency's facilities. These arrangements are best made before the need arises. Having completed an architectural audit, one knows the capacity of the facility to be readily accessible to and usable by people with disabilities.

D. Staff Training and Development In-service training is an integral component of ongoing professional training and development, and it typically is offered within organized municipal park and recreation agencies. Training topics vary according to the current or anticipated needs of the staff (McKinney & Lowrey, 1987) and may cover issues such as disability awareness and sensitivity, program planning and implementation, activity analysis, marketing and recruitment, fiscal responsibility, personnel concerns, and leisure trends. Various training materials addressing the ADA and related community recreation needs of people with disabilities have been developed and disseminated (Burkhour, 1992; Hill, Perkins, & Thompson, 1992; LIFE Project Staff, 1992; Ray, 1991; Schleien & McAvoy, 1989;

Schleien, Rynders, Heyne, & Tabourne, 1995; Stensrud, 1993; Swanson & Rivard, 1995). Both full-time and seasonal staff are expected to attend these in-service training programs as part of their professional responsibilities.

An important element that should be present in any comprehensive in-service training plan is a segment devoted to delivering inclusive leisure services to children, teens, and adults with disabilities. Because many parks and recreation departments hire seasonal staff to cover summer day camp programs, for example, they offer yearly training to these new, as well as veteran, staff on state-of-the-art program practices related to inclusive services. The Rockford (Illinois) Park District (RPD) is an excellent example of a community agency that has made tremendous efforts to inform its staff and citizens of the importance of inclusive recreation services and to educate its staff. The RPD has published its own staff training guidebook, entitled *A Rockford Park District Survival Guide to Recing Your Life*[2] (Bowerman & Mitchell, 1995). Created by the RPD as an inclusion "tool," this publication attempts to address and meet the following goals.

1. Educating RPD staff and recreation providers on the benefits of inclusive recreation.
2. Providing staff with a guide to RPD inclusive services.
3. Educating recreation providers on the "what it takes" to create inclusive recreational environments and encouraging staff to ask "How can we make this work?"
4. Outlining the inclusive support process available through (the) Extended Services (Department).
5. Promoting the adapted equipment and resources available through RPD programs, facilities, and Extended Services.
6. Educating RPD staff and recreation providers on preferred terminology and etiquette when communicating with and referring to people with disabilities.
7. Creating recreation staff awareness of park, program, and facility accessibility. (p. 5)

This guide goes on to briefly explain the ADA and RPD's response to and active support of this law. It is a highly readable and usable manual for recreation professionals and is representative of how material in this text, when combined with other resources, can be developed into effective staff training material.

Because of the vast amount of information available in the literature concerning the characteristics of different disability types, the authors have elected not to include that information in this text. However, people coordinating in-service training programs are encouraged to write to nationally recognized organizations (see Appendix E) to receive information on disabilities represented in their community. Furthermore, it is recommended that an individual from the recreation agency contact his or her state or local chapter of these organizations to establish a contact for future networking and participant referral. Often, representatives from these organizations will come to the recreation agency to speak and to share information about their particular constituency group. Representatives or constituents of these agencies can be recruited for the leisure advisory board. In addition, a resource file on characteristics of disability groups, updated annually, could be created and made available for reference by recreation staff members. Pamphlets from advocacy groups; informational brochures from sports and recreation associations for people with disabilities; and comprehensive mailing lists of national, state, and local agencies serving people with disabilities could be included in this resource file.

To strengthen the linkage among various key players in the recreation and leisure network, in-service training coordinators and/or community recreation pro-

---

[2]For further information, contact Extended Services Dept. of RPD, (815) 987-1600.

fessionals should invite individuals within each category or advocacy group to participate in some aspect of the in-service program. In fact, individuals with disabilities from the community should be invited to participate in the in-service training sessions as speakers or as resource people. Having a person discuss his or her disability is a useful way of educating audiences and dispelling negative attitudes. It is useful for recreation staff to be exposed to the experiences of others who have either had contact with potential consumers of community leisure services or who themselves have a disability. This approach lends credibility to the in-service program and legitimizes the process used to achieve inclusive services. This outreach approach demonstrates to the community that the park and recreation agency is interested in and concerned about the services it offers. The approach also demonstrates the agency's desire to interact as an advocate with the community to increase the chances that appropriate programs serving the needs of all citizens are considered and made possible. These public relations efforts are practical and useful and could result in increased recreation participation by people with disabilities. They also may generate interest among people without disabilities to serve as volunteer advocates to provide program assistance to participants with disabilities.

SUMMARY

This chapter underscored the need for public park and recreation professionals to objectively and comprehensively appraise their niche in the community leisure service system in which they play a predominant role. It was suggested that they begin this appraisal by gaining a perspective on current community leisure service options for people with disabilities. Because of barriers of omission, some citizens with disabilities are overlooked when recreation planners consider the leisure needs, interests, and preferences of the community. As a result, these citizens may choose not to become involved in the leisure lifestyle of the community, remaining dependent on family members, care providers, therapists, school personnel, and advocacy agencies to address their leisure needs. Other options include *segregated* services, which group people together in special "handicapped only" recreation settings; *integrated* services, which systematically plan and implement programs in which people with and without disabilities receive overt support to participate alongside one another; and *inclusive* services, which enable individuals to freely choose, gain access to, and enjoy leisure experiences in a manner consistent with how people without disabilities typically meet their leisure needs.

A process model for inclusive leisure services also was articulated in order for public recreation agencies to better organize their delivery systems. Ten components of this inclusive community leisure service process model were listed, and tasks were identified and explained to enable recreation professionals to achieve a clear understanding of their roles and responsibilities as they plan, implement, and evaluate inclusive recreation offerings. Examples were given of how communities may diverge from this process when providing either segregated or general recreation programs.

Finally, this chapter proposed a variety of general strategies to ensure that community recreation services and settings are inclusive of and architecturally accessible to people with disabilities. Creating a networking matrix of local key players in the community leisure service delivery process is a necessary first step to ensuring that agencies and individuals work together on issues of inclusion. Roles and responsibilities of key players were articulated and are organized in Appendix C. The chapter also suggested that an active and viable community leisure advisory board should be established to address community leisure service issues concerning people with disabilities. Ten functions of this advisory group were highlighted. The community recreation professional also should implement a comprehensive building and facilities accessibility audit. Recommendations to upgrade accessibility of leisure settings would then be forwarded to park planning personnel. A reproducible building access survey is provided in Appendix D. In addition, providing on an ongoing basis continuing education and training of community recreation professionals, seasonal staff, and volunteers regarding developing, implementing, and evaluating community leisure programs and services for people with disabilities was stressed.

The strategies presented in this chapter are not setting or community specific. That is, even though urban and rural communities exhibit differences in population distribution, availability of resources, convenience of services, and leisure lifestyles (e.g., limited leisure options in certain areas), each strategy highlighted in this chapter can be implemented to a greater or lesser extent and can remain functional for that community setting. In fact, planners in isolated rural communities that do not have community leisure service agencies or advocacy groups may need to emphasize implementing these basic strategies, particularly related to networking and collaborating, to optimize leisure service delivery to people with disabilities. The authors recommend that readers contact their state park and recreation professional membership organization to assist them.

Identifying and Overcoming Obstacles to Inclusive Recreation

3

◆ ◆ ◆ ◆ ◆

Recreation professionals with experience in providing recreation services to people with disabilities realize that barriers to inclusive services may be encountered at any stage of the recreation service delivery process. Problems encountered could be a result of any number of circumstances related to organizing recreation services, to personal or professional attitudes, to individual skills, and to the disability characteristics of the potential user. The strategies selected by the recreation professional determine whether barriers to inclusion are resolved and whether participants achieve a positive inclusive leisure experience. As highlighted in Chapter 1 and further illustrated in subsequent chapters, successful inclusive leisure experiences for participants with and without disabilities often are dependent on leisure personnel and other key players to systematically plan and implement barrier-free programs.

One must not be discouraged by the presence of barriers because it is unusual for an agency not to encounter them. In fact, people without disabilities also may experience conflicts or difficulties when attempting to participate in recreation activities, even though they are not handicapped by a disability or do not typically experience a negative stigma from the community. Examples include lack of skills for an art class, lack of sufficient physical fitness for a jogging program, lack of funds for class fees, and lack of accessible and convenient transportation to and from a program.

Empathizing with people with disabilities may be an effective means of understanding barriers that everyone might experience at one time or another as he or she attempts to enter community recreation settings. A professional approach to understanding barriers should be tempered with this personal awareness of the potential for encountering barriers. This will permit the recreation professional to assess each situation as unique. One must be careful, however, not to empathize with people with disabilities to the point of becoming patronizing or paternalistic. These behaviors, which can be manifested as "talking down" to another individual in a parent–child manner, can further "devalue" the person with a disability by making him or her feel helpless, dependent, and, possibly, humiliated. Recreation professionals must be just that—professionals; that is, people who bring skills, training, motivation, enthusiasm, and commitment to their jobs, in this case, the systematic approach to providing barrier-free community recreation services.

There are many ways to categorize sources of barriers to inclusive community leisure services (Bedini & McCann, 1992; Kennedy, Smith, & Austin, 1991; Smith, 1985). This chapter categorizes them as either individual barriers or external barriers. Individual barriers stem from the nature (i.e., the level and extent) of the person's particular disability. External barriers further handicap people with disabilities and inhibit their full participation in community recreation experiences.

Because the municipal park and recreation agency has the ultimate responsibility for providing recreation services to all members of the community (Rossman, 1995; Schleien & Werder, 1985) and because external, or environmental, barriers are the leading factors that inhibit accessible and inclusive recreation services, external barriers are addressed first with proposed solutions. A discussion of individual barriers follows in a similar form. The recreation professional is challenged to identify and eliminate external barriers in his or her own community, including the leisure service agency, and to avoid the assumption that the individual with disabilities is the primary cause of obstacles to inclusive community leisure services.

EXTERNAL BARRIERS

External barriers are the most common barrier type cited by recreation professionals and others. Granted, the person's disability may inhibit his or her access to the full range of community recreation services and settings, but external forces place additional pressure on the individual, making the disability and, consequently, the individual the problem. People, agencies, and social systems further handicap and stigmatize people with disabilities in the following ways: financial constraints, lack of qualified recreation staff, lack of accessible and available transportation, lack of accessible facilities, poor communication, ineffective service systems, and negative attitudes (Ohio Developmental Disabilities Planning Council, 1995; Putnam, Werder, & Schleien, 1985; Ray, Schleien, Larson, Rutten, & Slick, 1986; Schleien & Ray, 1988; Schleien & Werder, 1985; Smith, 1985; Wheeler, Lynch, & Thom, 1984).

Financial Constraints

Financial constraints can relate to one or more of the following: 1) potential participants, 2) staff, and 3) facilities and equipment/materials. People with disabilities might have less discretionary funds to spend on recreation and leisure activity participation than would people without disabilities. The cause may be lack of employment, low pay, limited assistance from social services agencies such as Medicare or welfare, and greater expenses because of the need to purchase specialized or adapted equipment such as vans with wheelchair lifts and/or custom-made clothing. Municipal park and recreation departments are further constrained when public funds are restricted, thereby limiting development or acquisition of new services, equipment, facilities, accessible buildings, and qualified staff. Several solutions to this barrier follow.

If the financial constraints are participant centered, then a sliding-fee schedule for all participants—based on ability to afford the cost of the activity—could be implemented. If volunteer advocates are needed for the person to participate, then let them attend for free or at substantially reduced rates. Participants with disabilities also could donate services (e.g., reception or secretarial duties, horticultural work) to park and recreation agencies in exchange for program fees. Perhaps a scholarship fund could be created for people with financial needs. Various civic or corporate organizations can sponsor potential participants by assisting with fees or transportation. Donated in-kind services (e.g., photocopying, printing, mailings) by these same agencies could release monies to be applied to scholarships and fee reductions. PL 101-336, the Americans with Disabilities Act (ADA) of 1990, mandates that any additional expenses associated with inclusive programs and settings cannot be passed on solely to participants with disabilities. The agency or community itself must absorb these expenses if the leisure service agency cannot demonstrate and document a financial hardship.

If an agency believes that additional staff members are necessary to implement programs but lacks funds to hire them, then a consortium among agencies could be created to hire a "traveling," or itinerant, certified therapeutic recreation specialist (CTRS) to serve a consultative role with various park and recreation agencies and to provide assistance in such areas as activity modifications or evaluation when needed. Rather than relying on several expensive specialized staff members, it might be more cost-effective for the agency to create and fund a volunteer services coordinator staff position. The return on investment will occur when an extensive network of volunteers is developed and available for resource staff members to train and use as volunteer or trainer advocates. In addition, providing ongoing in-service training for existing staff members should eliminate the need for specialized staff.

Often, facilities must be made more architecturally accessible to people with mobility and sensory impairments. Also, adaptive materials and equipment, which may enhance program accessibility and partial participation, must be acquired. Agencies should pursue donations or corporate funding to purchase necessary equipment and materials such as accessible vans or bowling ramps. Private donations or corporate funding also can be utilized to produce media presentations such as slide shows or videotapes for use as promotional or staff training aids. In addition, communities could earmark funds from the municipal park and recreation department budget to improve the accessibility of recreation services. Because approximately 10%–15% of the U.S. population is classified as having a disability, a comparable amount of funds should be allocated to serve these people. State and federal grants are available to upgrade personnel development from the U.S. Department of Education, Office of Special Education and Rehabilitative Services. Furthermore, the U.S. Department of Transportation and Community Development Block Grants provide funds for upgrading facilities, and many states' Developmental Disabilities Planning Councils sometimes provide grants for program development. Select agency personnel could develop grant-writing skills to pursue new funding sources.[1]

---

[1]To develop your agency's grant-writing skills, contact the Grantsmanship Center, Post Office Box 17220, Los Angeles, CA 90017, (800) 421-9512 (telephone), (213) 482-9863 (FAX); and your local community education program, community college, or university.

Collaborating between public and private-sector leisure service agencies is a viable method of coping with scarce resources. Co-sponsoring programs with other agencies can provide access to additional resources such as materials, equipment, and funds. Finally, agencies should develop simplified, homemade equipment and material adaptations to replace commercially marketed adapted equipment that can cost significantly more to purchase and maintain.

Lack of Qualified Staff

Even though community recreation professionals claim to be generalists and are empowered to plan and provide programs and services to constituents within a particular geographic area, they often do not possess the skills, knowledge, or motivation to adequately or appropriately include people with disabilities in these programs. Because of these factors and for reasons often related to attitudes and past practices, municipal park and recreation agencies may believe that special population groups require services unrelated to those typically offered to constituents who do not have disabilities. Therefore, special staff members are hired to provide these services. However, agencies must be willing to provide more training to general leisure service personnel on ways to apply typical services in order to eliminate unnecessary reliance on specialized staff. Agencies also must inform staff of their roles and responsibilities in ensuring access to and inclusion in recreation programs and settings.

In-service training programs for current staff members and volunteers must be ongoing, comprehensive, and relevant. Agencies may want to hire a CTRS consultant to conduct this training and to facilitate the process of developing and implementing inclusive leisure services. Trained volunteers and student interns from local university recreation departments could be incorporated in programs and services to expand staff and, subsequently, opportunities for participants with disabilities. More practicum and internship sites must be developed within the municipal park and recreation agency to enhance this potential. Leisure service agencies also could create a professional staff position called a community leisure planner (CLP) or community leisure facilitator (CLF) (Moon, 1994; Ray, 1991). This person(s) could be employed by advocacy groups, local schools, and recreation agencies with the primary function of ensuring that community members with disabilities are appropriately accommodated in recreation programs and settings. Other titles sometimes used by agencies to refer to people who function in a similar capacity are leisure coach, inclusion (integration) specialist/coordinator/facilitator, special needs director, and adaptive recreation specialist. Table 3.1 identifies the chief characteristics of a CLP, and Appendix C lists the roles and responsibilities. Job descriptions must be developed or revised to affirm the role of the community recreation professional as a facilitator of inclusive leisure services. Figure 3.1 is a sample job description for a CLP.

Special education teachers and part-time assistants from local schools may want to serve as staff members or consultants during the summer months. Additional training must be provided at the preservice level to university undergraduate and graduate students on those competencies needed to be an effective community recreation professional. This instruction should include training methods for including people with disabilities in recreation programs and settings, as well as the vital importance and critical necessity of establishing networks of communication among key players.

Table 3.1. Chief characteristics of a community leisure planner (CLP)

A VISIONARY	• Knows the future is inclusion, where all people belong
	• Understands and practices values of inclusion
	• Knows that inclusion "makes good sense," and everyone benefits
AN ADVOCATE	• Knows and understands the legal mandates for inclusion
	• Convinces others of the value and importance of inclusive leisure as a means of enhancing quality of life
	• Respects, empowers, and solicits input from families and individuals with disabilities
	• Speaks up and out about inclusion within the agency and throughout the community
	• Shares stories about successful inclusion efforts
AN AUTHORITY	• Has personal and professional standing within the agency and the community, which enhances credibility with key players
	• Is a good listener; respects and is respected by key players
	• Understands roles and responsibilities as a key player; knows when to step in—and when to step back to let others who are empowered take charge
	• Knows inclusion is a process; familiar with state-of-the-art approaches and strategies
ACTION ORIENTED	• Takes initiative within agency and community to promote and foster inclusion efforts
	• Educates staff and administration on inclusion
	• Knows or finds key players and actively networks
	• Takes a leadership role on Community Leisure Advisory Board
	• Is "proactive" versus "reactive"

Adapted from Ray (1991).

Lack of Transportation

Some of the most prevalent concerns that people with disabilities have are the availability and quality of transportation services to community recreation settings; transportation systems such as public buses or taxis may not be physically accessible. In addition, taxis may be too expensive. If adapted vehicles are used, they may only be available on a limited, reservation-only basis. Because of the large number of segregated programs being offered in centralized locations and the apparent lack of accessible neighborhood recreation programs and facilities, people with disabilities must rely totally on alternative transportation systems. These transportation options, however, are not always available. Solutions to this problem do exist.

Because transportation issues are addressed in the ADA, local communities are obligated not to discriminate if they provide transportation to other community members. The cost of including accessible buses in the transportation fleet, however, may make more immediate and practical measures necessary in the interim. For example, the person with a disability or his or her advocate could contact public (e.g., city transit authority) and private (e.g., ambulance service) transportation agencies to determine the availability of vehicles accessible to people with disabilities, costs, and scheduling information. Corporations that use employee carpooling and that have corporate-owned vehicles may be willing to donate transportation services during times when the vehicles are not in use. Privately owned taxicab

JOB TITLE: Community Leisure Planner

SUPERVISOR:

FTE: Full-time

SALARY RANGE:

GENERAL FUNCTION:

The Community Leisure Planner facilitates the inclusion of youths and adults with disabilities in existing programs offered by the YMCA of metropolitan Minneapolis branches. Responsibilities include outreach, assessment, adapting programs, evaluating outcomes, and training staff members to meet the needs of youths and adults with disabilities.

REQUIREMENTS:

- Master's or bachelor's degree in therapeutic recreation, special education, adaptive physical education, rehabilitation, or related field.
- Knowledge of and minimum of 2 years experience working with broad array of disability populations in a direct service capacity.
- Knowledge of YMCA service delivery system, disability resources, and techniques for adaptations in equipment, teaching strategies, and activities.
- Knowledge of the philosophy of inclusion and the ability to communicate that philosophy.
- Knowledge of the Americans with Disabilities Act and clear understanding of professional boundaries and applicable regulations regarding data privacy, confidentiality, and vulnerable adult status.
- Ability to deal effectively with parents, program participants, community agencies, and the general public in an effective, tactful, and courteous manner.
- Ability to function independently with a minimum of day-to-day supervision and in a team situation.
- Current, pending, or ability to secure CPR/First Aid certification.
- Ability to work flexible hours, including some evenings and weekends.

PRINCIPAL ACTIVITIES:

- *Train* staff about disability awareness, inclusion, and program adaptations.
- *Develop* an outreach plan to increase public awareness, promote programs, and encourage people with disabilities to participate in programs.
- Serve as point person for participants with disabilities to *provide* information, *perform* assessments (if needed), and *ensure* that participant needs will be met. *Facilitate* team meetings with staff, participants, and parents as necessary.
- *Develop, implement,* and *monitor* a system to track the level of participation of people with disabilities in YMCA programs to determine whether outreach efforts have been successful.
- *Develop, implement,* and *monitor* a system to measure the effectiveness of adaptations made and the satisfaction of participants with disabilities, their families, and staff with their experience at the program.
- *Ensure* that public relations, marketing, and informational materials promote the YMCA's inclusive philosophy and that the YMCA's physical environment is welcoming for all potential participants.
- *Assist* with developing and implementing a transition plan to meet ADA requirements.
- *Promote* a positive image of individuals with disabilities, and create an atmosphere of acceptance in the community.
- *Respect* the privacy of participants by limiting the sharing of personal information to a need-to-know basis.
- *Perform* other duties as assigned.

Figure 3.1. Job description for a community leisure planner (CLP) for the YMCA of metropolitan Minneapolis. (*Source:* Swanson and Rivard, 1995.)

companies could offer rate reductions and convenient services for users of community recreation services. In addition, organizing carpools using volunteers, parents, and care providers is a proven method of overcoming transportation barriers for people with disabilities. Churches often own buses and vans and may be contacted to determine whether these vehicles are available during slow times. Finally, potential participants must be taught how to independently take advantage of available transportation systems. This is an extremely important leisure skill that parents, care providers, teachers, and therapeutic recreation specialists should teach to people with disabilities.

Lack of Accessible Facilities

Federal laws mandate that public facilities and services, including those providing recreation in the community, must be architecturally accessible for people who have disabilities such as mobility and sensory impairments. Individuals with disabilities cannot successfully participate in park and recreation programs if they are unable to enter or to make their way around facilities and park areas. Burkhour (1992) defined a physical barrier as "a condition of the physical environment that restricts or complicates access, movement, or participation by individuals attempting to use recreation facilities or areas" (p. 20). Physical barriers can be manmade (e.g., stairs, narrow doors, curbs, steep ramps) or natural (e.g., hills, sand, thick vegetation, rocks) and, therefore, have different implications for people with and without disabilities. Architectural barriers in the environment can be minimized in the following ways.

Architectural accessibility surveys of indoor and outdoor environments, using the Americans with Disabilities Act Accessibility Guidelines (ADAAG), should be conducted under the direction of the leisure service agency and the recreation staff. State (e.g., Council for the Handicapped) and national (e.g., Architectural and Transportation Barriers Compliance Board) boards and commissions may be contacted for standards and recommendations regarding physical accessibility of facilities (see also Building Access Survey sample forms in Appendix D). Many communities have "accessibility specialists" who can serve as agency consultants. They can conduct surveys, make recommendations, and prepare and deliver reports on their findings to park and recreation personnel and boards. Federal and state funding may be available for removing existing physical barriers. Communities may offer low-interest loans (e.g., 3%) to businesses that seek to comply with accessibility standards.

In the event that facilities and areas cannot be made totally accessible, program modifications such as conducting nature hikes on blacktop trails or switching classrooms must be considered. If outdoor environments are being used, then small teams of individuals can be assembled to assist each other to move through the natural environment. For example, two people can walk with one person in a wheelchair, or a sighted guide can accompany a blind skier. In one creative example, upon learning that a young student who uses a wheelchair was in a class arriving for a nature study program and hike, nature center staff members coordinated with a local golf course to have a golf cart delivered so that the student would be able to negotiate the unimproved nature trails with his classmates. If necessary, arrange with other leisure service organizations such as YMCAs or YWCAs, churches, synagogues, community centers, or sports and health clubs to use their facilities, if these are more accessible. Finally, recreation agency personnel must be apprised of accessibility issues in their communities in order to provide knowledgeable service to potential consumers who may contact them to determine accessibility features. It may be useful to summarize accessibility features and issues in a three-ring binder that is convenient to staff members and easily revised and updated as facilities are improved.

Poor Communication

For those individuals whose speech and language abilities are affected by certain developmental disabilities (e.g., cerebral palsy, hearing impairments), communication may be limited. Unfortunately, recreation planners can compound this problem if they lack necessary skills (e.g., sign language, interpreting communication boards) and telecommunications systems (e.g., TDD) to "talk" with them. Again, recreation agencies are responsible under the ADA to acquire the necessary systems and skills, as well as to establish policies that allow people with communications difficulties to communicate with them. Lacking such systems and skills is predominantly an external barrier issue, even though having such impairments is an individual barrier encountered by the potential consumer.

Speech impediments are only one manifestation of poor communication. Unclear communication also may be found in those situations in which recreation professionals are "hearing" but not "listening" to potential participants. Because people with disabilities represent only a small minority group within a community, recreation professionals usually design most of their programs for the majority population—those without disabilities. Potential users with disabilities may express their needs, preferences, and suggestions; but if community recreation professionals are not "listening," then inclusive programs will not result. Thus, unclear lines of communication can be a significant obstacle.

In addition to unclear interpersonal communication, lack of communication across agencies also can be a problem. For example, ineffective networks can "muddy" lines of communication. This can result from a lack of a unified process that involves active collaboration and communication, or networking, between individuals and agencies with similar interests and missions. This can lead to redundant or duplicate services, inefficient utilization of scarce resources, and, worse, assumptions that leisure services for people with disabilities are being provided appropriately by people and/or agencies other than leisure service providers when they are not.

One solution to poor networking is for community recreation professionals to invite an allied health professional such as a speech-language pathologist or a communication disorders specialist to make an in-service presentation on communication disorders and alternative communication systems (e.g., sign language, Blissymbolics, word boards, electronic devices). In addition, recreation staff members could enroll in sign-language classes at the local technical-vocational institute or university. A meeting between potential participants and the recreation staff also may be useful. The person with disabilities and/or his or her care provider should explain to the recreation staff the participant's communication needs for the recreation activity in which he or she is planning to participate. The ADA obligates agencies to provide sign-language interpreters as a necessary accommodation for individuals who need it. Volunteer advocates who understand the participant's communication system may serve as liaisons or intermediaries between the recreation staff and the participant with the speech impairment. Community recreation professionals also should avoid using jargon and professional terminology when meeting with parents and care providers. As a final approach to solving interpersonal communication barriers, the community recreation professional should heed the following guidelines:

- Be an active listener.
- Maintain direct eye contact.
- Talk to the individual (not to the volunteer advocate or care provider).
- Ask for clarification if what is being said is unclear (if necessary, have the person repeat him- or herself).
- Speak in two- to three-word phrases.
- Invite the volunteer advocate or care provider to assist, when appropriate.

To further enhance communication across individuals and agencies, the following solutions are proposed. The community recreation professional should communicate regularly with parents and care providers to provide feedback on participation by people with disabilities in the recreation program and to determine whether skills learned at the recreation site are being generalized to the home. Community recreation personnel also could help to create a community leisure advisory board made up of key players in the inclusion process. Recreation personnel can be advocates of inclusive community leisure services, as well as personal advocates for specific individuals with disabilities, at local government meetings and state legislation sessions in which decisions concerning community recreation funding or service delivery are being made. In addition, personnel can plan to participate in advocacy group meetings or special education councils or to serve on associated task forces formed by these groups. Clearer communication through networking will occur if participants express care, concern, and understanding of others.

Ineffective Service Systems

Although community recreation professionals may support the tenets of normalization and inclusion, often the park and recreation systems within which they operate can confound their efforts by being slow to change traditional service delivery processes. Ineffective service systems may result from a combination of obstacles in the environment, including barriers of omission, and rules and regulations barriers. Often it is what is not provided by a service system that limits participation by people with disabilities. Because people with disabilities are a minority and generally not as visible in the community, they may not be remembered or included when new programs and services are being developed by recreation departments. The result: barriers of omission.

Rules and regulations typically are developed by people who do not have disabilities and who seldom take into account the needs of people with disabilities. The result is that participation by people with disabilities in recreation often is limited:

1. People in wheelchairs often must sit in aisles and walkways when attending events at inaccessible theaters and sports complexes. This is against fire regulations.
2. Most games, whether board/table games or athletics, have prescribed rules for participants or else penalties are imposed. Rather than deviating from the

rules, people with disabilities frequently choose to be spectators rather than participants.

3. The separate restrooms and locker rooms provided for men and women can present problems for an individual whose attendant is not of the same gender.

4. Public tennis courts often have restricted openings to prevent bicycles from damaging the surface of the courts. These openings also keep wheelchair users off.

Many solutions to barriers imposed by ineffective service systems exist. Administrators and recreation programmers should carefully assess their roles and responsibilities to determine the optimal approach to overcoming these significant barriers. For example, professionals can become aware of the unique needs of people with disabilities by examining the present system of leisure service delivery to identify obstacles created by service gaps. Also, professionals can take preventive measures by actively implementing a systematic process for service delivery to all people with and without disabilities. This will prevent obstacles from occurring in the first place. Others are involving community members through focus groups (Heyne, Schleien, & McAvoy, 1993) and other collaborative efforts such as "action planning" teams (Pedlar, Gilbert, & Gove, 1994) and personal futures planning teams (Mount & Zwernik, 1988). In addition, professionals can develop and assume an active role on a community leisure advisory board to enhance awareness and interpersonal and interagency communication through networking with schools, municipal park and recreation departments, and community education agencies. Board members could use brainstorming meetings as a forum to exchange ideas on program delivery and activities. This process will be beneficial for a number of reasons: 1) participation and advocacy would increase; 2) professional staff, educators, students, and advocacy groups would be encouraged to research the effectiveness of implementing the strategies within the inclusive community leisure service process; and 3) service providers would receive current information on consumer needs with regard to programmatic and architectural accessibility.

There are a variety of ways to advertise recreation and leisure services to ensure that people are aware that services are open and accessible: 1) advertising on gas, water, or electric bills or in bank statement envelopes; 2) inserting program brochures into newspapers and advocacy group newsletters; 3) creating public service announcements to be broadcast on the radio and TV; 4) inviting media coverage of inclusive programs; and 5) leaving brochures with neighborhood businesses, such as laundromats, grocery stores, or banks, for distribution.

A concern expressed by parents is that the "legalese" nondiscrimination statements on program brochures are impersonal and tend to discourage participation. Agencies must develop a more personal nondiscrimination statement to be included in all program brochures and advertisements. (See p. 36 for examples of nondiscrimination statements.) Recreation professionals also must take the initiative to contact local and statewide social services agencies, especially those that provide services to people with disabilities, for assistance in locating potential consumers of leisure services.

Finally, continuing concerns for park and recreation agencies are safety, risk management, and legal liability (Brademus, 1991; Gold, 1994; Stensrud, 1993). Concerns stem mainly from activity offerings and administration (Edginton & Ford, 1985), facility design (Kaiser & Mertes, 1991), type and extent of insurance coverage (Brademus, 1991), volunteer involvement (Henderson & Bedini, 1991), and participant characteristics (Gold, 1994). Local governments must continue to accept a level of responsibility to ensure the general health, safety, and welfare of users of their programs and facilities. As stated by Gold (1994), a "professional standard of care that reflects the state-of-the-art technology and information should be used in the design and management of public parks" (p. 35). This is consistent with trends that suggest that these types of concerns, raised by recreation administrators, will continue in the future to have an impact on leisure service provision in public recreation settings (Whyte, 1992) and, when this level of care is missing, may be a reason that potential participants stay away from programs (McCarville & Smale, 1993).

Although it is important to develop risk-management plans and to be concerned about liability issues, recreation administrators must be very cautious when discussing the implications of people with disabilities and inclusive recreation programs and environments (Council of Better Business Bureaus' Foundation, 1992). Section 35.130 of the ADA, General Prohibitions Against Discrimination (28 CFR Part 35; Department of Justice), states that recreation service providers are obligated not to act in ways that may further discriminate against or cause the segregation of people with disabilities. Recreation agencies, therefore, must take appropriate steps to ensure that people with disabilities and their family members, care providers, and volunteer supports are not a primary liability or risk concern but rather are included in discussions and risk-management planning to the benefit of *all* park and recreation users.

Recreation professionals are strongly encouraged to raise these issues with insurance providers, legal counsel, advocacy agency personnel, community councils, people with disabilities and their families, and others to gain appropriate and relevant perspectives on potential risk and liability issues, to become sensitive to possible discriminatory practices, and to learn better ways to assist community members with disabilities so that they can enjoy and be equal participants in public park and recreation services. Although the ADA, state insurance and liability statutes, and professional literature may provide guidelines for addressing these issues, recreation professionals must look inward to their own attitudes about inclusion, as well as strive to design and implement, to the best of their professional ability, programs and facilities that meet the true needs of *all* community members.

Negative Attitudes

One of the most powerful obstacles faced by individuals with disabilities who are attempting to be included in community recreation programs is the misinformed attitudes of people without disabilities, particularly professional service providers (Burkhour, 1992; Germ, 1993; LIFE Project Staff, 1992; McGill, 1984) and co-participants in leisure experiences (Heyne et al., 1993; Rynders & Schleien, 1991). Generally, American society has taken an ambivalent attitude toward people with disabilities. This attitude is manifested in different ways. For example, people without disabilities openly admire people with disabilities at times, believing that they are entitled to the "good things in life." Individuals without disabilities believe that they, themselves, have a responsibility to make contributions to improving the quality of life of people with disabilities, who they feel are less fortunate than themselves. However, because of society's generally misinformed attitudes about disability, the efforts of people without disabilities to improve the quality of life of people with disabilities are conducted in ways that keep people with disabilities socially distant, thus building an invisible wall of exclusion. This invisible wall becomes more pronounced as the severity of one's disability increases. Attitudes toward people with more severe disabilities and disability characteristics that appear to be more threatening (e.g., mental illness) tend to be considerably more negative than attitudes toward people with mild and/or more familiar disabilities (Roth & Smith, 1983). Individuals without disabilities may further accentuate differences by the manner in which they interact, or do not interact, with people with disabilities. Included among the variety of unpleasant behaviors that a person without a disability may manifest toward an individual with a disability are paternalistic behaviors (e.g., head patting, age-inappropriate talk, excessive praise), avoidance (i.e., not acknowledging his or her presence), and teasing behaviors (e.g., mocking, name calling).

Admiring people with disabilities often leads to an unhealthy attitude of *social altruism* that may decrease, rather than increase, opportunities for full inclusion. People without disabilities believe that they have a responsibility to help people with disabilities, rather than recognize the possibilities of developing appropriate relations and include them in community environments. Many people still believe that people with disabilities are somewhat "sick" and dependent and that relationships, if any, are vertical; that is, people without disabilities are the "helpers" and people with disabilities are the "helpees," dependent on others to ensure their participation in society.

During a meeting of a local civic club, for example, members demonstrated their social altruism by describing the extent of their volunteer work with community members who have disabilities. Admittedly, their contributions were worthy, as the club of 25 members totaled more than 200 person-hours of volunteer assistance with the local Special Olympics event. Yet none of the members considered recruiting people with disabilities, especially those adults with cognitive disabilities whom they may have assisted at the athletic event, to be members of their civic club. A similar example concerns a student-run community service club at a large Midwestern high school that believes that one purpose of the group is to "serve" less fortunate people (e.g., neighborhood elders, low-income families, fellow students with disabilities). The club sponsored a dance for students with disabilities at which club members picked "buddies," gave them candy, and danced to age-inappropriate music (e.g., Bunny Hop). The students with disabilities became a "project" of the club and, therefore, were not viewed as potential members of the club. Actions like these, as well as many other efforts conducted under the guise of "helping" people with disabilities, maintain walls of exclusion and continue to keep people with disabilities "comfortably away" from the rest of society.

Societal attitudes and perceptions also are reflected in the types of leisure service delivery systems that are established in communities. Sessoms (1984) pointed out that in complex societies, delivery systems are developed to meet specific societal needs. For example, leisure service systems were created to answer society's need to engage in recreational activities that permit one to escape the demands of work or of everyday life. But society is made up of diverse individuals with varying recreational interests and needs. Community recreation personnel must make it a priority to regard themselves as "generalists" endeavoring to meet the leisure and recreation requirements of a demographically and culturally diverse constituency. By applying a systematic and inclusive planning process and planning in collaboration with key players, recreation professionals will have a greater chance of ensuring that all members of the community have their leisure needs addressed to the greatest extent possible.

Interviews with community recreation personnel revealed that resistance to providing leisure services to people with disabilities may be a result of an organizational stigma (West, 1982). *Organizational stigma* refers to the situation wherein recreation professionals attach their own preconceived values about a person's leisure needs and abilities to the type and extent of services offered, thus limiting service diversity and flexibility. West (1984) also found that people with disabilities are able to perceive this stigma and thus tend to maintain a "self-imposed exile from active participation in community recreation" (p. 41). Each view reinforces the other and prevents successful inclusion from taking place. For example, a recreation professional may offer primarily athletic programs, but people with physical disabilities are unable to participate in such programs. The professional assumes that "handicapped people" are not interested in these programs because they are never heard from, nor are they seen at the park. Furthering this cycle, the recreation professional offers the same programs each year. People with disabilities continue to stay away from the park because they cannot participate. Community and organizational stigmas are thus reinforced. People with disabilities disappear into the home or are shunted into segregated, special recreation programs.

One of the many negative results of society's attitude that people with disabilities are sick, dependent, or even deviant is that people with disabilities themselves begin to accept this perception. This *self-fulfilling prophecy* may be the result of focusing on differences among people rather than seeking out similarities (Dattilo & Smith, 1990) and labeling individuals by their disability characteristics. Labeling begins a process whereby people who are perceived to be different (i.e., people with disabilities) are separated from the mainstream of society and are reinforced for accepting an outcast role and behaving in a manner consistent with society's preconceived and often negative expectations (Hutchison & Lord, 1979). The result is that because society expects people with disabilities to be different from people without disabilities, they, in fact, become different and begin to accept a lifestyle that is removed from the community. An example that illustrates this point concerns a social-recreational club for young adults with cognitive and other learning disabilities that moved from being sponsored and staffed by a local chapter of The Arc to becoming a part of a local YMCA outreach program. Club members were used to having The Arc staff organize, plan, and implement activities in rooms adjacent to The Arc offices—all they had to do was show up. When sponsorship moved, YMCA staff members attempted to engage club members in program planning and running the club, as well as integrating club activities within typical YMCA leisure environments. Because members had been dependent on The Arc staff for so many years and because they did not receive leisure education or opportunities to learn skills to be active partners either in planning and implementing activities or in how to use a leisure environment like the YMCA, club members were unable to have a positive leisure experience. They expressed that they wanted the club "back the way it used to be."

Because negative attitudes are, perhaps, the most pervasive of obstacles, it is extremely important that significant efforts be made to arrive at solutions that minimize these barriers. The influence of Wolfensberger (1975, 1983, 1995) frequently is cited by advocates who have made efforts to dispel myths and stereotypes about disability. Through his work and his writings, one can truly appreciate that people with disabilities have an inherent right to live full, complete lives similar to and typical of people who do not have disabilities. With this viewpoint have come new approaches to referring to people with disabilities. A "people first" philosophy is the most prevalent approach and concerns the specific manner and ways in which one refers to people with disabilities (Dattilo & Smith, 1990). No longer is it acceptable to refer to a class of people as "the handicapped" or "the disabled." Instead and in recognition that they too live, work, are educated, and play in typical communities and neighborhoods, people with disabilities are always referred to as "people" first, with the disability characteristic or label second, if relevant (e.g., all-star baseball pitcher with a physical impairment vs. one-armed baseball player; National Merit Scholar with a disability vs. handicapped kid from math class). This recognizes that the person's role in life (e.g., athlete, business person, health care provider, parent, student) transcends the disability characteristic and is more valued than the disability in the eyes of others in the community. A term gaining wider acceptance, for example, is "mixed-ability groups." This affirms that all people within the group have inherent skills and abilities that they bring to the group, each able to contribute in a meaningful way without the need to separate the group into people with and people without disabilities, thereby making an inappropriate assumption that people without disabilities have more skills and abilities.

The service focus, therefore, is on identifying which types of leisure experiences the individual with a disability needs or has an interest in (Ray, 1994; Wells & Wells, 1995), not how professionals should program for a class of individuals (e.g., segregated programs for only people with mental retardation, multiple sclerosis, cerebral palsy). Therefore, as was discussed in Chapter 2, the programming service focus is shifting from programs "for the retarded, disabled, handicapped, blind, and so forth" to understanding which programs that are already available to the general public fit the interests, dreams, desires, and capacities of the person, who also happens to have a disability and may need extra support to engage or be reasonably accommodated in a leisure experience (Amado, Conklin, & Wells, 1990; Mount & Zwernik, 1988; Vandercook, York, & Forest, 1989). Although the passage of laws such as the ADA helps provide impetus for changing the ways in which leisure services are provided at the community level, it is the change in attitudes of professionals and providers themselves that is enabling the public to view people with disabilities differently and in more valued and accepting ways.

Creating more accepting attitudes about people with disabilities may seem like a difficult task, but it is necessary if full inclusion is to succeed (Bedini, 1991). Many of the laws that have been enacted to guarantee and protect the rights of people with disabilities living in our communities cannot mandate changes in attitudes. Attitude changes can be made only by willing participants. Cnaan, Adler, and Ramot (1986) suggested a two-step strategy for changing attitudes: 1) address the issue of attitudes of the general public toward people with disabilities, and 2) address attitudes as they relate to increasing social contact.

Including welcoming language and photos of participants with disabilities in recreation department literature is a good objective of step 1 and should enhance positive perceptions of the public. Making people with disabilities feel that they "belong" in recreation centers and other leisure environments and that positive relationships and friendships can be created, nurtured, and reinforced in these environments will enable people without disabilities to feel and act more positively toward co-participants who happen to have disabilities. Baker and Salon (1986) emphasized that minimizing negative social behaviors is imperative for social interaction and positive public attitudes. Including people with disabilities in recreation programs provides opportunities for them to use participants without disabilities as appropriate behavioral role models (Rynders & Schleien, 1991).

There are many national and grass-roots efforts that alert communities to the barriers that prevent inclusion of citizens with disabilities. Disability awareness events are staged in communities across the country and provide opportunities for community residents to learn about disability, related technology, and inclusion supports. In addition, various advocacy agencies (e.g., The Arc) and other nonprofit groups are alerting media professionals to more appropriate ways of portraying people with disabilities in articles, photographs, and advertising. Internationally known fast-food chains, clothing manufacturers, and department stores using actors and models with disabilities to market familiar goods and services, without focusing on the person and/or the disabling condition, presents to the viewing public a positive portrayal of these people. This ultimately may change attitudes and stereotypes, clearing the way for more open and inclusive service systems for people with disabilities.

Employing a combination of extrinsic and intrinsic strategies is necessary for improving attitudes. Intervention techniques that address societal attitudes are further examined in Chapter 6. One general suggestion is to have local advocacy groups such as The Arc, the Multiple Sclerosis Society, or special education parent groups present workshops on disability awareness. Professional and educational associations such as the Division of Recreation, Park, and Leisure Studies at local universities could present workshops, conferences, and courses on leisure and disability issues. Also, it might be helpful for recreation personnel to visit neighborhood group homes, nursing facilities, and "natural" homes of people with disabilities to understand how people with disabilities experience their lives (e.g., through observation, naturalistic inquiry, interviews, surveys). Agency supervisors should make every effort to educate and train staff members on the importance of demonstrating accepting and caring behaviors to all people. Another suggestion is to have volunteers with disabilities lead awareness programs or training workshops. Hiring qualified individuals with disabilities as staff members is another useful way to help dispel negative attitudes because these individuals can serve in leadership positions (i.e., "helper" roles) and be appropriate role models to other individuals with disabilities. These activities have proved to be effective in heightening staff awareness of the needs of special population groups (Dattilo & Smith, 1990; Stensrud, 1993).

INDIVIDUAL BARRIERS

Individual barriers pertain to such issues as limitations in social, leisure, or functional skills; extent of dependence on others for assistance to participate; health or fitness levels; and knowledge of recreational opportunities.

Skill Limitations

Skill limitations may be attributed to lack of social competencies, limited leisure skill repertoires/lack of leisure education opportunities, and lack of functional skill development as a result of the particular manifestation of the disability. Because people with disabilities traditionally have been excluded from opportunities to socially interact with peers without disabilities, they often lack the interpersonal skills that promote positive and appropriate interactions within community recreation settings. The community recreation setting is an ideal place for an individual with disabilities to gain social skills and, perhaps, to develop genuine friendships within the context of an enjoyable recreation activity.

People with disabilities lack sufficient opportunities to develop expertise in recreation activities. Even if they possess the fundamental social, motor, and cognitive skills to participate in an activity, people with disabilities may not have sufficient opportunities to engage in these activities. If people with disabilities do not possess sufficient leisure-related skills and are not being taught those skills by recreation staff members and family members, then they may be relegated exclusively to activities that require passive, low-level skills or that are age inappropriate (e.g., adults participating in a cut-and-paste activity rather than in an art appreciation class). Because a person may be perceived as being "not ready for" inclusive programs as a result of his or her skill limitations, he or she may participate very little or not at all in community recreation settings.

Because leisure skill instruction is vitally important, the authors suggest several solutions for overcoming obstacles related to skill limitations. Teachers and parents or care providers are encouraged to provide social and leisure skills training in chronological age–suitable leisure activities at school, at home, and in community settings. Also, programs should be designed to encourage socialization among participants through, for example, cooperative grouping arrangement strategies, table games, and noncompetitive team games. Recreation professionals can collaborate with other key players to design leisure education curricula and allow use of their facilities for education and training by instructors (Ray, 1994; Schleien, Meyer, Heyne, & Brandt, 1995).

Appropriate social skills (e.g., greetings, shaking hands, social praise) and leisure skills should be modeled during the program in the recreation setting and should be consistently practiced with participants at home and throughout the length of the program. Through participation in inclusive programs, people with disabilities can learn skills by imitating their peers without disabilities. Children and adults without disabilities can be taught to be volunteer advocates and peer companions (i.e., support people) using narrated slide presentations, puppets, and question/discussion sessions (Amado et al., 1990; Heyne et al., 1993; Rynders & Schleien, 1991). These volunteer advocates may be needed as facilitators of socialization and leisure skill development in programs to enhance inclusion. Structured programs more than 1 hour in length may need to have breaks part of the way through to enable participants to have opportunities to informally socialize with peers. Stumbo (1995) provided for recreation professionals a comprehensive listing and review of 48 commercially available resources for social skills intervention, most with implications for leisure settings and individual skill development.

Finally, prerequisite core skills—those that are basic and vital to participation—should not be exclusionary in nature. Participants could develop core skills within the context of age-appropriate activity. Thus, activities could be task analyzed to determine the participants' strengths, general abilities, and skill limitations (Dark & Wright, 1988; Schleien, Meyer, et al., 1995). Programs could be designed to be sufficiently flexible to permit participants to enter them at different skill levels yet offer opportunities to improve over time (e.g., bowling, video games, art, music, aerobics). See Chapter 8 for a more in-depth description of these assessment and instructional strategies.

Functional skill limitations generally are a result of the unique disability characteristics of the individual. Recreation professionals are encouraged to discuss a potential participant's current skills and abilities with the participant and his or her parents, care providers, teachers, and others who know the person well. These key players can talk about past participation patterns and behaviors and any limitations and barriers related to functional skills. With permission (and, possibly, a signed release form), functional assessments conducted by a CTRS, physical and occupational therapists, and special education teachers may be shared with recreation program planners. Conducting comprehensive task and activity analysis during the inclusion process will inform recreation professionals about issues related to functional skills. Recreation professionals must obtain a clear understanding of the physical, social, emotional, and other related demands of the leisure activity and environment (see Chapter 5) in order to understand and appreciate the participant "fit" and methods for making reasonable accommodations to ensure the participant's partial or full participation.

Dependence on Others

Whether limited by disability, restrictive social service systems, or overprotective families and acquaintances, people with disabilities either lose or never gain the ability to function independently in the community (Hawkins, 1991). Personal growth and development are not achievable if people with disabilities become "handicapped" by a lack of control over their environments. They consequently become limited in their abilities to make decisions and choices and must depend on significant others to have their recreation needs met. Following are some guidelines for decreasing or eliminating barriers caused by dependency.

First, people with disabilities should be afforded the same respect and understanding as anyone else. One should relate to the person with disabilities in an age-appropriate manner; one should never "talk down" to the person. Give the participant opportunities to make decisions. If necessary, provide decision-making training to individuals with disabilities (Abery, Dahl, & Shelberg, 1993; Mahon, 1994) and assist them to become *self-advocates*—people with disabilities who can speak up and speak out for themselves (Allen, 1989; Arndt, Rudrud, & Sorenson, 1994). Second, people with disabilities should be given opportunities to understand and select from a wide array of community leisure options according to their own interests and preferences (Mount & Zwernick, 1988). Third, one should encourage family members and care providers to allow the individual with disabilities to independently use a community recreation setting with only minimal assistance. Other people should assist only if necessary. Finally, the recreation professional can determine, through use of the Recreation Inventory for Inclusive Participation (see Chapter 5), those times when personal assistance for the individual is absolutely necessary for such tasks as toileting, dressing, self-care, and eating. Program modifications can then be made that permit appropriate levels of interdependence while allowing opportunities for maximum independence.

Health and Fitness

The health and fitness needs of a person with disabilities generally are determined by the nature of the person's disability. For example, people with multiple sclerosis may fatigue easily, and people with quadriplegia are susceptible to hypothermia because of poor blood circulation. As a result, endurance, stamina, and strength to participate in a variety of recreation and sports activities may be severely limited.

Public recreation, park, and leisure services long have been recognized as being essential to the health and welfare of the community (Hartsoe, 1985; Tindall, 1995). Benefits of these services, therefore, should be of primary concern to recreation professionals (Godbey, 1991; Godbey, Graefe, & James, 1993; Whyte, 1992). Several strategies are available to a recreation professional to assess the health and fitness needs of potential participants to maximize their safety, welfare, and enjoyment during the recreation experience. Initially, the recreation professional should discuss with participants, physicians, advocacy groups, parents or care providers, and other pertinent allied health professionals the general health concerns of people with disabilities. If the professional requires information on a specific participant's health status during registration, then the following should be considered: 1) extent and level of disability, 2) current medications, 3) fitness level (e.g., flexibility, coordination, strength, balance), 4) emergency notification procedures, and 5) allergies. Throughout the duration of the recreation program, instructional and program staff should monitor physical status (e.g., skin color, fatigue, breathing) of people with disabilities (e.g., people with multiple sclerosis, diabetes, epilepsy, Down syndrome) who have been determined, through the initial assessments, to be at some health or fitness risk (e.g., atlantoaxial instability and dislocation in individuals with Down syndrome). Before enrolling in any active sports program, participants should undergo a physical examination by their physician. Also, recreation professionals could contact the American Red Cross and/or specific advocacy groups to determine what, if any, appropriate measures should be taken with people with disabilities concerning administration of cardiopulmonary resuscitation (CPR) or first aid. (When in doubt, always ask the participant with the disability first!) Of course, all personal information about a participant's health and fitness condition should be kept confidential and shared only among pertinent people and only with permission of the participant and/or his or her family. An astute recreation professional will realize that *all* participants should be asked at the time of registration to disclose any information about their personal health and fitness status prior to participating in activities in which this may be a concern. Barriers related to health and fitness are not just limited to people with disabilities as many "weekend warriors" (i.e., part-time athletes) have come to learn.

Lack of Knowledge

If people lack information about community recreation programs and services or knowledge of the support systems available to help make recreation opportunities inclusive, then their participation will be inhibited or nonexistent. A leisure education program, sponsored by the recreation agency or initiated in collaboration with a school system or community education organization, could be instituted to develop awareness of accessible and inclusive recreation programming. Facilitating a leisure education program could be a primary responsibility of the CTRS consultant, community leisure planner, inclusion specialist, or the like. Some communities hold resource "fairs" for community members with disabilities and their families in order to showcase recreational options and available supports for participation. These fairs have been held in schools, community colleges, neighborhood recreation centers, and other accessible public places.

Another suggestion is to develop a resource booklet that describes inclusive recreation programs available throughout the community. All recreational opportunities, such as museums, theaters, nature centers, neighborhood parks, community centers, and so forth, would be listed with specific information about accessibility features. This could be a specific task of the community leisure advisory board, which could disseminate it to people with disabilities and their family members/care providers and interested others. Other suggestions include developing a seasonal program brochure outlining all programs offered, including descriptions, dates, times, fees, and skill and clothing requirements. Newsletters, published quarterly, for instance, could highlight inclusion efforts, such as personal inclusion stories, staff training topics, and administrative response to achieving physical accessibility at various facilities. Other suggested activities include advertising programs in the local media (e.g., community newspapers) and posting program brochures or fliers in public places (e.g., grocery stores) that are frequented by many people, including people with disabilities. Finally, volunteers could be trained to serve as communication links between community recreation centers and other agencies serving people with disabilities, such as residential facilities, day activity programs, or counseling services, to make certain that program and resource information is being shared.

SUMMARY

Although the mandate for inclusive and accessible leisure services seems clear, there continue to be any number of barriers that may impede progress toward achieving the goal of full inclusion. Society's negative role perceptions of people with disabilities, as well as its low tolerance for individual differences, increase the likelihood that obstacles such as community and organizational stigmas and other pervasive negative attitudes will continue to decrease leisure service delivery and to diminish rates of participation by people with disabilities. A more positive view that the individual with a disability is a person first may help change societal perceptions. A change toward more open and inclusive service systems could be a reflection of these perception and attitude changes. Passing the ADA, including its comprehensive discussions on rules regulating recreational environments, is reflective of these attitude changes and provides helpful guidelines for ensuring that citizens with disabilities are reasonably accommodated and ultimately included in leisure settings.

This chapter identified and categorized for recreational professionals persistent obstacles to the community recreation inclusion of people with disabilities. It is the authors' firm belief that many of these obstacles could be avoided or eliminated if community recreation agencies incorporate the strategies presented throughout this text to change and improve existing leisure service delivery systems. Taken as a whole, this chapter presented a process for leisure service delivery that is welcoming to people with disabilities who want to participate in community recreation experiences and that enhances their feelings and sense of belonging to the communities and neighborhoods in which they live, work, and play. Ongoing communication and collaboration with key players will ensure that the recreation needs of people with disabilities are met in the community, where physical and social inclusion with peers without disabilities is stressed, and the spirit and intent of the Americans with Disabilities Act is realized. Community recreation professionals are reminded to take a proactive rather than a reactive approach to systems and personnel change and to avoid making the erroneous assumption that barriers to inclusion and accessibility are created or caused by the individual characteristics of people with disabilities.

If recreation professionals follow the techniques and strategies presented here, they will have progressed in developing and appropriately manifesting positive, accepting attitudes toward consumers with disabilities, as citizens in Sweden have done. According to Pedlar (1990), the people of Sweden have adopted a social sense of collective responsibility, whereby all members of the community are valued for who they are. Efforts are made to discover the value and talents of each individual so that each individual can make his or her unique contribution for the good of all. As a result, all members of this society are viewed as valuable, and it is understood and accepted that all people with disabilities will receive whatever support is necessary to become active and contributing members of society.

Building Bridges Between Families and Providers of Community Leisure Services

Jennifer B. Mactavish

◆ ◆ ◆ ◆ ◆

The practice and the profession of recreation and leisure have undergone many changes since the early 20th century. Among the most significant of these changes is society's recognition that recreation plays an integral role in the lives of all people, regardless of whether a person has a disability. Consequently, individuals with disabilities have greater opportunities than ever before to participate in recreation.

Despite these changes and increases in opportunities, recreation participation by people with disabilities continues to be fairly low. Some researchers in therapeutic recreation have come to believe that limited participation, particularly among children, is a result of the way that services and programs are provided (Schleien, Rynders, Heyne, & Tabourne, 1995). Most recreation service professionals focus exclusively on the child with a disability and his or her needs once the child has arrived at a program. Although this approach is important for those attending programs, it does little to encourage the involvement of nonparticipants. To reach these children (and adults, for that matter) and to improve programs in general requires a different strategy—one that acknowledges the importance of families in facilitating the recreation experiences of individuals with disabilities. In other words, understanding families and their recreation is the key to building bridges between family and community recreation options. This chapter illustrates the fundamental importance of establishing this link by sharing knowledge about family recreation and by providing ideas for fostering connections between leisure service professionals and families that include members with disabilities.

OVERVIEW OF THE INFLUENCE OF FAMILY RECREATION

A popular belief within Western cultures, advanced by the recreation and leisure profession, is that a "family that plays together stays together" (Orthner & Mancini, 1990, p. 129). Supporting this belief are numerous studies that indicate that family recreation contributes—sometimes negatively but more often positively—to family relationships and overall satisfaction with the quality of family life (Hill, 1988; Holman & Jacquart, 1988; Orthner & Mancini, 1980; Palisi, 1984). In fact, in a national study involving more than 300 self-described "happy" families, "doing things together" was identified as one of the key determinants of their success as a cohesive family (Stinnett, Sanders, DeFrain, & Parkhurst, 1982). Furthermore, 500 professionals who work with families noted in a survey that "shared recreation/leisure time" was 1 of 15 common qualities found among "healthy" families (Curran, 1983). Authors of a report on American culture concluded that "based on the strong tie that exists between leisure and family values," recreation is an emerging "therapeutic ideology" of the family (Orthner & Mancini, 1990, p. 126). In short, evidence is emerging that supports family recreation as a powerful vehicle for bringing and, possibly, keeping families together.

Beyond having positive impacts on the overall quality of family life, family recreation carries special significance for children because for most, this constitutes their first exposure to recreation. Interacting with other family members—siblings, parents, grandparents, aunts, and uncles—provides a context in which children begin to acquire the skills (e.g., social, physical, recreation) and develop the interests that have the capacity to influence—positively and/or negatively—their lifelong involvement in recreation.

Although it is tempting to acknowledge family recreation as a beneficial force within the lives of families and their individual members, the supporting research has several substantive limitations. Of particular concern is the extremely narrow range of families and family types that have been considered in studies of family recreation. One casualty of this limitation is the knowledge about the potential contribution of family recreation to the life experiences of families that include children with disabilities. This is a significant oversight, particularly in light of the preceding discussion about families that do not include children with disabilities and the role of family recreation in promoting healthy family functioning and child development. In addition, knowledge about families that include children with disabilities underscores the need for greater knowledge about these families and their recreation.

CREATING THE CONTEXT:
FAMILIES THAT INCLUDE CHILDREN WITH DISABILITIES

Historically, a large proportion of children with disabilities did not live with their families (Landesman & Vietze, 1987). Institutionalization was the norm, which typically afforded little opportunity for contact between children and their families (Landesman & Vietze, 1987). This began to change in the early 1970s with the emergence of the principle of normalization. Normalization is the philosophical cornerstone of movements aimed at furthering the rights of people with disabilities to experience, to the fullest degree possible, culturally normative conditions of life (Perrin & Nirje, 1985; Wolfensberger, 1972). Since that time, normalization in tandem with a range of supporting legislation has resulted in significant increases in the number of individuals with disabilities who live with their families (Landesman & Vietze, 1987).[1]

Research interest within a number of disciplines (e.g., educational psychology) has accompanied the trend toward maintaining children with disabilities in their family homes. Some of this interest concerns the positive influences of these children on family functioning (e.g., Turnbull & Turnbull, 1990); however, the converse typically has been the focus (Glidden, 1993). As noted by Glidden (1993), much of this work has been and continues to be guided by the belief that "a family with a child who has a disability is a family with a disability" (p. 482). It is not surprising, therefore, that children with disabilities reportedly have negative effects on an array of family variables (e.g., marital relationship, sibling relationships, finances, planning of daily activities and family vacations) (Blacher, 1984). Implicit in almost all of these studies is the assumption that the presence of a child with a disability results in elevated levels of family stress (Glidden, 1993).

Although in some cases this assumption may be true, it also must be noted that not all families respond negatively (e.g., with stress) to the presence of a child with a disability (Glidden, 1993; Turnbull & Turnbull, 1990). Unfortunately, this has not been the prevailing perspective. Much has been written about the problems that beleaguer these families but little about "families who meet the crisis of a handicap as they meet other crises, with resilience and common sense" (Blacher, 1984, p. 30). Furthermore, relatively few studies have examined the strategies that families employ to combat the stress that may accompany the presence of children with disabilities. What has been done, however, suggests that recreation may be an important coping mechanism for families. For example, in a study of families with children with spina bifida, Nevin and McCubbin (1979) reported that an active "recreation orientation" was, among other things, a useful means for reducing family stress. Similar findings also have been reported in studies of families with children with autism and mental retardation (Blacher, 1984). Although this research did not directly assess recreation as a stress-reduction strategy, it did indicate recreation's potential importance and utility for this purpose.

Another aspect of recreation that has increasingly become the focus of attention, particularly within the community therapeutic recreation field, is the involvement of children with disabilities in integrated community recreation programs and services (Schleien & Ray, 1988). Much of this attention has centered on the benefits that individuals with and without disabilities derive from participating in such programs: 1) physical and psychological health, 2) development of new skills, 3) opportunities for friendships, and 4) connections with others in the community (Schleien, Green, & Heyne, 1993; Schleien & Ray, 1988). These benefits contribute to the overall enhancement of the quality of life. Although this evidence suggests that recreation plays a powerful and positive role in the lives of individuals with disabilities, it provides little insight regarding recreation within these individuals' families.

---

[1]Examples of supporting legislation appear in Table 1.1.

Despite the limited understanding of recreation in families that include children with disabilities, it has been noted that these families are pivotal in providing recreation activities and opportunities for their children (Cameron, 1989; Mactavish, 1995; Rynders & Schleien, 1991; Schleien, Cameron, Rynders, & Slick, 1988). Recognizing this, researchers have started to generate strategies for facilitating greater collaboration among families, care providers, and service delivery systems (Rynders & Schleien, 1991; Schleien et al., 1993; Schleien, Heyne, Rynders, & McAvoy, 1990; Schleien, Rynders, et al., 1995).

The literature has devoted little attention to recreation in families that include children with disabilities. In spite of this neglect, there are at least two compelling reasons for developing a stronger understanding of family recreation within these families. First, from studies of families that do not include children with disabilities, evidence suggests that a strong relationship exists between interactions in family recreation and "healthy and happy" family lives (Orthner & Mancini, 1990). Second, within the therapeutic recreation literature is increasing recognition that initiating sustainable participation by children with disabilities in home, school, and community recreation environments is largely contingent on family support (Schleien et al., 1993). One approach to gaining such support is to provide school and community programs that build on and reflect family recreation experiences, needs, and interests.

FAMILY RECREATION IN FAMILIES
THAT INCLUDE CHILDREN WITH DISABILITIES

As of 1996, family recreation in families that include children with disabilities has been the subject of only one study. In this exploratory investigation, parents from 65 families shared their perspectives on family recreation[2] and its impact on their lives and the lives of their children with and without a developmental disability (Mactavish, 1994). The families in this study came from diverse backgrounds (e.g., race/ethnicity, education, income, number of children, level of disability, family composition). The "average" family, however, was of Caucasian/European ancestry, included two parents of the opposite sex who had at least some college education, held either full- or part-time employment outside the home, earned less than $45,000 per year, and had two to three children. These children were almost evenly divided between those with a developmental disability (74) and those without (76). Table 4.1 provides an overview of the key characteristics of the children with disabilities. Surveys and interviews were the principal sources of information. The survey contained open/closed-response format questions, and the interviews employed an interview guide approach (i.e., flexible questions that enable the interviewer to pursue issues and lines of questioning that emerge during the interview) (Patton, 1990). The interviews involved multiple adult members of the same family, usually two parents, and were conducted in the family home. Although only one study, it revealed a number of important insights about the nature and benefits of

---

[2]Family recreation, also referred to as "shared recreation," was defined in this study as "any activity (or activities) that two or more members of the same household enjoyed participating in together. Participation in these activities could occur anywhere and could be spontaneous play activities and/or formally organized engagements." This definition was used to guide parents' thinking about family recreation without precluding the possibility of family-by-family variations in meaning.

Table 4.1. Key characteristics of the children with disabilities in the family recreation study

Number of children by sex	Age range (years)	Average age (years)	Standard deviation (years)
47 Males	2–19	9.47	3.86
27 Females	4–22	12.13	4.97

and constraints on family recreation in families that include children with developmental disabilities.[3] The remaining sections of this chapter highlight the major results of this research and implications for leisure service providers.

NATURE OF FAMILY RECREATION

The "nature" of family recreation was operationally defined, for the purposes of this study, according to patterns and forms of participation. That is, the nature of family recreation was examined by considering two distinct issues: where and with whom activities transpired (i.e., pattern) and the type of activities (i.e., form) pursued. As noted by Kelly (1974): "What is done, not where or with whom, is the sole criterion of differentiation" (p. 183) between patterns and forms of recreation.

Three patterns of participation characterized the family recreation experiences of most of the families in this study: 1) an *all family* pattern, which involved everyone within the immediate family; 2) a *subunit/subgroup* pattern, whereby small groups within the family engaged in activities together; and 3) an *equal combination* pattern, in which participation alternated between small-group activities and those involving the entire family. Those subscribing to the latter pattern described the small-group activities as the *weekday version* of family recreation, and the *weekend version* involved the whole family.

> Every weekday morning I'm up and walking out the door when the rest of the family is just getting up. When I get home we balance getting what needs done - done . . . so family recreation during the week is pretty much mixed up with one of us doing the things that have to be done and one of us trying to do something fun with the kids so they don't feel as though it's all work and no play. Weekends. Now that's another story. Weekends are family time—family recreation time. We try to do at least one activity together—all of us.

Overall, small-group (i.e., subunit pattern) activities tended to dominate the recreation experiences of the families in this study. These groupings typically involved one parent—most often mothers—in activities with their children with developmental disabilities or all of their children. Based on discussions with parents, the subgroup pattern appeared to serve two important functions. First, activities including small groups within the family appeared to be a conscious strategy for ensuring that family recreation opportunities occurred despite busy schedules and often competing demands.

---

[3]In keeping with the exploratory and naturalistic nature of this study, the intention was not to offer generalizations about the recreation experiences of *all* families that include children with developmental disabilities and/or any other type of disability. The results of this research are discussed in a way that recognizes their specificity to the families from which they were drawn; however, these families' experiences may have relevance to a wider range of families. Hence, some of the strongest findings from this research have become the basis for a series of practical suggestions (final portions of this chapter) that will positively assist efforts to build bridges between families and recreation service systems and providers.

> Our weekdays are hectic. I work full time, Mike works full time, the kids go to school and day care . . . so one of us tries to make sure that some part of every day is time for doing something fun with each of the kids. This isn't always something special. But just spending time with them individually is special for them.

Second, in families that included children with more significant developmental disabilities, parents noted that recreation involving small groups of family members was essential to making these activities more manageable.

> The kids all have very different interests, abilities, and activities that they are into. Abilities are probably the biggest thing to get around, though. To be perfectly honest, Jeremy needs so much care and attention that it's almost impossible to do things that involve more than say me, him, and maybe one of his older sisters. So doing smaller group things is really about making things work better for all of us.

Independent of who participated, most families believed that the majority of their recreation occurred with equal frequency in home and community settings. In contrast, a smaller number of families reported that most involvements took place at home, and even fewer noted that the community was the site of most of their family's recreation. Reintroducing a sense of spontaneity and providing changes in scenery were two of the most common themes illustrating the underlying popularity of non–home-based recreation.

> Planning, planning, planning! That's what it takes to get any family recreation activity going in our family—probably in any family with a kid with a disability. On the up side, this is one way of making sure that everybody has a good time. On the down side, nothing is ever very spontaneous . . . so family recreation has a tendency to get boring. Getting out of the house and doing things out in the community help to make things feel a little less routine, less predictable.
>
> Getting out of the house, even for a short while, gives me and the kids a big lift. We don't have to do anything really special, just getting that change in scenery can be a big deal.

For single-parent families, the opportunity to socialize with other adults was a strong motivation for involving the family in activities in the community.

> We spend a lot of time at activities run by the church and this parents-of-preschool-children group that goes on at the community center. I see these activities as being good for the kids, but more to the point—I just need to get out of the house and have a chance to get some adult socialization . . . as much as I love my kids, there's just no substitute for the kind of conversations adults can share.

Implicit in this parent's thoughts are several suggestions that service providers could adopt in an effort to enhance the involvement of single-parent families in community recreation programs. Specifically, programs should incorporate opportunities for parents to be active participants with their children, but they also should include activities that foster parent-to-parent interactions. This could be done by interspersing the program with activities for the children only or by providing social time at the beginning and/or conclusion of the program.

Moving beyond the needs of single-parent families, what was learned about patterns (who is involved and where it takes place) of family recreation in general suggests a number of areas in which leisure service providers could have positive impacts. For example, service providers could go a long way toward facilitating family recreation by

- Increasing the availability of family-centered programs

- Providing family-centered programs that 1) expose families to a range of activities and ideas that they could generalize to their leisure involvements at home, 2) do not require families to make long-term commitments, and 3) do not require a great deal of preplanning (e.g., simplified registration procedures, drop-in).
- Enhancing the range of community and home supports that would enable families to participate in meaningful and enjoyable family recreation activities. Examples include 1) having staff (e.g., therapeutic recreation specialists) who will do what it takes to include people of all abilities in recreation, 2) providing extra volunteers, 3) having adaptive equipment available, and 4) providing co-ed washroom/changing facilities.

In addition to considering patterns of family recreation, the forms of family activities were examined. Based on parents' reports of their family involvements, five categories of activities were identified: 1) passive (e.g., watching TV), 2) play (e.g., board games), 3) physical (e.g., swimming), 4) social (e.g., visiting extended family members), and 5) entertainment/special events (e.g., going to the movies).

A number of factors (e.g., employment status, type of household) influenced the frequency with which families engaged in specific activities. For example, families of children with more significant disabilities tended to participate in more passive and play-oriented activities; families of children with less significant disabilities took part in more physical activities and entertainment/special events. Family recreation, therefore, may not provide exposure to as wide a range of recreation skill–building activities for children with more significant levels of disability.

From a service provider's perspective, this finding suggests three important considerations:

1. Children with more significant disabilities may require individual and family recreation programs that offer a stronger skill development focus than what typically is needed by children with milder forms of disability.
2. Children with significant disabilities would benefit from therapeutic recreation programs and services that teach their families creative strategies for involving them in a diverse range of family activities.
3. The nature of an individual's disability (e.g., level of disability, type of disability) may influence choices—the individual's and/or the parents'—of programs and services; therefore, providing opportunities that attract a wide range of participants, including those with more significant levels of disability, requires an awareness of potential differences in program interests and a willingness to address these differences by developing programs around preferred activities and modes (e.g., competitive, cooperative, inclusive) of participation.

Despite the variations based on level of disability and other factors, a large proportion of families reported physical activities—specifically swimming, walking, and biking—as their most popular and most frequent forms of family recreation. The passive (e.g., watching TV/videos), play (e.g., board/video/computer games), and social (e.g., visiting family and friends, attending church) categories of activities shared lower yet comparable levels of popularity and participation.

In sum, what is known about the nature of family recreation suggests that it primarily involves two or more, but not all, family members in equal combinations of home- and community-based physical activities. Also, although they often occur in community settings, these activities are almost exclusively child centered, informal, and family initiated. Typically, mothers are the initiators of these activities and the gatekeepers to involvements outside of the home.

Benefits of Family Recreation

To set the foundation for a discussion of the benefits of family recreation, it is necessary first to consider the importance of these interactions. As was noted previously, studies of families that do not include children with disabilities indicate that family recreation is a valued and important focal point in the lives of many. According to this research, simply taking part in enjoyable activities together helps strengthen relationships and generally makes for healthier and happier families.

Based on the study of parents from 65 families that include children with a developmental disability, family recreation appears to be very important to them as well. This importance was described in many different ways, but family recreation was most commonly described as a way of reestablishing a sense of what is important in life.

> Life as a family can be stressful . . . with kids going out to school, both parents working, trying to make ends meet . . . Well, you get the picture—things can seem like drudgery after a while. So for both of us, sharing fun activities with the kids and one another is probably the most important thing we can do as a family to balance things out.

> So much of life is about getting along—surviving from one pay cheque to the next. To me, family recreation is about remembering what's important in life. It's about the best way I know of honoring one another as people and as members of your family.

Adding to this view, some parents talked about shared recreation as an integrated experience that was of value and importance for immediate and extended family members.

> Everybody in our family lives within 5 or so miles of here . . . so almost everything we do includes one or more of them. Andrea does everything we do and I think it's been really positive—she gets to be around people, kids, and adults that aren't handicapped. Probably more important, though, is they get to be around someone who is.

> When Nicholas was first born, my parents and sisters and stuff were pretty freaked out . . . but going to the cabin, Sunday dinners, and just hanging out together has really helped them get a better outlook on children—I guess you could say people in general—with disabilities.

> I always laugh when they [service providers] talk about "adaptive rec" and the like, being sort of a new idea or at least something that you people [recreation service providers] are into these days . . . we've been adapting and integrating within our own family for years now . . . .

Building on comments about the importance of family recreation, parents also spoke at great length about the benefits of taking part in activities as a family. Most of the time, these conversations centered on how family recreation "made families closer," "gave them something fun to do," and "improved quality and satisfaction with family life." Illustrating the meaning of each of these outcomes to families, consider the words of three different parents:

> Making and keeping love and compassion between all of us is a priority in this family. The time we spend together, the activities we do . . . even if it's just a walk in the park . . . helps us do that. It just helps us bond as a family.

Family recreation gives everyone a chance to do something extra—something that's fun. It's a time to let go of case notes, assessments, advocacy . . . it's a time to be a family.

Mainly family recreation helps make us be more satisfied with our family life in general. I guess you could say that it makes the quality of all of our lives better.

It appears that these interactions are as important in families that include children with disabilities as they are in those that do not. Family activities are viewed as valuable opportunities for 1) spending quality time together, 2) reestablishing a focus on life priorities (e.g., family), and 3) providing integrated experiences that are beneficial for the family as a whole and for the children with disabilities. Furthermore, while recreation within the family context is considered important for all children—it is within the family that most children are first exposed to recreation and begin to learn the skills (e.g., social, physical, recreation) that set in motion their long-term interests in participation—it is of particular significance for those with disabilities. Specifically, family recreation not only serves as a catalyst for these children's skill and interest development but also continues as their primary participation outlet well beyond when their siblings without disabilities graduate to individual recreation pursuits in the community. An intense emphasis is placed on these family recreation experiences to help children connect with other family members, develop skills, and set foundations for the future.

I give my child my undivided attention when we do activities together—where else is he going to get that? Also, I do things with him in the hope that they'll carry over to other things he does later on in life.

I try to help our daughter, when we're playing, on the skills she needs so that she might do better later on. The other thing, though, is she's never going to get the kind of connection with other people that she gets with our family. That might be the most important benefit of all—belonging.

Our son is behind in most skills, so one of the benefits to doing things as a family is he gets a chance to work on these things in a fun way and have unconditional acceptance and support along the way. I'm not sure there are many other situations in his life where that is possible . . . but maybe if he learns how to do some of these things now—at home—he'll have a better chance of making friends to do things on his own with.

Obvious in the words of these parents are strong beliefs in the importance of family recreation and the hope that skills learned in the home will be useful later on—perhaps in individual activities in the community. While reflecting optimism about potential long-term benefits, these comments also acknowledge a less positive and all too frequent reality for many children with disabilities: Despite their best efforts, their children with disabilities are unlikely to develop lasting interpersonal relationships and meaningful recreation involvements outside the family unit.

During more in-depth discussions, it became clear that the importance of family recreation shifted with children's ages and the presence or absence of a disability. Parents of children with and without disabilities under age 10 generally viewed activities with the family as highly important. By the time children without disabilities had reached age 12 or so, individual options became somewhat more important than family recreation for these children. Meanwhile, participating in family activities continued to be the most important recreation outlet for children with disabilities. When parents explained their views on this, it was as though they spoke with one voice:

Let's face it . . . as much as they say things are changing and as much as I hope they are, family recreation is really the only option for our two with a disability. Well at least the option that we can really be sure about. As for the other ones—well, it's just natural at their age to want to do their own thing. Recreation-wise, it's just so much easier for them . . . they can go off to the park or some kind of program and we don't have to worry all the time about them being okay.

From a service provider's perspective, it also is crucial to recognize how important and beneficial family recreation is to families. This information is critical because it provides the foundation for programs and services that meet family needs by building on their interests and experiences. Opinions about service providers, program quality, and the ability of staff to provide meaningful experiences for children with disabilities have powerful influences on the willingness of families to seek access to community leisure programs and services. Parents' opinions of these programs are not always the result of direct experiences but are often formed on the basis of discussions with other parents and, at times, without the benefit of anything other than the assumption that programs and services will not meet family and/or individual needs. In short, leisure service providers who are committed to providing top quality programs and services must provide ways for parents to communicate their interests and needs regarding family and individual recreation options involving children with disabilities. This could be accomplished in a variety of formal and informal ways:

Formal
- Needs assessment inventories

- Surveys

- Family focus groups

Informal
- Talking with family program participants

- Involving parents in planning new programs

- Providing a suggestion box so that parents could offer their opinions anonymously

Constraints on Family Recreation

Despite the benefits associated with family recreation, the realities of busy lives often make it difficult for individuals, let alone groups of individuals, to participate in recreation as often as they would like. To explore this issue, parents were asked how often 13 items drawn from previous constraints research limited their family recreation. These items included structural (e.g., work responsibilities, lack of time), interpersonal (e.g., lack of common interests), and intrapersonal (e.g., lack of energy) constraints (Crawford, Jackson, & Godbey, 1991). Taken as a whole, parents reported that the listed constraints "seldom" to "sometimes" had negative impacts on their families' recreation. When exceptions to this occurred they typically involved limitations imposed by work responsibilities and/or a lack of time (i.e., these items had an effect "most of the time").

In addition to asking about the listed constraints (13 items), families were invited, via an open-ended survey question and during interviews, to discuss any other constraining influence(s) that affected their shared recreation. From this information, it became apparent that work responsibilities and a lack of time were less significant challenges to family recreation than was being able to coordinate family members' schedules.

I don't think lack of time would be the way I would describe it . . . we all have the same number of hours to deal with. The problem really comes down to trying to work around work, school, appointments—that's the real challenge . . . getting our schedules together.

Everyone in this family is on some kind of schedule. From the baby's feeding and nap schedule to my husband's court dates . . . you name it, we've got a schedule for it . . . so when it comes to family recreation, a lot of times it's really difficult to fit in . . . and you know how that goes—not scheduled, doesn't happen.

Time, time, time . . . it's not really about that. It's about trying to use what we have better. That takes juggling around with everyone's schedule so we can fit in that movie, day at the park . . . when you've got five people to work around it gets tough.

Another major impediment to family recreation was difficulties associated with finding activities that could accommodate wide ranges in age and skill level.

Age differences, that's the biggest part of the problem . . . with kids aged 9, 4, and 2, it gets challenging to find activities that they can all do and that will be fun for us, too.

I think knowing that Tracy is 12 and the other two are not in school full time is the best example of how the children's ages make it hard to find activities that we all can do . . . the skill level just isn't the same . . . interests too, but skills are the big ones.

An open-ended survey question asked parents about the constraints that made family recreation "most difficult" for the child with a disability. The most frequent responses related to domain-specific skill limitations (e.g., physical, social, recreation) and health concerns/care needs. From the interviews, a series of different constraining influences emerged—ones that complemented and extended those noted in reference to the entire family. For example, parents shared various perspectives on how the presence of a child with a disability affected efforts to find activities that could accommodate wide ranges in age and skill level. Interestingly, in families with children under the age of 12, the constraining affects of variations in abilities were consistently attributed to the age differences between the children and did not appear to be related to the presence or absence of a disability.

Differences in abilities don't really have anything to do with Adrian's disability. It [differences in ability] has a lot to do with him and the other younger one's just not having the skills . . . it makes it hard on family recreation activities.

Parents of older children (i.e., over age 14) and/or those spanning wider ranges in age (e.g., 6–20), however, tended to connect their children's disabilities and the difficulties associated with finding family activities that were flexible enough to accommodate mixed abilities.

Probably the biggest difficulty for us to do recreation together are differences in our children's abilities. There are a lot of things Damon just can't do because of his disability—physically it's impossible . . . it makes it really hard to find things we can all do together.

Shannon just hasn't learned all the skills, yet, that she needs to fully take part in all the activities we like to do as a family . . . but we learned a long time ago that what's difficult for Shannon is difficult for all of us . . . we just do what we can to work around it.

The finding that most consistently arose from the interview data clearly suggested an interconnection between family and individual constraints. Specifically, the difficulties imposed by trying to coordinate family members' schedules often were further complicated by the degree of preplanning (planning demands) required to orchestrate family recreation activities. Distinguishing between coordinating schedules and planning, emphasizing the importance of the latter, parents noted,

> Scheduling and planning—well, to me they mean different things . . . scheduling is balancing out what needs to get done, like work and those kinds of things, and still having time to do fun things together. Planning has to do with organizing, finding out what's going on, whether it's accessible . . . the stuff that makes it possible for us to actually take part in a fun activity together.

> Scheduling is about working around other commitments, planning is really the nuts and bolts part of making sure we can do whatever it is we want to do . . . Shawn's needs are so great that everything we do requires a lot of advance work.

> By the time I've got the schedules worked out and have done all the background planning . . . well, sometimes that's it. Time's up!

> Sometimes it's so complicated . . . getting things coordinated and planning everything to the last detail . . . it's just a lot of work and we always seem to put more time into getting ready than anything else.

At first glance, the implications of these findings for service agencies and/or providers are not particularly obvious. Realistically, it could be argued that leisure service providers are limited in their ability to directly assist families in dealing with the challenges of coordinating their schedules, addressing planning demands, and finding activities that could accommodate the abilities and interests of everyone in the family. A couple of suggestions offered previously in this chapter, however, could be helpful:

1. Providing family-centered programs that use a drop-in format and have extra volunteer support to allow the flexibility that busy families need in order to fit family recreation into their hectic schedules
2. Providing family-centered community programs that expose families to activities reflecting a wide range of abilities and interests, which, in turn, would provide parents with ideas they could try at home

A final constraint emerged from discussions about the factors that made it difficult for children with disabilities to participate in family recreation. This involved parents' concerns about the messages—the information—they received from recreation service agencies. Most of the time these concerns revolved around marketing and promotional materials that did not provide enough information or the kind of information needed to decide whether existing programs were appropriate and of interest.

> I eliminate a lot of things because of the messages I pick up from the information recreation places give. If they told me about stuff like—is the place accessible, do they have the equipment we need to take part, do they have co-ed bathrooms, a place to change diapers, who to call if I have questions . . . then I'd have something to go on. There just has to be a better way of communicating with people—welcoming and encouraging tax paying potential customers. Why do I always have to do all the calling and digging?

> I'm always looking through the information that comes from parks, the Y—we have a family membership at the Y. They all seem to have that generic statement, something about no one being excluded . . . yet I never find anything in it that makes me feel like they are really wanting me to call or to come. It gives you the impression that they are more concerned with appearing to be open to everyone. So even though we belong—we pay our dues—it's just not all that inviting . . . we don't go and do as much as we would like as a family and we sure don't send our son off to do things on his own.

Implicit in these points is the critical importance of providing parents with the type of information that they need to make informed decisions about whether a program and/or service is appropriate. For example, it would be extremely helpful if service providers made available the answers to the following questions:

- Are staff trained to include participants of all abilities?
- What is the staff/volunteer-to-participant ratio?
- In what ways is the program and/or service being promoted a good one?
- What kinds of benefits can participants anticipate gaining from the program?
- What do other families—particularly those that include children with disabilities—have to say about the quality of the promoted program/service?

A final, more general, implication also can be drawn from what was learned about constraints to family recreation. In the past, service providers primarily concerned themselves with factors that make it difficult, if not impossible, for individuals with disabilities to participate in community programs. By looking exclusively at the individual, particularly when that individual is very young and/or a person with a disability, one risks underestimating the impact of constraints that come from other sources. For example, in the study of family recreation, it became apparent that an accumulation of factors specific to the children (e.g., lack of skills), adults (e.g., not knowing how to include everyone), and service agencies (e.g., poor quality of information) often worked together, which made participating in family recreation a challenge. Those interested in helping people with disabilities overcome constraints to family and individual recreation must extend their focus to include factors faced by the family as a whole.

SUMMARY

Families that include children with disabilities, like other families, view family recreation as a valuable part of their lives together. These interactions help strengthen family relationships and provide children, particularly those with disabilities, with chances to learn lifelong leisure skills in supportive and nurturing environments. Moreover, because of experiences gained through family recreation, parents often have a good understanding of what it takes to successfully include their children in programs. Taking this knowledge and adding beliefs about the quality of community recreation programs, however, has made parents cautious gatekeepers when it comes to activities outside of the family—especially for their children with disabilities. To change this situation requires that strong bridges be built between families and providers of community leisure services.

One of the most obvious ways of facilitating this goal is to increase the number of family-centered program opportunities. This type of programming could make a positive contribution by promoting and supporting what families are already doing within their self-initiated recreation. To achieve this aim, service providers should focus on creating program options that

1. Take into account the interests and needs of families and their members.
2. Accommodate wide ranges in age and ability so that the whole family can participate together.
3. Provide opportunities for interacting with other families.
4. Introduce simple, low-cost activities that families can try at home.

In addition to increasing the number of family-centered programs, service providers must ensure that existing programs are open and willing to welcome all potential participants. This is particularly important in light of the previous discussion about constraints in which parents suggested that service providers seemed more concerned with "appearing to be open to everyone." Consequently, parents believed that little attention was paid to the issues (e.g., accessibility, trained staff, support, family focus) that needed to be addressed before they would feel comfortable involving their family and children with disabilities in community recreation settings. As a step toward changing this view, leisure service providers must take the lead by communicating or, better yet, demonstrating that

1. They are prepared to accommodate and welcome all potential participants.
2. Services are or could be made available to facilitate positive and meaningful participation (e.g., therapeutic recreation specialists are available to help if needed).
3. A contact person is present to address families' questions, concerns, and complaints.

In addition to becoming more responsive to the needs of families that express interest in progams, service providers should adhere to three important service delivery principles that could enhance family recreation and the individual activities of children with disabilities:

1. Effectively market available program options, and communicate the potential benefits of these activities for families and their individual members.
2. Take into account challenges faced by the family and their interests and needs.
3. Ask and listen to parents' views and concerns.

The practical strategies introduced throughout this chapter provide some tools for building bridges between families and providers of community leisure services. To put these tools to work, however, requires a shift in the way that leisure services are perceived and delivered. In other words, there is a need to move beyond an exclusive individual orientation to one that includes a family focus. This is a logical extension, particularly when one considers that families are, in essence, the first "recreation delivery systems" from whom individuals receive "services"; and, in the case of individuals with disabilities, perhaps the most enduring provider of recreation opportunities.

Thinking about families in this way helps to illustrate the importance of understanding families and their recreation. What are families interested in? What are the positive outcomes that families and their individual members hope to gain from their recreation experiences? What challenges and/or constrains the abilities of families to engage in recreation together? Asking questions as simple as these and being sensitive to families' answers will help service providers demonstrate that they are concerned with the needs, interests, and experiences of families. In turn, these insights will build the bridge between family and community recreation and, in the process, will enhance the quality of leisure programs, services, and, more important, people's experiences.

Recreation Inventory for Inclusive Participation

5

◆ ◆ ◆ ◆ ◆

Human services professionals have attempted to provide services to individuals with disabilities in community and other noninstitutional settings. The term *least restrictive environment* (LRE) is commonly used to describe this noninstitutional service approach. Leisure and discretionary time use in the LRE refers to the acquisition and performance of leisure skills by people with disabilities in normalized community environments. Using the adjective *normalized* is critical to distinguishing this service approach from programs in the community that are in segregated (i.e., nonnormalized) settings.

Acquiring functional leisure skills (i.e., skills that are naturally occurring, are frequently demanded, and have a specific purpose) that are age appropriate (i.e., activities typically performed by people in a particular age group) and comparable to the skill performance of peers without disabilities is a powerful tool for including people with disabilities in normalized community environments. The selection of leisure skills for individuals with disabilities should reflect this potential benefit. Only those skills or activities that have the potential of being performed in the presence of or in interaction with peers without disabilities should be selected for instruction. Anything short of this goal will do little to mitigate the unnecessary, long-term segregation of people with disabilities and could result in the acquisition of leisure skills that meet only the substandard performance demands of protective segregated settings. This chapter details the process of including people in community recreation and presents a strategy, adapted from an approach to analyze vocational tasks (Belmore & Brown, 1976), as a guide to developing leisure skill instructional content that is based on the skill performance of individuals without disabilities.

The Recreation Inventory for Inclusive Participation (RIIP) (Schleien, Green, & Heyne, 1993) was designed to provide the community recreation professional, educator, parent, and consumer with relevant instructional content and the information needed to make viable leisure education instructional decisions. It identifies specific needs of individuals with disabilities and provides an excellent starting point from which to consider necessary program modifications to enhance successful participation. Using the RIIP provides the recreation professional and the parent or care provider with a systematic approach to facilitating the successful involvement of people with disabilities in community recreation settings. The versatility and utility of this instrument can be attributed to its task-analytic nature, which breaks down the recreation skills into steps that the participants can learn more easily and provides descriptions of the behaviors required so that they can be performed by participants of varying abilities.

By following the specific steps spelled out in the RIIP, people with disabilities—with the help of a community recreation professional, educator, or parent—can gain access to community recreation activities and settings and improve their quality of life. Children with disabilities can begin at an early age to develop leisure and social skills that are functional and appropriate, allowing them to participate in activities with their peers in schools and neighborhoods. The RIIP approach will help adolescents and young adults make the transition to adulthood as they learn to participate successfully in community recreation. Ideally, as children, youths, and adults develop inclusive recreation skills, friendships will develop, and social networks will expand. This environmental inventory approach can be applied in the home, in schools, in vocational and community settings, and in recreation settings. The authors acknowledge that the RIIP process is long and initially tedious; however, this tool helps develop functional, age-appropriate, and inclusive recreation skills. Skill development is a benefit that far outweighs the inconvenience of completing the RIIP. The RIIP is beneficial in a variety of other ways:

1. It provides step-by-step procedures for including people with disabilities in community leisure services.
2. It offers an individualized approach to community recreation participation by people with disabilities.
3. It provides helpful information to care providers (e.g., how to plan and prepare for the leisure experience) and community recreation personnel (e.g., guidance and direction in planning and delivering of leisure services for current and future program instructors).
4. It identifies basic and vital skills and other useful information for participating in the targeted activity and is compared with performance of peers without disabilities. This information can be used repeatedly. For example, whenever a person with a disability is identified as a potential participant, the inventory data from previously completed inventories can be used again and again.

It appears that most participants or consumers of recreation services follow a particular step-by-step procedure when using community recreation settings. The RIIP, in its simplest version, consists of the following four general steps:

1. Identify a community leisure setting or recreation activity that is of interest to the individual with a disability.
2. Make the necessary arrangements to arrive at the setting or activity.
3. Participate in the activity.

4. Determine whether a return to the recreation setting for future participation is desired.

A more comprehensive examination of each element of this procedure follows.

PROCESS FOR PARTICIPATING IN A COMMUNITY RECREATION ACTIVITY

Procedures for the Participant/Consumer

A. Identify the preferred leisure setting/recreation activity.

  1. Become aware of a community recreation setting/activity by reading about it in a newspaper, magazine, or program brochure; or by hearing about it on the radio or TV or from a friend, family member, or teacher.
  2. Express interest in attending the community recreation setting/activity.
  3. If needed, request additional information about location and directions to facility; request program brochure for specific information on activity, dates, time, orientation meeting, and activity fees, if appropriate.

B. Make arrangements to attend the leisure setting.

  1. Determine tasks to be completed before participating. Tasks could include the following:
     a. Completing registration procedure (Potential participant may need to determine an ideal time to travel to the setting to complete registration procedures.)
     b. Obtaining parent/guardian permission (if under a certain age restriction)
     c. Determining program costs
     d. Arranging transportation for future visits to agency
     e. Determining appropriate dress for activity
     f. Obtaining necessary materials/equipment (e.g., for tennis, one would need a tennis racquet and three tennis balls, shorts, tennis shoes, sweat socks)
     g. Inviting a friend or family member to participate with you
  2. At the appropriate time, gather necessary material and equipment, such as clothing, money, racquet, and balls, appropriate to the activity.

C. Travel to recreation program.

  1. Travel to the selected recreation setting using previously arranged transportation.

D. Arrive at and enter the recreation setting.

  1. Exit vehicle and safely cross streets and/or parking lot. (Participant may first locate entrance from vehicle.)
  2. Locate main entrance.
  3. Proceed in the direction of the facility's entrance.
  4. Enter the facility and locate the activity or program area.

E. Participate in recreation activity.

  1. Request information about the selected activity from the information desk.
  2. Complete equipment/material check-out procedures.

3. Locate the appropriate area to engage in the activity.
4. Participate in the activity; demonstrate appropriate behaviors.
5. Return equipment/materials following termination of the activity.
6. Leave the program area.

F. Leave community leisure setting.

1. Exit the community recreation facility.
2. Cross streets and/or parking lot safely, and enter vehicle.
3. Return to place of residence or other prearranged location (e.g., restaurant).

G. Consider future involvement (optional).

1. Return to community recreation facility for future participation.

When participating in a community recreation setting, the individual without a disability can perform many of the steps of this process without extensive planning. To illustrate this process, two scenarios are presented next.

Participation in Community Recreation by People without Disabilities

Mark Lamorte, while on his way home from work, hears an advertisement on his car radio for a new physical exercise class at the neighborhood recreation center. The advertisement states that new members who register and pay for 20 sessions will receive 5 free bonus sessions. This is an activity that Mark has been interested in pursuing for quite some time. From the directions given on the radio broadcast, he knows that the recreation center is in proximity to his home. Mark also makes a mental note of the activity schedule, program costs, and registration procedures.

After relaxing at home and "psyching" himself up to enroll in the exercise class, Mark decides to call his friend and let her know about this exciting offer. Mark's friend also expresses an interest in the program and decides to meet Mark within the hour. Mark understands the appropriate attire needed for participating in the program and the amount of time required to get to the recreation agency. After changing into his exercise clothes, he grabs his wallet, keys, and coat. He leaves, excited in anticipation of this new experience. Mark and his friend arrive at the community recreation center 15 minutes early, with ample time to request assistance with the registration procedure. They are directed to the multipurpose room where the exercise instructor can answer any of their questions. They are informed that the first class, to be held that evening, is a general orientation and that they can attend for only $1. In addition, a medical liability release form has to be read and signed. Following the orientation class, participants can register for the 20-session exercise program and take advantage of the new-member bonus offer.

Mark and his friend enjoy the exercise orientation class. They learn about exercise, health, and fitness and meet others their age. Before leaving, they register for the 20-session class. For three evenings per week, they enjoy participating in this healthful, educational, and enjoyable community leisure experience. In addition, Mark and his friend discover other activities, such as the pottery workshop, the holiday dances, and the neighborhood picnic, that also are held at the recreation center throughout the year.

Mark's continued involvement in these activities has facilitated his personal growth and development and has greatly improved his health, quality of life, and leisure lifestyle. The program has helped him become an active participant in the community. He has invited other friends and family members to share in his leisure and social experiences at the community recreation center.

Now one might ask: "If a person with a disability had an interest in participating in the same recreation activity as had Mark, would the procedures for participation be identical?" The next scenario describes a situation wherein the participant has a developmental disability.

Participation in Community Recreation by People with Disabilities

While listening to the radio in her bedroom at the group home, Debbie Cox hears the same advertisement for the physical exercise program. She believes that this activity would be worthwhile and enjoyable. Debbie understands that the exercise class meets several days a week and includes a participation fee.

Debbie is a 22-year-old woman with a developmental disability living in a group home with five other individuals also diagnosed with developmental disabilities. The residents (ages 22–37 years) have mental retardation requiring limited to extensive support. Debbie has mental retardation requiring limited support with an IQ of 48. She has limited expressive language (e.g., uses simple words and phrases) and frequently exhibits inappropriate social behaviors (e.g., vocalizes loudly at inappropriate times, touches others inappropriately, forgets to attend to personal hygiene). Debbie is ambulatory but has an unsteady gait and a noticeable limp. At times, she requires assistance with dressing, such as putting on her coat, buttoning her blouse, and tying her shoelaces, because of the limited use of her disabled right arm. Debbie attends a sheltered workshop during the day and independently commutes there on a public bus. The only consistently planned leisure activity in which Debbie participates is a segregated Tuesday evening Bible study class sponsored by the local church and conducted solely for people who have mental retardation. Occasionally, she participates in large group recreational field trips that are planned by the group home staff (e.g., movies, The Arc's monthly dances, trips to a local restaurant for coffee). At other times, Debbie and the other residents are left with a substantial amount of unstructured discretionary time.

For the past 5 years, Debbie has resided in a supported living environment; much of the decision making and planning in her life is conducted by a paid professional staff on her behalf. Unlike Mark, Debbie is not encouraged to decide on her own where and in what she will participate. She must undergo a completely different process to become involved in the community recreation center program.

How does Debbie express her interest in participating in the exercise class to her care providers? Each time Debbie hears the radio advertisement for the exercise class, she becomes anxious at the thought of participating. One evening, Debbie expresses her desire to participate in the class by pointing to the radio, nodding her head, and laughing in the presence of a care provider as the advertisement is broadcast over the radio. Her care provider acknowledges her attempt to communicate by stating that she has already received information about the exercise class through the mail in a community recreation center brochure. The care provider explains to Debbie that she will contact the recreation center director later in the week to receive additional information about the course. However, she will first discuss Debbie's potential participation in the class with the group home director and other staff members.

During a weekly staff meeting shortly after this exchange, Debbie's care provider shares with the other staff members Debbie's interest in the program and her request to participate. The group home director and staff identify several problems or barriers that could prevent Debbie from participating successfully. Staff members cite insufficient staffing, the lack of personal and agency finances, and the unavailability of transportation as major obstacles that they may not be able to overcome at present. The staff's decision to deny Debbie's participation in the program is communicated to her, although she fails to understand the reasons behind this decision that lacked her input. Debbie's excitement about the program remains high, and she seeks staff attention every time she hears the exercise class promotion on the radio. Staff members continue to respond: "Debbie, we're looking into it for you!" Debbie remains hopeful, but as time progresses, she becomes frustrated and begins to experience feelings of helplessness. Group home staff members begin to have difficulty controlling her inappropriate behaviors; for example, she throws a tantrum every time a radio is turned on in her presence. The group home staff members find that they are not able to motivate her to participate in other recreational and social activities at home or elsewhere.

At the next staff meeting, it is decided that action must be taken to effect Debbie's involvement in an exercise program. A group home care provider telephones the community recreation center to solicit additional information regarding the program and to notify the agency of Debbie's interest in participating. Having been informed that Debbie is a potential participant with special needs because of her mental and physical limitations, the recreation center director responds:

> Since we attempt to meet the leisure needs of all persons in our community, including those individuals with disabilities, I am pleased that you called. Let's discuss Debbie's needs and then the particular exercise class that she wants to participate in. I must ask you several questions to determine if this class is an appropriate and feasible leisure option for her. If it is, then we will want to discuss the best ways to involve Debbie so that she, as well as other participants, will benefit from the program. I could ask you these questions over the telephone or in person, whichever is most convenient for you and Debbie. We look forward to having Debbie in our program, and I look forward to meeting you. Thank you for your call.

COMPLETING A RECREATION
INVENTORY FOR INCLUSIVE PARTICIPATION

The community recreation center director asks the instructor of the exercise class to use the Recreation Inventory for Inclusive Participation to facilitate Debbie's participation in the class. The RIIP is a four-part tool used during the initial stages of program development. This planning process includes identifying an appropriate activity/setting and addressing preplanning issues and tasks such as program dates and times, activity costs, and transportation needs. The RIIP includes a general analysis of the program and a discrepancy analysis to determine how well the participant's abilities match the overall skills necessary to participate successfully in the activity. This inventory process includes identifying possible program modifications to enhance the participation of individuals who may need such alterations.

Applying the RIIP to Debbie's participation in the inclusive community exercise class is presented next. Each section of the inventory is accompanied by a discussion of its implementation and usefulness, including completing all necessary forms. A flow chart illustrating the use of the inventory follows the implementation example. All forms described next reappear in Appendix F for your future use.

Part I: (A) Appropriateness of Recreation Activity/Setting (Figure 5.1) and Part I: (B) General Program and Participant Information (Figure 5.2) are completed during a second telephone conversation between the care provider and the agency staff member.

Part I is viewed as an initial assessment or screening device. The seven questions in Section A and the general information in Section B address critical areas of concern that could help determine whether the recreation experience under consideration for a particular individual will be a successful one.

For Debbie, the exercise class at the community recreation center is deemed a *chronologically age-appropriate* activity (Question 1). The appropriateness of this activity is determined by observing peers without disabilities participating in the same activity.

It is apparent that Debbie has demonstrated a *preference* for this activity by continually seeking out staff attention and by smiling each time the exercise class is advertised over the radio. In the past, Debbie exhibited similar behaviors when

---

RECREATION INVENTORY FOR INCLUSIVE PARTICIPATION (RIIP)
PART I: (A) APPROPRIATENESS OF RECREATION ACTIVITY/SETTING

When an activity or setting is being examined for recreation involvement, several key areas should be addressed prior to implementing the program. These areas relate to the *appropriateness* of the activity or setting to an individual's needs, preferences, and skill level.

With such a wide variety of leisure-related activities and settings available to individuals with disabilities, the information gained from the following questions will assist the person with a disability, his or her care providers, and the recreation staff in determining the appropriateness of the activity and setting for participation. In situations in which a decision between two or more activities must be made, this information may assist in determining the most ideal activity to meet the individual's needs and skill level.

Record the participant's name, activity, setting, and date, and check the appropriate responses to the following seven questions. If the responses to the questions are affirmative (i.e., yes), proceed to the next step of the RIIP (Part II: Activity/Discrepancy Analysis). If the responses to these questions fail to show positive results, an alternative recreation activity or setting should be selected for analysis and potential participation.

Name of Participant: _Debbie Cox_ Date: _3-3-97_

Activity/Skill: _Exercise Class_

Community Leisure Setting: _Hiawatha Recreation Center_

Parent/Professional Filling Out Form _Patrick O'Morrow_

1. Is the activity or setting selected appropriate for people without disabilities of the same chronological age?
   _X_ yes ___ no

2. Does the individual demonstrate a preference for this activity, or could he/she benefit (i.e., individual has related goals/objectives stated in program plan, IEP, IHP) from participating in this particular activity or setting?
   _X_ yes ___ no

3. Can the individual financially afford/receive financial assistance to gain access to this specific activity/setting?
   _X_ yes ___ no

4. If materials or equipment are necessary for participating in the activity or setting, does the individual own or have access to the necessary materials/equipment (e.g., borrow from recreation center, family, friend)?
   _X_ yes ___ no

5. If necessary, are material and/or procedural adaptations available?
   _X_ yes ___ no

6. Does the individual have access to some form of transportation to get to the leisure setting?
   _X_ yes ___ no

7. If physical accessibility is a special consideration for participating, does the setting provide easy access (e.g., handicapped parking, curb cuts, accessible restrooms, ramp to entrance)?
   _X_ yes ___ no

Figure 5.1. Appropriateness of recreation activity/setting.

RECREATION INVENTORY FOR INCLUSIVE PARTICIPATION (RIIP)
PART I: (B) GENERAL PROGRAM AND PARTICIPANT INFORMATION

General Information

Recreation Program Experience: _Exercise Class_
Directions: Check or write in the requested information on the following items. If necessary, use space on back.

1. Dates: from _3-17-97_ to _5-19-97_
   Days/times: _M, W, F 5 to 6 p.m._
   Number of sessions: _20 plus 5 free sessions Total: 25 (Approx. 9 weeks)_

2. Registration required: _X_ yes ___ no
   Procedure: _X_ in person ___ mail ___ phone
   Deadline date: _none *_
   * This class is ongoing. One can register at any time.

3. Guardian permission required:
   ___ no _X_ yes Comment: _Medical release form must be signed._

4. Fee charged or money required: _X_ yes ___ no
   Amount: $ _6.00_ Payment procedure: _Pay instructor each session—maximum $20._
   Are memberships available for free or reduced entrance fee?
   _X_ no ___ yes; Cost: ___ Good for how long? ___

5. Transportation provided: ___ yes _X_ no
   If yes, is it handicapped accessible (e.g., wheelchair lift)? ___ yes
   ___ no
   Other comments: ___

6. Comment on type of dress worn: _Exercise clothes; Tennis shoes required_

7. List required equipment and materials:
   a. Facility owned: _Exercise mats_
   b. Participant owned: _None_
      Optional: Exercise weights

8. Special rules related to this activity (e.g., appropriate dress): _No eating during class; work at your own pace._

Participant Information

Name: _Debbie Cox_ Date: _3-3-97_
Directions: Refer to item in left column. Check correct response for participant. Add comments when appropriate.

1. _X_ Can participate
   ___ Any conflicts (i.e., arrive late, leave early)?; Comment: ___

2. ___ Registration not required
   ___ Can register independently
   _X_ Needs assistance; Comment: _Staff from group home will assist as needed_

3. ___ Permission not needed
   _X_ Permission granted (consent form attached)

4. _X_ Participant can afford financial costs.
   ___ Other arrangements; Comment: ___

5. Participant's transportation choice(s):
   ___ Walk ___ Drive _X_ Bus ___ Bike
   ___ Dropped off ___ Other: ___
   Assistance needed: _X_ yes ___ no
   Initial bus training required

6. _X_ Participant has appropriate attire.
   ___ Other; Comment: ___

7. _X_ Equipment/materials are supplied
   ___ Participant has equipment
   ___ Equipment/materials need to be purchased
   ___ Other; Comment: ___

8. _X_ Participant can meet requirement
   ___ Other; Comment: ___

Figure 5.2. General program and participant information.

92

she enjoyed herself in other highly preferred activities. Upon further investigation, it is determined that her participation in the exercise class is consistent with the goals and objectives contained in her individualized program plan (Question 2).

Staff members confirm that, with careful budgeting, Debbie can *financially afford* to participate in the recreation class (Question 3). If an activity or setting has a user fee, then it must be determined in advance whether one can afford the costs to participate, either through personal resources or through access to financial assistance. Most recreation agencies, including private for-profit ones, usually offer some type of financial assistance package, such as a full or partial scholarship, to help those individuals with financial needs participate in their facilities and programs. This recreation agency informed the group home staff that it can apply a sliding fee schedule to help Debbie pay her way.

Debbie possesses the necessary *materials and equipment*—in this case, exercise clothing and tennis shoes—for participating in the exercise class (Question 4). Owning or having access to the required materials and equipment is necessary for complete and functional participation in the recreation environment.

Debbie's minimal physical limitations do not present a problem for participation; therefore, material and/or procedural *adaptations* were not necessary, at least initially (Question 5). However, for individuals with significant physical and/or cognitive limitations who may require additional assistance, it would be necessary to implement material and/or procedural adaptations to promote participation, success, and enjoyment. (See Chapter 6 for a detailed description of adaptation alternatives and partial participation strategies.)

Debbie demonstrates independent *transportation* skills (e.g., riding the city bus to and from the sheltered workshop). With additional training, she could learn to ride the bus that makes stops at the recreation center and one block from her group home (Question 6). Incorporating additional transportation skills training into Debbie's program could prove to be of great value in her attempts to participate in the community in the future.

Physical accessibility is not a special consideration that could hinder Debbie's participation in this setting (Question 7). Further investigation reveals that the recreation center is physically accessible; there are, for example, handicapped parking spaces, curb cuts, no steps with which to contend, accessible restrooms, and lowered drinking fountains with push plates. These factors likely will facilitate Debbie's (as well as other participants') independent, functional, and successful participation in the program.

Together, the exercise class instructor and the care provider complete Part I: (B) General Program and Participant Information (Figure 5.2) to identify preplanning tasks.

Based on the information previously collected, the exercise class is deemed appropriate for Debbie's participation. Following the directions stated in Part I, a meeting is arranged for the recreation center director, a group home care provider, and the exercise class instructor to complete Part II: Activity/Discrepancy Analysis (Figure 5.3). Completing Part II provides an overall inventory of the basic and vital skills necessary for Debbie's successful participation in the activity. It helps these key players identify the critical physical, cognitive, and social/emotional demands and expectations of participating with one's peers.

After completing and reviewing Part II, Part III: Specific Activity Requirements (Figure 5.4) is completed. The *social/emotional skill requirements* of the ex-

RECREATION INVENTORY FOR INCLUSIVE PARTICIPATION (RIIP)
PART II: ACTIVITY/DISCREPANCY ANALYSIS

Leisure Skill Inventory

Activity/Skill: _Exercise Class_

Leisure Setting: _Hiawatha Recreation Center_

Directions: Below, give a step-by-step breakdown of those *basic* and *vital* skills a person without disabilities would need in order to participate in the activity. Include all components (e.g., breaks, using restrooms, drinking fountain, telephone).

Inventory for Participant with Disability

Name: _Debbie Cox_

Directions: Read the step(s) in left column. If participant can perform the step, mark a plus (+) in the center column. If the participant cannot perform the step, make a minus (−) in the center column. If the participant's performance is marked (−), identify a teaching procedure or adaptation/modification for that step in the right column. Upon completion, go to Part III: SPECIFIC ACTIVITY REQUIREMENTS.

STEPS (Activity Analysis):	−	+	Teaching Procedure, Adaptation/Modification, Strategy for Partial Participation
1. Enter the recreation center.		+	1.
2. Acknowledge recreation staff and others, if appropriate.	−		2. Initially, group home staff will appropriately model interactions with rec. staff and others. (Staff may not be available.)
3. Locate and proceed to the multipurpose center.	−		3.
4. Locate coat rack along the wall and proceed in that direction.	−		4. Initially, group home staff will model and assist Debbie in this step.
5. Take coat off, hang on coat rack or place it with other belongings (e.g., sport bag, purse) along the wall.		+	5.
6. Find a space on the exercise mat and proceed in that direction.	−		6. Initially, group home staff will model and assist Debbie in this step.

(continued)

Figure 5.3. Activity/discrepancy analysis.

(continued)

Step	Rating	Notes
7. Wait for class to begin.		7.
8. Optional: Appropriately speak with others and stretch out.	+	8. Appropriate role modeling needed.
9. When class starts, listen to and follow instructor's directions.		9.
10. Do warm-up exercises.	+	10.
11. Do strength training exercises.	−	11. Debbie may have difficulty with some of these exercises. The instructor will provide modified exer. or assistance as needed.
12. When instructor offers a break, use drinking fountain if necessary.	+	12.
13. Do aerobic exercises.		13. Assistance/modification as needed.
14. Check heart rate (3 x).		14. Assistance/modification as needed.
15. Do cool-down exercises.	+	15.
16. Upon completion of class, help put mats away.		16. Appropriate role modeling/teaching may be needed.

(continued)

(continued)

STEPS (Activity Analysis):	+	–	Teaching Procedure, Adaptation/Modification, Strategy for Partial Participation
17. Optional: Talk to other participants			17. Group home staff will appropriately model interactions with others.
18. Optional: Use drinking fountain/restroom, if necessary.			18.
19. Collect personal belongings.			19.
20. Put on coat.			20.
21. Exit recreation center.			21.
22.			22.
23.			23.
24.			24.
25.			25.

(If needed, use additional space on back)

ercise class that would be expected of Debbie are areas of concern (see Part IV: [C] Social/Emotional Considerations in Appendix F) (implementation example found in Figure 5.5).

Part IV: (C) Social/Emotional Considerations of the inventory is then completed to further analyze the social and emotional skill requirements of the exercise class that would need to be addressed prior to Debbie's participation. In this manner, social and emotional difficulties can be alleviated with additional training and activity modifications, as necessary. Strategies to enhance Debbie's participation are jointly developed by Debbie, group home staff members, and the exercise class instructor. The accompaniment of a volunteer advocate (see Chapter 6), additional social skills training, and peer social reinforcement and role modeling are identified as potential strategies to facilitate a successful experience for Debbie. If the assessment would have "red flagged" additional skill limitations relative to the exercise class demands in the physical and/or cognitive/academic areas, then Sections A and B (i.e., Physical Skill Requirements and Cognitive/Academic Skill Requirements), respectively, would have been addressed as well. Copies of these Further Activity Considerations—Sections A–C appear in Appendix F.

Using the four-part RIIP allows for an individualized and systematic approach to including people with disabilities in community recreation settings. To follow the RIIP process in its entirety, refer to the flow chart illustrated in Figure 5.6. Blank forms from the RIIP are in Appendix F and may be reproduced for personal and agency use.

INVENTORY SUMMARY

As used here, the RIIP outlines a systematic method for conducting an observation of an event as it occurs in a natural setting under typical conditions. Utilizing an inventory approach to developing instructional sequences and related information provides recreation professionals, parents, teachers, and consumers with accurate, detailed descriptions of recreation activities. As such descriptions are generated by observing peers without disabilities, the necessary skills for successful participation can be compared with performance criteria exhibited by people without disabil-

---

RECREATION INVENTORY FOR INCLUSIVE PARTICIPATION (RIIP)
PART III: SPECIFIC ACTIVITY REQUIREMENTS

Name: **Debbie Cox**   Date: **3-3-97**

Question: After completing and reviewing the ACTIVITY/DISCREPANCY ANALYSIS, if particular responses would be difficult for the participant to perform, would special material/procedural adaptations or teaching procedures be readily available to enable at least partial participation?

＿＿ yes   **X** no

If *yes*, participate in the program.

If *no*, please check the area(s) of concern listed below. This allows for an in-depth analysis of the specific requirements needed for this activity in the identified area of concern (e.g., physical, cognitive/academic, social/emotional).

＿＿   Physical Skill Requirements: refer to RIIP PART IV (A).

＿＿   Cognitive/Academic Skill Requirements: refer to RIIP PART IV (B).

X   Social/Emotional Skill Requirements: refer to RIIP PART IV (C).

Figure 5.4.   Specific activity requirements.

RECREATION INVENTORY FOR INCLUSIVE PARTICIPATION (RIIP)

PART IV: FURTHER ACTIVITY CONSIDERATIONS—(C) SOCIAL/EMOTIONAL CONSIDERATIONS

Activity: __Exercise Class__

Name: __Debbie Cox__   Date: __3-3-97__

Directions: Check, circle, or write in the correct information.

Directions: Refer to information in left column. Answer yes or no as to whether the participant can participate at the level requested. If the answer is "no," comment on the assistance that is required.*

1. a. This activity occurs: ____ alone ____ with 2 ____ in small group (3–8) __X__ in large group (8 or more)

   b. This activity is structured:
   __X__ class structure ____ no structure ____ combination

   c. Comment on the type and amount of supervision:
   __One exercise instructor leading the group.__

2. This activity involves: __X__ females __X__ males
   Age range: ____ preschool (under 5) ____ teens (13–19)
   ____ children (5–12) ____ senior citizens (65+)
   __X__ adults (20–64)

3. a. Check the social interactions listed below that pertain to this activity.
   __X__ Share materials ____ Take turns ____ Compete
   __X__ Communicate with other participants
   ____ Have physical contact with other participants
   b. Noise level: ____ quiet ____ medium __X__ loud ____ mixed

4. List words or common phrases associated with or used during this activity (e.g., nice shot).
   __Stretching out counting 1-2-3, work it, jog, bend to the left, right, down on the mat, arms in front, legs out, etc.__

---

1. a. __X__ yes ____ no
      Comments:

   b. __X__ yes ____ no
   c. __X__ yes ____ no
      Comments:

2. __X__ yes ____ no
   Comments:

3. a. ____ yes __X__ no → Debbie displays inappropriate
      Comments: social skills (e.g., vocalizes loudly).
      If a group home staff person cannot assist
      w/ approp. role modeling and ver-
   b. __X__ yes ____ no bal correction, it may be necessary to
      Comments: solicit a class participant (volunteer)
      advocate to assist, as needed.

4. ____ yes __X__ no
   Comments: __Debbie__ will require additional
   training and peer social reinforcement
   and modeling to respond to
   instructors directions.

---

*If social/emotional considerations have been met, proceed as planned. If not, an alternative activity or setting should be considered for investigation and potential participation.

Figure 5.5. Social/emotional considerations.

98

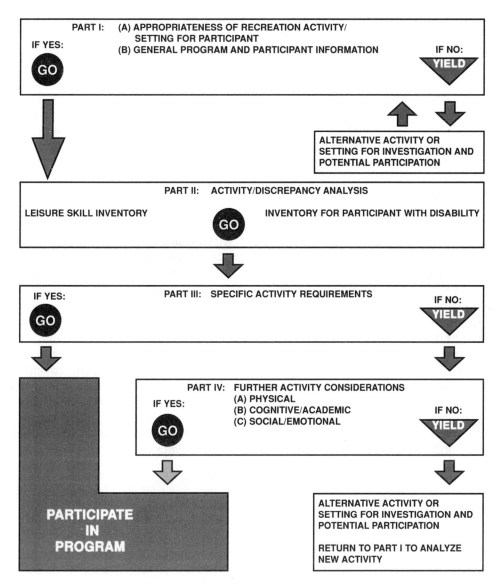

Figure 5.6. Recreation Inventory for Inclusive Participation (RIIP) flow chart.

ities. As a result, important yet subtle component responses, such as finding an un-occupied space on the exercise mat or waiting one's turn for a drink at the water fountain, or qualitative response characteristics that might be easily ignored, such as performing warm-up exercises for the appropriate amount of time, are high-lighted and subsequently targeted for instruction. Incorporating such subtle com-ponent or qualitative responses can minimize unnecessary performance discrepan-cies between participants with and without disabilities who are jointly using a recreation environment or who are simply performing the same leisure skill. In ad-dition, using an observational inventory requires recreation professionals, thera-peutic recreation specialists, and teachers to leave residential facilities and school buildings and requires parents and consumers to leave homes in order to develop instructional content (i.e., recreation curriculum). A visit to the recreation agency by the individual with a disability or his or her parents or care provider to determine the program's and setting's appropriateness for recreation participation and instruction can be useful. Such a visit would reveal, for example, the variety of support elements needed by the participant, such as available transportation, or the number and complexity of location cues within the facility or the types of activities available to the individual as part of his or her leisure education. Completing the RIIP can provide a broader and more comprehensive view of recreation activities and environments. In this manner, subsequent instruction and participation will be more relevant, functional, and successful for all of the participants.

SUMMARY

This chapter presented a conceptual framework for community recreation programming and leisure skill instruction for people with disabilities. People with disabilities should be taught functional, age-appropriate leisure skills that are comparable to those used by individuals without disabilities and that lead to successful performance in inclusive community recreation settings. Through the selection of such leisure skills, maximum gains in independent community performance may be expected, over time, to accrue. The Recreation Inventory for Inclusive Participation (RIIP) helps facilitate this transition to more functional leisure education. This recreation skill and facility inventory was designed to modify or eliminate the various obstacles that people with disabilities often encounter. Following this inventory process could allow an individual to overcome obstacles that interfere with selecting and implementing functional, age-appropriate leisure skills in community recreation environments. Overcoming such obstacles would permit interactions between people with and without disabilities and development of age-appropriate leisure skills within inclusive community recreation contexts.

Intervention Strategies for Inclusive Recreation

6

John E. Rynders and
Maurice K. Fahnestock

◆ ◆ ◆ ◆ ◆

This chapter, designed to introduce and illustrate strategies that promote the successful inclusion of individuals with disabilities in recreation programs, is divided into three sections. The first summarizes the status of opportunity for inclusive recreation and offers a preliminary set of recommended professional practices for promoting inclusion. The second describes five specific strategies for enhancing the inclusion of participants with disabilities. The third is a case study of a municipal park and recreation department that has been implementing inclusive recreation since the early 1970s.

STATUS OF INCLUSIVE RECREATION

Even though legislative rulings such as Section 504 of the Rehabilitation Act of 1973 (PL 93-112) and the Americans with Disabilities Act (ADA) of 1990 (PL 101-336) have mandated inclusive opportunities, studies show that inclusion often is not experienced by individuals with disabilities. In fact, a national survey of 336 adults with mental retardation living in foster and small group homes (Hayden, Lakin, Hill, Bruininks, & Copher, 1992) reported that a large proportion of residents participate in relatively passive, often solitary, in-home activities with low demands for socializing, such as TV watching.

Two other studies shed light on the status of inclusion from a service-provider standpoint. Germ (1993) surveyed all of the park and recreation and community education departments in the state of Minnesota, focusing on the status of their inclusionary programming and the use of best professional inclusionary practices. The study categorized each department's self-report of inclusion into one of five levels—A, B, C, D, and E—indicating the level of inclusion and use of best professional practices. The A-level category included "agencies that serve persons with developmental disabilities in existing services; that list five or more integrated programs; and that use eight or more best professional practices." Of the 484 agencies surveyed statewide, only 13 (2.6%) met the A-level criterion of providing "successful integration" services to people with developmental disabilities. The criteria for the B level of service were "agencies that serve persons with developmental disabilities; that list one to four integrated programs; and that use one to seven best professional practices." Of the agencies surveyed, 220 (45%) met the B-level criterion of engaging in "some integration." The C-level category included agencies that "serve persons with disabilities but not developmental disabilities, or reported serving persons with developmental disabilities but listed no integrated programs." Of the 484 agencies, 136 (28.1%) fit into the category of providing "hypothetical inclusion." The D-level category included the agencies "serving persons with disabilities in segregated community recreation programs only." Fifteen agencies (3.1%) reported that segregated programs were their only offering to constituents with disabilities. The E-level category was defined as "agencies that do not currently serve persons with disabilities in their programs." Of the agencies surveyed, 100 (20.6%) reported not currently serving people with disabilities in their recreation programs. In other words, when Germ looked at all of the park and recreation and community education departments in the state of Minnesota, 3 years after the passing of the Americans with Disabilities Act, less than half of the agencies were doing "some integration," and only 2.6% felt successful at including people with disabilities in five or more of their programs, using at least eight best professional practices.

In 1995, the Ohio Developmental Disabilities Planning Council surveyed 71 park and recreation agencies throughout the state of Ohio. The survey asked agency representatives to give their impression of their agency's present ability to welcome and support people with disabilities. Seventeen percent responded as having an "excellent" inclusive approach to recreation and leisure; 38% had a "good" approach; 34% reported having a "fair" approach; and 11% reported that they had a "poor" approach to inclusion. Two other questions revealed constraints that the agencies felt toward their ability to deliver inclusionary services. In response to a question on the "availability of leisure aides" to support a participant with a disability, only 7% of the agency representatives said that their agency did an "excellent" job of providing aides; 25% felt that they were doing a "good" job, while 33% and 35% stated that they were "fair to poor" at providing an aide. Another question asked about the use of the recommended professional practice of providing "individualized planning sessions" to prepare staff for the inclusion of the participant with a disability. Only 4% of the agencies responded as doing an "excellent" job; 25% reported doing a "good" job, while 32% and 39% reported doing a "fair" to "poor" job respectively. As evidenced by these studies, the status of providing inclusive recreation in the United States is not at all impressive.

Identifying indicators of quality for inclusionary purposes may be helpful for shaping the attitude of recreation professionals toward inclusion. These indicators of quality create—for recreation providers, participants, and parents—a basis for asking questions, promote planning of better programs, and offer a "checklist" for evaluating programs more fully.

Schleien, Rynders, Heyne, and Tabourne (1995) have identified three types of indicators, based on a review of the literature: 1) logistical and environmental, 2) techniques and methods, and 3) individual programming. Examples from each of these areas follow.

1. Logistical and environmental

    • Programming occurs with peers who have a wide range of abilities, including peers who do not have a disability.
    • Participants are enrolled in programs that are chronological-age appropriate, reflecting participation in the type of activities typical of a comparable age group without disabilities.
    • Budgets are sufficient to support successful inclusionary efforts.
    • Scheduling reflects a sensitivity to times and places that are readily accessible to people with disabilities, including access to public transportation.
    • Avenues are developed to keep "key players" in continued communication with each other.

2. Techniques and methods

    • Inclusive program offerings provide effective techniques such as partial participation, companionship training, task adaptation, cooperative learning, and teaching of new social and recreation skills with appropriate behavioral techniques (e.g., task analysis, prompting, sequencing, correction and reinforcement, shaping, fading).
    • Ongoing modifications of activities and materials occur, and use of adaptive devices and techniques is reduced as appropriate.
    • Assessment of skill, experience, and interest levels of participants with disabilities occurs as part of the program plan and accommodation assessment.
    • A welcoming orientation exists for participants and families as they are introduced to inclusive programs and adaptive strategies. Once introduced to inclusionary programming, families are invited to participate in activities, assessment procedures, and program evaluation.
    • An ongoing evaluation of environmental and task quality and individual leisure needs, preferences, skills, and enjoyment is conducted and includes families as fully as possible.
    • Staff are well trained to conduct the program and receive administrative support and assistance.

3. Individualized programming

    • Activities are based on needs and preferences of individual participants.
    • Activities develop skills, leisure knowledge, attitudes, and resource awareness that are transferable to community settings and that accommodate time constraints of the individual.
    • Adaptations are geared to the individual, are designed to increase independence within the activity, and are oriented toward enhancing mastery of recreation and social skills including a plan to fade out adaptations when possible.
    • Activities afford a spectrum of choice.
    • An allowance is made for personal challenge and dignity of reasonable risk.

Agencies that want to become truly welcoming and supportive to everyone in their community must go beyond the letter of the law. They must develop a number of inclusionary strategies so that they can actually carry out the intent of the law.

FIVE INCLUSIONARY STRATEGIES

Harvesting the fruits of environmental preparation for accommodating services, as described in this chapter and in Chapter 5, will depend in large measure on the success of inclusionary strategies. Among these strategies, five are of special importance because they are under the direct control of community recreation professionals and because they meld peer-to-peer interactions and leisure activities into a rewarding experience for everyone. More than 20 years of research and development efforts have proved the worth of the following five strategies (cf. Rynders et al., 1993; Schleien, Meyer, Heyne, & Brandt, 1995):

1. Structuring inclusive activities for cooperative, heterogeneous, peer-to-peer interaction outcomes
2. Preparing peers without disabilities to be cooperative companions, cooperative tutors, or both and supporting that interactive role within a cooperative structure
3. Creating a team of adults (e.g., parents and professionals) and peers without disabilities, who can program activities collaboratively
4. Adapting tasks to promote multi-ability access while implementing specific skill training with the individual with a disability
5. Constructing activity plans that help "put it all together" from a cooperative structuring standpoint

Strategy 1: Structuring Inclusive Activities for Cooperative, Heterogeneous, Peer-to-Peer Interaction Outcomes

Unless an inclusive situation is structured for cooperative interactions, participants without disabilities often feel discomfort and uncertainty in interacting with peers who have disabilities. Furthermore, if a setting is not structured for cooperative learning experiences, then negative competition is likely to emerge and may actually socialize children without disabilities to reject peers who have a disability (e.g., Rynders et al., 1993). What does it mean specifically to structure an activity for cooperative interactions?

Usually, one to three models of activity structure are used when groups of people are learning something: competitive, individualistic, and/or cooperative. Each is legitimate and has strengths in particular situations. Furthermore, they often can be combined in a program.

A *competitive* learning structure, in its traditional application, leads to one person in a group winning and all other group members losing. If it is used in a group in which one of the members has a disability that makes successful task participation difficult, it will be likely that the participant with a disability will "come in last." An example of competitive structuring from the world of camping is to imagine five children, some of whom have movement-related disabilities, lining up at the edge of a lake for a canoe race. Each has a canoe and a paddle to use. The recreation leader tells them that the person who reaches the other side of the lake first will win a miniature canoe paddle. It does not take much imagination to realize that children with movement disabilities (e.g., coordination problems, low muscle tone) have little chance of competing successfully. Informed program leaders would not use a competitive goal structure in this manner, of course; they would either modify the competitive situation or would rely on one or both of the other structures instead.

In an *individualistic* learning structure, each member of a group works to improve his or her past performance. Potentially, every member of the group, including members with a movement disability, can win a prize for improvement if the target for improved performance is not set too high or is not inappropriately matched with a disability condition. Using the canoe example again, suppose that the recreation leader lines up the group on the shore of the lake and tells them that when they paddled across the lake last week each person's crossing time was recorded. Then, the recreation leader says that each person will win a miniature canoe paddle if he or she improves his or her time, even if the improvement is very small. Now everyone can be a winner. This structure often is used in amateur athletics in which a child is encouraged to "beat his or her own past best time."

A *cooperative* learning structure (if handled properly) creates a natural, socially positive interdependence because the group's attainment of an objective, with everyone contributing in some manner, is the quality that determines winning. Using the canoe illustration, the recreation leader might have the five children climb into a group canoe, give each person a paddle, and tell them that they each are to paddle as well as they can and that they all will win a miniature canoe paddle if they work together to keep the canoe inside some floating markers (placed in such a way that perfection in paddling is not required). The recreation leader will need to paddle alongside to determine that everyone is paddling and to encourage them to support and assist one another.

To promote positive *social* interactions between participants with and without disabilities, the cooperative structure will nearly always work better than the other two. Why? Because in a competitive situation, each child is concentrating on paddling the fastest; he or she doesn't have an incentive for interacting socially. Similarly, in an individualistic structure, each child is concentrating on bettering his or her own past performance; again, there is no incentive for interacting socially. In the cooperative structure, however, each person is inclined to encourage and assist every person in the group to achieve the group goal. This promotes positive interactions such as encouragement, cheering, pats on the back, and informal assistance.

Strategy 2: Preparing Peers without Disabilities to Be Cooperative Social Companions, Cooperative Tutors, or Both and Supporting that Interactive Role in a Cooperative Structure

The usual focus of a cooperative *peer teaching (tutor)* program is to have a peer without a disability teach a skill to a peer with a disability. For example, a 12-year-old child without disabilities works on a one-to-one basis to teach picture sequencing skills to a 6-year-old child with a disability. The focus of a cooperative *peer companionship (friendship)* program is to promote positive social interactions between a child with a disability and a child without a disability. In a typical application of this arrangement, two young peers of the same age—one with a disability and one without—make a giant puzzle, painting the pieces together, gluing macaroni and yarn on the pieces together, and so forth. The material that follows describes how to structure the two types of activities/roles.

Structuring an Activity for Cooperative Peer Companionship

1. *Age of Peers* Peers without disabilities and peers with disabilities should be approximately the same age so as to create an expectation of friendly socialization, turn taking, sharing, and so forth. If peers without disabilities are 1–2 years older that is fine; but for encouraging ongoing friendships, peers without disabilities generally should not be younger than peers with disabilities. Research shows that when people with disabilities are more than 2 years older than their partners without disabilities social awkwardness often occurs (Cole, Vandercook, & Rynders, 1988). Same-age peer interactions can be thought of as "horizontal"; that is, relatively equal and reciprocal on a socialization contribution basis (Sailor & Guess, 1983).

2. *Activity* Choose activities that are not highly project-skill oriented but are socializing oriented. Structure task directions so that mutual effort, not individual effort, is rewarded (e.g., a peer with a disability and a peer without a disability together put ingredients on a pizza, sharing in eating it later).

3. *Preparing Peers without Disabilities for Socialization*

   - Show them how to prompt cooperative interaction (e.g., "Chris, let's paint this picture together").
   - Show them how to encourage their partner's cooperative participation (e.g., "Bill, I'll bet that you are good at sanding. Can you help me sand this tray?").
   - Show them how to reinforce their partner for trying (e.g., "I like the way we painted the fence together. You're a good painter!").

4. *Recreation Professional's Role During Peer Socialization Interactions*

   - *Encourage* cooperative activity (e.g., "Mary, I'd like to see you and Joan take turns kicking the soccer ball").
   - *Reinforce* cooperative interactions (e.g., "I like the way you're setting the table together").
   - *Redirect* participants back to the cooperative task when one or both become distracted.
   - *Step in* if a socialization problem occurs between participants.

5. *Limitations* The purpose of cooperative peer companionship is to promote positive social interactions. It will not necessarily lead to increased skill development in a specific task in a child with a disability (unless, of course, the skill itself is of a social nature). So, if the leader's goal is to assist a child with a disability to become a more proficient reader, then an older peer without a disability (peer tutor) or an adult will need to provide reading instruction and guided reading practice. Cooperative socialization-based companionship would not meet this task skill development goal very well.

Structuring an Activity for Cooperative Peer Tutoring

1. *Age of Peers* Peers without disabilities should be considerably older than the partner with a disability (twice as old is a good rule of thumb) because the primary purpose of teaching is to enhance the tutoring recipient's skill in some task. This relationship is a vertical one (Sailor & Guess, 1983) ("I'm the 'teacher,' you're the student"). Because it is a vertical relationship, the real

teacher must supervise it so that it does not become "dictatorial" or "over mothering" on the part of the partner without disabilities.

2. *Activity*   Activities should feature cooperative skill teaching practice instead of socialization. For example, the older student without disabilities teaches the younger child with disabilities to use a hand mixer. After giving the child with a disability a chance to demonstrate the steps that he or she can do correctly, the peer tutor teaches the younger child the steps that he or she cannot do. For instance, if the child with a disability does not know how to identify the various speeds on the mixer's control dial, then the peer tutor will label each setting verbally while pointing to the corresponding printed words on the dial. The tutor will show how the printed word on the dial translates into mixer speed as the dial is moved from speed to speed. After that, the tutor might print the words on pieces of cardboard and use them like flash cards until the child with a disability can identify them very quickly and accurately. After that is accomplished, dial position commands are given (e.g., "Turn to high") with the tutor watching for errors and hesitations, correcting errors if they occur. Finally, the speed-dial operation is reinserted into the whole task of using a mixer to mix batter for a cake. Food becomes the reward for achieving this cooperative tutorial outcome, with both individuals enjoying a piece of cake together for their joint effort.

3. *Preparing Peers without Disabilities for Tutoring*

    • If old enough, show them how to use a variety of instructional techniques such as modeling, reinforcing, prompting, fading, and so forth to promote task achievement.
    • Show them how to create and use a task analysis.

4. *Recreation Professional's Role During Interactions*

    • *Reward* tutorial attempts by the child without disabilities, and reward attempts of the child with a disability to respond to the tutoring.
    • *Model* good instructional techniques.
    • *Step* in to prevent/correct instructional problems.
    • *Redirect* participants if off-task behavior occurs.

5. *Limitations*

    • A tutoring situation's social dynamics can turn autocratic if not monitored carefully.
    • The tutor may lose interest in instruction if the partner's progress is very slow. The teacher can blunt this possibility by keeping the cooperative structure in place, tying rewards to something under the tutor's control (e.g., number of practice trials given), rather than to the recipient's success (though success usually occurs when the task or step of the task is broken down into small, simplified pieces). The outcome of the task that is taught often can be rewarding itself, as in the case of the cake batter–mixing task in which the pieces of the finished cake become a reward for both participants.

A third type of structure—one that should see increasing popularity in community recreation programs—is the *cooperative tutoring / cooperative companionship* combination whereby, for example, an older peer without a disability tutors a younger peer with a disability while a peer without a disability of the same age as the child with a disability serves as a social companion. This trio structure may have at least three advantages. First, because of the participants' age differences, peers without disabilities can assume either a teaching or socializing role, one that feels comfortable to them and suits the task. Second, if teaching becomes necessary to achieve a task then there is an older peer without a disability in the group to teach while the younger peer without a disability concentrates on socializing. Third, this structure (dubbed the "one-room school" model), with its various participant ages, takes advantage of the age and ability differences, which are familiar because they occur naturally in families. For example, a young child without a disability and a young child with autism, both of whom are nearly the same age, ride horses together at the local stable (cooperative companionship). At the same time, an older peer without a disability teaches riding skills to both of the younger children (cooperative tutoring).

Strategy 3: Creating a Team of Adults and Peers without Disabilities Who Can Program Activities Collaboratively

A first step in creating a collaborative support group of adults and peers in an inclusionary program is to recruit and train volunteers (and, later, evaluate their efforts and recognize their contributions). Because some individuals with disabilities need personal assistance to participate successfully in a recreation program (based on the Recreation Inventory for Inclusive Participation [RIIP]), volunteers become essential. Therefore, adding a volunteer advocate (usually an adult without disabilities) who can individually assist the participant with disabilities when and if necessary is helpful to the recreation leader. The tasks of the volunteer advocate might include

1. Assisting the participant with a disability during registration
2. Explaining to peers without disabilities the nature of a partner's disability, if the partner with a disability is not able to do so him- or herself
3. Managing problem behaviors if they occur
4. Facilitating interpersonal relationships with classmates
5. Physically prompting the participant to perform a task (e.g., helping a person with poor balance to bend over to touch toes in an exercise class)
6. Task analyzing and teaching leisure skills to the participant
7. Evaluating participant involvement in the recreation program
8. Providing transportation assistance to and from the recreation program site
9. Assisting during toileting, dressing, and grooming
10. Assisting throughout program (e.g., pushing wheelchair, walking beside person with a disability, providing needed support)
11. Providing assistance as determined by the RIIP and recommendations of the recreation leader

A legal interpretation may be needed, but the program is responsible for providing the supports necessary for the participant with a disability to reach the goals of the program; this could include the use of a volunteer advocate. It is sometimes difficult, however, to identify individuals to assume this role. Parents, siblings, friends, classmates, and neighbors of people with disabilities should be contacted as potential volunteer advocates. In addition, agencies providing youth services, such as Boy Scouts and Girl Scouts, 4-H clubs, or YMCAs/YWCAs, often look for service projects for their membership. Volunteer advocacy is an excellent way to involve these groups. Corporations also have been known to provide volunteer resources for recreation programs and special events in which people with disabilities are expected to participate.

An important role of the community recreation professional is to identify volunteer advocates and the skills that they might need. There are two important steps for recruiting and retaining volunteers in case the need for volunteer advocates arises:

1. Develop a Volunteer Advocate Job Description format that outlines specific responsibilities and expectations. Include the following:

   a. Title   (e.g., volunteer advocate, special tutor, special friend)
   b. Job description   (based on individual participant needs)
   c. Days needed   (consult program brochure)
   d. Hours needed   (consult program brochure)
   e. Length of program   (consult program brochure)
   f. Location of program   (facility; classroom)
   g. Immediate supervisor   (program leader's name)
   h. Special skills needed   (based on individual participant needs)
   i. Description of participant with disabilities and his or her needs (from registration form)
   j. Other considerations   (e.g., transportation needs, self-care)

2. Recruit potential volunteer advocates from the community, youth service agencies, businesses, and so forth. Appropriate methods to solicit involvement include the following:

   a. Advertising in municipal park and recreation program brochures
   b. Distributing news releases to the media
   c. Writing public service announcements for local radio, TV, and cable network stations
   d. Creating a speaker's bureau made up of parents, consumers, and advocates to speak to agencies and organizations such as schools, parent groups, advocacy groups, and senior centers
   e. Registering the municipal park and recreation department and/or individual community centers with the local volunteer clearinghouse

The following list suggests ways to follow up on the volunteer advocate recruitment process:

1. Send out a Volunteer Application (see Appendix G) and job descriptions to interested people who respond. (*Note:* Be sure to include a stamped, addressed return envelope with the application. The easier it is for a prospective volunteer to respond to the agency, the greater the likelihood of successfully recruiting him or her.) Complete the Volunteer Advocate Call Sheet (see Appendix G).
2. Follow up with a telephone call to the individual asking whether he or she has received the application and whether he or she has any questions. At this point, it is a good idea to ask the volunteer candidate to identify a specific task of interest.
3. Review the application and call the applicant to set up a personal interview.

4. During the interview, clarify the volunteer's goals, specific talents and preferences, and hours during which he or she can volunteer time.

5. Match volunteer advocate with a program and a participant with disabilities. Fill out a Volunteer Advocate–Participant Match Form (see Appendix G). Complete the job description, and give a copy to the volunteer.

6. Arrange for the volunteer to meet the participant with a disability before the program begins. Be sure that the community recreation professional or another representative from the agency is present at the first meeting. Once the volunteer has made a commitment, it is the recreation professional's responsibility to provide comprehensive preservice and in-service training to the volunteer advocate. Training topics could include site orientation, goals and objectives of the program, and policies and procedures of the agency, including emergency policies and procedures. Depending on how many volunteers have been recruited, it might be easier and more efficient to provide volunteer orientation concurrently with staff orientation.

To assess whether the individual volunteer's needs and the needs of the agency have been met, it is essential to conduct program and volunteer evaluations upon completion of the program. The program staff should evaluate the volunteer not only to assess the person's personal competencies but also to determine whether the volunteer was actually needed and, if so, whether the volunteer enhanced the program and the recreation experience of the participant with a disability. The volunteer should assess his or her experience by evaluating whether the training and supervision were adequate and whether the volunteer was respected by other staff members. (Evaluation formats are presented in Appendix G.)

Volunteers need to feel important about their work. Indeed, many activities could not be accomplished without them. Because the recreation agency has invested time and energy in recruiting and training a volunteer, it is important that the volunteer continue his or her program involvement. Volunteer recognition is the best way to ensure that trained volunteers return and provide the necessary program continuity and support for people with disabilities. Recognition can be handled in a number of ways. Regular and sincere praise is the most natural way to reinforce volunteers. Awarding certificates of recognition and organizing small social events such as pizza parties and picnics, as well as full-scale annual recognition dinners with awards, are additional methods to honor and reward volunteers.

Strategies 1 and 2 in this chapter contain information about how to promote cooperative interactions directly (e.g., how the recreation professional rewards cooperative tutorial or cooperative socialization interactions when they occur). Also, there are techniques that a recreation leader can use that grow out of a group counseling tradition—techniques that bring adults' and youths' thoughts together for a common purpose. Two of these techniques, each of which shares the cooperative planning approach but from a slightly differing perspective, are Circle of Friends and the McGill Action Planning system (MAPs). These two often are used together, often sequentially. (See Chapter 7, pp. 136–137, for a description of Circle of Friends because it is primarily a sociometric technique rather than an inclusion strategy per se.)

In the MAP system (Vandercook, York, & Forest, 1989), the recreation professional assembles people who are important in the child's life (especially those in the inner one or two circles of the circle of friends). Often, a parent becomes the most important member of the planning group, although the recreation professional often acts as the facilitator. Sitting around a table, the child's parent, siblings, one or two peers, a teacher or two, a volunteer advocate, perhaps a scout leader or other community-based person who is important in the child's life, and other people including the child who has a disability "think out loud" about the following points, keeping in mind that successful inclusion in the community is the primary goal: 1) What is the individual's history? 2) What is your dream for him or her? 3) What is your nightmare? 4) Who is the individual? 5) What are his or her strengths and weaknesses? 6) What are the individual's needs? and 7) What would his or her ideal day look like, and what must be done to achieve the ideal? These points are written at the top of large sheets of paper, becoming a "map" to the future for the individual. From the notes generated through this method, short-term and long-term goals are written, followed by a list of steps/tasks that must be accomplished for the goals to be attained.

The following is an example of the MAP system in action. Megg is a 10-year-old with Down syndrome who attends a neighborhood school in which she is integrated into several curricular areas and has a general class as a homeroom base. Megg is easy to have around; unfortunately, too easy to have around sometimes because she is very withdrawn socially. Her pencil-drawn circle of friends shows no child, older or younger or of the same age, who can be considered an indispensable ("best") friend. Her mother does show two girls' names in the second circle (the good friends circle), though—girls who are in Megg's 4-H Club and have shared pizza with her a few times at club meetings.

Working closely with Megg's mother, individuals important to her life, including the two 4-H companions, are brought together to develop a MAP for her. One of the first things that is brought out is Megg's mother's nightmare. She is afraid that Megg will be totally without friends as an adult and that Megg will be placed in a highly segregated and geographically isolated residential facility when her mother dies, spending her days in a lonely and depressed state.

On the brighter side, Megg's 4-H leader says that Megg has a nice smile (when she displays it, which is not often) and good manners. The group decides to build on these, creating opportunities in which social interaction demands will be moved up a notch but will not be overwhelming for her. Her 4-H leader decides that Megg will have a nonspeaking role in the next Share the Fun skit, not a big role but one that will perhaps draw her out a little bit from a socialization standpoint.

Megg's mother and teacher decide that Megg also will be encouraged to train for the Special Olympics volleyball event, joining teammates with and without disabilities through a Unified Sports program that meets at her school twice each week. (Megg enjoys volleyball very much and does reasonably well in it.) The volleyball coach becomes part of the MAP system, learning more about how to structure cooperative activities for athletes with and without disabilities so that they succeed collectively as well as individually.

Megg is beginning to grow in her socialization abilities as a result of combining MAPs, Circle of Friends, and cooperative goal structuring techniques. Her day-to-day life shows new vitality too: new friends (both with and without disabilities), more variety in her socialization sphere, and a schedule that regularly gets her out of the house and into worthwhile activities.

Strategy 4:   Adapting Tasks to Promote Multi-ability Access While Implementing Specific Skill Training with the Individual with a Disability

The following task adaptation principles must be considered by practitioners who are responsible for adapting community recreation activities because adaptations lead to greater access to activities, which, in turn, lead to greater inclusionary opportunities (Wehman & Schleien, 1981; Wehman, Schleien, & Kiernan, 1980).

1.   Adapt enough to increase participation, success, and enjoyment, but adapt only when necessary. In Debbie's situation (see Chapter 5), the RIIP and, in particular, the discrepancy analysis sections identified Debbie's need for assistance for successful and enjoyable participation.

2.   View any changes or adaptations as temporary. Work toward engaging in original, nonmodified activity. Unless the adaptation is continuously necessary (e.g., prosthetic adaptation such as a built-up tennis shoe for people with a shorter leg, a sighted guide for a blind cross-country skier), program modifications must be designed as temporary changes so that the person requiring the changes can learn the necessary skills and can participate eventually in a standard fashion, if possible, like his or her peers without disabilities. For example, initial volunteer advocates for Debbie may be close acquaintances, such as care providers; later, the advocates may be other class participants, such as new friends. Ultimately, the need for a volunteer advocate is discontinued as Debbie participates in community recreation programs independently.

3.   Make adaptations on an individual basis meeting individual needs. When the community recreation professional discovered Debbie's need for specific program adaptations, he based his findings on the information that he gathered from the RIIP. He did not have any preconceived notion that people "like Debbie" (e.g., people with mental retardation) are "special" and should automatically require one-to-one attention during participation in recreation programs. The analysis by the community recreation professional, however, determined that Debbie initially would require some type of one-to-one arrangement, a volunteer advocate in her case, to increase Debbie's chance for successful and enjoyable participation in the exercise class. Other modifications were noted in Part II: Activity/Discrepancy Analysis (Figure 5.3), described in Chapter 5.

After making certain that all of the foregoing principles are considered thoroughly and deemed necessary, the community recreation professional, in collaboration with key others, considers what types of adaptations must be made in recreation activities prior to Debbie's participation. The recreation professional identifies five areas of the program that could be modified: 1) activity materials or equipment, 2) rules of the activity or game, 3) skill sequence, 4) facility and environment, and 5) lead-up activities. Following is a list of possible modifications that can be made in these five program areas. Modifications specific to Debbie's participation in the exercise class are followed by a more general list of modifications that can be made to accommodate other participants with disabilities in a variety of recreation activities.

1.   Activity Materials or Equipment: Leisure materials or equipment are modified to facilitate participation of people with disabilities.

   Modifications for Debbie: Built-up tennis shoes or orthotic insert

Other Types of Activity Modifications:
- Tubular steel bowling ramp
- Lowered basketball backboard and rim
- Built-up handles on paint brushes
- Sport versus standard wheelchair
- Braille reading materials
- Close-captioned videotapes
- Soft versus hard rubber balls
- Picture card of recreation center activities to make activity selection easier
- Handicapped-accessible playground equipment
- Tee-ball versus pitched baseball

2. Rules of the Activity or Game: Change the original rules to simplify activity.

Modifications for Debbie: Because of limited income, Debbie makes partial payments rather than lump-sum payments for lessons.

Other Types of Activity Modifications:
- Stand closer to horseshoe pit to ensure greater accuracy
- Allow two-handed basketball dribble
- Require one-handed versus two-handed play on foosball table
- Allow table tennis ball to hit same side before going over net
- Use personal item versus driver's license as collateral to borrow games in recreation center

3. Skill Sequence: Rearrange component steps of an activity to enhance safety and efficiency.

Modifications for Debbie:
- Dresses in exercise clothing at home
- Does not perform activity until instructor verbalizes then demonstrates exercises
- Does one half of the normally required exercise repetitions

Other Types of Activity Modifications:
- Place finger on camera's shutter release button before raising camera to eye level
- Enter recreation center earlier than other participants
- Place food item in oven before turning oven on

4. Facility and Environment: Renovate or construct facilities and outdoor environments that are physically accessible.

Modifications for Debbie: None

Other Types of Facility Modifications:
- Ramp curbs and steps
- Handrails from building to ice-skating rink
- Installation of accessible toilets, sinks, and water fountains
- Asphalt versus sand or dirt walking paths
- Tree branches trimmed so as not to injure people with visual impairments

5. Lead-Up Activities: Simplify version of traditional activity allowing practice in component skill of the game leading to full participation in the future.

    Modifications for Debbie:
    • Uses a chair when necessary to aid balance
    • Practices exercises at home
    • Works with a volunteer advocate

    Other Types of Lead-Up Activities:
    • Kickball leads to game of softball
    • Tricycle leads to bicycle
    • Using only low numbers on dart board as scoring numbers in cricket dart game
    • Boot hockey leads to skate hockey
    • Game of "catch" over a net leads to volleyball
    • Having a volunteer advocate leads to participating with friend or independent access

Strategy 5: Constructing Activity Plans that Help "Put it All Together" from a Cooperative Structuring Standpoint

For adults who are just beginning to structure peer-to-peer activities for cooperative learning, it can be helpful to "seed" the planning process with a few completed activity plans that have a built-in cooperative orientation. The three that follow are based on a handbook for 4-H leaders (Rynders & Schleien, 1991) and illustrate how peer involvement takes on a cooperative orientation in the activity itself and how the recreation leader organizes and supports the collaborative effort. Because the five strategies in this chapter are embedded in the activity plans, the program leader should make notes in the margins of the plans to help him or her remember nonembedded (or not fully represented) strategy possibilities.

ACTIVITY PLAN #1
Laughing Line Mural

(For kindergarten through early elementary)

(Cooperative structure: peer friendship)

Introduction

In this cooperative art project, participants work together to create a vibrantly patterned mural. A large sheet of mural paper is decorated with a variety of "laughing lines," which are either painted or cut from construction paper.

Resources/Materials

- White mural paper 36–48 inches wide, 6–10 feet long, depending on number of participants (1 foot of paper per person is a good rule of thumb)
- Scissors that are safe for participants
- Black construction paper
- Red, blue, and yellow tempera paint
- Sponges
- Trays for paint supplies
- Painting smock for each person
- Water containers

Preparing the Environment

Work in a room with a floor that is easily cleaned. With some groups, you may want to have participants sit on the floor around the edge of the mural paper.

For each group of three or four people, prepare a tray with three jars of paint (red, yellow, blue), brushes (one for each person), a water container, and a sponge. Keep the paint within easy reach of all.

Instructions to Group Leaders

1. Discuss art as being about ideas. How is a mural different from other types of paintings? It is BIG! The first murals were drawn on the walls of caves. Ask whether anyone has seen a mural on the wall of a building. What did it look like?
2. Talk about lines. What kind of lines are there? Lines have size and direction. Lines that stand up straight are awake, at attention, and lively! Lines that lie down are tired, sleepy, and lazy! How can you give a line a feeling? How can you make a line laugh? (Curve it upward? Make it zigzag?) How does it feel when you laugh? What does your body do?
3. Discuss that, as a group, participants will create a mural of laughing lines. They will cut lines out of black paper and glue them to the mural. Then they will paint red, blue, and yellow lines around the black lines. The mural will have no "right" side up; participants will work from all sides.

The authors thank Kathy Tilton for designing this cooperative art activity. Kathy is a professional artist and art educator.

4. Demonstrate cutting different lines from black paper. Use glue to attach several lines to the mural paper.
5. Demonstrate applying the paint. Make several painted lines. Encourage participants to look at the mural before making their lines so that there is variety in color and style. Stress the thorough washing of the brush before changing colors as an important step.
6. Pass out tray of materials and instruct participants to proceed.
7. If spaces look blank or too crowded with one color, then you may want to make suggestions about variety and balance. Some participants may want to stand up to get a better view. For some participants, it may be helpful to mark their space with a light pencil mark.

Instructions to Companions

1. With your partner, get the supplies: scissors, glue, black paper, etc.
2. Side by side, cut some laughing lines and glue them to the mural. Take turns.
3. When the adult group leader brings the painting tray, encourage your partner to choose his or her favorite color to use for the laughing lines.
4. If needed, show your partner how to use paints, and assist him or her in applying paint to the mural paper. Share materials. Take turns.
5. When the mural paper is well covered, help your partner clean up your working area and return the scissors and glue.

Expanding the Activity

1. After clean-up, ask group to look at the mural. (It will be easier to view if it is hanging up, but that may not be feasible if the paint is drippy.) Look for interesting shapes/feelings within the mural.
2. Visit a building on which a mural is painted on an outside wall, and discuss colors, shapes, feelings, and the message of the mural.

ACTIVITY PLAN #2
Life in the Pond

(For elementary)

(Cooperative structure: primarily peer friendship)

Introduction

In this activity, participants discover that there is a great variety of living organisms in a pond or lake. A single drop of pond water is full of an unbelievable number of different creatures. Zooplankton, one type of animal living in ponds and lakes, are very small. Many lakes house literally trillions of them during the summer. They eat algae (the Greek word for "plant"), and they are, in turn, eaten by many kinds of fish, including bluegills and sunfish.

Resources/Materials

- White or light-colored shallow wash basins, dishpans, or similar containers (not buckets): one for every 3–5 participants
- Pond study nets (one per group)
- Cups or small containers
- Magnifying glass: one per group

Instructions to Group Leaders

1. Emphasize to the group that zooplankton, though small, are living creatures and need to be handled very gently. Also, tell the participants that, as much as possible, they should avoid disturbing the zooplankton's home environment while collecting specimens.
2. Ask the participants to watch as you demonstrate how to collect pond specimens.
3. Fill pan with water (to half an inch from top).
4. Move net through water, low enough to brush through weeds but not on the bottom.
5. Bring up net and quickly turn inside-out over pan, dipping it into the water in the pan to release any small creatures clinging to the bottom of the net.
6. Tell participants to be sure to keep the creatures in water. When they have completed their observations, they should gently return the creatures to the pond.

Instructions for Companions

1. With your partner, fill the shallow pan with water up to half an inch from the top.
2. While your partner holds the pan, move the net slowly through the water to collect pond specimens, taking turns holding the pan and collecting specimens.
3. Together, look carefully in the pan for moving creatures.

The authors thank the Bell Museum of Natural History, Imprint, Vol. III, #2, Spring 1986 for some of the content in this activity plan.

4. Capture some creatures with a cup and view closely with a hand lens or magnifying glass. With your partner, take turns holding the cup and observing the specimens. *Note:* Be sure to handle creatures with care! It's easy to injure or kill such small creatures.
5. When you are finished observing the creatures, return them to the pond. Keeping the edge of the pan or cup near the surface of the pond, slowly pour the creatures back into the pond.

Expanding the Activity

1. Note which creatures are active on the surface and which move about beneath it.
2. Determine, if you can, whether the animal composition varies with water depth, bottom type, exposure to light, water temperature, vegetative cover, time of day, and season of the year.

Apple-Head Doll

(For adult)

(Cooperative structure: peer friendship and peer tutor)

Introduction

Apple-head dolls, long considered a tradition of early New England, actually were developed by the Seneca Indians of the New York area more than 500 years ago. Called Loose Feet, the doll represented a very old and wise spirit who was a guardian of children.

The doll of the Seneca Indians was slightly different in both construction and appearance from the dolls we make today. The Seneca method was to core a slightly green apple and mold the face as the apple dried. In the final stages, a wooden plug or corncob, bound with a top knot of feathers, was inserted into the hole where the core had been. The bottom of the apple was fitted with a roughly carved piece of wood representing a neck and shoulders. Cornhusks were bunched together around the front, and legs and feet were formed by binding the cornhusks above and below the knees and at the ankles. A wide husk was tied at the waist to form a kilt-type garment.

This project adapts the Native American craft to create the attractive apple-head dolls seen today. The intrigue lies in the simplicity of the process that creates apple faces, each different in appearance.

Resources/Materials (needed for each pair of participants)

- Two firm, large, unbruised apples
- Small paring knife
- Teaspoon
- Lemon juice concentrate (optional)
- Small bowl
- Whole cloves or round-headed pins for eyes
- Wire: 16 or 18 gauge
- Scissors
- Masking tape
- String
- Batting, cotton, or soft cloth cut into 1-inch-wide strips
- Cotton, yarn, or polyester fiberfill for hair
- White glue
- Toothpicks and extra apple for hands (optional)
- Fabric for clothing

Preparing the Environment

This activity will need to be completed in two stages. Steps 1–11 of Instructions to Companions describe how to make the doll's head and hands. Steps 12–19 describe how to make the doll's body. The doll's head and hands will need to dry for 2–3 weeks. *Note:* It is best to let the apple dry naturally, but if you must shorten the drying time, you may dry the carved apple overnight, then submerge it completely in silica gel. Cover tightly for at least 36 hours. Allow to air dry until ready (7–10 days). Make a doll before participants arrive so that you will feel comfortable with the steps and will have an example to show.

The authors thank Caye Nelson, Carol Shields, and Marlene Stoehr, 4-H professionals and consultants, for their contributions to this plan.

Instructions to Group Leaders

Explain to companions that they may need to demonstrate to their partners how to complete the activity steps and should offer assistance as needed.

Instructions to Companions

To make doll's head and arms

1. Assist your partner as you each select a firm, unbruised apple; the bigger the better because the apple will shrink to nearly half its size.
2. Peel the apples. A small section of peel may be left at both the stem and the blossom ends. Do not core apples. Help your partner peel his or her apple as needed (help probably will be needed because knives can be dangerous and must be handled carefully).
3. About one third of the way down from the stem end, scrape two hollows for eyes, leaving a ridge between the hollows for a nose. Using just the tip of a teaspoon, shape indentations where the eyes will be located.
4. On each apple, form a nose with the spoon tip by scraping away apple, creating a triangle shape, with the base slightly below the center of the face.
5. On each apple, make a slit with the knife; it will become the mouth as the apple dries. (Be careful with the knife.)
6. If ear detail is desired, scrape away apple with the spoon tip, making a half-moon shape on both sides of the head.
7. Apples dry in various shades of brown. If you wish to keep the face a lighter shade, then dip the carved apple in lemon juice concentrate.
8. Insert whole cloves or round-headed pins for eyes.
9. To add greater detail to the doll, you may make apple hands. From another apple, cut two wedges about one fourth–inch thick. Cut into a mitten shape. Cut slits to form four fingers, and put hands on toothpicks to dry. These will later be inserted into the arms of the doll's clothing.
10. For each doll, cut a piece of wire 20 inches long. Fold it in half and insert the bent end into the apple from the bottom to the top of the head.
11. Insert a string through the loop of each wire. Hang the apples in an airy spot to dry, away from direct sunlight. Features may be emphasized by molding them as the drying process takes place. Continue to push in the eyes. Complete drying takes about 2–3 weeks.

To make doll's body

12. When an apple feels pithy and does not cave under slight pressure, remove the hanging string, and complete the following steps.
13. To shape the body from the wire sticking out of the head, first bend the ends of the wire 1 inch from the bottom to form feet. Form a small loop in the wire ends for feet.
14. Cut a piece of wire 7 inches long. Form arms by winding this length of wire half an inch below the head. Form small loops in the wire ends for hands.
15. Pad the body by wrapping it with the batting, cotton, or soft cloth cut into 1-inch-wide strips. Hold these in place with stitching or tape.
16. Wrap the feet and hands with masking tape, or add dried hands.
17. Form hair by gluing on cotton, yarn, or polyester fiberfill.

18. Bend the doll to form a sitting or standing pose. The knee joint should be about 2 inches from the top of the leg. To make the doll look old, bend the shoulders forward slightly.

19. Dress the doll. With alterations in clothing and hair style, the doll can be either male or female. Place dolls on paper and trace around bodies, arms, and legs. Using these shapes as guides, cut out simple patterns for desired garments. Allow for a three eighths–inch seam. Stitch main seams, and complete stitching right on the doll to achieve a finished look. Aprons, shawls, bonnets, vests, kerchiefs, and other accessories can be added if you like.

Expanding the Activity

1. Visit a museum featuring paintings and models of how Native Americans lived long ago. Notice, particularly, the geometric shapes on the clothing, the materials from which clothing articles were made, and the ornaments that were part of their garments. Decorate doll garments accordingly.

2. In advance of the activity, visit an orchard with the group to collect apples. If that visit is not feasible, go to the supermarket together to select the apples to be used.

CUSTOMER SERVICE BUILDS BETTER PROGRAMS: BLOOMINGTON PARKS AND RECREATION

So far, this chapter has examined indicators of inclusionary program quality, along with intervention strategies that can produce these qualities. The strategies can be viewed as intervention "tools"; the quality indicators represent the products of those tools. But using tools and tool products without a process for guiding their use is similar to building a home without a blueprint. In the following case study, a process ("blueprint") for guiding implementation is described, and its use is illustrated.

The Parks and Recreation Division of the city of Bloomington, Minnesota, has been dedicated to serving individuals with disabilities since the early 1970s when a parent movement helped create its Adaptive Recreation program. In 1988, Bloomington's Adaptive Recreation program joined three surrounding city park and recreation departments and their corresponding school districts to form the Adaptive Recreation and Learning Exchange (ARLE) cooperative. Today, the Bloomington Adaptive Recreation program, in collaboration with ARLE, offers a wide variety of year-round recreation and education opportunities, as well as supported inclusion in all of the parks and recreation programs offered to the general public. In 1995, almost 200 participants with disabilities took part in Bloomington's more than 20 different recreation programs.

In 1991, the Adaptive Recreation program in Bloomington was recognized by the University of Minnesota's School of Kinesiology and Leisure Studies as 1 of 13 sites that used "best practices" in integrated recreation in Minnesota (Germ, 1993). This case study explores some of the aspects of the Bloomington program that make it a "best practices" site.

Planning for Successful Inclusion and a Broad Range of Inclusive Programs

To understand the policies and practices used by Bloomington, refer to Figure 6.1.

In the first phase of the service delivery model—annual planning—staff members at Bloomington work closely with the ARLE cooperative staff and the ARLE Advisory Board. The ARLE Advisory Board is made up of parents of children with disabilities, adults with disabilities, professionals in the field of disability services, school personnel, and ARLE program staff members. This Advisory Board is divided into subcommittees, which focus their efforts in four areas: marketing, education, programming, and special events.

The programming subcommittee is responsible for reviewing the overall comprehensiveness of programming, collecting and reviewing programming suggestions from participants and parents, and making programming recommendations to the ARLE Board and agencies to create new programs. This subcommittee allows consumers and their parents to have direct input into the offerings of the ARLE cooperative. Another subcommittee, marketing, is responsible for generating new and creative ways to market programs. One of the recommendations made by the marketing committee in 1995 was to try new strategies to reach school personnel and to assist them in communicating community recreation and learning options effectively to parents during special education conferences. In the past, Bloomington

This case study was developed with the help of Crystie Dufon, CTRS, Adaptive Recreation Supervisor, Bloomington Parks and Recreation, Bloomington, Minnesota.

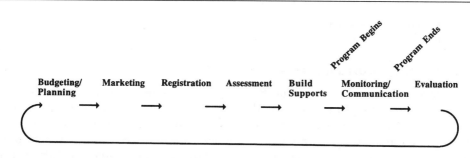

Figure 6.1. Delivery of inclusionary programs.

staff members attempted to send fliers and brochures home with special education students through the school, but no tracking system existed to determine how (or if) the fliers were actually reaching parents. Now the marketing committee and program staff have created a three-ring notebook labeled "ARLE Adaptive Recreation/Learning Exchange: ACTIVITIES for Students." Each child study team (CST) leader in every school building has a copy of the notebook available to him or her. An additional copy is available to all of the other special and general education teachers in the resource rooms. Bloomington staff members make a presentation at an all-district CST leader meeting to introduce the concept of inclusion, distribute notebooks, and explain how they can assist parents to gain access to ARLE and Bloomington programs.

Each notebook contains a variety of information that describes adaptive recreation and explains how to gain access to programs. It also includes the following items:

- Introductory program brochures
- Introductory letters explaining the purpose of ARLE, the purpose of the binder, and the contents of the notebook
- Guidelines for selecting a recreation program
- ARLE guidelines for inclusion
- ARLE brochure
- Breakdown listing of individual city brochures and program offerings

The purpose of the notebook is to consolidate the flow of information to school personnel and parents of school-age children, creating a way to track marketing efforts. To continue to expand services, a variety of other marketing techniques also are utilized.

Marketing and Outreach Efforts to People with Disabilities

Bloomington Parks and Recreation employs several methods for advertising its programs and reaching out to families that include children with disabilities. These marketing and outreach efforts include

- Word of mouth
- Quarterly brochures
- Articles and/or press releases in local newspapers
- General brochures
- ARLE information notebooks to CST lead teachers
- Special education advisory boards

- Group-home presentations
- Leisure Discovery Day
- Rally Days
- Presentations to disability organizations

Leisure Discovery Day is one of Bloomington's unique marketing techniques. It is a 1-day event, open to students with disabilities who attend local high schools and technical colleges. The goals of the event are to 1) give students opportunities to choose and participate in three recreation activities at no cost; 2) give community recreation professionals opportunities to introduce themselves to future constituents; and 3) provide participants with information packets, which include resources and contact names of professionals to use when selecting activities that interest them.

During Rally Days, a representative from Bloomington Parks and Recreation makes presentations at local semi-independent living apartment complexes and group homes. The representative describes the activities and programs that are available and helps individuals choose activities and fill out registration forms. The representative also assists people with registering for TRAIL (Transportation Resource to Aid Independent Living) service.

A group of dedicated parents and individuals with disabilities in the ARLE cooperative rallied together to create TRAIL, a nonprofit transportation service for individuals who live alone and do not have transportation services from a human services provider such as a group home. TRAIL holds annual fund-raisers and contracts with a local transportation service to provide rides. These transportation services are available for a small fee to qualified ARLE program participants. Most of the participants would not be able to attend ARLE programs without TRAIL service because the Bloomington community public transportation service has a limited route and schedule.

An essential "best practice" that Bloomington Adaptive Recreation staff members demonstrate is to keep lines of communication open among everyone involved in the inclusion process. This means that as soon as parents register their children for programs, the communication process begins. For some programs, the registrant simply indicates whether he or she has a disability and whether the person wants a staff member to contact him or her to assist in inclusion efforts. The communication and assessment process then rests in the hands of the adaptive recreation staff member who is responsible for initiating contact with the parent. In other programs, a written assessment form is sent with the registration form, and a staff member follows up with a parent interview once the forms are received.

Bloomington staff members receive extensive training in how to interview parents and participants while in the assessment phase. During the interview, staff members first explain to parents and participants the goals and objectives of the program, the typical staffing levels (additional staff members are added only if necessary), the staff members' background and training, the routine and schedule of the program, and the activities planned for the program. This background information allows parents and participants to participate in making decisions about the kind of assistance that the participant might need, how long assistance will be required, and the type of program and curriculum adaptations that may be needed. With the parents' permission, special education teachers, adaptive physical education teachers, and other program leaders who have worked with the participant are contacted to assist in the assessment and support-building process. Parents and the participants are kept informed of all support-building activities, and, if necessary, a meeting is set up between the assisting aide and the participant and parents before the program begins.

Once the program begins, communication is the key to monitoring the inclusion process successfully. The participant, parents, on-site staff members, and supervisory staff members all must have a clear understanding of day-to-day operations and how things are going. Parents are asked how they would like to be informed of programming. Staff-to-parent communication can take different forms. It might be a brief discussion at child pick-up time, a daily or every-other-day telephone call, or a journal entry. To assist participants who do not read or speak, Bloomington staff members use pictorial agendas for each day of the program. In programs such as day camp, the camper is given a half sheet of paper with pictures of each activity (e.g., hiking, eating, crafts, swimming) to represent the day's agenda. At the end of each day, staff members make certain that the camper takes the agenda home to be shared with his or her family. Parents have praised staff members for this form of communication, indicating how wonderful it is to be able to speak with their child about what occurred in the program that day. At the end of the program, everyone's experiences—staff members', participants', and parents'—are evaluated.

Evaluation

Parents, participants with and without disabilities, and staff members fill out program evaluation forms. Questions such as "What worked well?" and "What could be done to improve the program?" are asked. The answers are collected and compiled for use in quarterly and annual program reports, as well as to be reviewed for the following year's program preparations. This allows for an open process of evaluation, one that seeks to refine and improve each program continually. Open communication among all of the parties involved builds trust and the willingness to call on one another to solve problems or prevent them. It also is one of the best methods of marketing.

Two Success Stories

Michael's Story   Michael has been involved with the Bloomington Parks and Recreation program since 1990 when he was integrated into the preschool-age Discovery program. Today, he is a 7-year-old who has an appealing personality, is shy, and has a developmental disability. Over the years, Bloomington staff members have continuously nurtured a relationship with Michael and his mother and have built a high level of trust between them. Recently, when Michael's mother called to discuss Michael's possible participation in the Killebrew Baseball League, staff members were able to weigh the program's positive and negative aspects for Michael together. The Adaptive Recreation staff met with Michael and his parents before he got involved in the baseball program to help identify his strengths and weaknesses and to prepare for a successful outcome. During these meetings, Michael's mother revealed that she was afraid that he would not fit in, that other children would tease him, and that his skills would not be strong enough. After discussing her fears with the adaptive recreation supervisor, she felt more comfortable. Together, the program staff and Michael's mother decided to try the program with the active support of an inclusion aide (i.e., volunteer advocate). Staff members spoke with his team's coaches and had the volunteer advocate meet with the family in advance of the program. During the games, Michael fit in well as a Killebrew player and team member. His favorite activity was "hitting the ball," his least favorite was "losing" (a typical response from a 9-year-old boy!). By working together, the season ended successfully.

Michael's mother was happy that the staff encouraged him to join the baseball league. She said, "Michael loves sports, and this made him feel part of the team." She also believed that the volunteer advocate provided Michael with the freedom that he required to feel independent when he wanted it and with adequate assistance when he needed it. His mother summed it up as follows: "This was a good first-time experience for him." Bloomington staff members attribute the program's success to Michael's desire to play baseball, his mother's courage to take a risk, and the level of trust and quality of communication built between the professionals and family.

Scott's Story   After Scott participated in summer playground and day camp programs, a photo of three smiling children and the following note were sent to a Bloomington staff member. On the back of the picture, Scott's parents wrote the following:

> I thought you'd enjoy this picture. Scott, Dana, and Jesse met at Camp Kota. Scott sees Jesse often, they eat lunch together at Oak Grove Intermediate School and are taking an after-school class together. Thanks for your part in making this possible.

> —Curt & Julie

One of the primary goals of the day camp program was to introduce the children to each other and to provide a welcoming and supportive environment in which children could become friends. Scott has muscular dystrophy and uses a wheelchair for mobility. At camp, he participated in many challenging activities including hiking, nature study, swimming, and the overnight camp out. From the smiles in the photo and the note from Scott's parents, it is apparent that the program reached its goal of helping Scott and the other participants build positive relationships with one another.

Youth-at-Risk Outreach Program

Another, perhaps unique, program created in Bloomington is a youth-at-risk outreach program that began in the spring of 1991. The program offers personal assistance to fifth- through ninth-grade youths and their parents in identifying and gaining access to summer recreation programs. Every spring, the outreach program staff members work in coordination with Bloomington School District personnel to identify youths who are in trouble at school, at home, or in the community. Program fliers are mailed to each family. The program offers three levels of assistance to youths and their families: 1) information and referral, 2) assessment meeting and program placement, and 3) program support and ongoing monitoring.

At the first level, each youth is identified, and his or her parent receives a flier describing the outreach support program, along with a listing of all of the summer opportunities that are available in the city. Following the mailing, each family is contacted by telephone to determine whether additional information or assistance is needed.

At the second and third levels, an assessment and program placement meeting takes place in which an outreach staff member meets with youths to discuss their interests in programs and presents detailed information on possible programs. If a youth or parent believes that further assistance would be helpful, then necessary services and supports are implemented. These services and supports could include introducing the program staff to the participant before the program begins, recruiting a peer to support the participant in the program as a companion, and providing direct assistance from the outreach staff member during the program. Program service and support also can include providing a one-to-one aide, ongoing monitoring of the child's progress, and a high level of communication between program staff members and parents. At the end of the program, each family is contacted by telephone to conduct a final interview, a part of which involves evaluating the program.

In its first year, 308 youths were identified as being at risk, and 91 (30%) attended recreation programs that summer. In 1993, 457 youths were served in programs. The overall program, evolving over the years, now offers an after-school program and a summer outreach program.

Bloomington has used a customer service approach to enhance its services to all of its citizens. This has been an evolutionary process that has engaged all of the main players (parents, participants, and staff) in making it work. Following are some suggestions for participating parents.

Know what types of programs and program outcomes you want for your child, and be specific about requesting them. If you are looking for learning opportunities or skill-building programming, competitive sports, social-friendship–building programming, or just plain fun, then let the staff know of these desires. If you are searching for relationship building or leisure-skills programming, then ask staff members for particulars about how they provide participants with social and skill-learning opportunities.

Interview staff about the program. Ask them about the following areas:

- Particular program's goals
- Anticipated outcomes for the participants, parents, and staff
- Staffing—including staff-to-participant ratios—and their training, background, and experience with the program and with participants who have disabilities
- Physical setting for the program and how accessible it is
- Specific activities for participants, including each day's agenda
- Agency experience in serving participants with disabilities

Be certain to ask staff whether the program is an established one or one they are trying to launch. Ask your neighbors and friends about which programs have been successful for their children. As you share your goals with staff members, be honest about your "nightmares," if any, about inclusion so that the staff can attempt to avoid their occurring.

Offer staff members the names of other professionals (e.g., certified therapeutic recreation specialist, special education teacher, adapted physical educator) who know your child and who would be willing to share their experiences and make suggestions as to how to make implementation successful.

Get to know the recreation professionals. Build a trusting relationship with them so that both you and staff members feel comfortable calling one another to answer questions, solving problems, and—most important of all—planning for success. Give them honest, immediate feedback throughout the program, and request daily, or at least regular, brief progress reports. To facilitate communication, give your child a communication notebook. Also, speak briefly with staff members when you pick up your child, or make a telephone call to "check in." Offer thoughtful constructive criticism and suggestions with all of the participants in mind, demonstrating concern for every participant, not just your own child.

Finally, fill out the evaluation form, providing honest opinions and thoughtful suggestions. (If the agencies with whom you are working do not evaluate their programs, then call or write a letter to the supervisors who are responsible for the recreation programs to which you want to gain access.)

These agency strategies can be very effective in building customer-centered programs and services of high quality. Moreover, when combined with the other strategies for inclusion that are described throughout this chapter, the entire community can become a much better place in which to live—not only for individuals with disabilities and their families but for everyone.

SUMMARY

Even with federal legislation mandating inclusive opportunities, people with disabilities often do not experience inclusion. Although dramatic progress has been made since the early 1970s when institutionalization was popular and the first laws providing equal opportunity and access for people with disabilities were being passed, the attitudes of recreation professionals must be shaped even further toward inclusion. Recommended professional practices for overcoming this and other barriers were presented in the chapter.

To determine whether and to what extent programs are inclusive, this chapter identified indicators of quality in inclusive programming. To fully carry out the intent of the law, however, recreation professionals must develop inclusionary strategies. Five strategies for promoting the inclusion of people with disabilities in recreation programs were presented, along with the outcomes of a park and recreation department's inclusive programming. The authors hope that readers can benefit from these strategies and successes and develop successful inclusive programs of their own.

Friendship

with Linda A. Heyne

◆ ◆ ◆ ◆ ◆

A discussion on community recreation inclusion without a discussion on friendship would be incomplete. From one perspective, friendship and recreation are irrevocably intertwined: as dependent on each other as are love and family. Friendship enhances the recreation experience; even the best recreation experience can be made better by sharing it with a friend. Recreation activities provide opportunities to meet new people in situations in which differences in abilities are often minimized in favor of enjoyment, play, and camaraderie. Friendships typically grow and develop through shared recreation experiences. In fact, some researchers argue that joint recreation experiences serve as the fundamental vehicle for friendship development (Green & Schleien, 1991). Without the mutual satisfaction of shared recreation experiences, relationships would remain relatively void of fulfillment.

The relationship between friendship and recreation should be an important consideration when exploring how to facilitate community recreation experiences for people with disabilities. People with disabilities often have unique barriers that inhibit developing and maintaining friendship, even when the individuals are participating in the friendship-conducive environment of community recreation. These barriers, however, are not insurmountable limitations that must preclude friendship development. Rather, these barriers should serve to challenge the creative teacher, family member, or recreation programmer to incorporate strategies for promoting friendship within the context of community recreation.

As each individual with a disability is unique, the barriers to friendship development and subsequent strategies for facilitating friendship necessarily vary. Understanding friendship and its symbiotic relationship with recreation is an essential first step toward recognizing the barriers to friendship that individuals with disabilities face. A broadened perspective on friendship will enable one to select the appropriate strategy (or strategies) for facilitating friendship in community recreation and to evaluate the effectiveness of those efforts.

This chapter defines friendship and elaborates on the important link between recreation and friendships for people with and without disabilities. It also discusses strategies for promoting friendships within the context of community recreation and presents a practical tool for measuring and documenting friendship acquisition.

DEFINING FRIENDSHIP

To better understand the connections among recreation, friendship, and people with disabilities, it may be revealing to first examine the nature of friendship in general. As simple as this may sound, it is not an easy task. As noted by MacAndrew and Edgerton (1966), there may be as many definitions of friendship as there are people defining it. Most people agree, however, that friendship entails certain common attributes: 1) friends freely choose each other (Heyne, Schleien, & McAvoy, 1993), 2) friendship is mutual and reciprocal (Green & Schleien, 1991; Rubenstein, 1984), and 3) friendship is strongest when it is consistent and expected to endure (Stainback & Stainback, 1987; Young, 1986). Friendship is an affective tie between two individuals that is mutually preferred and enjoyed. Friendship usually is demonstrated behaviorally as two people engage in meaningful interactions (Howes, 1984) and participate in leisure activities together (Green, Schleien, Mactavish, & Benepe, 1995). This association between friendship and leisure reaffirms the importance of addressing friendship within the context of community recreation programs. As noted previously, many people would agree that friendship and recreation go hand in hand. In fact, the word *friend* frequently is defined as a person with whom one shares free time and leisure experiences (Green & Schleien, 1991; Pogrebin, 1987).

IMPORTANCE OF FRIENDSHIP

No matter what one's age may be, friendship appears to play an important role. Rubenstein (1984) noted that childhood friendships allow children to share affection, support, companionship, and assistance. In fact, children are resources for each other in ways that adults cannot be. Through play, children teach each other social skills (e.g., how to communicate, be tactful, handle conflict) and give each other a sense of self-hood and of social realities. These skills lay the foundation for developing friendships later in life.

During adolescence, the need for intimacy and companionship tends to lead to forming bonds with peers of the same gender who are similar in age, background, and interests (Rubin, 1985). These relationships often are characterized by intense closeness, emotional sharing, and adjusting one's behavior to meet the mutual needs of the relationship. Adolescents spend much of their leisure time with friends, often "hanging out" with a core clique that serves as a haven for developing and expressing growing social personality (Duck, 1991). Membership in a social clique often depends on an appropriate (relatively speaking) range of social and leisure skills.

Adult friendship builds on the entire culmination of skills and sensibilities that have developed during childhood and adolescence. Friendship among adults is characterized by intellectual stimulation and social interconnectedness (Rubin, 1985), reciprocity in affection (Green & Schleien, 1991), and the desire and ability to share responsibility for nurturing and maintaining the relationship (Stainback & Stainback, 1987). Rubin (1985) maintained that adult friendship has an enduring quality that often is lacking in children's friendships and that adult friends often are expected to accept and grow with the changes that occur in the lives of their intimate friends. At every stage in life, friendship anchors us by providing emotional support, reassurance of personal worth, opportunities to reveal ourselves, and a sense of belonging.

What happens when one has no or few friends? In his classic work, *The Broken Heart: The Medical Consequences of Loneliness*, Lynch (1977) presented an extensive review of research on the effects of social-emotional factors on physical health. He concluded that isolation ultimately erodes longevity; if one fails to fulfill the human need for loving relationships, then one's physical health and ability to resist disease will suffer. House, Umberson, and Landis (1988) cautioned that social isolation is an even greater mortality risk than smoking. They asserted that individuals with few or weak social ties are twice as likely to die at a given age as those with strong ties. Not surprisingly, some experts have deemed friendship so essential that it has been called not an expendable luxury but a necessity to life itself (Amado, 1993; Lynch, 1977).

FRIENDSHIP AND PEOPLE WITH DISABILITIES

Researchers generally have noted that even though people with disabilities may have many opportunities to interact with peers, their actual social networks of friends and intimate relationships are substantially smaller than are the social networks of people without disabilities (Abery & Fahnestock, 1994; Vandercook, York, & Forest, 1989). Kennedy, Horner, and Newton (1989) reported that adult residents of a group home had social contact with an average of 63.5 different people (not including housemates and people paid to provide support) during a 30-month period. These data were supported by the findings of Sparrow and Mayne (1990), who concluded that adults with intellectual disabilities were participating in recreation with friends (as opposed to "alone" or "with family") in near-typical patterns of frequency. Contrary to these findings, Amado (1993) noted that people with disabilities actually have far fewer relationships than do peers without disabilities and in far fewer areas of life. These relationships typically are limited to family members, acquaintances with disabilities, and people who are paid to interact with them. Kennedy et al. (1989) concurred, predicting that the residents in their study probably would not sustain authentic friendship relationships over time. The continuous process of people entering and exiting the residents' lives created the false impression that friendships were forming; in actuality, the relationships were only fleeting acquaintanceships.

Green and Schleien (1991) referred to this false impression as a "facade to a life of social isolation" (p. 30). They proposed that adults with mental retardation and their peers without disabilities often develop different perceptions of a shared relationship. For instance, although adults with mental retardation may believe that they are sharing a friendship relationship, their peers without disabilities develop a completely different perception. Adults with mental retardation often perceive relationships with peers without disabilities who are nice to them as friendships. These relationships appear to mirror a pattern similar to the dynamic between children and adults, whereby children declare friendships with adults who do something unexpectedly nice for them (Duck, 1991).

In a follow-up study, Green et al. (1995) found that adults without disabilities who participated in social recreation activities with partners with mental retardation often expressed positive friendship-like feelings about the relationships; however, they described the relationships in terms that distinguished them from friendships with peers without disabilities. Rather than basing these relationships on reciprocated affective ties with mutual sharing of the responsibilities for nurturing and maintaining the relationship, the peers without disabilities perceived their roles to be primarily based on a sense of obligation to provide assistance. A similar feeling of obligation is common among siblings of different ages but rare among friends. Clegg and Standen (1991) explained this difference in perception by reporting that relationships between people with and without disabilities often lack intimacy and empathy—key ingredients that distinguish true friendship from other types of relationships.

According to Abery and Fahnestock (1994), people with disabilities more commonly make friends with other people with disabilities, regardless of age, than with peers without disabilities. These relationships provide the individuals with a significant amount of support but often are dependent on a specific social context, thus precluding the extension of the friendships to a variety of social settings. As a result, these relationships do not generate the social support necessary for developing extended social networks. As noted by Green and Schleien (1991), friendships between peers with disabilities are fulfilling and should be encouraged. True community inclusion, however, does not occur unless people with disabilities who are gaining access to the community also are making friends with peers without disabilities.

Contrary to these findings, evidence exists that meaningful friendships can and do develop between individuals with and without disabilities. Amado, Conklin, and Wells (1990) recounted several stories of mutually rewarding friendships between adults with disabilities and typical community members. In fact, social connections promoted positive changes in the behavior of the adults with disabilities. For example, in instances in which traditional behavioral interventions had previously failed, establishing connections with community members encouraged adults with disabilities to adopt positive behavior patterns such as rising from bed in the morning, finishing breakfast, grooming, trying new activities, and joining Weight Watchers.

In addition, Heyne et al. (1993) documented the positive relationships that can occur between elementary-age students with differing abilities. The relationships of children with and without disabilities were followed during a 2-year period as the children participated in a variety of recreation activities together. Nearly every time that they were interviewed, the children with and without disabilities consistently and mutually identified each other as "friends" or "best friends." In fact, children without disabilities appeared to benefit as much, if not more, from the relationships than did their peers with disabilities. Children without disabilities reported that they learned how to be a friend, developed new play skills, and discovered what it was like to have a disability. They also reported a heightened awareness and acceptance of differences, particularly related to disabilities.

WHAT PREVENTS FRIENDSHIP FROM DEVELOPING

It would be optimistic to say that it is not necessarily the disability that prevents friendship but rather the limitations associated with a disability that prevent friendship. Unfortunately, that may not always be true. Barriers to friendship appear to be a combination of individual social limitations and negative attitudes associated with disabilities.

The limitations that result from having a disability often make social interactions with peers difficult. For example, the absence of appropriate expressive communication skills may make it difficult to share thoughts and intimate feelings with potential friends. Abery and Fahnestock (1994) identified additional social-skill limitations that often are barriers to social inclusion: 1) insufficient social skills for gaining access to social environments (Schloss, Smith, & Kiehl, 1986), 2) insufficient knowledge of available community resources (Schleien & Ray, 1988), 3) inadequate transportation skills (Schleien & Ray, 1988), and 4) an increased anxiety in social situations as one becomes self-aware of the limitations and differences associated with his or her disability.

Friendship and social inclusion can be inhibited by society's negative attitudes toward disabilities and people who have them. Preconceived negative attitudes can make it difficult for peers without disabilities to get to know a person with a disability. Consequently, an individual's abilities often are overlooked. Gibbons (1985) demonstrated that children as young as 4 years could distinguish between people with and without disabilities. Given the opportunity to express a preference, children more often chose a person without a disability over a same-age person with a disability, suggesting that the perception that people without disabilities are more attractive than are people with disabilities may develop at an early age.

STRATEGIES FOR FACILITATING FRIENDSHIP

As more individuals with disabilities gain access to the community, the strategies for promoting social inclusion multiply and improve. Unfortunately, there is no universal, magical strategy that will guarantee meaningful friendships for all people. It is, therefore, wise to become familiar with the many methods for facilitating friendships that exist in order to develop a plan that meets the unique needs of each individual. It is important to note that many strategies for promoting friendship among children often are ineffectual and inappropriate for promoting friendship among adults.

For the purpose of classification and discussion, the strategies for promoting friendship that are presented here are divided into two groups: *extrinsic* and *intrinsic*. Although the value of using an extrinsic or intrinsic strategy in a given situation may be debatable, it is the opinion of the authors that a combination of both strategies, working in harmony, best encourages friendship development. Extrinsic strategies often are highly effective in recreation programs designed to promote friendship among children. This may be a result of children's natural, unprejudiced inclination—once given the opportunity to learn about and interact with peers with disabilities in an inclusive recreation environment—to accept individual differences.

Intrinsic strategies may be most effective when applied to complement extrinsic strategies. By empowering individuals with disabilities with the leisure and social skills necessary for making friends, acceptance into prepared environments is enhanced. In addition, intrinsic strategies are particularly useful for adults because programmers are not as free to manipulate or control the play environment. In either case, approaches to promoting friendship should be individualized using a combination of strategies that will best meet the person's needs.

Extrinsic Strategies

Extrinsic strategies are designed to manipulate or change the environment by creating settings that are conducive to friendship development. Extrinsic strategies are useful in that the individual with a disability is not expected to change, nor is change within the individual deemed necessary for forming relationships. This approach accepts the assumptions that society has the responsibility to accommodate the needs of people with disabilities, every individual has the right to have a friend, and every person has the inherent positive personal qualities necessary to become a friend. Environmental constraints and attitudinal constraints by others, of course, often inhibit the discovery of these traits by potential friends. Extrinsic strategies thus are designed to change the play environment enough to encourage positive social interactions, allowing the members of a group to discover and share common interests and experiences. Extrinsic interventions attempt to create fertile environments in which people can meet, learn about each other, and become friends.

This section presents three extrinsic strategies that are especially effective with children: sociometry (Moreno, 1934), circle of friends (O'Brien, Forest, Snow, & Hasbury, 1989), and cooperative peer companionships (Rynders, Johnson, Johnson, & Schmidt, 1980; Rynders & Schleien, 1988, 1991). An extrinsic process for building social connections between adults with disabilities and community members (Amado, 1993) also is presented.

Sociometry Sociometry (Moreno, 1934) is a procedure for restructuring play groups to identify and integrate isolated group members (Schleien, Fahnestock, Green, & Rynders, 1990). Program planners begin by identifying the qualitative dimensions of a play group, including group cohesiveness, existence of subgroups, interpersonal attractions and rejections between members, and the social rankings of each member by his or her peers. Groups are then restructured to promote positive interactions among members. Sociometry promotes the development of friendship during recreation programs by creating a play environment of subgroups of individuals who have the potential to form positive social relationships.

Sociometry is best suited for a play-group setting in which a large group can be broken down into smaller subgroups. For example, a summer camp counselor can use sociometry to assign cabin members to groups for projects. Sociometric procedures can help ensure that a positive social environment exists in each of the cabin groups. Note the following steps using the summer camp example as a reference:

1. Identify the limits of the large group. The group would be limited to the children in the counselor's cabin.
2. Ask each member of the large group to choose or exclude other members of the group based on a specific criterion. The specific criterion could be a desire to

share a canoe. For instance, the cabin members would be asked, "With whom would you like to share a canoe?" and, "With whom would you not like to share a canoe?" The children could select as many or as few of the other members of their cabin as they pleased. This step is the most crucial. Programmers should take precautions to ensure that the children understand the questions, that the opinions expressed by each child are kept confidential, and that the questions will lead to the information needed by the programmer (validity).

3. Construct a sociogram using the initials of each member of the group (see Figure 7.1). A sociogram is a diagram that indicates the direction of the members' choices. To indicate a positive attraction, a solid line is used to connect the initials of two members. An arrow is added to the end of the line to indicate the direction of the attraction. If two members select each other, the arrowheads are eliminated, and a slash is marked across the line. A broken line with an arrowhead indicates a member's exclusion of another member, with the arrowhead again indicating the direction of the exclusion.

4. Restructure the group into smaller subgroups. The leader should begin by focusing on the excluded and isolated members of the group. In this case, LW, MM, and SS are considered isolated members because they have not been selected by other group members. These individuals should be placed in groups with other members whom they have selected as desirable and away from members who have excluded them. While carefully considering the requests, the programmer can structure positive play groups by placing each member with other individuals with whom there appears to be an attraction (see Figure 7.2). Leaders can avoid placing individuals together who may be in conflict.

5. Repeat the process throughout the life of the group to ensure continued nurturing of positive and supportive social play groups.

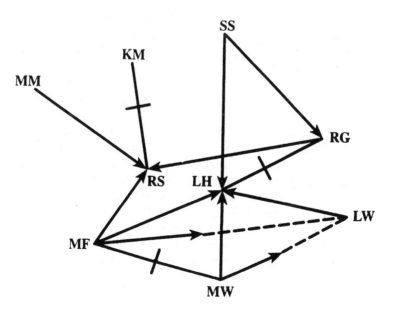

Figure 7.1. Sociogram of the cabin members.

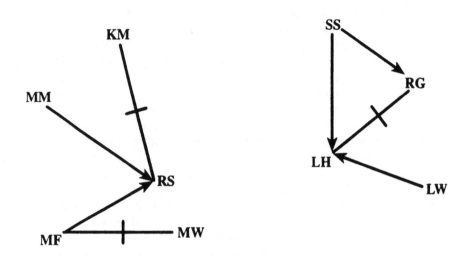

Figure 7.2. Cabin members restructured into two groups.

Circle of Friends Circle of friends is an intervention for promoting the social inclusion of individuals who may have difficulty entering a group (O'Brien et al., 1989; Schleien, Fahnestock, et al., 1990). This technique is used to prepare a small group, or circle of friends, to assist an individual to overcome barriers to belonging to a group. The circle is composed of group members, peers, friends, family, and other concerned individuals who play a significant role in the life of the individual with a disability. This circle of friends uses its knowledge of the target individual and the demands of the play setting to identify potential barriers to social inclusion and to create an environment that is conducive to cultivating friendship. Conduct the following procedures:

1. Assess the target individual's current social relationships. This procedure can best be accomplished by using a modified version of the Social Relationships Assessment Scale (Green, 1992; Schleien, Green, & Heyne 1993), examined later in this chapter. With the assistance of parents and/or guardians (if necessary), the facilitator identifies all of the people with whom the individual currently has a relationship. These relationships are then categorized as friends, acquaintances, or service providers. Because friendship is the goal of the program, friendship relationships are further dichotomized into close friends and casual friends. It is important to remember that family members often can be described as friends, acquaintances, and/or service providers. Leaders may want to make a distinction between family and nonfamily members when constructing the Circle of Friends Diagram (see next step).

2. Construct a Circle of Friends Diagram (see Figure 7.3). In this diagram, each circle represents a different type of relationship. All of the close friends can be placed on the inner circle, represented by either a square (for family) or a dot (for nonfamily). The second circle includes all remaining friends (i.e., casual friends). The third circle encompasses all acquaintances, and the final circle is used to represent all remaining individuals, both professional and volunteer, who provide a service to the individual.

3. Select a small circle of friends (approximately 5–10 individuals) from the diagram to serve as a support group. This group should include friends, family, ac-

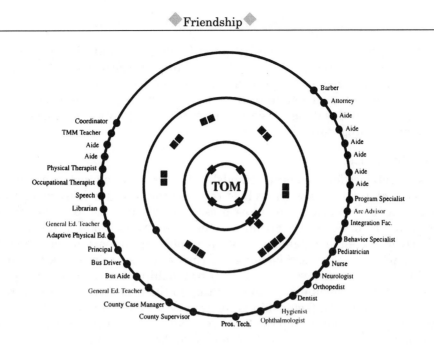

Figure 7.3. Tom's circle of friends. (● = family; ■ = nonfamily)

quaintances, and service providers. All group members should be familiar with the target individual and the setting in which integration will occur. Friends or "peer acquaintances" who are accepted members of the targeted group are especially valuable members of the circle of friends.

4. The leader guides the circle of friends through a brainstorming session to identify all of the potential barriers to social inclusion. The target individual's skills, limitations, and fears also are identified, as are the extrinsic barriers (e.g., group attitudes, competitive nature of group activities) that may inhibit social inclusion.

5. Conduct a follow-up brainstorming session to focus on solutions to overcoming the barriers to social inclusion. In this session, each member of the group commits his or her support to promoting the social inclusion of the target individual by declaring the role he or she will assume. For example, parents may commit to driving the individual to after-school activities. Teachers and recreation leaders may commit to placing a priority on friendship development as a goal during recreation activities. Finally, and most important, friends and peers may commit to overlooking the disability and differences, accepting the person as an equal member of the group, and introducing their new friend to other members of the group.

Cooperative Peer Companionships Cooperative peer companionships is a planning strategy for social inclusion with an emphasis on actively promoting person-to-person interactions. Within a holistic approach to friendship facilitation, cooperative peer companionship programs supplement and enhance the effectiveness of sociometry and circle of friends. Whereas sociometry is designed to ensure that isolated individuals are placed in supportive group environments, cooperative peer companionship programs can promote opportunities for positive interactions among peers within newly formed groups. With careful planning on the part of the group leader, the interdependence required for group goal attainment becomes an avenue for accentuating the potential contribution of each member regardless of ability level. As positive interaction becomes the focal point for group success, misconceptions about a person's disability are minimized, and positive social relationships are developed. See Chapter 6 for a detailed discussion of peer companionship programs.

Intrinsic Strategies

Intrinsic strategies for promoting friendship are designed to promote change *within* the individual. Intrinsic strategies hold that reciprocity is a necessary ingredient of friendship and that each person must possess certain friendship skills and characteristics that he or she can contribute to the relationship. These skills and characteristics (e.g., listening, extending invitations, offering support, providing feedback) play an important role in establishing, nurturing, and sustaining relationships and typically lay the groundwork for lasting friendships. Unless both members of a dyad share the responsibility of contributing to the friendship equally, a relationship less intimate than friendship is likely to occur (Green et al., 1995). Intrinsic strategies are designed to help the individual with a disability develop the personal characteristics and skills that may be offered to the relationship.

Although extrinsic strategies have proved successful in promoting friendship in recreation settings, it is the environment, not the individual, that becomes more conducive to friendship development. Should the environment change for any reason (e.g., the individual changes residence, a peer companion moves away), the individual may continue to lack the skills necessary to sustain a relationship, interact with peers, and make a new friend. For this reason, extrinsic strategies are best combined with intrinsic strategies to ensure that an individual with a disability is prepared to make friends throughout his or her lifetime. Intrinsic strategies are designed to teach age-appropriate, socially valid recreation and social skills to individuals with disabilities. The individual with a disability is taught skills that make him or her more attractive to potential friends and better prepared to take an active role in establishing and maintaining friendships and other social relationships.

Friendship is a complicated dynamic requiring a myriad of social and leisure skills (Furman, 1984). Developing friendship skills could take a lifetime of effort. Social skills often are especially difficult to master for individuals with significant cognitive disabilities. Social competence often is directly tied to the subtle dynamics of a particular social situation, requiring the individual to use abstract thinking skills to interpret social cues and respond appropriately. As a result, social-skill acquisition often takes time, long-term interdisciplinary effort, and sufficient opportunities for practice. This section offers two intrinsic strategies for promoting the friendship and social skills of people with disabilities: friendly action circle and developing leisure interests and skills.

Friendly Action Circle An intrinsic strategy for developing the friendship skills of young children, kindergarten to grade 4, is a game called the "Friendly Action Circle" (Vandercook et al., 1994). This activity is designed to give children with and without disabilities opportunities to practice typical friendship behaviors in a group of peers. As one person acts out a friendly action, the other group members watch and, similar to a game of charades, try to guess the behaviors that are being demonstrated.

Friendly actions that are taught to younger children, kindergarten to grade 2, include thanking someone; sharing; offering help; and indicating "no" by talking, signing, or shaking one's head. Older children, grades 2–4, are taught these same actions (except for indicating "no"), along with the more complicated friendship behaviors of giving a compliment, suggesting an activity, and apologizing to someone. This activity could be used by a teacher in a classroom, a camp counselor, a parent volunteer leading a Girl Scout or Boy Scout troop, a Sunday school teacher, or a group leader of any children's social club.

The game uses a series of "friendly action cards" to teach the children the friendship behaviors. The friendly action cards for the younger age group show illustrations of children acting out the different behaviors. For example, the "sharing" action card shows two children putting together a puzzle, with the caption "sharing." The cards for the older children describe the action with words only. For example, the sharing action card is titled, "Friendly Action: Share Something." The card reads, "Your job is to share something with someone in the group." Examples of sharing are provided, such as, "Jason, do you want to use my markers for your project?" and "Tashina, do you want to use one of my new stickers?" Samples of friendly action cards are provided in the appendix of the curriculum that Vandercook et al. (1994) have developed, or a group leader could design his or her own cards by using illustrations from magazines and examples that more personally reflect the qualities and interests of the children in the group.

The group leader can set the stage for the game by reading aloud to the children a book about making friends. The book that Vandercook and her colleagues recommend is *Arnie and the New Kid* (Carlson, 1990). After reading the book, the leader can lead the children in a discussion about such topics as teasing, how people feel when they are teased, how people become friends, and what friends do for each other.

Procedures for Children in Kindergarten to Grade 2

1. The group leader introduces each of the friendly action cards, one at a time, to the group of children. The word or words describing the action (e.g., "sharing") should be printed on a chalkboard or poster paper, with the picture or card illustrating the action taped beside it. The group leader asks the children to suggest ideas about what is happening in the picture and what the action means. The group leader should clarify the meaning of the action by providing a simple definition of the word. She or he also should help the children associate the illustration with the printed and spoken words.
2. The group leader tells the children that they will be acting out the friendly actions that are printed on the cards while other group members try to guess what the action is. If the group is large, then the leader tells the children that they will first play the game in the large group, then move into smaller groups.
3. The leader demonstrates the friendly actions for the group, one at a time, asking for volunteers to act them out. At first, the children may need suggestions for what action to demonstrate to the group. Later, the children should be encouraged to decide for themselves which action to show. The children who are observing then guess what the action is by verbally identifying the behavior, pointing to the picture on the friendly action card, or moving a paper clip (or similar object) to the particular item.
4. When the children in the large group understand the rules of the game, they can move into smaller groups. The children take turns acting out the friendly actions while the children who are not acting try to guess the behaviors. The group leader or older children who are assisting the groups should encourage

the children to identify the clues that were given that divulged the friendly action.

Procedures for Children Grades 2–4

1. The children are divided into "friendship circles" of six children each. The object of the game is for each friendship circle to guess all six of the friendly actions (see previous procedures) as they are acted out, one by one, by the group members.
2. Each child selects a friendly action card that he or she would like to act out for the group. Each child is then given a "guessing card" that lists the six friendly actions and has blank spaces for the participants to write the names of the actors and the actions that they think are being demonstrated. (Sample guessing cards are included in the appendix of the curriculum.)
3. One at a time, the children act out their friendly actions.
4. As each action is portrayed, group members record on their guessing cards their "best guesses" of what they think the person is doing. Let children know that they may change their guesses later, so they do not need to worry about getting the "right" answer (and perhaps miss the point of the game—to learn about and understand friendship behaviors).
5. After each child has acted out his or her friendly action, the children immediately share their answers and discuss any differences of opinion they might have. The children continue to take turns acting out their friendly actions until all of the children have participated.

Developing Leisure Interests and Skills   How can a well-designed recreation program contribute to developing friendship skills? Although recreation appears to provide an ideal environment for friendship development, it may be erroneous to place the responsibility for developing friendship skills solely on recreation professionals (and volunteers). Rather, recreation professionals can make their own distinct contribution to an individualized program. For example, Stainback and Stainback (1987) identified six specific skills necessary for making and keeping friends. Of these, developing common interests may be the most appropriate target for intervention by the recreation professional. As members of interdisciplinary teams, recreation professionals can contribute to the development of friendship skills by assisting the individual in developing age-appropriate and socially valid leisure skills that can serve as a basis for future friendships. Recreation professionals may design their intrinsic strategies by adhering to the following procedures:

1. Facilitate the development of an appropriate leisure lifestyle. Although teaching recreation activity skills may appear to be the most efficient way to develop interests that can be shared with friends, professionals should teach these skills within the context of a holistic leisure lifestyle. A holistic approach to leisure lifestyle development focuses on empowering the individual to make personal decisions concerning leisure participation and on developing a wide range of skills (e.g., choice making, self-help, communication, transportation) to independently pursue a satisfying leisure lifestyle (Datillo & Murphy, 1991).
2. Identify recreation activity skills that are attractive and personally satisfying to each individual. In some cases, developing recreation activity skills will take months or even years. Activities that the individual finds appealing will help

ensure continued participation long after instruction has ceased. Refer to Schleien, Meyer, Heyne, and Brandt (1995) for a detailed description of preference assessments and guidelines for selecting appropriate activities.

3. Select leisure activities for instruction that are easily accessible and popular among peers. The Recreation Inventory for Inclusive Participation (see Chapter 5) will assist the leader in selecting appropriate activities.

4. Consider the long-range and permanent impact of skill acquisition. Acquiring skills in activities that do not reflect the principle of social values and that are not age appropriate may actually delay the process of making friends.

Building Community Connections for Adults

Amado (1993) has offered a series of strategies for encouraging friendships between adults with disabilities and community members. The strategies she suggested combine both extrinsic and intrinsic approaches by shaping external strategies around the unique capacities, interests, and talents of adults with disabilities. Calling attention to a person's positive attributes in the planning stages of friendship development allows those inherent qualities to grow and flourish throughout the relationship.

When assisting adults with disabilities in developing friendships with members of the community, Amado emphasized three basic principles. First, she advised to "act as if almost anything can happen" (p. 311). Most successful matches have begun with a strong, confident belief in the benefits of these relationships and a trust in both the person with a disability and the community member. Second, "start small—one-to-one" (p. 311). A staff person may be tempted to seek friends for everyone with whom he or she works. Friendship building, however, is hard work that can entail a considerable amount of time, effort, ingenuity, and perseverance. It also is easier for community members to relate to only one person at a time, rather than several people at once. Third, planning and implementing strategies to make friends must be grounded in a "capacity-based view of the person" (p. 312). Traditional methods of planning interventions have tended to focus on what individuals lack. Friendship building requires appreciating the positive attributes and gifts of individuals and recognizing the contributions they can offer others.

The following steps for building friendship are presented, not as a linear step-by-step process but as guideposts to follow. Because every person is unique, no one method will work for all people. Each person's individual situation must be carefully considered when planning and implementing strategies to promote social connections.

Identify the person's interests, gifts, and contributions. Because friendships often are formed around shared interests, it is important to learn about the things that give meaning to the person's life. For some people, interests may be obvious. They may be able to tell you or show you their preferences for games, sports, or hobbies or for kinds of food, clothing, movies, or music. For other individuals, spending time with the person may be required in order to detect the small ways in which his or her interests are expressed. Or, one may need to talk with others, such as family members or direct care staff, who know the person well on a day-to-day basis.

A person's gifts are those attributes that attract other people to the person. A gift may be a cheerful attitude, a good sense of humor, an ability to accept others as they are, or being a hard worker. Identifying gifts highlights what the individual has to offer other people and lays the groundwork for identifying places in which gifts can be expressed and appreciated by community members.

Explore and identify possible connections with people and places in the community. Amado (1993) suggested several ways that one may explore possible connections. First, generate a list of all of the places in which the person expresses a particular interest or gift, as well as a list of all of the places in which the interest or gift could potentially be expressed. After generating the list, ask: Who do I know in these places? Who can I ask to be involved?

Second, identify opportunities for the person to form consistent community relationships. Community inclusion often has focused on creating opportunities for people to participate in activities, rather than opportunities to meet people and explore relationships. Two important considerations are 1) Where will the person be able to see the same people over time? and 2) Are there regular opportunities for exchange? Situations that could provide opportunities for ongoing interaction are belonging to a club, participating on a team, or volunteering at a neighborhood site.

Third, look for settings that would potentially welcome the person. Explore local businesses, community building projects, neighborhood groups and clubs, and public agencies and institutions (e.g., parks, libraries, universities, hospitals, churches, synagogues, associations), and assess their receptivity to people with disabilities. Consider how the person might become involved in these places. A good rule to follow when matching people with settings is "one person, one environment."

Fourth, identify people who might be interested in becoming friends with the person with a disability. Consider one's own social networks, and assess one's own willingness to develop a new relationship. Consider people who have never before interacted with people with disabilities. Ask people directly whether they would like to be the person's friend, with the understanding that being a friend is different from being a volunteer. That is, volunteers usually are involved in time-limited, formalized assignments in which they are doing something *for* someone else. Friends, however, genuinely like each other and mutually benefit from and contribute to the relationship.

Introduce the person to new people in the community setting. A personal one-to-one approach is the most effective way to make introductions. The manner in which the person with a disability is introduced and what is said about him or her can naturally affect how community members view the individual. The person making the introduction, therefore, will need to think carefully about what information and how much information to provide. When telling community members about the individual, emphasize the person's interests, gifts, and qualities that others appreciate. Generally, both the participant with a disability and the community member should be given enough information so that they both feel comfortable.

If the person is being introduced into a group of people, such as a social club or an association, then identify a group member who can serve as a "host" for the individual with a disability. This host can act as a sponsor, helping the individual gain entry into the group by introducing him or her to other group members.

Work to continue to support the relationship. Relationships will vary in the amount of support and the kind of support they will require. Sometimes a relationship requires considerable encouragement to grow; other times, the relationship works best if it is allowed to happen on its own. Occasionally, no matter how much assistance is given, the relationship never develops into a friendship.

One must be sensitive to the people and the situation involved to understand how much support to offer and when to offer it. Three general principles can help guide this process of supporting relationships. First, the person facilitating the friendship must genuinely care about the individual with a disability and be willing to engage in a personal friendship with him or her. Second, one must trust in the openness and willingness of community members to extend themselves to people with disabilities. Third, one must believe in the value of building community for people with disabilities, as well as for society as a whole.

ASSESSING AND EVALUATING FRIENDSHIP

Finding an accepted method of measuring friendship may be as difficult as finding a universally accepted definition (Green, 1992). House et al. (1988) claimed that, far too often, friendship or social support is regarded as an independent variable in research, with research aimed at determining how friendship has an impact on personal lifestyles and quality-of-life issues. They called for research that views friendship as a dependent variable, with the hope that a growing understanding of the many variables that affect the development of friendship will result. They argued that, in spite of attempts to study social support and friendship, most research is being conducted without a theoretical or empirical definition of the variable.

For parents and practitioners, a simple yet valid method for measuring friendship would be invaluable. A facilitator of friendship could use a friendship assessment to identify the existence or absence of friendships in the life of individual participants. Furthermore, relationship patterns could be explored to determine the extent of social connections. Finally, pre- and post-assessments would allow parents and practitioners to evaluate the effectiveness of strategies, as well as to justify expending time and effort to facilitate friendship.

A simple method for measuring friendship, however, does not appear to exist. Multiple and relative definitions make friendship an elusive variable to define and measure. Even though the number of friends a person has could be counted, how many friends one must have to be considered "friend healthy" is not measurable. Duck (1991) suggested that the number of friends that make up our social network changes with age. Can a "normal" number of friendships be established? Probably not, yet the need to measure friendship still exists.

A variety of methods have been used in recreation to attempt to measure social inclusion and friendship. However, the variables that each method measures should be examined carefully. Green (1992) noted that social interaction and popularity often are used interchangeably with friendship for the purpose of assessment and evaluation. Although closely linked, these concepts differ from friendship. Social interaction presumably implies friendship (Howes, 1984); however, social interactions are only one vital component of friendship (Furman, 1984). Friendship may depend on social interaction for both initial development and eventual maintenance of friendship; but social interaction only reflects a shared experience; the motivation underlying the shared experience is undetermined. Unless an intrinsic, mutual desire to interact and a shared responsibility for maintaining the bonds of affection exist, social interactions are not equivalent to friendships (Green, 1992). Popularity refers to the state of being widely liked or appreciated (*American Her-*

itage Dictionary, 1994). Popularity is a status measure indicating social acceptance, differing from friendship in that reciprocity is not a necessary, nor expected, component (Rubenstein, 1984). Popularity often is achieved by adhering to specific social expectations and often reflects one's attractiveness by a higher-than-normal quantity of people (Kutner, 1990). Regarding the quality of an individual's life, however, the friendship of one person may be more significant than the adulation of many.

Although they do not necessarily measure friendship, two assessment procedures discussed in Chapter 8 can be used to measure changes in related variables that influence friendship. First, sociometric assessment, when repeated periodically over the course of a recreation program, can measure changes in attraction and acceptance by other group members. Sociometric assessment is more a measure of popularity than of friendship. Thus, the validity of sociometric assessment as a measure of friendship is questionable. For example, at the beginning of a canoe trip, the children were asked to identify members of the group with whom they would like to share a canoe. This information would allow the leader to identify isolated and less popular children. If this question were again asked at the conclusion of the canoe expedition, then the leaders would be able to note changes in an individual's popularity over the course of the trip. As stated previously, although popularity may be an indicator of potential friendship, it is not interchangeable with friendship. The most popular children may be the ones who receive a constant supply of homemade cookies in the mail, thus making them desirable canoe partners. Measures of friendship need to progress beyond measures of popularity or social isolation.

Second, measures of social interaction may provide additional information related to an individual's social inclusion. If, for example, Joe begins to interact more frequently with partners during play activities, then leaders can conclude that he is becoming more socially included with his peers. The validity of claims that friendship is developing, however, is once again in question. Increased interaction could be a result of a number of factors, and these factors may or may not be related to friendship development. Again, the frequency and quality of interactions are important components of friendship but are not necessarily equivalent to friendship. Measures of friendship should take into account the content of the relationships as well as the existence and frequency of interactions.

Social Relationships Assessment Procedure

The Social Relationships Assessment Procedure (Green, 1992; Schleien, Green, et al., 1993) can be used to measure the existence of current and potential friendships. This procedure is used to assess an individual's network of social relationships, utilizing the content of the relationship as a defining variable. The result of the assessment is a social diagram of existing relationships that can identify potential friends and can be used to assess changes in relationship patterns over time. The Social Relationships Assessment Procedure has five steps:

1. Identify all of the people with whom the target individual has interacted in the past year. Label these individuals as "relationships." Any contact that is recognized by both members of the dyad is considered an interaction. Recreation leaders, parents, teachers, and other care providers may assist in identifying these relationships.

2. Categorize relationships by name or other identifying feature (e.g., camp counselor, softball teammate) according to the "primary relationship" that they have with the individual. Note that relatives and family members often play dual roles in the lives of individuals with disabilities. Be sure also to categorize according to their primary relationships. The three mutually exclusive relationship categories used for assessment are the following:

   A. **Friends**—people with whom the individual has a significant, mutual, and reciprocal emotional relationship and with whom he or she has a reciprocated desire to spend time and share experiences

   B. **Acquaintances**—people with whom the individual has had recent (in the past year), relatively brief or impersonal interactions, either by chance meetings or on a planned basis. Co-workers, classmates, and other people with whom the individual interacts yet does not seek out for joint recreation participation are considered acquaintances.

   C. **Service providers**—people for whom the relationship with the individual is primarily based on an obligation to provide any of a variety of services (e.g., teacher, dentist, therapeutic recreation specialist) or people who bear most of the responsibility for continuing the relationship

3. **Friends** are further categorized according to the quality of the relationship and the reciprocated desire to spend time together:

   A. **Significant others**—friends with whom the individual shares a significant and reciprocated emotional or sexual bond and with whom the individual prefers, above all others, to share time and experiences

   B. **Best friends**—friends with whom the individual shares a significant and reciprocated emotional bond and with whom the individual prefers, above all others, to share time and experiences

   C. **Friends**—people with whom the individual shares a significant and reciprocated emotional bond and with whom the individual has a reciprocated desire to spend time and share experiences

4. **Acquaintances** are further defined according to the frequency of contact, and the familiarity of the target individual with his or her dyadic partner:

   A. **Frequent acquaintances**—acquaintances with whom the individual has had recent, frequent contacts and social interactions and about whom the individual knows personal information (e.g., name, telephone number, address)

   B. **Acquaintances**—people with whom the individual has had recent interaction, either by chance or coincidental planned meetings, and about whom the individual knows a little personal information

   C. **Distant acquaintances**—people with whom the individual has infrequent interaction or knows very little, if any, information about or people whom the individual does not particularly enjoy

5. **Service providers** are further defined according to the purpose of the relationship and the percentage of responsibility that they assume for maintaining the relationship:

   A. **Big brothers/big sisters**—service providers with whom the individual considers to be friends but who assume a higher percentage of the responsibility for maintaining the relationship or who assume some responsibility for caring for or providing services

B. **Service providers**—people with whom the relationship is based on one member's obligation to provide any of a variety of services to the other member or people with whom the responsibility for maintaining the relationship is not equally shared

C. **Care providers**—service providers whose primary responsibility in the relationship is to provide custodial services necessary for daily functioning

An example of a social map that uses the Social Relationships Assessment Procedure is presented in Table 7.1. As often occurs for individuals with significant disabilities, few, if any, friends appear on the social map. This deficit is partially explained by Green and Schleien (1991), who argued that individuals with and without disabilities often have different perceptions of friendship and that friendship as it is perceived by individuals with disabilities is not always friendship as it is defined by peers without disabilities. Green et al. (1995) also asserted that the often abundant big brother/big sister relationships are quality relationships that individuals with disabilities consider to be as personally satisfying as friendship relationships. Although this assertion is valid, it reflects the importance of conducting an assessment to accurately measure existing relationships without assessing the value of each relationship.

This particular social map indicates that although Joe does not have any close friends, he is socially connected to potential friends and others who care about him. The big brother/big sister relationships may be important and satisfying to him, but the need exists for Joe to develop significant and reciprocal emotional bonds (or friendships) with peers. The information from this map may assist program leaders in identifying candidates for the circle of friends (e.g., big brothers and sisters) and identifying individuals who may be considered potential friends (e.g., frequent acquaintances). From this point, leaders can choose a combination of intrinsic and ex-

Table 7.1.   Social map using the Social Relationships Assessment Procedure

Friends	Acquaintances	Service providers
Significant others -0-	Frequent acquaintances • 5 classmates who sit near him at school • 2 peers who live in the neighborhood • 3 peers who talk to him at recess	Big brothers/sisters • Grandmother • Volunteer companion from high school
Best friends -0-	Acquaintances • 20 classmates • 10 bus riders	Service providers • Teacher • Doctor, dentist, etc. • Day camp director
Friends -0-	Distant acquaintances • Father • Most relatives • Former classmates	Care providers • Mother

trinsic strategies to facilitate friendship development, and, at a later time, again conduct the Social Relationships Assessment Procedure to document the changes in Joe's social relationships.

Family Focus Groups

Family focus groups, colloquially known as family friendship groups, are another means of assessing and evaluating friendships for children with disabilities. They also may be used as a means for developing intrinsic or extrinsic strategies for promoting friendship development, depending on the nature of the questions that are asked and the problem solving that occurs during a focus-group session.

Family focus groups are composed of children with disabilities and their family members, preferred peers without disabilities and their family members, and anyone else who is in a position to support the children's relationships. A supportive group member may be a certified therapeutic recreation specialist, classroom teacher, teacher's aide, school social worker, community recreation professional, or inclusion specialist.

Heyne et al. (1993) have written about the use of family focus groups in their 2-year study of the relationships of elementary-age students with and without disabilities. Throughout the study, families were brought together four to six times each year to discuss three main questions: 1) What is the nature of the children's relationships and friendships? 2) What barriers prevent friendships from developing? and 3) How can the relationships and friendships be encouraged and maintained over time? These same questions may be relevant for other family groups that want to explore and support their children's relationships; however, family focus groups are encouraged to develop their own set of questions related to their children's specific needs and concerns.

The format for focus groups presented here is based on an educational model developed by Krueger (1988). A focus group may be defined as a guided group discussion that brings together people to freely share their perspectives on a given topic without judgment or censorship. A step-by-step process for planning, conducting, and evaluating family focus groups is offered next. Keep in mind, however, that these guidelines are intended to be flexible, and procedures should be tailored to suit individual group needs.

Planning the Family Focus Group   The value and utility of a family focus group depend largely on the careful planning that precedes the meeting. Thoughtful consideration should be given to each of the following tasks, even though they need not necessarily be performed in sequence, to prevent any unexpected events from disrupting the discussion:

1. Clearly define and communicate the purpose of the meeting. Clarifying the purpose of the meeting is the most important planning task; it also may be the most difficult. A clear purpose will help generate enthusiasm, guide the discussion, and assist in evaluating outcomes.
2. Determine the family–focus-group members. Identify peers without disabilities with whom the child with a disability shares a mutual attraction. Peers may be classmates, playmates from the neighborhood, or fellow participants in a community recreation program. Also identify adults in a child's life who can play an active role in assessing, observing, supporting, and monitoring the relationships.

3. Develop a written plan of action. Summarize the problem, outline the purpose, describe how participants will be recruited, indicate who will be responsible for which tasks, and indicate where and when the meeting(s) will take place.
4. Recruit the focus-group members. Friendship-group participants most likely will be hand-picked, so it will be important to schedule meetings at times and places that are convenient for the majority of the group members. Advance notice, follow-up telephone calls, personalized confirmation letters, and central meeting places all can encourage a high participant turnout.
5. Formulate the discussion questions. Consider the most pressing issues and questions (e.g., lack of opportunities to get together, differences in social skills, transportation) related to the children's relationships. Arrange the questions in a logical sequence. Try to develop questions that begin with "How" or "What" and that tend to generate thoughtful, in-depth responses. Avoid questions that begin with "Why" and that usually put respondents on the defense. Also avoid questions that can be answered solely with a "yes" or "no."
6. Secure a meeting site that is accessible, is easy to locate, and has free parking. A site that is familiar to all of the participants, such as a school or recreation center, is a good choice for a meeting place. Other potential sites are libraries, churches, synagogues, hotels, and private homes.
7. Provide for relaxed, comfortable seating, preferably in a circle, in which participants can easily see each other.
8. Add a touch of hospitality, and create a social environment by planning for light refreshments.

Leading the Family Focus Group The moderator of the family focus group plays a key role in creating a nonthreatening, supportive environment in which people feel comfortable speaking. A moderator may be a parent, a certified therapeutic recreation specialist, a classroom teacher, or anyone else interested in friendship development for the children with and without disabilities. Following are some tips for moderators:

1. Create a warm, friendly atmosphere.
2. Be knowledgeable about the issues related to the children's relationships.
3. Memorize the discussion questions so that you can look directly at the participants, not at your notes.
4. Be genuinely interested, and listen with empathy.
5. Allow group members ample time to respond. (It is sometimes necessary to wait up to 10 seconds after asking a question.)
6. Emphasize that every opinion is important. Be aware of quiet and domineering group members. Sit shy people across from you where your eye contact can encourage them to speak. Invite domineering group members to sit on the sides, where eye contact can be more easily diverted from them.
7. Avoid expressing personal opinions or evaluating participants' comments. Try to be neutral, or "beige," in your reactions.
8. Maintain control of the group dynamics in an unobtrusive manner. Be flexible, but keep the discussion on track. Gauge when to explore an issue more fully and when to move ahead to the next question.
9. Keep a sense of humor and an air of congeniality.
10. To conclude the discussion, ask a final wrap-up question, request additional comments, and/or provide a brief summary of the main points expressed dur-

ing the meeting. Be sure to thank group members as they leave, and be available to answer any questions that they might have.

Evaluating the Family Focus Group Many issues, opinions, concerns, and ideas may come to light during an animated family–focus-group discussion. It may seem difficult, if not impossible, to assimilate all of the comments that are expressed and draw accurate conclusions. To help digest the information and evaluate the outcomes, it may be helpful to ask the following questions:

1. What was the general mood or tone of the meeting?
2. What were the characteristics of the group members?
3. What did the participants' body language, nonverbal communication, or other behaviors suggest?
4. What themes, comments, or opinions recurred during the meeting?
5. What divergent opinions were expressed?
6. What shifts in mood, philosophy, tone, discussion, or opinions occurred during the course of the meeting?
7. What new questions or information emerged related to the relationships and friendships of the children?
8. What solutions to problems or strategies for developing friendships were generated?
9. How well did the discussion meet the original purpose of the meeting?
10. As a result of the meeting, what action is now required? Who will be responsible for following up on the action?

SUMMARY

Friendship can be considered an essential component of quality of life. Friendship fulfills the need for intimacy, allows one to share affection and support, and contributes to the maintenance of positive physical and mental health. Yet for many people with disabilities, friendship often is elusive.

Many barriers can inhibit the development of friendship for people with disabilities. Individuals may have restricted opportunities to interact with same-age peers or may be denied the opportunity to develop friendship skills. In addition, attitudes of people both with and without disabilities may hinder friendship development. Peers without disabilities often are willing to spend time with partners with disabilities, but they all too often perceive their role in the relationship to be as a care provider. Their partners with disabilities develop the misperception that friendly assistance from well-intentioned people is indicative of friendship.

This chapter presented a variety of strategies for facilitating friendship for people with disabilities. Sociometry, circle of friends, cooperative peer companionships, and building community connections for adults were discussed as examples of extrinsic strategies. These strategies facilitate friendship by manipulating the environment to make it more conducive to friendship development. Friendly action circle and strategies for developing leisure interests and skills were presented as intrinsic strategies, or strategies designed to promote change within the individual.

This chapter concluded with procedures for assessing and evaluating the development of friendship. The Social Relationships Assessment Procedure measures the existence of current and potential friendships. It is designed to monitor changes in an individual's social relationships and to identify people currently in an individual's social network who may be considered potential friends. Family focus groups subjectively measure the extent and quality of one's social network. It is a versatile procedure that also can be used for developing intrinisic or extrinsic strategies for promoting friendship.

Evaluating Community Recreation Programs

8

◆ ◆ ◆ ◆ ◆

As is clearly described and illustrated in the preceding chapters, individuals with disabilities can be physically and socially included in recreation activities and settings. Physical inclusion has been shown to have positive effects on the participants if the needs of the individual with a disability are met (Rynders et al., 1993; Stainback, Stainback, & Jackson, 1992). Evaluating physical inclusion of community recreation programs, however, typically has been conducted by simply counting the number of people who participated and the individuals' participation rates. This method of evaluation provides *quantitative* information only and cannot determine whether a person's needs are being met. A qualitative analysis is necessary.

PARTICIPANT ASSESSMENT AND PROGRAM EVALUATION: QUANTITATIVE AND QUALITATIVE ANALYSES

Quantitative information allows a practitioner to determine whether the number of people participating in a program is increasing or decreasing; such information also reveals frequency of participation. This method of evaluation alone, however, may not provide the needed information concerning the *quality* of the participants' recreation and social experiences.

Qualitative information could be gained by evaluating the social aspects of the inclusive community recreation program. The success of social inclusion of participants may be determined by observing certain behaviors and outcomes between participants with and without disabilities. These behaviors may include initiating and receiving social interactions, eye contact between peers, physical proximity between participants, appropriate physical contact, sharing or offering equipment or materials, appropriately participating in a cooperative activity, making friends, and changing attitudes toward other participants. These potential participant outcomes must be evaluated to better understand the impact and effectiveness of the recreation program on the participants.

Why must the recreation professional go beyond quantitative evaluation strategies and attempt to evaluate the qualitative aspects of the program? The most salient benefits may be that qualitative evaluation could

1. Provide valuable information to the program instructor for subsequent program decisions and revisions
2. Enhance accountability to administrators, family members, and participants
3. Help the recreation staff gain support for the program from administrators, professional colleagues, parents, and consumers
4. Enable the program leader, participants, and family members to better understand how the program is improving the participants' quality of life
5. Provide information that could be used to solicit funding for future program endeavors
6. Assist in recruiting other participants and volunteers
7. Increase community awareness of the values of the recreation program by providing concise information concerning the impact that the program is having on participants
8. Assist in determining whether program goals and participant learning objectives are being met

Consumers and their care providers, program staff, and agency administrators typically ask several questions that lend themselves to a comprehensive program evaluation when an agency attempts to socially include participants with and without disabilities in its recreation programs:

1. Are the participants acquiring the recreation and social skills that are targeted for instruction?
2. Are participants with disabilities interacting appropriately, sharing conversation, and making friends with their peers who do not have disabilities, and vice versa?
3. Can other individuals be identified as potential participants to increase participation and socialization within the group?
4. Are attitudes of the participants without disabilities changing toward their peers with disabilities, and vice versa?
5. Are participants' levels of self-concept increasing as a result of their participation in the program?
6. Are the participants' quality of life improving as a result of their participation in the program?

Qualitative program evaluation and the strategies and tools used for this purpose are presented in this chapter and may assist community recreation professionals and participants in answering many of these questions. Program evaluation—the process of gathering information about the efficacy of a program in order to make decisions—is essential to good recreation programs. It must be a systematic procedure that is formative or ongoing in nature (see Figure 8.1). This process may include the following 11 components:

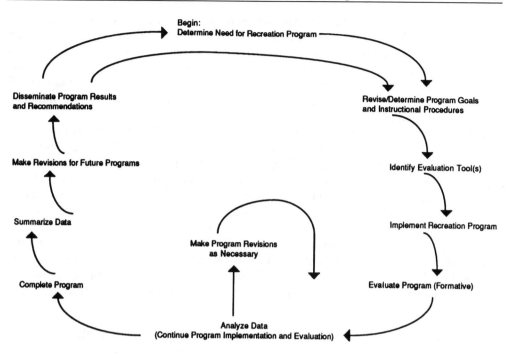

Figure 8.1. Process of recreation program evaluation.

1. Determining the need for the recreation program
2. Determining program goals and instructional procedures
3. Selecting evaluation tool(s) that will determine whether program goals are being met
4. Implementing the recreation program
5. Gathering data on the performance of participants
6. Analyzing the data
7. Incorporating necessary revisions into the program
8. Concluding the program
9. Summarizing the data following the conclusion of the program
10. Making program revisions and recommendations and disseminating (sharing) these to administrators, participants, family members, care providers, and other interested people
11. Implementing a new program with revised goals and instructional strategies.

The process of program evaluation is a dynamic one. The program evaluator must continue to seek ways to improve the program to benefit the participants. To provide optimal recreation services, evaluation must be viewed as a helpful process that allows the professional to gain important insight, feedback, and information concerning the impact of the program on its service recipients, as well as on the agency itself. It is only through systematic and ongoing evaluation that the community recreation program will continue to benefit all of its participants.

Evaluation is a crucial step in planning and implementing inclusive community recreation programs. Two major forms of evaluation influence the success of a program. The first is baseline assessment, an initial observation of the participants' needs and ability levels before actual implementation of a program. The second form of evaluation is ongoing, or formative, evaluation of the progress that the participants are making throughout the program's duration. Both forms of evaluation are essential to an inclusive recreation program because without baseline assessment, it is impossible to determine the individual's level of competency on the activities and skills that are to be taught; and without ongoing evaluation, it may be difficult to verify the progress (e.g., skill acquisition, friendship development) made by the participants and program quality.

"Disability rights" legislation such as the Education for All Handicapped Children Act of 1975 (PL 94-142), the Education of the Handicapped Act Amendments of 1986 (PL 99-457), and the Individuals with Disabilities Education Act (IDEA) of 1990 (PL 101-476) have created a heightened awareness of the importance of program evaluation by mandating that program evaluation data must be provided in a student's individualized education program (IEP) or an adult participant's individualized habilitation or service plan (IHP, ISP) and periodically updated.

This chapter discusses relevant program evaluation in the context of designing and implementing inclusive community recreation programs. The relationship of program evaluation to an individual's IEP or IHP; the frequency, reliability, and validity of evaluation; and detailed descriptions of six program evaluation strategies are discussed.

Relationship of the IEP or IHP to Evaluating Participants with Disabilities

Every individual's education or program plan requires an annual evaluation of short- and long-term instructional objectives. The individual's program is evaluated by an interdisciplinary team of which a therapeutic recreation specialist often is a member. These are minimal standards for evaluation and they are, in the authors' opinion, far too limited.

For a participant's IEP or IHP to be properly developed, the therapeutic recreation specialist, teacher, and family member or care provider must make evaluation a continuous, ongoing process as opposed to following time periods for review that have been set arbitrarily. For instance, the recreation professional must regularly communicate the participant's most current level of performance to significant others. Evaluating skill mastery will confirm the individual's strengths and weaknesses in different activity and curriculum areas (e.g., sports, games, socialization) throughout the year as well as address program quality.

Other reasons exist for evaluating programs and individuals as a critical aspect of the IEP or IHP process. Following the initial assessment of the participant's performance levels, frequent follow-up assessments provide for tracking overall progress in each activity area. Weekly, or at least bimonthly, evaluation of recreation objectives can indicate the effectiveness of programs.

The dynamic process of regularly evaluating instructional procedures, as well as short-term learning objectives, will make the IEP or IHP a more vital blueprint of the individual's recreational and educational progress and not simply a piece of paper to be shuffled into one corner of the desk or placed in a file cabinet. The progress of each participant should be followed systematically throughout the year and reported periodically to supervisors, teachers, and family members or care providers.

Considerations in Evaluating Progress

Frequency of Evaluation A decision that must be made, usually by the recreation program leader, is to determine exactly how often short-term instructional objectives will be evaluated. Objectives may be evaluated at the end of each programming day; or they may be evaluated weekly, biweekly, or once per month. As a general rule, the individual's progress on a specific skill or in a particular activity should be monitored often enough for the instructor and participant to

1. Receive helpful feedback on the progress of the participant. The more frequently the participant's skill level and abilities are evaluated, the easier it is to assess problem areas and build on strengths.
2. Make necessary modifications in methods or materials, and ascertain whether the instructional protocol is effective.
3. Verify that the participant has attained the learning objective(s). Once the participant has acquired the targeted skill and met the objective, the next skill in the instructional sequence can be taught with the newly acquired skill being reviewed periodically.

It is advisable, however, to evaluate measures continuously; that is, in a formative manner. For example, one should evaluate at each session the progress of individuals who do not display clear-cut gains in their programs. Keeping a chart or plotting a graph of the participant's performance (which the authors believe is absolutely necessary) will reveal the rate of the individual's mastery of the skill. If the program is effective, then there will be an ascending rate of progress. For those who serve individuals with significant disabilities, charting and continuously evaluating are critical for determining whether any progress is being made.

Reliability of Evaluation The reliability, or accuracy, of data is dependent on a number of factors, including the method by which data are collected. The process of monitoring the participant's progress can be influenced by a number of factors. If the participant or instructor is ill, for example, or if the same individual does not always do the evaluating or if there is confusion or inconsistency about the method of evaluation or what is to be measured, then the data collected will be suspect and not very reliable.

One means of increasing the reliability of observations is to have a second trained observer collect data independent of the primary observer. For example, to achieve a reliability of agreement that the target behavior actually is occurring at a given rate, two or more independent observers must simultaneously assess the participant. In this way, an index of the consistency of agreement may be established. Reliably recording behavior is the foundation of a good evaluation. Inconsistent agreement between observers casts serious doubt on the credibility of evaluative data. Data collected from observations must be reliable before the evaluation can be considered valid.

Validity of Assessment The validity of the evaluation technique addresses the question, "Does the instrument that is used to assess the participant's progress measure what it purports to?" For data to be considered valid, participants must be evaluated with instruments that provide a true picture of the individual's performance level.

One way to ensure validity of evaluation measures is to employ different types of techniques. For example, if a community recreation instructor is interested in improving a participant's basketball-shooting accuracy, then an observational assessment of percentage of successful field goals achieved by the participant might be computed and recorded daily. This would be an example of a *criterion-referenced* evaluation.

As an initial evaluation, however, the participant's basketball-shooting accuracy could be compared with the scores of other individuals of the same chronological age. This procedure is *norm-referenced*; that is, performance levels are computed on the basis of how well a large number of other respondents have performed the same task.

By utilizing the two types of evaluation—criterion- and norm-referenced—participant performance can be cross-checked. Although improvement on one measure, observational assessment, might not be mirrored by similar advances in the norm-referenced standardized tests, these measures allow for two independent methods for tracking an individual's progress. Only criterion-referenced evaluation tools, however, are described in this chapter. For more comprehensive reviews of criterion-referenced and norm-referenced evaluations in therapeutic recreation and special education, refer to Cullen and Pratt (1992) and Wehman and Schleien (1980).

Following are six program evaluation strategies. Each evaluation strategy is accompanied by an introduction/rationale, step-by-step procedures for implementing the tool, and directions for summarizing the data. Examples of completed evaluation forms are included. Blank forms of all of the evaluation tools, suitable for duplication, appear in Appendix F.

◆ ◆ ◆ ◆ ◆

EVALUATION STRATEGY #1
Skill Acquisition Evaluation Tool:
Task Analytic Assessment

Although there are a number of areas that can be assessed in a recreation environment, an initial question that must be answered to determine the first area of study is whether the individual knows how to interact appropriately with the recreation materials. Also, can the individual use the facility independently? Stated another way, when placed in a recreation environment and supplied with recreation materials, can the participant use the materials appropriately? If not, then systematic instruction is required.

What is required for evaluating leisure-skill proficiency is task analytic assessment (Browder, 1991; Nietupski, Hamre-Nietupski, & Ayres, 1984; Wehman, Renzaglia, & Bates, 1985). An instructional objective must be written for a specific behavior or activity. This objective should reflect the specific skill that the instructor wants the participant to learn.

There are multiple advantages to this type of observational assessment. First, the information collected about the participant performing a particular leisure skill or participating in a specific recreation environment helps the instructor pinpoint the exact area in which instruction should begin or assistance should be provided so that the participant does not receive instruction on skills in which he or she is already proficient. Another advantage is that step-by-step individualized instruction is facilitated. Evaluating the participant's proficiency with different materials or in different environments over an extended period of time also will be more objective and precise and will be less subject to instructor bias.

The Skill Acquisition/Task Analytic Evaluation Tool (Figure 8.2) could be used to determine which parts of a larger leisure skill or recreation activity have been acquired by the participant and at what rate the participant is acquiring the skill.

SKILL ACQUISITION/TASK ANALYTIC EVALUATION

A. Name: _Debbie Cox_

Date: _3-3-97_

D. Program: _Exercise Class_

B. Goal Statement: _To independently participate in an exercise class M,W,F : 5-6 p.m._

C. Verbal Cue: _"Debbie, we're here for your exercise class."_

F.

Task Analysis Steps	a	b	1	2	3	4	5	6	7	8	9	10	11	12	13	14	15	16	17	18	19	20	21
25																							
24																							
23																							
22																							
21 Exit the recreation center.	–	–	+	+	+	+	+	+	+	+	+	+	+	+	+	Ⓞ	+	+					
20 Put coat on.	–	–	+	+	+	+	+	+	+	+	+	+	+	+	Ⓞ	+	+	+					
19 Collect personal belongings.	–	–	+	+	+	+	+	+	+	+	+	+	+	Ⓞ	+	+	+	+					
18 Optional: use drinking fountain/restroom.	–	–	+	+	+	+	+	+	+	+	+	+	Ⓞ	+	+	+	+	+					
17 Optional: talk to other participants.	–	–	+	+	+	+	+	+	+	+	+	Ⓞ+	+	+	+	+	+	+					
16 At the end of class, help put mats away.	–	–	+	+	+	+	+	+	+	+	Ⓞ	–	–	–	–	–	+	+					
15 Do cool-down exercises.	–	–	–	–	–	–	–	–	–	Ⓞ	+	–	–	–	–	–	–	–					
14 Check heart rate (3 x).	–	–	+	+	+	+	+	Ⓞ	+	+	+	–	–	–	–	–	–	–					
13 Do aerobic exercises.	–	–	+	+	+	+	Ⓞ	+	+	+	+	–	–	–	–	–	–	–					
12 When instructor offers break, use drinking fountain.	–	–	–	–	–	–	–	–	Ⓞ	–	–	–	–	–	–	–	–	–					
11 Do strength training exercises.	–	–	–	–	–	Ⓞ	–	–	–	+	+	+	+	+	+	+	+	+					
10 Do warm-up exercises.	–	–	+	+	+	+	+	+	+	+	+	+	+	+	+	+	+	+					
9 When class starts, listen to and follow instructor	–	–	–	–	Ⓞ	–	–	–	+	+	+	+	+	+	+	+	+	+					
8 Optional: approx. speak w/others; stretch out	–	–	+	+	+	+	Ⓞ	–	–	–	+	+	+	+	+	+	+	+					
7 Wait for class to begin.	–	–	–	–	–	Ⓞ	–	–	–	–	–	–	–	–	–	–	–	–					
6 Find a space on the mats & go in that direction.	–	–	–	–	–	–	Ⓞ	+	+	+	+	+	+	+	+	+	+	+					
5 Take off coat, hang it on coat rack.	–	–	–	–	–	–	–	–	–	–	Ⓞ	–	–	–	–	–	–	–					
4 Locate coat rack along wall; walk in that direction	–	–	–	–	–	–	–	–	Ⓞ	–	–	–	–	–	–	–	–	–					
3 Locate & proceed to the multipurpose room.	–	–	–	–	–	–	–	Ⓞ	+	+	+	+	+	+	+	+	+	+					
2 Acknowledge rec. staff & others, if approp.	–	–	–	–	–	–	–	Ⓞ	+	+	+	+	+	+	+	+	+	+					
1 Enter the recreation center.	–	–	+	+	+	+	+	+	Ⓞ+	+	+	+	+	+	+	+	+	+					

E.

Sessions

G. Total # of +'s

	a	b	1	2	3	4	5	6	7	8	9	10	11	12	13	14	15	16	17
Total # of +'s	0	0	5	7	8	8	11	12	14	16	16	17	15	17	19				
Your initials																			
Date	3/1	3/19	3/21	3/24	3/26	3/28	3/31	4/2	4/4	4/7	4/9	4/11	4/14	4/16	4/19	4/21	4/23		

H. Your initials

I. Date

J. _Partic. in comm. rec. program_

Skill

157

To conduct the assessment, the evaluator must familiarize him- or herself with the completed Skill Acquisition/Task Analytic Evaluation Tool.

The process begins when the instructor identifies and lists on the evaluation form each step that is required for the participant to independently complete the selected skill. The steps should be listed sequentially. In each session, following the completion of instruction on the selected skill, a verbal cue can be provided to the participant that instructs him or her to begin the activity. Without offering any reinforcement to the participant, such as giving positive feedback for his or her performance, the instructor observes the participant attempting to complete the task or skill. During observation and recording, the instructor records a plus (+) by each step of the task analysis that the participant completes independently and a minus (−) by those steps not performed independently. The recorded "+" signs reveal which steps of the skill the participant has mastered. The beginning of consecutive "−" signs determines the point at which instruction should begin in the following session. By totaling the number of "+" signs, the instructor can determine the participant's progress in learning the skill and quantify the rate of skill acquisition.

Skill acquisition evaluation enables the instructor to provide individualized instruction on a specific step of the skill that has not been mastered by the participant. It also gives the instructor immediate feedback about the progress that each participant is making on the targeted skill in the program.

DIRECTIONS FOR SKILL ACQUISITION/TASK ANALYTIC EVALUATION TOOL

Before the Program Begins

1. Write the participant's name on line "A."
2. Determine a skill relevant to the program that the participant needs to acquire. Write the skill on line "J."
3. Write the goal statement on line "B."
4. Determine a phrase (i.e., verbal cue) that you will consistently use to instruct the participant to begin the task. Write this verbal cue on line "C."
5. Write on line "D" the name of the program, the days it meets, and the time the sessions are held.
6. Observe an individual who has already mastered the skill, and perform this skill by yourself so that you may write in the "Task Analysis Steps" column each step that is necessary to independently complete the skill. Write step 1 on line "E.1," step 2 above it on line 2, and so forth.

Note: Your targeted skill may require more or less than the 25 rows provided; modify the form as necessary.

Evaluating the Initial Sessions

1. To begin instruction on the targeted skill, give the participant the general verbal cue; record each step of the task analysis that the participant performs independently with a plus (+) and those not performed independently with a minus (−). Record your observation under "F" in column "a." Repeat the procedure during each session, and record your observation under "F" in column "b," and so forth.

2. A plus (+) or minus (−) should appear after each step listed in the task analysis in column "F," in both the "a" and "b" columns, by the end of the first two evaluation periods.

3. The information gathered during the first two sessions is referred to as the *baseline assessment*. This baseline assessment identifies the participant's current level of mastery of the task before instruction begins. At least two assessment probes on different days should be conducted to establish a true baseline rate. When the baseline rate appears stable (i.e., forms a horizontal line), instruction on the targeted skill should commence. A stable baseline followed by an increase of steps mastered in the task analysis documents the effectiveness of the recreation program (i.e., leisure skills instruction).

4. To complete the remainder of the form, refer to the directions on "Evaluating All Other Sessions During Instruction."

Evaluating All Other Sessions During Instruction

1. Begin instruction on the targeted leisure skill by giving the participant the general verbal cue.

2. Following the completion of instruction on the targeted leisure skill for a particular session, give the participant another general verbal cue (on line "C") to signal him or her to perform the activity without any assistance.

3. In the column that coincides with the number of that session (e.g., session 2: record in column 2), record a plus (+) next to each step that the participant performs independently and a minus (−) next to those steps that are not performed independently during the nonreinforced data probe. A plus or minus should appear in each step of the task analysis at the end of the evaluation.

4. On line "G," write the total number of plus signs (+) recorded in that session.

5. On line "H," write your initials.

6. On line "I," write the date that you made your observation.

7. Circle the box (in the column that was just recorded) that coincides with the number of the "Total # of +'s" box. For example, if the total is eight correct steps in session 3, then circle the box on line 8 in column 3.

8. Draw a line graph across sessions by connecting the circles that were drawn in step 7. This line will create a graph that illustrates the participant's level of mastery of the task throughout the program.

9. Locate two consecutive minus signs in the column in which you just recorded the data. The first, or lower, of the two recorded minus signs is the step of the task analysis at which to begin instruction during the next session.

EVALUATION STRATEGY #2
Social Interaction Evaluation Tool

For many participants of recreation programs—particularly those individuals with disabilities who often are socially isolated—an important instructional goal is to initiate, receive, and sustain interactions with peers more frequently. A relatively common occurrence is the presence of several children with and without disabilities playing separately from each other during free play (Schleien, Rynders, Mustonen, & Fox, 1990). During these play situations, the potential benefits of social interaction and friendship development are not accrued.

One way of assessing social interaction is to count the number of times a child initiates an interaction, receives an interaction, sustains an interaction, or terminates an interaction. Duration assessment may be used to measure the length of the interaction, in seconds or minutes, between peers and also between participants and adults in the recreation setting. A second means of gathering more social interaction information is coding specific types of interactions. Carney and her colleagues (1977) identified 20 interaction skills under four categories (receive, initiate, sustain, and terminate). In addition to providing sequence, these skills may be task analyzed to determine the individual's proficiency on selected behaviors (see Evaluation Strategy #1).

Analyzing the direction of interactions (i.e., who initiates to whom) can be helpful in assessing which individuals in the environment are reinforcing to the participant and which may become friends. As Beveridge, Spencer, and Miller (1978) observed, child–instructor interactions occur more frequently than do child–child interactions, especially among children with significant disabilities. Structured intervention by an adult is the action usually required to increase child–child interactions (Rynders & Schleien, 1991; Shores, Hester, & Strain, 1976). The direction of interactions should be assessed during home visits while observing the child playing with siblings or with neighborhood peers. The interactions between individuals with disabilities and their peers without disabilities should be recorded. This type of behavioral analysis can be revealing because most children without disabilities do not include children with disabilities in play unless prompted and reinforced by adults (Rynders & Schleien, 1991; Schleien, Meyer, Heyne, & Brandt, 1995).

To identify the individuals with whom the participants are interacting during a program and to determine whether participants are increasing or decreasing their interactions toward an individual or a selected group of people, the Social Interaction Evaluation Tool can be implemented. This evaluation procedure incorporates a data-collection method referred to as a *time sampling*. The time-sampling procedure requires the instructor to momentarily observe (e.g., for 2–3 seconds) a participant at predetermined times, with a minimum of three observation times per hour, during the program. These observation times should be evenly distributed within the program time and should vary from session to session. For example, if the program is held from 3 P.M. to 4 P.M. on Mondays and Wednesdays, then the instructor may record observations on Mondays at 3:05 P.M., 3:35 P.M., and 3:55 P.M. On Wednesdays, the observation times may be 3:15 P.M., 3:30 P.M., and 3:45 P.M. At these predetermined times, the instructor should observe the participant for an instant and record with whom the participant was interacting, if an interaction was occurring, and whether that interaction was appropriate or inappropriate. Appropriate and inappropriate social interactions and any other actions or behaviors that could help describe the social environment should be *operationally defined*. In this manner, the evaluator has a standard, predetermined criterion on which to make accurate and reliable observational judgments. Examples of possible definitions for appropriate and inappropriate social interactions are provided in this chapter. It is important to understand that the more times a participant is observed during a program, the greater the amount of information will be obtained from which to evaluate the participant's progress and the overall effectiveness of the program.

Two variations of the Social Interaction Evaluation Tool (Figures 8.3 and 8.4) are included in this chapter as examples. The first tool could be used to collect information on one participant; the second tool is used for two or more participants.

SOCIAL INTERACTION EVALUATION FOR ONE PARTICIPANT

A. Program Title: _Talking Art_

B. Program Goal: _increasing social interaction between part._

C. Name: _Debbie Cox_

D. Date: _5-9-97_   Evaluator: _E. Fullen_

E. Level of Interaction

Time (preset)	None	Staff	Part. w/dis.	Part. w/o dis.	Other	Activity	Comments
3:05	A					Taking coat off	
3:10				A		Sitting at table	
3:15				I		Throwing clay	Debbie was being ignored by staff and peers
3:25		A				Asking for help	
3:40	A					Working on project	
3:45				I		Pushing mess to neighbor's space	Possibly seeking attention from peer in close proximity
3:55				A		Putting coat on	

H. Totals

	A	2	0	1	0	0	2	0
	I	2	0	0	0	2	2	0

Key

A = Appropriate Social Interaction
I = Inappropriate Social Interaction

Figure 8.3. Social interaction evaluation—completed.

SOCIAL INTERACTION EVALUATION FOR TWO OR MORE PARTICIPANTS

A. Program Title: _Talking Art_

B. Program Goal: _To increase social interactions_

D. Date: _6-11-97_

E. Times to Observe: 1. _6:10 p.m._ 2. _6:30 p.m._ 3. _6:45 p.m._

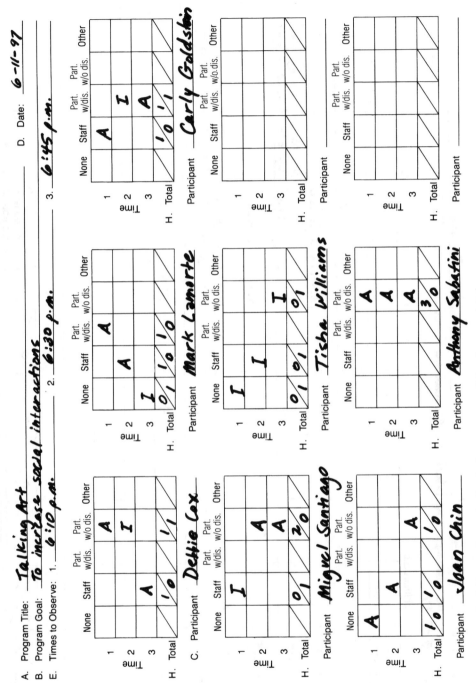

Figure 8.4. Social interaction evaluation for two or more participants—completed.

The instructions for using both instruments are identical. This evaluation procedure can be used to gain information on many different social aspects of the community recreation program. For example, if one wishes to evaluate changes in the participants' sportsmanship during an inclusive softball program, then the targeted behavior—sportsmanship—must be operationally defined (e.g., assisting another participant during the game, not screaming at opponents, taking turns coming to bat). One should then conduct a baseline assessment (refer to the Skill Acquisition Evaluation Tool for this procedure), conduct the softball program, observe the participants, record and graph the participants' behaviors, and summarize the results.

Before proceeding, the reader should become familiar with the completed Social Interaction Evaluation sample forms that follow.

The benefits of implementing the Social Interaction Evaluation Tool could include 1) identifying the individuals with whom participants are primarily interacting (e.g., staff, participant without a disability, participant with a disability, no interactions occurring) and 2) documenting changes in the level of interaction between participants.

OPERATIONAL DEFINITIONS

Appropriate Social Interaction

1. *Initiates Positive Interaction* Participant actively seeks positive contact with a specific peer or adult by touching, gesturing to, or vocalizing/verbalizing to individual. Interaction may be a facial expression (e.g., smiles), vocal tone (e.g., pleasant), verbal content (e.g., praise, giving directions, encouragement), nonverbal vocalizations (e.g., laughs, giggles), appropriate touch (e.g., guidance or assistance, hugs, pats on the back), or gestures or verbal behavior that seeks to recruit peer's attention.
2. *Receives Positive Interaction* Participant with a disability is touched, gestured to, commented to, given directions, or questioned by peer or adult in a nonderogatory, nonthreatening manner. Interaction may be a facial expression (e.g., smiles), vocal tone (e.g., pleasant), verbal content (e.g., praise, being given directions, encouragement), nonverbal vocalizations (e.g., laughs, giggles), and/or appropriate touch (e.g., guidance or assistance, hugs, pats on the back).

Inappropriate Social Interaction

1. *Initiates Negative Interaction* Participant touches, gestures to, gives directions to, or questions peer or adult in a hostile, derisive, or threatening manner. Interaction may be a facial expression (e.g., frowns, grimaces), vocal tone (e.g., sharp, loud, whiney), verbal content (e.g., "No!"; punitive, threatening or disapproving remarks; swearing, derogatory, or derisive comments), nonverbal vocalizations (e.g., crying, moaning, groaning, growling), and/or aggressive physical contact (e.g., hitting, slapping, flailing at, pushing, pulling, scratching, biting).
2. *Receives Negative Interaction* Participant is touched, gestured to, commented to, given directions, or questioned by peer or adult in a derisive, threatening, or hostile manner. Interactions may be a facial expression (e.g., frowns, pouts), vocal tone (e.g., loud, whiney, sharp, angry), verbal content (e.g., "No!"; punitive,

threatening, or disapproving remarks; swearing or derogatory comments), and/or nonverbal vocalizations (e.g., crying, moaning, groaning, growling).

KEY FOR THE SOCIAL INTERACTION EVALUATION TOOL

None = The individual with a disability is not interacting with anyone.

Staff = The individual with a disability is interacting with a staff person/program instructor.

Part. w/dis. = The individual with a disability is interacting with another participant (peer) with a disability.

Part. w/o dis. = The individual with a disability is interacting with a participant (peer) without a disability.

Other = The individual with a disability is not present for the observation (e.g., he or she is in the restroom, has gone home early).

DIRECTIONS FOR SOCIAL INTERACTION EVALUATION TOOL (BOTH FORMS)

Before the Program Begins

1. Write the name of the program on line "A."
2. Write the goal(s) of the program on line "B."
3. Write the participant's name on line(s) "C."
4. Write the date that you will conduct the evaluation on line "D."
5. Determine the times at which you will observe each participant in the session. Write these times in column "E."
6. Position a clock or wristwatch so that you can accurately observe the participant at the designated times.

Evaluating

1. At predetermined times, observe the participant for a brief moment (approximately 2–3 seconds) and record in the correct column (e.g., None, Staff, Part. w/dis.) an "A" for appropriate social interaction or an "I" for inappropriate social interaction.
2. If you are observing more than one participant concurrently, list the participants in a predetermined order. At the appropriate observe/record time (e.g., 5:20 P.M.), observe for a brief moment the first participant on the list (e.g., Debbie Cox), record her behavior, and then observe the next participant (e.g., Mark Lamorte) on the list. Continue this observe/record procedure until all of the participants on the list have been observed. At the next designated observation time, repeat this procedure.
3. Write in column "F" a brief description (1–3 words) of the activity in which the participant was engaged during your observation. (This description is omitted from the form for two or more participants because of space and time limitations. If possible, write your comments on a separate sheet of paper.)
4. Write in column "G" any comments that you believe would clarify the information you recorded. These would be the comments omitted from the form designated for two or more participants.

5. After the session has ended, determine the total number of appropriate social interactions in each category, and place that number on the left side of the slash in the box (see "H") directly beneath that column. On the right side of the slash, place the number of inappropriate social interactions recorded in that column.

6. Transcribe the data from the Social Interaction Evaluation Tool onto the Social Interaction Evaluation Summary Sheet (see Figure 8.5).

Completing the Social Interaction Evaluation Summary

1. Write the name of the program on line "A."

2. Write the program instructor's name on line "B."

3. Write on line "C" the names of other staff members who assisted in the program.

4. Write on line "D" the beginning and ending dates and year of the program. Include at the end of line "D" the date this summary sheet was completed.

5. Write the participant's name on line(s) "E" (bottom of form).

6. In each of the columns, add the "A's" (appropriate social interactions) recorded in all of the sessions during the first half of the program semester. Write the totals in the appropriate boxes on line "F." Repeat this procedure with the "I's" (inappropriate social interactions).

7. Color half of each column up to the number that corresponds to the number in the "Total" box.

8. The completed graph illustrates the frequency of interactions by each participant and identifies the people with whom he or she was interacting.

9. Repeat steps 6 and 7 after the final session to summarize the interactions of the second half of the program semester. Write the totals in the appropriate boxes on line "G." A comparison of the graphs from the first to the second half of the program semester will display an increase, decrease, or stable rate of appropriate and inappropriate social interactions between participants.

EVALUATION STRATEGY #3
Sociometry Evaluation Tool

The term *sociometry* derives from the Latin term for social or companion measurement. Although sociometry is widely accepted and used in industry and in summer recreational camps, schools continue to be the most prevalent setting in which this technique is applied. It has been used by teachers to analyze the social structures of students in group situations and the extent to which students are accepted by their peers.

The ease with which sociometry can be developed and administered makes it a practical and convenient tool for use by community recreation professionals to supplement their personal judgment of a group's dynamics. Sociometry can be used to evaluate the emotional climate of a group and the attitudes of participants within a group toward each other; to identify any friendships that are being established, especially between individuals with and without disabilities; and to document changes in the patterns of social interactions. In short, the sociometric structure addresses the network of interpersonal relationships between participants. This network is presented in the form of a *sociogram*.

SOCIAL INTERACTION EVALUATION SUMMARY SHEET

A. Program Title: _Talking Art_

B. Program Instructor: _E. Fullen_

C. Other Staff: _A. Bartlett, R. Thomas_

D. Duration of Program: _6 weeks (6-3-97 to 7-15-97)_ Date: _7-15-97_

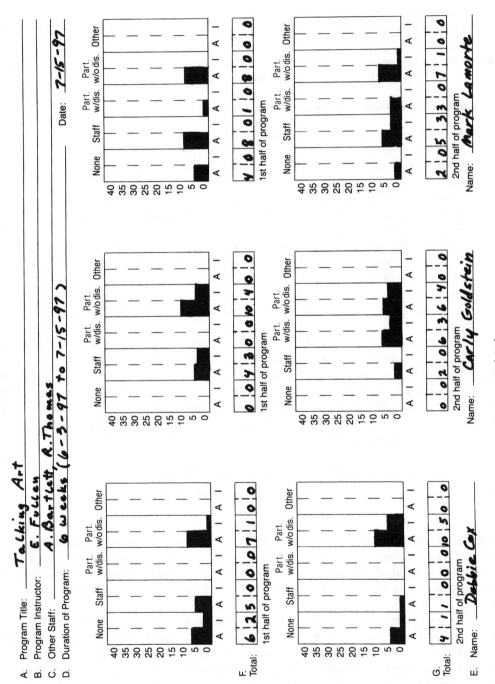

F. Total: | 6 | 25 | 00 | 07 | 10 | 0 |

G. Total: | 4 | 11 | 00 | 00 | 50 | 0 |

E. Name: _Debbie Cox_

Total: | 0 | 04 | 30 | 06 | 04 | 0 |

2nd half of program
Name: _Carly Goldstein_

Total: | 4 | 08 | 01 | 08 | 00 | 0 |

2nd half of program
Name: _Mark Lamorte_

Figure 8.5. Social interaction evaluation summary sheet—completed.

To use sociometry to measure social experiences, a sociometric question is posed to each participant. For example, "Whom would you like as a partner on the nature hike?" Participants' responses are then documented on the Sociometry Evaluation Information Form. Interpreting and diagramming this information in a sociogram could be completed at other times following the program. The sociometric technique can be implemented on three separate occasions: 1) during the first day of the program to establish the current levels of interaction between participants, 2) at the midway point of the program to reveal any changes in levels of interaction and to identify areas in which changes could still be made, and 3) during the final day of the program to document the total number of changes that have occurred throughout the program.

Before proceeding with the directions, the reader should become familiar with the completed Sociometry Evaluation Information Form sample (see Figure 8.6).

DIRECTIONS FOR SOCIOMETRY EVALUATION TOOL

Before the Program Begins

1. Write the name of the program on line "A."
2. Write the program's goal(s) on line "B."
3. Write the date of the evaluation on line "C."
4. Write each participant's name in the "Participant" column beginning on line "D.1."
5. Use the number to the left of the participant's name for his or her identification number.
6. If the participant has a disability, then draw a triangle (△) in the "Symbol" column after his or her name. If the participant does not have a disability, then draw a circle (○) there.
7. Write the participant's identification number inside his or her symbol (e.g., △).
8. Write on line "E" the sociometric question(s) that will be asked. The question must require the participants to name others in the group with whom they would like to interact. For example, "If you were going on a week-long vacation, who would you choose to accompany you?" or "If I gave you $5, who would you like to take to the ice cream shop?" are sociometric questions. Of course, the sociometric question(s) must be appropriate for the chronological ages of the participants and should reflect realistic scenarios or concerns for the respondents.
9. More than one question can be asked to assess whether the participants respond in a similar manner. This would serve as a reliability check and would be an optional procedure. If more than one sociometric question is asked, then the response to the second question should be recorded using a different symbol from that of the first (e.g., use "X's" or "O's").
10. Write the evaluator's name on line "F."

During the Program: Evaluating

1. During the first, midpoint, and final sessions of the recreation program, ask each participant the sociometric question(s) that is (are) recorded on line "E."

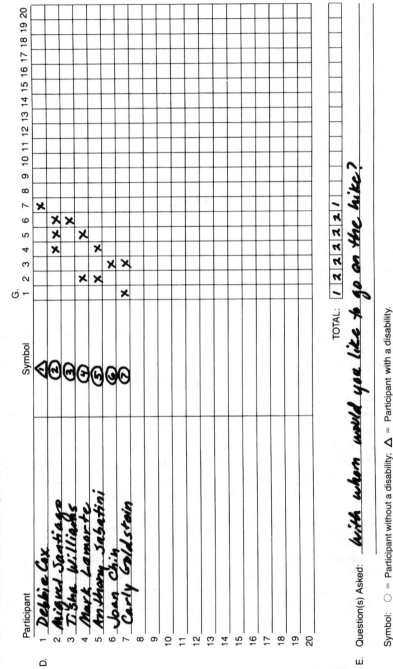

Figure 8.6. Sociometry evaluation information tool—completed.

168

2. Record each participant's response on the Sociometry Evaluation Information Form. For example, if Debbie (#1) said that she would select Carly (#7), then place a mark on line 1 in column 7.
3. Repeat this procedure until responses are received and recorded for each participant.

After the Program: Summarizing

1. Tally the number of marks in each column, beginning in column "G," and place the total number of marks in the "Total" box at the bottom of each column.
2. The number at the top of each column coincides with the participant's identification number, and, therefore, the information in that column pertains to him or her. For example, column 4 has a total of two recorded marks; therefore, two participants selected Mark as a companion to take on the nature hike.

Graphing the Information on a Sociogram

1. On the Sociogram Evaluation Graphing Form (see Figure 8.7), seven rings appear; these are numbered 0–6. Each ring represents the total number of times a participant was selected by another respondent.
2. Draw the participants' symbols and identification numbers, as they appear in the "Symbol" column (e.g., △), in the ring that matches the number in the "Total" box at the bottom of each participant's column. For example, the number in

SOCIOGRAM EVALUATION GRAPHING FORM

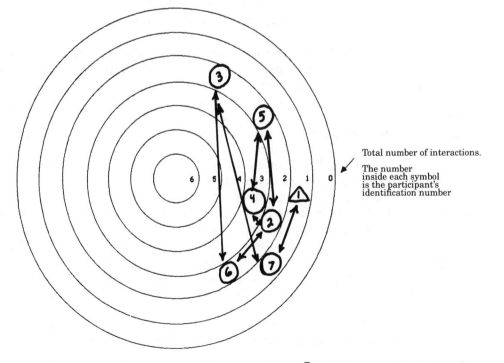

Total number of interactions.

The number inside each symbol is the participant's identification number

Figure 8.7. Sociogram evaluation graphing form—completed. (○ = Participant without a disability; △ = Participant with a disability.)

Debbie's "Total" box is 1. Draw her symbol (△), with her identification number inside of it (1), in the ring where the #1 appears.

3. Using the information recorded on the same line as the participants' names, draw an arrow from each participant's symbol to the individual he or she selected. For example, Debbie (#1) selected Carly (#7) in response to the sociometric question. Draw an arrow from symbol #1 to symbol #7. Note: If Carly (#7) also selected Debbie (#1), then draw an arrowhead on both ends of the line that has been drawn between the two participants' symbols to illustrate a mutual, or reciprocal, selection.

Interpreting the Sociogram

When interpreting these data, one might ask questions that are important to the success of the program: Are participants without disabilities interacting with their peers with disabilities? Are socially withdrawn participants becoming more involved in the recreation program? Who are the most popular participants, and are they being regarded as role models by the other participants? Other questions include:

1. Are there any social isolates (i.e., individuals who were not selected)?
2. Is there a leader among the group or an individual whom many participants selected?
3. Is there a difference in selection rates between participants with and without disabilities?
4. Are there participants who selected each other in a reciprocal manner?

EVALUATION STRATEGY #4
Peer Acceptance Evaluation Tool

Voeltz (1980, 1982) developed a method to evaluate changes in attitude or in levels of acceptance as demonstrated by individuals without disabilities toward their peers with disabilities. The Peer Acceptance Survey (Figure 8.8) is a modified version of Voeltz's survey. Within the context of community recreation programs, instructors can improve the level of peer acceptance among the participants by role modeling, planning cooperatively goal-structured activities, and providing social-skills instruction to the participants.

One method of evaluating peer acceptance is by using a pretest and posttest of acceptance level of the other participants. Prior to the first program session, the Peer Acceptance Survey can be administered to each participant. The results can be scored using the Peer Acceptance Survey Answer Key (see Appendix F) and documented outside of program or class time. During or immediately following the final meeting, the survey can be administered again to the participants; results are recorded on the summary sheet. Similarly, the Peer Acceptance Survey Evaluation Summary Form (Figure 8.9) is easy to implement and provides objective information concerning the attitude changes of the participants toward each other throughout the recreation program.

Before proceeding with the instructions, the reader should become familiar with the completed Peer Acceptance Survey Evaluation Summary Form.

PEER ACCEPTANCE SURVEY

Name: ___Erik Lankenau___

1. I don't have any friends who have mental retardation or a disability.
Agree ____ Disagree _X_ Undecided ____

2. If my sister or brother had mental retardation, I wouldn't talk about it to anyone.
Agree ____ Disagree _X_ Undecided ____

3. I have talked to people who use wheelchairs.
Agree ____ Disagree _X_ Undecided ____

4. If I found out that someone I hang around with has mental retardation, I would still be his/her friend.
Agree ____ Disagree _X_ Undecided ____

5. I have talked with some people with mental retardation at the park.
Agree ____ Disagree ____ Undecided _X_

6. It snows in Minnesota in the winter.
Agree _X_ Disagree ____ Undecided ____

7. There is no reason for me to spend time with anyone who has a disability.
Agree _X_ Disagree ____ Undecided ____

8. I think that a student who is deaf or blind could be in my recreation program.
Agree ____ Disagree ____ Undecided _X_

9. I wouldn't want a person with a disability to be my partner in an activity.
Agree ____ Disagree ____ Undecided _X_

10. I believe that I could become close friends with a person who has a disability.
Agree ____ Disagree ____ Undecided _X_

11. I have helped some people who are in wheelchairs.
Agree ____ Disagree _X_ Undecided ____

12. Minneapolis is a large city in Minnesota.
Agree _X_ Disagree ____ Undecided ____

13. People who have mental retardation should not come to the park for activities.
Agree _X_ Disagree ____ Undecided ____

14. I wish I could become friends with a person who has mental retardation.
Agree ____ Disagree _X_ Undecided ____

15. I would not like to be around a person who looked or acted different.
Agree _X_ Disagree ____ Undecided ____

16. If someone told me about a new TV program about disabilities, I would probably watch it.
Agree ____ Disagree ____ Undecided _X_

17. I have never talked with a person who is paralyzed or couldn't walk.
Agree _X_ Disagree ____ Undecided ____

18. I don't say "Hi" to people who have mental retardation.
Agree _X_ Disagree ____ Undecided ____

19. Minnesota has many lakes.
Agree _X_ Disagree ____ Undecided ____

20. I believe students with disabilities should participate with other people in the recreation department's programs.
Agree ____ Disagree _X_ Undecided ____

Finished! Thank you for completing the survey.

Figure 8.8. Peer acceptance survey—completed. (This questionnaire was adapted from Voeltz, L. [1980]. Children's attitudes toward handicapped peers. *American Journal of Mental Deficiency, 84,* 455–464.)

PEER ACCEPTANCE SURVEY EVALUATION SUMMARY FORM

A. Name: _Erik Lankenau_

B. Program Title: _New Games_

C. Program Goal: _to participate cooperatively in groups_

D. Objective: _Erik Lankenau_ _____ will increase (his)/her
    (name)
    posttest score __8__ points above (his)/her pretest score after attending __8__ sessions
    (number)   (number)
    of _New Games_ _____.
    (program)

Total number of points possible = 40.

Date	Pretest Score	Date	Posttest Score	Difference between Pretest and Posttest Score
E. 6-12-97	F. 13	I. 7-10-97	J. 34	K. (J. − F.) 21

G. Number of program sessions __8__.

L. Number of sessions attended by the participant __8__.

Activities engaged in by the participant:

	Date	Activity	Comment	Initial
H.	6-17	knots	Erik didn't want to hold hands	of
	6-19	new frisbee	This activity was enjoyed	of
	6-24	group juggling	Erik found this fun but	of
	6-26	instant replay	Erik needed much instruction, difficult	of
	7-1	hug tag	Activity was enjoyed by group	of
	7-3	human pinball	Jim was inapprop. at first	of
	7-8	taffy pull	Erik played well in his group	of
	7-10	people pyramids	Erik was very cooperative	of

Figure 8.9. Peer acceptance evaluation summary form—completed.

DIRECTIONS FOR PEER ACCEPTANCE
SURVEY EVALUATION SUMMARY FORM

1. Write the targeted participant's name on line "A."
2. Write on line "B" the name of the program that the participant will be attending.
3. Write the program goal(s) on line "C."
4. Fill in the blanks on line "D" to complete the objective.
5. During or prior to the first session, administer the Peer Acceptance Survey to each participant. Ask the participants to answer each question individually. Reassure them that there are no right or wrong answers and that their answers are strictly confidential.
6. Score the Peer Acceptance Surveys by referring to the Peer Acceptance Survey Answer Key to determine the point value for the response given to each statement. Add the point values for all 20 statements for all of the participants who completed the survey, and divide that number by the total number of respondents to arrive at a total pretest score.

7. Write on line "E" the date that the survey was completed.
8. Write on line "F" the participant's pretest score.
9. Write on line "G" the total number of program sessions.
10. On line "H," write the date of the first session, the activities in which the participant was involved, any comment that may assist with interpreting the data (e.g., Erik did not want to hold hands with his partner), and your initials.
11. Repeat step 10 until the program has terminated.
12. During the final session, or shortly thereafter, administer the questionnaire once again to all of the participants. Remind the participants that their answers are strictly confidential, that there are no right or wrong answers, and that they must complete the survey individually.
13. Score the Peer Acceptance Surveys in the identical manner as in step 6.
14. Write the date of the posttest on line "I."
15. Write the posttest score on line "J."
16. Subtract the number on line "F" from the number on line "J" and write the total on line "K" (i.e., J − F = K).
17. Write the total number of sessions that the participant attended on line "L."

*(Note: In addition to the evaluation strategies described throughout this chapter that address social interactions and peer attitudes, the **Social Relationships Assessment Procedure** is described in detail in Chapter 7 as it relates to friendship development.)*

EVALUATION STRATEGY #5
Self-Concept Evaluation Tool

One of the most important results of participation by people with disabilities in recreation programs is the opportunity for participants to develop their self-concept or self-esteem. The Self-Concept Questionnaire (Figure 8.10) is a pretest and posttest measurement strategy for determining levels of self-esteem. This 30-item questionnaire is administered to all of the participants before the program begins. The scores are then tallied using the Self-Concept Questionnaire Answer Key (see Appendix F) and recorded on the Self-Concept Evaluation Summary Form (Figure 8.11). Additional questions on the summary sheet must be completed by the program instructor. During the final session, or shortly thereafter, the identical questionnaire is once again administered to each participant, and the score is recorded on the summary form. The Self-Concept Evaluation strategy is simple to implement and score. It could complement the data collected from the other evaluation procedures described in this chapter and elsewhere. For example, information gained from the Social Interaction Evaluation Tool (this chapter) or the Social Relationships Assessment Procedure (see Chapter 7) might illustrate that the participant with a disability only interacts with staff members, not with his or her peers, and has made few friends. The Self-Concept Questionnaire may reveal that this participant has low self-esteem and, consequently, has a difficult time pursuing others as friends or even as social acquaintances. Based on these data, the program instructor could suggest that the individual receive additional social-skills training and encourage the participant to interact with his or her peers. Also, an instructor could provide positive social reinforcement such as social praise and continu-

SELF-CONCEPT QUESTIONNAIRE

Name: _Debbie Cox_

Date: _8-4-97_

1.	I feel like I can improve how I look.	Never	**(Seldom)**	Sometimes	Often	Always
2.	Others think of me as a leader.	**(Never)**	Seldom	Sometimes	Often	Always
3.	I make friends easily.	Never	**(Seldom)**	Sometimes	Often	Always
4.	I learn how to play games fast.	Never	Seldom	**(Sometimes)**	Often	Always
5.	I consider myself smart.	Never	**(Seldom)**	Sometimes	Often	Always
6.	Others tease me.	Never	Seldom	Sometimes	**(Often)**	Always
7.	I want to be like someone else.	Never	Seldom	Sometimes	Often	**(Always)**
8.	I enjoy making decisions.	**(Never)**	Seldom	Sometimes	Often	Always
9.	I get picked last in games.	Never	Seldom	Sometimes	Often	**(Always)**
10.	I feel good when I learn something new.	Never	Seldom	Sometimes	**(Often)**	Always
11.	When I look in the mirror, I like myself.	Never	**(Seldom)**	Sometimes	Often	Always
12.	I am a leader when with others my own age.	**(Never)**	Seldom	Sometimes	Often	Always
13.	I like to play alone.	Never	Seldom	Sometimes	Often	**(Always)**
14.	Others consider me smart.	**(Never)**	Seldom	Sometimes	Often	Always
15.	Others like playing games with me.	Never	**(Seldom)**	Sometimes	Often	Always
16.	Others ask me to be their friend.	Never	**(Seldom)**	Sometimes	Often	Always
17.	I feel bad when my team loses.	Never	Seldom	Sometimes	**(Often)**	Always
18.	Others tell me what to do.	Never	Seldom	Sometimes	**(Often)**	Always
19.	I can make up my own mind.	Never	Seldom	**(Sometimes)**	Often	Always
20.	I enjoy playing by myself.	Never	Seldom	Sometimes	**(Often)**	Always
21.	I only like to play if I win.	Never	Seldom	**(Sometimes)**	Often	Always
22.	I get mad when someone teases me.	Never	Seldom	Sometimes	Often	**(Always)**
23.	I get picked first in games.	**(Never)**	Seldom	Sometimes	Often	Always
24.	I like to play with others.	Never	**(Seldom)**	Sometimes	Often	Always
25.	I feel like I can get things done.	Never	Seldom	**(Sometimes)**	Often	Always
26.	I get what I can from others.	Never	**(Seldom)**	Sometimes	Often	Always
27.	I feel it's my fault when my team loses.	Never	Seldom	Sometimes	Often	**(Always)**
28.	Others enjoy being with me.	Never	**(Seldom)**	Sometimes	Often	Always
29.	I can choose what to do during my free time.	Never	**(Seldom)**	Sometimes	Often	Always
30.	Others like to be around me.	Never	**(Seldom)**	Sometimes	Often	Always

Finished! Thank you for completing the survey.

Figure 8.10. Self-concept questionnaire—completed.

SELF-CONCEPT EVALUATION SUMMARY FORM

A. Name: _Debbie Cox_

B. Program Title: _Just for Me_

C. Program Goal: _To increase personal understanding of 'self'_

D. Objective: _Debbie Cox_ _____ will increase his/her
      (name)
   posttest score _15_ points above his/her pretest score after attending _8_ sessions
              (number)   (number)
   of _Just for Me_ .
      (program)

Total number of points possible = 150.

Date	Pretest Score	Date	Posttest Score	Difference between Pretest and Posttest Score
E. 8-4-97	F. 66	I. 8-27-97	J. 104	K. (J. − F.) 38

G. Number of program sessions _8_ .

L. Number of sessions attended by the participant _8_ .

Activities engaged in by the participant:

	Date	Activity	Comment	Initial
H.	8-4-97	Interest Survey	Said "I can't do anything right"	
	8-6-97	Talent Collage	One picture of watching TV	
	8-11-97	Leadership Skills	Limited but good interaction	
	8-13-97	New Games	Appeared to enjoy them	
	8-18-97	Self-Portraits	Used bright colors	
	8-20-97	Being Positive	Made no comments	
	8-25-97	Growing from Failure	Added to the discussion	
	8-27-97	Party	Socially involved w/peers	

Figure 8.11. Self-concept evaluation summary form—completed.

ous feedback to strengthen the participant's self-esteem and friendship-making abilities.

Before proceeding with the directions for implementing the Self-Concept Evaluation strategy, the reader should become familiar with the completed Self-Concept Evaluation Summary Form.

DIRECTIONS FOR THE SELF-CONCEPT EVALUATION STRATEGY

1. Write the participant's name on line "A."
2. Write the name of the program on line "B."
3. Write the program goal(s) on line "C."
4. Fill in the blanks on line "D" to complete the objective.
5. Administer the questionnaire to each participant. Ask the participants to complete the questionnaire individually. Reassure them that their answers are strictly confidential and that there are no right or wrong answers.
6. Score the questionnaires by referring to the Self-Concept Questionnaire Answer Key to determine the point value for the response given for each statement. Add the point values for all 30 statements to arrive at a total pretest score.

7. Write on line "E" the date that the questionnaire was completed.
8. Write the participant's pretest score on line "F."
9. Write on line "G" the number of sessions in the program.
10. On line "H," write the date of the first session, the activities in which the participant was involved, and any comments that could assist in interpreting the data. For example, "Debbie was not feeling well and did not participate for most of the session and said, 'I can't do anything right!'" Initial your entry.
11. Repeat step 10 throughout the sessions.
12. During the final session, or shortly thereafter, administer the questionnaire to each participant. Remind the respondents that their answers are strictly confidential and that there are no right or wrong answers.
13. Score the questionnaires in the identical manner as in step 6.
14. Write the date of the posttest on line "I."
15. Write the score of the posttest on line "J."
16. Subtract the number on line "F" from the number on line "J" and write the total on line "K" (i.e., $J - F = K$).
17. Write on line "L" the number of sessions that the participant attended.

EVALUATION STRATEGY #6
Numerical Evaluation Tool

A numerical evaluation strategy should be used only in conjunction with the other methods of evaluation described in this chapter. Numerical evaluation as the *only* method of evaluation typically does not provide sufficient information to allow the program leader to make the necessary program decisions and revisions. Numerical evaluation is simply documenting the number of individuals who have participated in the program or the duration of time that the targeted individual participated in the activity. These data could be compared over time with attendance records of similar programs or the average duration of time that the participants without disabilities engage in an activity. An understanding of which programs have high registration rates and interest levels could be gained. Numerical evaluation also should take into consideration duration (for how long the participants are involved in the programs), program costs, and other features that affect the success of programs.

Before proceeding with the directions, the reader should become familiar with the completed Numerical Evaluation Information Form (see Figure 8.12).

DIRECTIONS FOR NUMERICAL EVALUATION TOOL

1. Write the program's title on line "A."
2. Write the name of the program site on line "B."
3. Write the goal(s) of the program on line "C."
4. On line "D," write the requested program information.
5. On the line in column "E," write the number of participants without disabilities who attended the session.
6. On the line in column "F," write the number of participants with disabilities who attended the session.
7. In column "G," write the date that the session was conducted.

NUMERICAL EVALUATION INFORMATION FORM

A. Program Title: _Me and My Friend_

B. Program Site: _North Commons Recreation Center_

C. Program Goal: _To include people with and without disabilities into a variety of recreation activities at the center._

D. Program Information (include cost, meeting times, duration, day held, age of participants, etc.):

No charge. Program meets Thursdays from 6:30-7:30 p.m. for 6 weeks. The participants are 8 to 11 years of age.

	E. Number of participants without disabilities	F. Number of participants with disabilities	G. Program date	H. Comment
Session				
1	17	4	9-4-97	
2	18	4	9-11-97	
3	18	4	9-18-97	
4	18	3	9-25-97	
5	18	4	10-3-97	
6	18	4	10-10-97	
7				
8				
9				
10				

I. Total number of participants without disabilities	J. Total number of participants with disabilities	K. Total number of participants (with and without disabilities)
107	23	130

L. Number of sessions conducted	M. Average number of participants per session	N. Number of participants registered
6	21.67	22

Figure 8.12. Numerical evaluation information form—completed.

8. If a dramatic shift in attendance for a given session occurred, then write the presumed reason (e.g., snowstorm in Minnesota, excessive heat in Miami) in column "H."

9. Repeat steps 5–8 following each session until the program's termination.

10. On line "I," calculate the total number of participants without disabilities throughout all sessions.

11. On line "J," calculate the total number of participants with disabilities throughout all sessions.

12. On line "K," calculate the total number of participants (with and without disabilities) (i.e., I + J = K).
13. On line "L," write the total number of sessions conducted.
14. Write on line "M" the average number of participants in attendance per session. (To calculate the average number of participants per session, divide the total number of participants [line "K"] by the total number of sessions conducted [line "L"]. 130 participants with and without disabilities ÷ 6 sessions = 21.67).
15. Write on line "N" the total number of registered participants in the program.

SUMMARY

This chapter discussed the benefits of carefully and comprehensively evaluating community recreation programs and described six strategies for conducting program evaluations. It is strongly recommended that some combination of these tools be used to present a comprehensive "picture" of program results and benefits to the participants. The Social Relationships Assessment Procedure (see Chapter 7) should be implemented to assist in evaluating friendship and other social relationship development throughout the recreation program.

Evaluative data are unnecessary and a waste of time unless they are shared with key stakeholders in the program. It is not until the consumers of services, their family members, and agency management also receive this information that these results can be considered (socially) valid and useful. Also, it is the responsibility of the program evaluator to disseminate program findings to professionals in the fields of therapeutic recreation and recreation, park, and leisure services in general to further advance the recreation and leisure services field. It also is necessary to disseminate program results to professionals in related disciplines, such as special education, social work, and rehabilitation, through professional publication and presentation to inform as broad an audience as possible of the results of program efforts.

Exemplary Programs in Inclusive Community Recreation

9

◆ ◆ ◆ ◆ ◆

In the first edition of this book, the authors offered examples of pilot programs that demonstrated the potential effectiveness of exemplary community recreation services to individuals with disabilities. At the time, they proclaimed that the primary responsibility for delivering community recreation services to people with disabilities should be assumed by community park and recreation agencies. Because it is the public recreation and park department's responsibility to meet the needs of all citizens of the community, it would follow that this agency should assume a primary leadership role in delivering community recreation services to people with disabilities. Besides, the principle of normalization has long guided recreation service providers toward including people with disabilities in community recreation, a concept that is now mandated by law.

Since that time, the authors have heard from many people who used the first edition of this book to initiate efforts to include people with disabilities in community recreation programs. Most of these readers have been professionals in related disciplines who were seeking better ways to include recreation as an integral component of a holistic lifestyle. The authors also heard from many park and recreation service providers who were looking forward to initiating services for people with disabilities in order to create a more inclusive community recreation environment. For the most part, all agreed that in an ideal society, park and recreation agencies should be the primary agency responsible for serving the recreation needs of individuals with disabilities. In reality, not all park and recreation agencies have the resources or the expertise to accept this responsibility. Rather, some of the most effective strategies for inclusion have been the results of collaborative efforts among a variety of disciplines. Progressive community park and recreation agencies not only are accepting the responsibility of including people with disabilities as equal members of their programs by providing comprehensive recreation services but also are accepting the advice and assistance from those professionals who have traditionally provided a myriad of services to people with disabilities. As a result, a variety of symbiotic relationships have formed for the purpose of including individuals with disabilities in community recreation.

Exemplary efforts to include people with disabilities are occurring in many recreation programs across the United States and in other countries. This chapter highlights just a few. A range of efforts is represented that reflects a commitment of many professionals to provide inclusive community recreation services for people with disabilities. In some cases, entire community recreation programs have undergone wholesale systems changes in order to be more accommodating and inclusive of citizens with disabilities. These positive steps toward inclusion are the results of collaborative efforts by highly trained professionals who apply innovative recommended practice strategies to change program service delivery (extrinsic strategies) and to support and prepare individuals with disabilities for inclusion (intrinsic strategies). Also presented is an example of an exemplary "homemade" strategy for inclusion, whereby community recreation professionals demonstrate their commitment to equality and inclusion by responding to the needs of one individual at a time. In all cases, readers are invited to share in this sampling of experiences as the following exemplary programs are presented by their designers.

◆ ◆ ◆ ◆

EXEMPLARY PROGRAM I
Project TRAIL (Transition Through Recreation and Integration for Life)

Gail Hoge, John Dattilo, Susanne Schneider, and Katie Bemisderfer

Barriers that restrict leisure choices often result in individuals with mental retardation participating in solitary, passive, home-based activities. One way to overcome barriers and increase the leisure choices of individuals with mental retardation is to provide systematic leisure education. Leisure education can be designed to help people gain knowledge of their leisure needs and interests, understand the relationship and role of recreation to a quality lifestyle, learn about available leisure opportunities, and learn recreation activity skills. The program described here is a component of a field-initiated research and demonstration project sponsored through the Department of Recreation and Leisure Studies at the University of Georgia. The purpose of the project is to meet the leisure needs of people with mental retardation by providing data-based solutions to problems that they experience in leisure. Project TRAIL focuses on helping youths with mental retardation who are completing high school to make a successful transition into community recreation settings. The Project TRAIL leisure education system contains four components that work together to facilitate transition to community leisure involvement: 1) leisure education course, 2) leisure coaching (similar to job coaching) in the community, 3) family and friend support, and 4) follow-up services.

METHODS

Participants

A total of 21 students labeled as having mental retardation requiring intermittent to limited supports from three area high schools in the Southeast participated in

Project TRAIL. The leisure educator and leisure coaches obtained information from each student's individualized education program (IEP) to help determine each student's strengths and needs. In addition, the following three assessments were used to identify the student's leisure needs: 1) the TRAIL Leisure Assessment Battery (T–LAB), 2) three adapted scales of the Leisure Diagnostic Battery (LDB), and 3) the TRAIL Social Relationship Scale (TSRS). The T–LAB consists of nine 8½"×11" laminated circles divided into five to seven sections that contain pictures of 132 recreation activities. Each circle represents a set of either home-based or community-based activities including 1) relaxing at home (e.g., watching TV, listening to music), 2) being creative at home (e.g., painting, drawing, sewing), 3) improving things at home (e.g., making repairs, taking care of animals and plants), 4) doing things at home (e.g., playing a board game, talking on the telephone), 5) learning new things (e.g., fitness classes, going to the library), 6) doing things with people (e.g., parties, shopping), 7) doing outdoor activities (e.g., hunting, picnics), 8) doing sports and exercise (e.g., walking, softball), and 9) doing things for fun that make you feel good (e.g., movies, going to church). The instrument also contains questions related to leisure behaviors (e.g., choice, socialization, enjoyment, assistance) and barriers. The LDB Short Form A provides information about each student's perceived freedom in leisure. Two follow-up LDB scales are barriers to leisure experiences and leisure preferences. The TSRS is used to gain insight into the social world of the participant (e.g., who are his or her friends, who are the people with whom he or she has a relationship and what is the nature of the relationship— friend, service provider, family member). Assessments are completed in approximately two 45-minute sessions, depending on the cognitive abilities of each student. After assessing each student, the leisure education system is implemented.

Leisure Education System

Leisure Education Course The first component of the system was a five-unit leisure education course designed to be taught over 18 weeks. The course was taught three times a week for 45 minutes with each student group. Lessons in each unit included a variety of both didactic and experiential activities. With these students, who had a variety of ability levels in reading and writing (some were unable to read or write), using active experiential games and activities was found to be very effective. The five units, which included leisure appreciation, social interaction and friendship, leisure resources, self-determination, and decision making, are presented in the following section.

The first unit of study in the course was leisure appreciation. In this unit, students gained an understanding of the meaning of leisure and learned about the role of leisure in society and about barriers to leisure. Some learning activities used in this unit included developing a class recreation inventory and role-playing situations involving barriers. In one role-playing activity, students role played a trip to an amusement park. They were told that they needed $24 at the ticket window and that they only had $20 among them. This learning activity was designed to encourage participants to plan some of their experiences to avoid barriers.

In the social interaction and friendship unit, students learned communication and social interaction skills (e.g., how to listen and how to speak to merchants, how to be a friend, how to develop friendships). One of the learning activities used a group of pictures showing people communicating in different ways. Students were asked to identify these forms of communication (e.g., talking, body language). They then practiced using body language to communicate feelings. Some experiential activities used to teach friendship skills were 1) developing an advertisement about the kind of friend they are (students were encouraged to think of qualities to describe themselves that would attract a friend), 2) writing a friendship recipe (students listed the qualities important in a friend), and 3) using the analogy of a tree to friendship and considering what is needed for a friendship to flourish. In addition, role playing was used to teach about friendship. In one role play, a student assumed the role of a friend and another student assumed the role of someone who was not a friend. Following the role play, all students discussed the qualities of friendship and identified who was the friend and who was not the friend in the role play.

In the leisure resources unit, students learned how to use printed resources about recreation activities, spent time identifying and exploring recreation opportunities, and discussed recreation activity ideas. One learning activity required students to generate a list of different activities and identify where those activities could take place in their town using the telephone book, newspaper, or brochures to locate the information needed. Another learning activity used "people resources." Students were taught that friends, family members, and schoolmates are potential sources of information and assistance for leisure participation. Various resource people shared their interests and knowledge on a variety of subjects such as photography, aerobic dance, and gardening. Self-contained instructional packages (SCIPs) were frequently used in this unit to help students learn more about local resources. SCIPs are leisure education games modeled after popular table games such as "Taboo," "Concentration," "Bingo," and "Connect Four," which students found especially enjoyable. Field trips to a variety of recreation, cultural, and volunteer settings were used to reinforce understanding of concepts being taught.

In the self-determination in leisure unit, students learned the value of making choices and taking responsibility for their actions and how to be assertive. Making choices is a skill with which many individuals with mental retardation have little experience. Every lesson gave each student an opportunity to make choices (e.g., choosing the color of pencil they wanted to use to draw, choosing teammates for a learning activity). Role playing helped students learn to differentiate between assertive and aggressive behaviors. Students role played these behaviors and then identified and discussed the behaviors. Another activity was for students to depict their ideal vacation using modeling clay. The intent of the ideal vacation was to have students choose what they wanted to do and then picture themselves actually engaged in the activity.

In the decision-making unit, students learned steps in making a decision by considering factors that influence decisions and associated outcomes. They learned a five-step decision-making model presented on cards (words with pictures). Students practiced making leisure decisions using the cards as a guide with the goal of putting the cards in the proper order for making an informed decision. This unit also involved leisure planning. Each student received a leisure activity planning folder. When thinking about planning an activity, students began with naming a desired recreation activity. They then used the folder to guide them in planning the activity. The plan helped students answer the following questions: 1) Where could I do that activity? 2) When do I want to do it? 3) With whom do I want to do the activity? and 4) What resources (e.g., equipment, cost, transportation) will I need? A typical learning assignment was to ask students to complete some of the steps needed to participate in a recreation activity (e.g., make telephone calls to a recreation department about tennis lessons).

Leisure Coaching The leisure education course was complemented with systematic community-based leisure instruction and support provided by leisure coaches. Similar to job coaches, leisure coaches provided assistance to students while they participated in inclusive community recreation settings and acted as advocates for the students. Initially, leisure coaches worked with students in the classroom. Once a rapport was established and the leisure coaches had thoroughly assessed the needs of the students and families, community-based leisure instruction began. The leisure coaches assisted students in developing and using skills that they learned in class. Leisure coaches helped the students identify personal leisure interests and recreation opportunities and develop skills necessary to pursue these opportunities (e.g., how to use the telephone book, how to gain access to other resources to determine when activities are offered and associated costs, how to get to an activity by using public or private transportation). To help students, the leisure coaches responded to questions and concerns about participating in the community. Direct recreation skills instruction was provided when needed. Once students were participating on a regular basis in an activity, the coaches faded their assistance and presence at the activity.

Leisure coaches also worked with and supported leisure service professionals by responding to questions and concerns and discussing available services. When appropriate, leisure coaches provided consultation to leisure service professionals (e.g., suggesting possible modifications that would promote inclusion).

Family and Friend Involvement An important component of the leisure education system was family and friend involvement. It was important for the success of Project TRAIL that family and friends supported students' independence in the community. To accomplish this task, workshops or personal meetings with the family and friends were held. During these meetings, family and friends were provided with information on a variety of topics including the purpose of leisure education and coaching, what the student was learning, the importance of leisure instruction to transition, and resources that the family might draw upon to assist their family member in developing independent leisure functioning. Family and friends were an important link to helping students maintain the skills that they acquired from their involvement with Project TRAIL.

Follow-Up The last component of the leisure education system was follow-up, which facilitated generalization and maintenance of leisure skills and knowledge. After fading their presence, leisure coaches stayed in contact with their students by telephone (or in person, if necessary) to determine the extent of students' current community leisure participation. If barriers to participation were identified, then the coaches would assist the students in overcoming the barriers. Coaches also maintained contact with the family to encourage their support for their family member's pursuit of leisure participation.

RESULTS OF PROJECT TRAIL FOR ONE STUDENT

The purpose of Project TRAIL was to provide youths with mental retardation with the skills necessary to make a successful transition to community recreation settings. The following case study illustrates the results of a student who experienced success in making this transition.

Assessment

Tracy[1] is a 16-year-old African American adolescent who had been diagnosed as having a mild intellectual impairment, with reading and arithmetic skills at approximately the third-grade level. She had well-developed social skills and cared for her own basic needs, but she had problems controlling her anger. She lived with her grandmother and had occasional contact with other family members. Two brothers in foster care visited her occasionally, and she maintained telephone contact with her mother, who was incarcerated at the time when Tracy was involved with Project TRAIL.

The LDB and the T–LAB indicated that Tracy enjoyed group activities. She perceived the lack of money, transportation, and opportunities as barriers to her leisure participation. These instruments indicated that she felt independent in her choice making and that she thought she needed little assistance in her chosen activities. The TSRS indicated that Tracy had quite a few friends and enjoyed spending time with them and with her family. Most of the activities she pursued were passive and home based, such as watching TV and videos, talking on the telephone, and visiting with family and friends. She seemed to have few community contacts and no established organized recreation pursuits or patterns.

Intervention

Tracy participated in the 18-week leisure education course in her high school, which allowed her a forum to frequently speak about her feelings and ideas. With the support of her leisure coach, Tracy applied the information that she learned in the classroom to community situations.

It was important for Tracy and her leisure coach to establish a trusting relationship. As a result of family issues, Tracy had been in a variety of living situations and had not had many opportunities to experience a stable relationship with an adult role model. Her leisure coach provided her with encouragement, support, and direction. Tracy and her leisure coach spent time identifying interests, gathering information, and participating in community activities. Tracy decided that she wanted to join a bowling league. She spoke to the manager at the local bowling alley and made arrangements for her and her coach to attend a meeting for new members. After a brief introductory period, Tracy made many new friends.

Outcomes

The league members were enthusiastic about having Tracy in their league and were very supportive. The bowling coaches took her aside to show her new techniques and make suggestions. One of the coaches gave Tracy a bowling ball, partially alleviating a monetary barrier. At the end of the first session of the league, Tracy received an award for the most-improved bowler.

Tracy's leisure coach gradually faded contact with her, encouraging Tracy's grandmother to be her primary source of transportation. As a result of an illness in the family, however, her grandmother became unable to transport Tracy to the bowling alley. At this point the leisure coach and Tracy resolved the problem through some assistance from one of the bowling coaches, who found Tracy a ride to the bowling alley. Tracy assumed responsibility for her own transportation from the

---

[1]The student's name has been changed to maintain confidentiality.

bowling alley by arranging for a family member to pick her up. At the time of this writing, Tracy is tied for most-improved bowler and continues to practice and enjoy the league. Her leisure coach keeps in contact with her by telephone and occasionally visits the bowling alley to watch Tracy in action.

Posttests with Tracy show that she is active in the community, participates in sports (organized and casual), and shows less preference for home-based activities. She identifies more than 100 people in her social world and prefers group activities to solitary pursuits. Tracy is included in a community leisure activity, enjoys the benefits of new friendships, and now takes responsibility for her leisure.

CONCLUDING REMARKS

The outcomes achieved by Tracy provide evidence that a leisure education system can be used as a technique to enhance community recreation inclusion for individuals with disabilities. With assistance in building lifelong leisure skills and support networks for maintaining leisure pursuits, individuals with disabilities are enabled to participate alongside their peers without disabilities in community recreation settings.

EXEMPLARY PROGRAM II

Inclusion Across the Life Span:
JCC Intergenerational Inclusive Preschool Program

Linda A. Heyne

When a parent is faced with making choices about educational services for his or her young child with a disability, inclusive preschool is not always a feasible option. Preschool placement is not mandated in every state, and, even when it is, many obstacles can stand in the way of providing inclusive services (see Chapter 3 for common barriers to inclusion). Not the least of these obstacles is recruiting and retaining someone who can consistently provide one-to-one assistance to a child who may need it in order to participate successfully in a classroom. The following case study describes a program at the Jewish Community Center (JCC) of the Greater St. Paul (MN) Area in which older adults from the community step forward to give children this personal assistance and make inclusion a viable option.

BENEFIT OF INTERGENERATIONAL PROGRAMMING

Interaction across multiple age groups actively involves older adults in their communities and instills in younger people an appreciation for experience and time-honored customs, values, and traditions. In today's age-segmented, youth-oriented society, intergenerational programming bridges communication across the age spectrum, promotes older adults as positive role models, provides opportunities for members of all age groups to learn from and respect each other's perspectives and stage in life, and encourages the preservation and regeneration of cultural ideas that can build and strengthen community life. From a necessarily pragmatic perspective, intergenerational programs also are cost efficient. They generally require small amounts of start-up and operating monies, tend to be self-perpetuating, and seldom necessitate extra staffing.

JEWISH COMMUNITY CENTER PROGRAMMING

The JCC offers a wide range of social, recreational, educational, and cultural programs to meet the needs of people across all age groups, from preschool to older adult. One of the JCC's many programs, the Early Childhood program, serves young children ages 3–5 in preschool classrooms. The Early Childhood curriculum addresses the cognitive, socioemotional, and physical development of each child, with an emphasis on allowing the child to grow at his or her own pace. Children's activities include art projects, dramatic play, music, swimming, gymnastics, computers, Jewish education, and free play, to name a few. Individualized goals and objectives serve as guideposts for developing teaching techniques and evaluating outcomes for each child. With such individual attention paid to every student, the Early Childhood curriculum is a naturally inviting venue for including preschoolers with disabilities.

The Senior Adult Department is another program area at the JCC. This department provides an array of services and programs for older adults including exercise programs, volunteer opportunities, social clubs and outings, congregate dining, dance classes, and transportation to and from the JCC. Many of the older adults at the JCC have grandchildren and even great-grandchildren who live outside of the state. The older adults rarely have contact with them and frequently miss them. Many of the older adults also derive satisfaction from donating their time to the various social and educational endeavors of the community. The staff members of the Senior Adult Department were well aware of the many benefits that can result when older people interact with young children and instinctively saw the benefit of including the older adults as "grandparents" in preschool classrooms.

In addition to serving people across the life span, the JCC has a commitment to serving people with disabilities. In 1984, the JCC initiated the Special Needs Program, which aimed to integrate children and youths with disabilities ages 6 months to 21 years into any age-appropriate JCC activity that a child's family requested. Funding was generated, and a certified therapeutic recreation specialist (CTRS) was hired to work with the JCC staff to develop a culture and a programmatic system that welcomed children and youths with disabilities. Many of the strategies recommended in Chapter 6 have been used to facilitate inclusion at the JCC. During the more than 10 years that the program has operated, nearly 200 children with disabilities have been served individually in numerous programs including theater, swimming, gymnastics, child care, basketball, modern dance, youth outings, and summer camp, among many others. Many of the children and youths have participated in programs over a period of several years. Its pioneering efforts in inclusion have won the JCC several awards from such national advocacy organizations as The Arc, The Association for Persons with Severe Handicaps, and the Jewish Welfare Board.

INTERGENERATIONAL INCLUSIVE PRESCHOOL PROGRAM

In the winter of 1994, the three JCC departments described previously—Early Childhood, Senior Adult, and Special Needs—collaborated with the University of Minnesota to form the Intergenerational Inclusive Preschool Program. The overall aim of the program was to bring together preschoolers with and without developmental disabilities ages 3–5 in integrated classrooms through the support and encouragement of older adults from the community. The program had three primary purposes:

1. To promote intergenerational interaction among older adults, classroom teachers, and preschoolers who do and do not have disabilities
2. To promote the play, social, and friendship skills of preschoolers with disabilities
3. To develop an understanding of the effects of the older adults' involvement in the program on their self-esteem, sense of self-efficacy, decision-making skills, and overall quality of life

The program had several corollary purposes. It was designed to give children with disabilities opportunities to play and interact with peers without disabilities at an early age. In addition, through regular exposure to and contact with children with disabilities, acceptance of children with disabilities by children without disabilities in the early years of life would be promoted. The program also aspired to provide families who had children with disabilities with "extended family" support through the involvement of older adults in their lives. Finally, it was designed to explore the many roles that older adults can assume as contributing community members and to understand the ways in which agencies can encourage those contributions.

The remainder of this report highlights the following program components: 1) how the needs and preferences of the children with disabilities and their families, as well as the older adults, were assessed; 2) effective inclusion strategies and recommendations for practitioners who might want to apply these practices at their agencies; and 3) program evaluation and outcomes.

Assessing Needs and Preferences

Assessing needs and preferences of the program participants took place with two groups of people: 1) the children with disabilities and their parents and 2) the older adults.

When a parent approached the JCC to enroll a child with a disability in the preschool, the child care services director reserved a spot for the child in a classroom based on the child's age, the number of hours the child would attend school, and the room capacity (usually 14–16 children). Families could choose from among several schedule options, ranging from 2 mornings a week to 5 full days a week. (This identical procedure was followed when parents of children without disabilities requested enrollment in the preschool.) Usually only one child with a disability was assigned per classroom to reflect the approximate number of people with disabilities that typically exists in society at large. With this natural proportion of students with disabilities to peers without disabilities, the classroom teachers could meet the needs of all of the students without feeling overextended, and the number of additional adults who might be needed as trainer advocates in a classroom could be minimized.

Upon confirming enrollment, which usually occurred several weeks, if not months, before the child's actual involvement in the classroom, the child care services director contacted the special needs director to facilitate the assessment of the child's needs, abilities, and preferences. A meeting was arranged with the family to discuss such issues as communication, physical handling, inappropriate behaviors, mobility, medication, transportation, recreation preferences, and the family's goals for inclusion. Information about the broad purposes of the Intergenerational Inclusive Preschool Program also was shared with parents, as well as the involvement of older adults in classrooms to promote inclusion. Based on the outcomes of this meeting, the degree of experience that classroom teachers had working with children with disabilities, as well as other classroom variables (e.g., the children's general activity level, their ability to play independently), a decision was made regarding the need to provide the child with a volunteer advocate (see Chapter 6 for more information about volunteer advocacy). This decision was made collaboratively, with input from parents, classroom teachers, the child care services director, and the special needs director.

In the meantime, individual meetings were set up with the older adults to assess their needs, abilities, and expectations and to discuss their roles in classrooms. In one-to-one interviews, the older adults were asked the following questions: What are your reasons for volunteering for this program? What prior experiences have you had interacting with children with disabilities? What unique contributions do you think older adults can offer young children in a preschool setting? What talents do you bring to the classroom? What are your expectations about working in the classrooms? What problems, if any, do you anticipate? What kind of training do you think you will need to work effectively with the children? Through this line of questioning, matches were made between the older adults and the children with disabilities, and the roles that the older adults would assume in the classrooms developed.

Approximately 2–3 weeks prior to the first day of school, the special needs director arranged a meeting among the important players in the inclusion process—the parent(s), the child with a disability, the classroom teachers, the older adult, and the trainer advocate (if one was needed). At this meeting, everyone had an opportunity to introduce him- or herself and to learn more about the family's needs, preferences, goals, and special considerations related to the child's participation in the classroom. Everyone also discussed the roles that each of the key players could play to promote inclusion. For example, a parent typically provided initial explanation about the child's needs and abilities, as well as ongoing feedback about participation. The teacher generally chose activities that emphasized socialization and cooperation, augmented the child's abilities, and created a welcoming environment for the child. The trainer advocate usually provided the child with one-to-one physical assistance, adaptations, and special behavioral instructions. The older adult often encouraged interaction with classmates, provided supportive comments and reinforcement, and served as a kind of "grandparent" mentor to all of the children in the classroom. This initial assessment process helped shape the child's instructional goals and objectives. It also gave the key players the grounding upon which to build future communication and collaboration.

Inclusion Strategies and Recommendations

As part of the JCC's commitment to providing inclusive recreation services to children and youths with disabilities, what have become known as *recommended professional practices* in inclusive recreation were consistently employed. These strategies included individualized needs and preference assessments, selection of age-appropriate and preferred activities, environmental and task analyses, individualized adaptations, trainer advocacy, behavioral teaching techniques, cooperative goal structuring, disability orientations for peers without disabilities, networking, ongoing monitoring, and program evaluation. In addition to these recommended strategies, other special techniques were used to attract, train, and involve older adults in the inclusion process, as well as to encourage agency staff members to work together to solve problems that arose. These special techniques, as well as suggestions for applying recommended practices to other sites, are described in the following sections.

Recruiting Older Adults   Several methods were used to recruit older adults from the community to assist the children with disabilities in preschool classrooms. Fliers that described the project and the roles that older adults would play were mailed to JCC members who were known to be age 65 or older. Recruitment talks were given at JCC events that older adults typically attended. An article about the program was published in the agency monthly newsletter. Announcements were posted on the Senior Adult Department bulletin board. Staff members from the Senior Adult Department approached individual older adults, encouraging their participation in the program. Word of mouth was another effective means of attracting older adults. Rather than relying on a single recruitment tactic, this combination of recruitment strategies was necessary to reach the broad range of older adults who took part in the many activities that the JCC offered.

When older adults were later asked what attracted them to the program, they commonly reported three compelling features of the program. First, the older adults looked forward to working one-to-one with a child with a disability. Forming a relationship with a child, learning about the child's disability, learning how to meet the child's needs in the classroom, and watching the child progress over time were dynamics that appealed to the older adults. Second, the older adults were attracted to the intergenerational aspect of the program. They believed that it was beneficial for all age groups to intermingle and learn from one another. They also believed that their experience gave them a special understanding of people that could benefit the students. Third, the older adults wanted to contribute to their communities, indeed felt a certain humanitarian obligation to do so. They wanted to make a concrete difference in someone's life.

Training Older Adults   Older people and young children often share a common learning style—they prefer to learn what they inquire about rather than what others prescribe. In developing the training curriculum for the older adults, therefore, suggestions were solicited from them regarding information that would be valuable for working with children in classrooms. The older adults typically responded that they would like to learn more about the children's disabilities, classroom protocol, and inclusion techniques. Based on these suggestions, the older-adult training was designed and implemented through both informal communications and formal, scheduled meetings.

To prepare the older adult to enter the classroom, he or she was invited to a preliminary meeting with the family to learn about the child, the disability, and the family's perspectives. To clearly identify older adults as Early Childhood staff members, they were given the same JCC staff name badges that were worn by all of the Early Childhood staff members. The older adults also were given a job description that outlined the general role that they would play in the classroom. This job description emphasized the importance of giving children opportunities to interact independently with play materials and classmates before offering assistance. It also outlined how a child's involvement in the group could be nurtured through providing verbal reminders and additional instructions, showing children how to use play materials, and encouraging social interaction with classmates.

To clarify the role of the older adults in classrooms, the teachers also were given job descriptions related to inclusion. Their role emphasized the importance of working as a team with the older adults to support inclusion. For instance, rather than expect the older adult to tend to all of the needs of a child with a disability, it was recommended that teachers also interact with the child and address his or her needs, just as they would typically address the needs of all children in the classroom. The teachers' active involvement in inclusion created a tone of acceptance and equal participation and gave older adults some latitude in assisting and forming relationships with other students.

As additional preparatory training, each older adult visited the classroom; observed classroom dynamics; and discussed with teachers the classroom environment, activities, rules, schedules, and children's goals. Based on the needs and concerns identified by the family, the special needs director provided additional instruction in inclusion strategies as appropriate, such as a special teaching technique, reinforcement procedure, or adaptation.

To supplement this individualized, child-centered training, the older adults took part in a series of four 2-hour training sessions that addressed the overall program goals. In designing and delivering the training, care was taken to structure lessons so that they would be interactive, engage the older adults in practicing methods and procedures, and promote concrete problem solving. This training was provided jointly by JCC and university staff members and included the following components:

- Early Childhood curriculum
- Special Needs Program overview, process, and goals
- Classroom emergency and accident policies
- Language that promotes dignity of people with disabilities
- Suggestions for communicating with people with disabilities
- Tips for leading activities
- Behavioral teaching techniques such as cueing, prompting, modeling, physical guidance, redirection, and positive reinforcement
- Policies, procedures, and guidelines for avoiding and addressing problem behaviors
- Problem-solving discussions

As older adults began working in classrooms, they received ongoing training through monthly staff meetings that all Early Childhood staff members attended. These meetings provided the staff with opportunities to work through problems, communicate, collaborate, and receive additional training related to early childhood education or inclusive recreation. The special needs director also provided the older adults with continuous training related to the specific needs of individual children as they arose throughout the program.

Involving Older Adults in Classrooms With this advance preparation and training, the older adult was introduced to the children in the classroom as a "new teacher" rather than as a "special helper" for a child with a disability. The introduction was made in this way to reduce the potential stigmatization that might be placed on a child who was assigned a special helper when no other student had a helper, as well as to give all of the children opportunities to benefit from contact and interaction with the older adult. Older adults typically assisted in classrooms two to three times a week for approximately 2–3 hours each time.

The first priority of the older adult was to provide whatever assistance the child with a disability might need to participate as fully and as successfully as possible in activities with the other children. In addition to this responsibility—and depending on how much assistance the child required—the older adult also fulfilled a number of other tasks in the classroom. For example, the older adult distributed play materials, assisted children with operating toys, read or told the children stories, played games, led craft activities, provided encouragement and positive feedback, and reminded children to respect each other and play well together.

Roles for the older adults were kept fluid and individualized to match classroom needs and the talents, goals, and limitations of older adults. For example, some older adults preferred to be very spontaneous in their interactions with the children; others preferred a more planned approach, with clearly defined tasks, expectations, and outcomes. Classroom dynamics and children's needs also influenced the roles that older adults played. In some classrooms, several children (in addition to the child with the disability) benefited from extra attention from the older adult. As a result, the older adult rotated from child to child as needed. In other classrooms, the child with the disability needed the support of a consistent, one-to-one relationship, so the older adult stayed close at hand.

Applying Case Study to Other Settings When presenting case-study recommendations, one risks the danger of intimating that all practices work equally well across all places. That, of course, is not the case, and each practitioner or parent will probably need to adapt the practices recommended here to fit his or her individual site. There also is the danger of creating an illusion that because the program has been identified as a "model" program, there were no pitfalls encountered along the way. That, of course, also is misleading. The remainder of this section offers some suggestions that will help others avoid some of the problems that were encountered in developing this program.

Communication among as many players as participated in this intergenerational program can be a challenge, especially when problems arise. First and foremost, teamwork and collaborative problem solving should be emphasized, along with open communication among all players. If direct communication among those actually involved in the classroom is difficult, then supervisory staff—such as a special needs director, child care services director, or senior adult supervisor—can serve as on-site contacts for facilitating communication. Program staff members can draw on their expertise in aging, early childhood education, and recreation inclusion to solve problems. Staff members also can call on them for counsel, to arrange meetings, to facilitate discussions, and to serve as mediators. It is important that each person involved in the program knows whom to consult if a problem should arise.

Confusion about roles in classrooms also can create problems. For instance, if a child with a disability happens to pinch another child, and a teacher observes the incident, then various questions can arise. Whose responsibility is it to intervene, the teacher's, the older adult's, or the trainer advocate's? How should the pinching incident be handled? Had the older adult observed the incident, would he or she have felt qualified to handle the situation? What follow-up is needed? Questions of this sort often are so classroom-specific that they can be resolved only by the people who work in the classroom. Roles, responsibilities, and classroom protocol may need to be clarified. Job descriptions may need to be developed, either verbally or in writing, that clearly specify each person's responsibilities. If job descriptions are developed for older adults, then they should be tailored to meet their individual needs. That is, some people may need only a few verbal directions to understand their roles; others may need activities clearly defined in writing. A staff person may need to strike a balance between giving an older adult very specific guidelines and allowing the person's natural, unique "grandparenting" skills to emerge. In general, one should avoid overscripting the older adult (unless, of course, the person finds this useful).

Agency staff members can play an important role in creating a work environment in which older adults feel comfortable. For instance, many older adults live active, busy lives. Because of this, staff members may need to be flexible in the demands they place on older adults' time and schedules. Staff members can teach older adults the games and activities that will be used in the classroom before they actually begin working with children. In doing so, older adults will feel more competent and prepared to do an effective job. It also is essential to share classroom procedures and rules with older adults so that they are aware of appropriate protocol to follow and boundaries that are important to respect. When identifying classroom tasks for older adults, staff members should keep in mind that some older adults might not be comfortable performing certain tasks, such as changing diapers, lifting children or heavy objects, pushing a wheelchair, or other physically demanding tasks. If this is the case, then classroom teachers, aides, or trainer advocates may need to share in these responsibilities. Frequent opportunities for older adults to practice safe handling or lifting procedures would be important to arrange. As older adults assist children, they may need to be cautioned about providing "too much" help and creating a dynamic of dependency between the older adult and the child. In addition, if an older adult appears discouraged that a child's progress is slow, then staff members may need to remind him or her that growth for the child may be realized in small segments and that changes may not be obvious except when viewed over time.

Last, and most important, staff members can play a critical role in frequently reminding older adults of the value of their efforts and contributions. Staff members' appreciation can be shown through a casual comment in a school hallway, a special acknowledgment at a staff recognition party, a newsletter article, or a birthday card. Older adults' unique contributions also can be recognized by inviting them to share information about their lives or lore about how things were done when they were children. For example, older adults can teach children the art of making latkes, share a game that was popular when they were children, provide instruction in their favorite hobby, or tell children stories about their families. Regular affirmation of the valuable roles that older adults play in the lives of all of the children in the intergenerational program will be greatly appreciated.

Evaluation and Outcomes

Program outcomes primarily were evaluated through regular one-to-one interviews with the older adults, classroom staff members, and parents. Questions were asked related to program benefits, problems, and new directions. Through the information gathered from these interviews, the following two case stories about Ida and Sid were developed.

◆ ◆ ◆

Ida, 85, volunteered to assist Maggie, 4, in her classroom because she "wanted to do something that's productive." Using a cane to enhance mobility, Ida walked five blocks to the JCC twice a week to assist Melanie. (In unfavorable Minnesota weather, she arranged a ride through the JCC Senior Shuttle.) Each morning, as Ida walked into the classroom, not only Maggie but all of the children would greet her with a big "Hi, Ida!"

Even though Ida said that she felt "inadequate" at times when assisting Maggie, she thought that it was important for her to take on the challenge. She explained, "There were a lot of times that I said, 'I don't think I can do that,' but then I said, 'Yes, you can.' Like when I picked up Maggie the first time. I was scared. I really was scared. She just jumped into my arms on the playground—all of the sudden there she was—so I just dug my knees into the sand [and caught her]." Ida believes that participating in this program has made a difference in how capable and valuable she feels. She said, "Well, I feel a sense of accomplishment. You try to do something that's productive, and I would say this is productive."

◆ ◆ ◆

When Sid, 73, read the recruitment flier that was mailed to his home, he called the JCC saying that he wanted to be involved in the program for humanitarian reasons and because he missed his grandchildren in Arizona. Sid was matched with Zach, 5, who was the same age as his grandson. "Zach's like a surrogate grandchild for me," Sid explained. "It's as if I'm playing with my own grandson."

In the classroom, Sid formed a rapport with Zach, helped him play and get along with the other children, and, when Zach's attention wandered, brought his focus back to the game or activity in front of him. Besides helping Zach, Sid also was there to help Zach's classmates. Sid assisted children in solving playground disagreements, provided an extra ear to listen to a child's lament, and helped children put on and take off their jackets. He laughed and said, "I'm known as the *zipper-upper!*"

As much as Sid helped Zach and his classmates, Sid thought that they did more for him than he did for them. Sid appreciated how the experience gave him something worthwhile to do after retirement. He observed, "I think there's a tendency for people like me to have a tough time getting used to retirement. I've only been retired for 2 years so it's still hard. I miss the social part of my work and this is a nice substitute." Sid continued, "I really feel I've done something to help. I feel that I am doing something useful. I get a kick out of [Zach's] reactions to me. Just seeing these kids—they keep me young! I get a lot of satisfaction out of it."

◆ ◆ ◆

When classroom teachers were asked what they thought about older adults joining their early childhood staff, they responded overwhelmingly with praise. Having an older adult in the classroom, they said, gave them extra time to provide individual assistance to children or to organize an activity. Staff members commented on the many ways that older adults helped out in classrooms, how the children "loved" them, and how the preschoolers would run up to them the minute they came into the room. The staff members' response was so favorable toward the older adults that teachers who did not have children with disabilities in their classrooms began to inquire, "Why can't I have an older adult in my classroom, too?"

Parents also believed that their children with disabilities benefited tremendously from the extra assistance that the older adults provided and from the intergenerational exposure. For instance, Maggie's mother, like many parents at one time or another, occasionally had difficulty coaxing Maggie to go to school. Her most persuasive strategy was to tell Maggie, "You'll get to see Ida today!" and she was ready to go. Another parent spoke eloquently about the value of the intergenerational component of the program: "I really like that 'grandparent' aspect. They have just everything to contribute—the mentorship, they have so much life experience—and their wealth of knowledge and patience after having been through so much over the years. Kids don't have too much experience with older adults. I think it's a vital connection that has really been lost in society today. I think it's real important to develop that relationship. I just think the extended network is very important."

CONCLUDING REMARKS

Intergenerational programming presents an opportunity to develop inclusive programs while simultaneously utilizing the talents often uniquely found among older adults. As children with disabilities become included in community recreation programs and as older adults are called upon to contribute their skills, knowledge, and resources, programmers begin to develop a truly inclusive community, improving the quality of life for everyone involved.

EXEMPLARY PROGRAM III

Northeast Passage: An Innovative Model for Community-Based Service Delivery

Janet Sable and Jill Gravink

Northeast Passage (NEP), a chapter of Disabled Sports, USA, is a nonprofit organization based in Durham, New Hampshire. Its mission is to create an environment in which individuals with physical disabilities can recreate with as much freedom of choice and independence as their peers without disabilities. NEP is founded on grass-roots support and is led by a consumer-steered Board of Directors. Program development is flexible and responsive to the desires and needs of its individual consumers.

The organization offers six distinctive programs, each designed to provide solutions to real problems. When conceptualizing the programs, NEP did not ask consumers what they did for fun; rather, it asked what was keeping them from doing what they wanted in leisure. Driven by consumer input, the decision was to not focus on a specific sport or activity because everyone's concept of recreation is different. Instead, NEP addressed what was preventing independent recreation. What was keeping someone from gaining access to recreation within one's community just like any other individual?

Certain themes emerged from the responses to these questions. Problems crystallized around specific themes: 1) lack of information, 2) lack of knowledge about equipment and individual modifications, 3) need for skill development, 4) the expense of adaptive equipment, 5) inaccessible facilities, and 6) a dearth of opportunity. NEP designed its programs to eliminate these problems and to clear the path to independent recreation involvement.

NEP facilitates the transition for individuals with physical disabilities from the rehabilitation facility to the home and community by developing functional and recreation skills, modifying and adapting equipment based on individual need, dispensing information on recreation resources, creating opportunities for sport, and offering access to adaptive equipment. At the same time, it works on opening the doors for opportunity within the community by providing in-services to recreation service providers and consultation with private and public providers to problem-solve individual needs.

NEP PROGRAMS

The six programs offered through NEP are

1. AIM for Independence—Activity Instructional Modules
2. Equipment Rental Program—offering expensive adaptive equipment at a low rental cost, which opens the door to independent involvement
3. Sports Development Program—in cooperation with other New England agencies, recreational wheelchair sports, competitive wheelchair sports, and youth development in wheelchair athletics are offered
4. Accessible Vacations—organized "get-aways"
5. Education and Advocacy—promoting equal access to recreation for people with disabilities
6. Resource File—an information and networking database connecting people with resources

AIM for Independence

This modular program was designed for consumers who want to be able to sample different activities without getting tied to a "special" program. Modules offer entry-level instructional clinics in various sports and recreation activities such as water skiing, scuba diving, handcycling, kayaking, conditioning, tennis, tai chi, stunt kite flying, and sledge hockey. Activities are selected based on the interest of members, and several new and different instructional modules are offered each year. Each module includes people with a variety of physical disabilities and those without disabilities. In addition, family members, significant others, and friends are introduced to the activity and the available adaptive equipment. Every module provides skilled instruction; adapted equipment; and ample support from friends, family, and volunteers. Each module provides the individual with a safe and positive first experience as well as all of the facts necessary to make an informed decision about continued involvement in the activity. Information on how and where to take part in the activity in the future is available at each module.

Equipment Rental Program

The Equipment Rental Program was created based on consumers' feedback that even if they knew how to participate in a sport and where to find an accessible environment, the cost of the equipment prevented their involvement; adapted recreation equipment often is prohibitively expensive. Designed to remove this barrier of cost, the Equipment Rental Program offers true freedom and independence. People rent equipment and recreate where they want, when they want, and with whom they want. With nearly $40,000 worth of equipment available, the program opens the door to 10 different sports and offers a progression of equipment to meet the needs of people with different disabilities (e.g., sit-skis, bi-skis, mono-skis). Similarly, a progression of equipment based on developing skill level is available (e.g., beginner water ski, intermediate, trick skis). Consumers use this program in a variety of ways. They may rent a particular piece of equipment several times per season. They may try out several different pieces of equipment to determine what they like before making a purchase. Others use the program to develop competency in a sport before initiating a purchase. For example, a member rented a beginner board for water skiing and then purchased a higher performance board for himself after he had acquired the skills. Community recreation departments and public schools have rented equipment to increase the accessibility and integration of their sponsored ski trips and skating parties. The demand for this program is best conveyed through a snapshot of one week's consumer use: During an average week in February, 19 pieces of rental equipment were used by 21 different consumers.

Sports Development Program

Sports Development, in cooperation with other organizations in New England, fills the void in wheelchair sports opportunities in northern New England. This is the only program offered that is an end in itself as opposed to a means to independent involvement in community recreation. Still, under the umbrella of this program, consumers are completely independent and responsible for coordinating the sport and future direction of the program.

The sports development program has three components: recreational wheelchair sports, competitive wheelchair sports, and youth development in wheelchair athletics. The recreational sports target pockets of interest to develop pick-up wheelchair basketball, sledge hockey, rowing, or other sports of interest. The focus is on a consistent opportunity for fun and fitness. If the interest becomes strong in a particular sport and consumers are interested in competition, then NEP facilitates developing a competitive team to join the national leagues. The decision to go competitive is entirely consumer based; consumers are the active catalysts to the sport's development.

Another identified subproblem of the lack of wheelchair sports opportunities is the limited number of opportunities for teenagers and young adults with newly acquired disabilities resulting in mobility impairments in New England to develop skills in competitive team and individual sports. NEP offers a summer residential skills camp in wheelchair basketball and wheelchair tennis. The camp is held at the University of New Hampshire when other sports camps for youths are in session so that although the sport is specific to individuals with physical disabilities, the setting is fully inclusive.

Accessible Vacations

Each planned vacation has three goals:

1. To provide a safe and accessible vacation experience for individuals with disabilities and their friends without disabilities in which the challenge is the activity, not accessibility
2. To work together with a community outfitter/service provider to offer an inclusive and accessible vacation experience
3. To establish future access of the outfitter's facilities and services so that they are able to accommodate individuals with disabilities in the flow of their daily operations

This approach ensures that NEP's involvement has an impact beyond a one-time trip. Consumers on NEP vacations are aware that they may be the first individuals with disabilities served by this agency. They come on the trip for the vacation experience but are willing to offer their expertise to improve service delivery for others who will follow. This offers a unique opportunity for teamwork among the community service provider, consumers, and NEP. For each vacation, NEP identifies an outfitter or service provider who is interested in improving the accessibility of its business. If necessary, NEP's connection with the outfitter can begin up to a year before the trip. NEP offers input on facility and program design and helps brainstorm equipment modifications to increase accessibility. NEP builds on the expertise at hand and the outfitter in the activity in modification and accessibility to create new opportunities. It returns to NEP's mission, which is to create an environment in which individuals with physical disabilities can recreate with as much freedom of choice and independence as their peers without disabilities.

Based on consumer requests, NEP's vacations have centered around outdoor adventure, sport, and wellness. NEP has offered weekends of dogsledding, sea kayaking, whitewater rafting, and a wellness retreat.

Education and Advocacy

Discussing, explaining, and teaching the techniques and benefits necessary for accessible recreation are consistent tasks of NEP and take place within every program offered. The Education and Advocacy program was specifically developed because consumers who are independent and ready to gain access to private and public recreation found that the community was not always ready to have them. NEP provides in-service education to public and private providers of recreation services to create more environments that are accessible and usable to individuals with disabilities. These in-services occur in a variety of settings. Staff members have conducted disability awareness trainings with public agencies and private corporations. They have brainstormed modifications for an activity or piece of equipment with a physical education teacher or recreation program director and assisted with an accessibility study for developing a new state park. A second focus of this program is increasing the awareness of consumers of potential recreation opportunities. NEP staff members work with the therapeutic recreation staff in a rehabilitation hospital and provide consultation to a patient prior to discharge to help with the transition to the community. In addition to rehabilitation hospitals, in-services are provided to other support agencies (e.g., independent living centers, National Spinal Cord Injury Association). Staff members offer telephone consultations with individual friends, families, and consumers living in the community.

Resource File

A computerized database of accessible equipment, programs, and sites is available to both consumers and providers in the New England region. One of NEP's objectives is to connect people with resources. NEP views the resource file as a means to providing a passage to independent recreation. At times, that can best be accomplished by just sharing information. NEP has a continuously expanding database including information on adapted equipment, specific programs, instructors, instruction, travel, and accessibility. If NEP staff members cannot answer a consumer's question, then they try to connect the consumer with someone who can.

CREATING PARTNERSHIPS

NEP is committed to using the existing resources and enhancing them to establish access for all. Guided by the vision of the organization as a "passage," NEP staff members work to establish access to recreation opportunities. NEP works to build the network and not duplicate services. This may best be articulated through the following example. Skiing is a substantial part of the winter recreation scene in New England. The instruction and equipment technology available to people with disabilities have progressed to a point that nearly everyone can experience the exhilaration of the sport. Six years ago, NEP offered instructional modules to introduce consumers to the sport of skiing and shared information on the limited number of instructional programs in the region. The clinic was always full. Over the course of several years, the existing adapted skiing programs grew stronger and larger, and several new ski programs emerged. There no longer was a need for NEP to provide ski instruction. Instead, NEP worked as a referral agency for other programs, providing their literature to NEP's consumers and listing their telephone numbers and special events in NEP's newsletter.

NEP's role shifted to creating independent access to those ski areas that did not have adapted ski programs. NEP attacked this need for more access on a number of fronts. It consulted with ski areas on improving accessibility and worked with several other chapters of Disabled Sports, USA, and the Professional Ski Instructors Association to design a consulting program for ski areas to increase overall access to their services. Simultaneously, NEP increased the amount of ski equipment available in the Equipment Rental Program so that independent skiers could go to the ski area of their choice. During one winter, NEP's equipment was on the mountains of 12 different ski areas in New England. Only six of those areas had any type of adaptive ski program. Independent skiers would have been unable to gain access to the other six areas without NEP's equipment. This example illustrates how NEP's role shifts and is flexible to respond to the needs of NEP's consumers. By working with other programs and service providers to create partnerships, as opposed to competition, NEP is reaching the goal of accessible recreation.

CONCLUDING REMARKS

The effectiveness of the Northeast Passage program is dependent on education and consumer input. People with disabilities who become aware of the myriad of recreation opportunities available to them can make informed decisions regarding personal recreation pursuits. Northeast Passage encourages others to work closely with consumers and the providers of community recreation services to ensure the inclusion of all interested participants.

EXEMPLARY PROGRAM IV

Rural Recreation Integration Project:
Connecting Recreation and Human Services Providers to Better Meet the Leisure Needs of People with Disabilities

Lynn Anderson, Carla Brown, and Patricia Soli

People with disabilities in North Dakota now reside primarily in communities, both large and small, across the state. This was not always the case. In the early 1980s, most people with disabilities lived in institutional settings such as state schools and state hospitals. In 1981, a lawsuit brought forward by the Association for Retarded Citizens (ARC) of North Dakota mandated deinstitutionalization (*ARC of*

North Dakota v. Olson, 1982). As a result of this court action, large numbers of people with disabilities were "placed" in a variety of less restrictive living environments throughout the state. Although communities may have been *physically* prepared to accept individuals with disabilities, they were not adequately prepared to *socially* include these individuals in their communities. Physical inclusion has been fostered by the human services system, which has met the housing and vocational needs of people with disabilities. Yet recreation and leisure needs, which would foster social inclusion, have not been adequately met. The leisure service system is the system that traditionally provides recreation services to communities. Recreation service providers in North Dakota have felt unprepared for including people with disabilities in the services that they provide. In addition, there is limited communication between the human services and leisure service delivery systems. Professionals working in the human services system are trained to work with people with disabilities and are highly aware of the leisure and social needs and barriers that people with disabilities encounter. Leisure service providers, however, have the facilities, resources, and expertise in recreation programming but lack awareness of the needs of people with disabilities living in their communities or how to meet them.

The Rural Recreation Integration Project (RRIP), a collaborative effort between the North Dakota Parks and Recreation Department and the University of North Dakota, has challenged itself to bridge the gap between these two service delivery systems. The intent of the program is to develop and help sustain naturally occurring networks in which resources and expertise can be shared to most effectively meet the recreation needs of people with disabilities in their communities. The purpose of the project is to facilitate the physical and social inclusion of people with disabilities in existing community recreation and leisure programs and services. By providing training and technical assistance, project staff members aid in developing skills, knowledge, and networks of leisure service providers and human services providers in North Dakota as they work to include people with disabilities. This is critical to a rural state in which resources are limited.

As a result, the efforts of the RRIP to promote and support inclusion of people with disabilities occur at both the systems level and the individual level. The following case study provides one example of the outcomes of this "top-down, bottom-up" approach. Collaborative efforts among The Arc of Upper Valley, the Pine to Prairie Girl Scout Council, and one child with a developmental disability to improve the inclusive nature of community recreation services are discussed. The efforts for inclusion required changes in administration of the agencies and in the individual child and neighborhood Girl Scout troop.

METHODS

Agency Level

The Arc of Upper Valley, with administrative offices in Grand Forks, North Dakota, provides services to the northeastern part of North Dakota as an advocacy and resource center for people with disabilities and their families. The Pine to Prairie Girl Scout Council, also with administrative offices in Grand Forks, oversees the Girl Scout troops, camps, and activities in eastern North Dakota and northwestern Minnesota. Both agencies completed the training provided by the RRIP.

Training on Inclusion   The following is an outline of curriculum topics covered in the 27-hour training:

Session 1:   What is inclusion; disability awareness
Session 2:   Physical disabilities; physical accessibility; universal design; ADA
Session 3:   Mental illness; social inclusion and programmatic accessibility; the inclusion process
Session 4:   Developmental disabilities; activity and equipment adaptations
Session 5:   Advocacy; facilitating friendship development
Session 6:   Administrative concerns with inclusion
Session 7:   Exemplary programs in inclusive recreation
Session 8:   The future of inclusion and people with disabilities
Session 9:   Structuring for social inclusion; discussion and questions—where do we go from here?

Forming Partnerships/Changes to Service Delivery   Assignments were an integral part of the training. Leisure service and human services agencies formed partnerships and completed the assignments together. Example assignments include critiquing mission statements, policies, procedures, and registration processes to assess them for their level of inclusion of people of all abilities. Another example is an architectural accessibility survey of one or more of the agencies' facilities used for recreation programming. The Arc and the Girl Scouts worked through the assignments together. They found many similarities in their missions. Although the Girl Scouts targeted girls as their primary group for service provision and The Arc targeted both children and adults with disabilities, they both were striving to provide a safe and comfortable place for people to discover the best in themselves and to learn to find the best in others, regardless of ability level. The Girl Scouts also identified the need to revise their annual field staff training to include disability awareness and inclusion as an important topic. The Arc and the RRIP staff assisted them with the training sessions. With a solid foundation of communication and a knowledge of each other's programs, goals, expertise, and resources, the two agencies were ready for the final assignment in the RRIP training—to identify individuals with disabilities and begin including them in leisure service programs. The Arc was able to easily identify girls with disabilities who were interested in participating in Girls Scouts. The Girl Scout Council was able to locate and initiate contact with the troop leaders in the girls' neighborhoods.

Individual Level

Assessing Leisure Needs and Barriers   Deanne, a 9-year-old with a developmental disability, was one of the girls identified as having an interest in becoming a Girl Scout. Deanne was an only child who lived with her mother in a new neighborhood. Deanne completed an interview, with her mother's assistance, to determine her needs and preferences for leisure, friendship, health, and other areas related to quality of life (see Table 9.1). She also completed an assessment of perceived barriers to leisure in her home, community, and school. From the assessment, it was determined that Deanne had only a few friends at school and no friends in her neighborhood. She had very few leisure skills and limited exposure to leisure choices. Much of her time was spent watching TV with her mother or playing by herself at the playground near her apartment. She expressed feelings of sadness when playing: "I don't think nobody likes to play with me . . . nobody ever plays with me." Barriers identified in the assessment were lack of community

Table 9.1. Topics assessed in the quality-of-life and barriers-to-leisure interview

Quality of life[a]	Barriers to leisure[b]
• Recreation participation	• Community resources
• Nature and quality of leisure	• Architectural barriers
• Choice/self-determination	• Family support
• Free-time usage	• Support services
• Friends	• Caregiver support
• Community involvement	• Transportation
• Values	• Money
• Health/fitness	
• Self-esteem	
• Physical environment	

[a]Qualitative, open-ended probes
[b]Three-point Likert scale

support and transportation difficulties, as her mother did not own or drive a car. Her identified needs included increasing her leisure experiences, being a part of a peer group, and making friends in her neighborhood. She was excited about the idea of joining Girl Scouts.

Working with the Family An important part of the inclusion process was working with Deanne's mother and helping her become comfortable with the inclusion process. She did not understand what the Girl Scouts were all about. She had fears of Deanne being teased, left out, and "made fun of." She also was concerned about the cost of Deanne being involved and transportation difficulties. Deanne's mother met with both the Girl Scouts and The Arc representatives to help address these concerns. They shared information on Girl Scouts, giving Deanne and her mother thorough orientation to the organization and its activities. They suggested providing an orientation with the girls without disabilities in which they would focus on Deanne's similarities with the other girls. They also suggested setting up an informal meeting with the troop leader and going to the house in which the meetings would be held to meet the leader and assess the environment. The Girl Scouts worked out a reduced fee for Deanne to attend the troop and participate in planned activities. They suggested that The Arc provide transportation for Deanne until she learned the route to walk from her house to the troop leader's house. All of these suggestions were welcomed by Deanne's mother and implemented.

Preparing the Program Environment After assessing Deanne's needs and interest in the Girl Scouts, a meeting was held among a representative from The Arc, a representative from the Girl Scout Council office, the neighborhood Girl Scout troop leader, and a staff member from RRIP. At the meeting, Deanne's needs, interests, and necessary accommodations for successful inclusion were discussed. In particular, the troop leader was given ideas on how to facilitate social inclusion. Because Deanne would be new to the group and had a tendency to isolate herself in uncomfortable situations, the participants in this planning meeting brainstormed suggestions to structure the social interaction at the first troop meeting. Activities to promote social inclusion included 1) developing a buddy system—on the first day, each girl was given a name tag with a colored dot and had to find her partner with the same color dot; 2) providing activities in which each girl had a portion of the materials necessary to complete a task; 3) providing activities that ensured equal status to all girls in the group; and 4) establishing a troop motto, name, and flag. In addition, the troop leader met with Deanne and her mother before the first meeting to minimize their fears and concerns.

The next step in the process was orienting the peers without disabilities in the group. The Arc representative met with the Girl Scout troop on the first day to share with them Deanne's interest and upcoming involvement in the troop. Because at times Deanne said or did things that were inappropriate, it was important for the girls to understand that she is still more alike than different from them. The Arc representative focused on what Deanne could do, as well as the similarities she had with the other troop members.

Implementing the Inclusion Program   The next step in the process was implementing the inclusion program. Deanne asked The Arc representative to walk her to the door on the first day because she was very nervous and was afraid that nobody would talk to her. The Arc representative remained there for about 10 minutes as the troop leader used the strategies previously discussed to begin including Deanne with the other girls.

Evaluating the Inclusion Program for Deanne   The primary method of evaluation in this case study was ongoing monitoring and interviewing of the key participants. One of the key participants was the leader of Troop #26. According to the troop leader, Deanne was included in the group without any negative comments ever being made about her. She was accepted and liked by the girls in the troop; the transition was a "smooth and fun experience." Deanne was active in the activities of the troop, and when needing assistance, the other girls willingly provided it. The troop leader emphasized the need to work together on all tasks, facilitating peer assistance among the girls. Overall, the troop leader felt that the inclusion process went well and actually improved her troop activities.

Deanne developed a friendship with one of the girls in the troop. The friendship was nurtured by The Arc representative as a solution to Deanne's transportation barriers, as this particular girl lived very near Deanne. The Arc representative helped Deanne learn the social skills first to offer her friend a ride with her and later to ask her friend to walk home from school and to the troop leader's house with her. This relationship has benefited both girls.

Deanne's teachers in school have made many comments to The Arc representative and Deanne's mother about her increased self-esteem in school. They observed that she began initiating conversations with others, increased her ability to listen, and interrupted less. They were impressed by her ability to ask for assistance in uncomfortable situations—situations in which she used to isolate herself.

Deanne's mother also has undergone a positive change as a result of this inclusive experience. She has become less overprotective of Deanne. She is beginning to allow Deanne to make more choices for herself regarding her recreation and leisure activities. According to The Arc representative, Deanne's mother's self-esteem improved as she realized that her daughter could be a successful part of a group of peers if given the proper support.

CONCLUDING REMARKS

The success that Deanne experienced in Girl Scout Troop #26 is representative of many of the rewards of inclusion efforts that take place when agencies in the human services and leisure service delivery systems share not only expertise, resources, and programs but also visions and dreams. It has been our experience in this project that very few leisure service agencies want to exclude people with disabilities, but they are overwhelmed with where to start the inclusion process. Given information and support, many agencies have found inclusion to be not only easier than they thought but also rewarding and fun. Starting with just one person with a disability at a time will cause a ripple effect that will do much to open up closed environments. Working with individuals and their own unique needs is an important part of the inclusion process in recreation services. Just as important is the need for agencies to examine the way in which they provide services and to adjust all components of the service delivery system to be welcoming and inclusive of all community members.

EXEMPLARY PROGRAM V
Trail Partners: A Creative Step Toward Access in Park Districts

Kim High and Erin Pearson

"Put the person before the disability." Although this statement often is cheered to the point of cliché among community recreation providers, rarely is it accomplished to its fullest potential. Indeed, such a statement calls for continuous work in responding to individuals' needs and desires—a goal that proves to be one of the most challenging in the recreation profession. To satisfy the needs of a variety of people participating in a myriad of services, providers must embrace a philosophy of alternatives, acknowledging that when faced with the question of how to increase accessibility, more than one right answer exists.

Fresh alternatives often are difficult to find; new ideas are limited by old directions and pervasive cultural misconceptions. For example, because creating accessibility historically has meant eliminating physical barriers, recreation professionals often perceive such action as the only way to proceed. Thus, park districts feel obligated to pave over green areas, overlooking other creative and, to some users, more desirable ways to accomplish the demand for access to all people.

The Trail Partners program, a service designed and implemented by the Metropolitan Park District of the Toledo (Ohio) Area, is one exception and an alternative to paving every trail. Trail Partners innovatively harnesses people power to increase access throughout its park system, especially in the more remote natural areas. The program trains volunteers to accompany and assist park visitors with disabilities on the trails and at the public programs of their choice.

The Trail Partners method is fairly simple. An individual wanting to visit a Metropark and/or attend a public event and desiring assistance contacts the park office. At that time, the individual is asked to complete a Trail Partners registration and release form to be kept on file with the park staff. Once a registration form is completed, the individual can request a Trail Partners volunteer at any time. Up to three Trail Partners volunteers can be requested if the individual feels that more than one is needed because of the severity of his or her disability or the difficult terrain of the trail that he or she has chosen. Office staff members then fulfill the request by telephoning volunteers. After confirming the outing with the individual who made the request, it gets recorded on the office calendar, becomes official, and proceeds as planned.[2]

One admirable quality of Trail Partners is that this method promotes independence and high self-esteem among its users. Based on the premise that the most ac-

---

[2]For details on the program and its implementation, see "Easy Access with Trail Partners," by Kim Bork in *Parks and Recreation*, December, 1989.

curate knowledge of the capabilities of any individual with a disability comes from that individual him- or herself, users are in charge of making their own decisions about what kinds of park activities they are interested in and can physically handle. They are provided with necessary information on terrain and event logistics and then make their own choices for trail use and event participation. They are responsible for giving directions to the Trail Partners volunteers during outings, and volunteers and staff members involved are encouraged to ask users about their needs and preferences and not to make assumptions based on preconceived and often incorrect notions. In this way, Trail Partners works successfully toward promoting independence as well as breaking down stereotypes.

Trail Partners' philosophy fosters a progressive style of training volunteers who work with people with disabilities: In many cases, individuals signing up to use Trail Partners also become trainers. The Trail Partners volunteer trainings are held approximately four times a year. As a result of the training, volunteers become familiar with trail terrain, acquire skills in maneuvering wheelchairs and lifting and transferring individuals, and receive information on the nature of the various disabilities among users. Although experts from support agencies often are called upon to deliver specialized training sessions, much of the training can be accomplished with the assistance of independent people in the community who have disabilities and are willing to spend time conversing and hiking with volunteers. Some of the most effective training comes from mentorships whereby new volunteers are simply sent on scheduled outings with more experienced volunteers and users.

The Trail Partners program emphasizes an inclusive approach to community recreation. The partnership concept offers a means by which park visitors with disabilities can be included in mainstreamed park events (e.g., nature walks) and enjoy the same trails used by the general public. An access statement printed in park event brochures invites all individuals to use Metropark's programs and facilities and highlights the Trail Partners option for individuals who desire assistance. The service also is marketed by park district staff members at public speaking engagements and advertised in support agency newsletters. The result is the inclusion of people with disabilities in daily park district events.

One of the most noteworthy features of Trail Partners is its versatility. Trail Partners is useful to a variety of populations for a variety of recreational pursuits. Since the service began in 1988, it has been used by people with visual impairments, people with mobility impairments, older adults who want someone to accompany them on their hikes, people recuperating from surgery and injury, children who need assistance for mainstreamed programs, and many others who have mild to severe disabilities. Although Trail Partners initially was designed to create greater access in nonpaved and remote natural areas for people with disabilities, users have requested volunteers for assistance at park activities as diverse as ice cream socials, jogging and exercise, holiday displays, and full-moon walks. While many requests are by users who simply seek accompaniment while leisurely enjoying nice weather in a pleasant park setting, a more adventurous user with a visual impairment has been requesting a volunteer for tandem bicycling. Trail Partners serves a greater range of purposes than originally anticipated, and its potential continues to grow.

The versatility of Trail Partners makes it a useful model for other recreation agencies. As the recipient of the New Programs Award from the Ohio Parks and Recreation Association in 1988, Trail Partners has received much attention. The idea has been adopted by several park districts throughout Ohio. In fact, recreation providers nationwide have contacted the Metroparks of the Toledo Area to inquire about the program's application in their regions. Trail Partners is a useful model primarily because it is cost and energy efficient and because it can be implemented on a variety of levels. For example, Trail Partners can be initiated by agencies on limited bases, perhaps at just one park in a system or for public events only, and then expanded after pilot attempts have succeeded. Furthermore, if park and recreation administrators are concerned about Trail Partners generating too much popularity and too many requests, then the service can be offered with registration limits. (Or park and recreation administrators can be gently reminded that their mission is to respond to the needs of clientele, regardless of ability levels of those desiring services.) However, such limits have not been necessary for the Toledo program. Trail Partners requests average approximately 50–75 participants per year, with some users making repeated visits and others participating just once or twice on special occasions. So although Trail Partners provides an important service, it has remained within a reasonable programmatic size. The Trail Partners option is not the choice for everybody; for some visitors, this kind of assistance is fulfilled by family members or other support people. For others, being alone in the park or using the physically accessible trails is preferred. The program is one alternative among several that promotes easier access.

Trail Partners as one option among many brings this discussion back to its most important point: The diverse needs of individual recreation users dictate that providers continuously seek a variety of alternatives in their efforts to increase access. The Metropark District of the Toledo Area offers a progressive access plan that includes, but is not limited to, accessible trails, TTDs and sign-language interpreters, employee access training, adaptive equipment at playgrounds, fishing areas, nature centers and historic sites, and Trail Partners. Such a plan allows for an increasing number of choices among users, thus working in favor of an ideal setting in which society really does "put the person before the disability."

CONCLUDING REMARKS

The success of the Trail Partners program rests on its simplicity. Potential users who are unable to gain access to Metropark facilities or events can request assistance from Trail Partners program staff members. Assistance is designed and provided on an individual basis, resulting in an inclusive community recreation environment that preserves the natural beauty of the park while maintaining the dignity of the individual.

EXEMPLARY PROGRAM VI
The Status of Community Recreation Programs for People with Disabilities in Israel

Shlomo Katz and Chaya Schwartz

The barriers to community inclusion for people with disabilities are not unique to North America. Efforts to include people with disabilities in community recreation in Israel have been under way since the mid-1970s. Like the United States, efforts at inclusion have resulted in a continuum of service options ranging from segregated recreation activities to opportunities for full inclusion.

Leisure time activities for people with disabilities in Israel generally are provided by volunteer organizations that focus services toward specific disability types (e.g., mental retardation, sensory impairments). Consequently, separate organizations exist that offer specific leisure programs for serving people with different types of disabilities. Most of these organizations plan social and recreational clubs in the afternoons and early evenings. Akim (Israel Association for the Rehabilitation of the Mentally Handicapped [sic]) is an example of one of these organizations. Akim is a volunteer parent organization that provides a variety of services for children and adults with mental retardation, including various recreational activities such as social clubs, outings, sport activities, and summer camps. The successful Akim programs have served as models for volunteer agencies that provide services to people with varying disabilities.

Akim established in 1975 the first five "special" programs for people with mental retardation. These clubs were located in the larger cities in Israel and functioned initially as segregated programs. Akim has evolved to include a number of community-based programs that enable children and adults with mental retardation to participate in leisure and recreational activities in their home communities. Together with local and governmental support, Akim now operates 60 clubs nationwide, with the majority of the clubs located in regular community centers. In addition to organizing and running the social and recreational clubs, Akim is responsible for operating the following four unique and nationally recognized leisure/recreation programs.

FLOWERS AND HEARTS

Flowers and Hearts is an annual meeting of various dance-group ensembles, bands, and choirs whose memberships consist primarily of individuals with mental retardation. Initially planned as a segregated cultural event to provide opportunities to meet new friends, Flowers and Hearts was designed from the beginning to encourage people with mental retardation to become involved in community events. Since 1991, this annual meeting has become an integral component of the Israeli Dance Festival that is held each summer in Karmiel. This inclusive festival exposes participants to professional choreographers who have begun working with dancers and singers with mental retardation. In addition to the increased opportunities to interact with peers without disabilities, several groups have been invited to participate in international festivals in other countries. More than 300 people with mental retardation participate in the program.

THE THEATRE

In 1990, Akim, in cooperation with the Ministry of Labor and Welfare's office for services to people with mental retardation, established The Theatre, an acting group consisting of 15 talented people with mental retardation. Professional directors work with this group of amateur actors, who perform for audiences throughout Israel. Their most widely known work is an original play written by the actors. Entitled "Fortunately There Is Night," the play describes the actors' experiences as people with mental retardation. Included in "Art for the People," a list of cultural activities recommended by the Ministry of Education, "Fortunately There Is Night" was recently added to the Acre Festival for Experimental Theatre. This program offers professional actors who play the role of an individual with mental retardation an opportunity to work with the theater group to establish a better understanding of the world from the eyes of a person with mental retardation.

THE CREATORS

Two hundred fifty adults with mental retardation participate in art workshops at the Israel Museum in Jerusalem, Tel-Aviv Museum, and Haifa Art Museum, the three largest art museums in Israel. The participants work side by side with the museums' regular staff members. The groups visit the different galleries to learn various techniques for self-expression through art. Many of their works are then sent to exhibitions in Israel and abroad. This project is associated with the Very Special Arts project founded by the Kennedy family in the United States.

ISRAELI ASSOCIATION FOR THE SPECIAL OLYMPICS

Akim established the Israeli branch of the International Association for the Special Olympics. Each year, more than 2,000 athletes with mental retardation participate in athletic competition through Special Olympics. More than 1,000 of these athletes eventually qualify for competition at the Wingate Institute for Sports in Israel, an annual sports meeting that also is sponsored by the Israeli branch of the International Special Olympics.

OTHER OPPORTUNITIES

In addition to Akim, two additional frameworks with roots as a volunteer organization have established opportunities for leisure and sport participation for individuals with disabilities. Not unlike many sports organizations for people with disabilities in the United States, these organizations are founded on segregated recreation opportunities. Yet additional efforts are under way to provide increasing opportunities for inclusive participation.

The Spivak Sport Center for Civilian Disabled [sic] primarily serves people with physical disabilities. The center was founded by Ilan, a parent organization that initially served people with polio and that subsequently began to serve people with cerebral palsy and other physical disabilities when the number of people with polio began to decline.

Beit Halochem, a sports program for veterans with disabilities, was initiated as a combined project of the Ministry of Defense, Department of Rehabilitation, and the Disabled Veterans Organization in Israel. In addition to providing various sporting activities, the center provides activity groups, theater, movies, and various cultural activities for veterans with disabilities and their families. The center has an olympic-size swimming pool, shooting range with adapted equipment for people with visual impairments, and facilities for other competitive sports.

The majority of sportsmen and sportswomen who represent Israel in international sports events and games for people with disabilities are affiliated with these two successful sports organizations. While the achievements of Israeli athletes without disabilities have totaled two bronze medals in the past Olympic games, Israeli athletes with disabilities have won many gold, silver, and bronze medals. These attainments are evidence of the important role that these two organizations play in encouraging and providing sport and recreation activities for people with disabilities. These achievements, however, often are cited by pro-segregationists as they argue for the need for segregated facilities for athletes with disabilities in order to retain success.

The success of these separate (segregated) organizations in providing leisure time activities for people with all types of disabilities and the satisfaction expressed by the participants and their families certainly have perpetuated the existence and growth of segregated programming. Other reasons often cited for the continued segregation of recreation programming are the lack of suitable equipment, inaccessibility of community facilities, inadequate instruction, and a lack of financial resources to pay for these services. As a result, the movement toward inclusion has only recently been offered as a viable alternative to segregated recreation and sport activities.

A number of organizations have been set up to facilitate the inclusion of people with disabilities in leisure activities. One of these organizations, Etgarim, was designed to allow people with disabilities the opportunity to participate in sport and recreation activities with peers without disabilities. Etgarim focuses on obtaining the resources necessary to overcome the obstacles (e.g., lack of equipment, inaccessibility) to inclusion.

People who join this nonprofit organization can participate in a variety of inclusive activities on land, in the water, and in the air. Land activities include skiing; horseback riding; bicycle riding; snappling; and tractor, jeep, and adventure touring. Water activities include snorkeling and scuba diving, water skiing, kayaking, sailing, wind surfing, and rafting. Air activities include parachuting, air surfing, and light aircraft flying.

In addition to offering specific activity courses, Etgarim provides material on new courses, helps individuals purchase the appropriate equipment at reduced prices, organizes outings and inclusive activities, and lobbies for support from the appropriate ministries and sport and leisure organizations. Etgarim also offers consultation services for community sports clubs, offering advice for including people with disabilities in existing clubs with peers without disabilities. The organization is creating a research unit that will develop and adapt new areas of activities for people with disabilities. The efforts of this organization have encouraged many people with disabilities to participate in inclusive sport and leisure activities. As a result, the number of inclusive recreation opportunities has increased dramatically.

CONCLUDING REMARKS

Israel, like the United States, is moving toward inclusive recreation programs for people with disabilities. Although many of the recreation programs are offered through segregated organizations, these organizations offer a variety of opportunities that reflect the myriad recreation interests of people with disabilities. It is hoped that these programs will serve as a catalyst for the expansion of inclusive leisure and recreation activities for people with disabilities throughout Israel.

EXEMPLARY PROGRAM VII
Community Recreation Inclusion Service

Laura Wetherald and Cathy Vigus

The Howard County (Maryland) Department of Recreation and Parks provides comprehensive services and opportunities for children, youths, and adults with disabilities. These services include more than 800 program opportunities that are open to all citizens in the county, regardless of ability. The purpose of these services is to provide quality inclusive recreation experiences for the estimated 21,000 (of a total population of 212,000) Howard County residents with disabilities. The inclusion services are designed to provide accommodations beyond the basic requirements of the Americans with Disabilities Act.

The Community Recreation Inclusion Service is part of a comprehensive Therapeutic Recreation Section that offers recreation programs including leisure education, skill development programs, teen and adult social clubs, and summer camps. Approximately 45–50 individuals with disabilities are included during the nonsummer months in the general recreation programs through the use of inclusion companions. This number dramatically increases during the summer with the inclusion of children in summer camps. During the 1995 summer season, approximately 140 individuals with disabilities participated in the department's nonsegregated recreation programs; over 50% of these individuals benefited from the services of inclusion companions. The success of the program has demonstrated the effectiveness of bringing together the human resources and community support necessary to provide quality inclusive services for individuals with disabilities.

IMPLEMENTATION PROCESS

The procedure for requesting accommodations is as simple as checking a box on the program registration form. The therapeutic recreation staff (TRS) then follow a step-by-step administrative process to ensure that the needs of each participant are met. The goal is to provide a comfortable transition into general recreation programs. It is the intent of the inclusion initiative to keep the approach as unobtrusive as possible by only providing essential accommodations. A summary of the administrative process, which was originally developed by the inclusion initiative in Montgomery County, Maryland, follows.

Step 1: Initial contact is made between the TRS and the registrant with a disability who has requested to be included in an advertised recreation program.

Step 2: If necessary, the TRS contacts the individual or parent/advocate who has requested inclusion placement to gain further information in order to provide proper accommodation.

Step 3: The TRS determines the appropriate accommodations needed. The extent of accommodations often is dependent on the individual's assessed challenge level (see Table 9.2). Some of the possible accommodations include

- *Transportation* arranged through different sources, including volunteer companions, assistance with public transportation access, and Urban Rural Transportation Administration (URTA)
- *Adaptive devices* owned by the department, obtained through various agencies, and/or ordered through catalogs
- *Accessible facilities* advocated for with assistance from the Accessibility Committee of the Commission for Individuals with Disabilities, a community-based organization
- *Financial assistance* offered to those individuals who qualify and administered with the Recreation and Parks Department
- *Inclusion companions* are the most important and effective accommodation in the inclusion initiative. The process includes an initial

Table 9.2. Community Recreation Inclusion Service model: Challenge level system

Challenge level	Characteristics
Challenge Level I *Independent Inclusion*	• No accommodations needed • Self-initiated • One-time informational telephone consultations
Challenge Level II *Complete Inclusion*	• Limited accommodations • Interpreter for sign language • Training staff and participant without disability • Adaptive devices • Mobility assistance • Accessibility of facilities • Transportation assistance • Financial assistance
Challenge Level III *Partial Inclusion*	• Substantial accommodations required • Community recreation companions needed • Includes recruiting, training, and coordinating a companion to assist individual with a disability to gain access to a program
Challenge Level IV *Foundational Inclusion*	• Therapeutic recreation programs are refocused to encourage inclusion experience Types of programs in Howard County: • Swimming instruction classes • Adult clubs and community outings • Creative art classes • Instructional sports skill classes • Leisure education classes • Outdoor recreation • After-school teen club

screening of the potential companion by a recreation staff member, placement interview, orientation and training, initial contact with the individual requesting the companion, arrangements to participate together in the activity, and official recognition of the companion

Step 4: General recreation leaders, companions, recreation specialists, and peers without disabilities receive appropriate training that may include disability awareness, sensitivity training, explanation of inclusion goals, terminology training, accommodations, and responsibilities.

Step 5: The individual attends the program or uses the facility.

Step 6: The TRS provides a follow-up service on the placement to ensure that everything is going smoothly for the participant and for the companion. Any concerns are addressed at this time. The TRS consults with the participant and the companion on future concerns.

Step 7: Both the participants and the companions are asked to evaluate the experience in order to identify the successes and failures. Evaluation is a vital component of the inclusion initiative because it provides the means to continuously improve the service.

Step 8: All general recreation sections and area programs are asked to complete record logs and return them to the TRS. This documentation procedure is an important means of data collection that will become the statistical base for the inclusion initiative and is invaluable for research and evaluation.

Step 9:   As a final action, the TRS encourages participants to become involved in other regular recreation programs. It is hoped that a successful inclusion experience will flow into increased inclusion participation in which the individual will build on his or her successes and begin regular participation in community life.

UNIQUE PROGRAM FEATURES

The success of the Howard County Community Recreation Inclusion Service can be attributed to three unique features of the program: 1) new participants are assessed and assigned to an appropriate level of accommodation; 2) the employment of inclusion companions has proved to be an invaluable "accommodation," one that is nearly universally applicable; and 3) a thorough training program has minimized the negative experiences of inclusion for program leaders and participants of all ability levels.

Levels of Accommodation—The Challenge Level System

It has to be assumed that individuals with disabilities will have individual needs, desires, skills, and limitations. It is the policy of the Howard County Recreation and Parks program, therefore, to offer a variety of accommodations. The concept of varying challenge levels has been developed to describe the many possible levels of accommodations based on individual limitations and need. This concept is not a progression, whereby an individual must achieve increasing independence in order to move up a level. Rather, each challenge level is a separate entity with no predictable vertical movement from one level to the next. Challenge levels have been designed to meet the needs of each individual and to provide flexibility and choice rather than limitations. An individual has the option of moving across levels to meet his or her own level of independence. For example, an individual may choose to function within Challenge Level I for a recreational swim program, while functioning within Level IV for the purpose of socialization (see Table 9.2).

Challenge Level I   Challenge Level I depicts the accommodations for independent inclusion in a recreation program or class. At this level, the individual does not require any specific accommodations to fully participate in a general recreation setting. In a majority of cases, the individual is not processed through the Therapeutic Recreation Section at all, although some individuals may contact the section merely for reassurance. Most individuals register independently for the specific recreation activity in the usual manner. The following is an independent inclusion example:

> Rose, a retired senior citizen, was interested in attending a craft fair sponsored by the recreation department. She noticed in the advertisements for the fair that individuals with disabilities that might require special accommodations were encouraged to call the department. Rose had had a stroke and used a wheelchair for mobility. She called the therapeutic recreation coordinator and explained her needs. The craft fair coordinator arranged for special parking accommodations for Rose's van. Because large crowds were expected, and Rose would have difficulty maneuvering in the crowded aisles, she also was allowed to enter the fair a half hour before it officially opened. This accommodation is routinely made at all the department's craft fairs.

Challenge Level II   Challenge Level II reflects limited accommodations for complete inclusion such as transportation, interpreters, financial assistance, additional training of staff, or equipment adaptations. Consultation with the participant and/or the parent/advocate often is provided to alleviate concerns. The following is a complete inclusion example:

> Rob and Tim enrolled in a golf instruction class for adults offered by the recreation department. Both were deaf and required the assistance of an interpreter to successfully complete the class. The therapeutic recreation coordinator for the department maintains a pool of sign-language interpreters and was able to acquire one to assist Rob and Tim during the class. An accommodation plan was written, and the sports coordinator as well as the class director were informed of the accommodations. Both participants were pleased with the accommodations and were able to gain as much from the program as were their hearing peers. As an unexpected, but pleasant, result of the arrangement, the interpreter was able to come away from the experience with newly developed golf skills.

Challenge Level III Challenge Level III, termed partial inclusion, tends to be the level that requires the most assistance from the therapeutic recreation specialist. The major difference between Challenge Level II and Challenge Level III is the added assistance of an inclusion companion. Other types of accommodations also may be required in a Challenge Level III placement for successful inclusion. The following is a partial inclusion example:

> Zachary, 7 years of age, was registered for a segregated therapeutic recreation summer camp for children with developmental disabilities. After 2 days, his mother decided to remove him from the program because he appeared bored. The therapeutic recreation coordinator suggested an inclusive summer camp program that would provide Zachary with more activity options and challenges. An accommodation plan was written, and the camp staff members were informed of the addition to their program. Information and training were provided to the camp staff to supplement the disability awareness training that they received at their initial camp in-service. An inclusion companion was hired and trained by the therapeutic recreation coordinator and placed with Zachary in a 6-week, full-day summer program. The companion worked very closely with Zachary's mother and school teacher to provide additional structure and to reinforce appropriate behaviors. Zachary successfully completed his first recreational inclusion experience without a negative incident and has subsequently enrolled in many other nonsegregated recreation programs with the assistance of an inclusion companion.

Challenge Level IV Challenge Level IV reflects the steps for restructuring special, separate therapeutic recreation programs to promote inclusion from within the special recreation programs. The following guidelines are used to promote foundational inclusion and to assist in providing normalizing experiences as a first step toward independence in leisure:

1. Utilize normal environments.
2. Choose age-appropriate activities.
3. Divide into small groups when going into the community for events to ensure that the ratio of people with and without disabilities approximates natural proportions (1:10).
4. Teach skills that support individuals in inclusion.
5. Promote self-esteem–building exercises.
6. Plan activities in community settings.
7. Emphasize people first and disability second. For example, refer to people as "individuals who have mental retardation" as opposed to "the mentally retarded."
8. Place people who are at the same ability levels together rather than mixing people with vastly different abilities.

9. Educate leaders concerning the process and goals of inclusion.
10. Check the accessibility and usability of targeted community facilities.
11. Encourage social interaction between individuals with and without disabilities.

The following is a foundational inclusion example:

> Alan, 50 years of age, has been a member of the Friday Night Social Club for adults with developmental disabilities for 8 years. He became involved in this program shortly after entering a community living facility after being institutionalized for most of his life. His lack of socialization skills and disruptive behavior made it difficult for him to integrate into the community. As a result of his continuous involvement in this program, his socialization skills and self-control have drastically improved. Alan enjoys interacting with his peers and developing new leisure skills and hopes to become involved in integrated community activities in the very near future.

A Closer Look at the Inclusion Companion

The inclusion companion is an innovative approach to successful inclusion. The companion provides grass-roots assistance to the individual for addressing his or her particular needs. The inclusion companion probably is the most functional accommodation for ensuring the success of an inclusion placement.

The function of an inclusion companion is to supply the individual with a disability with support and to eliminate barriers as follows:

- The companion acts as an ever-present advocate for highlighting the individual's abilities and his or her similarities to peers, diffusing subtle attitude barriers, and developing a climate of acceptance.
- The companion provides an opportunity for dismantling the intrinsic barriers to inclusion often found within the individual being included and replacing these barriers with skills and a healthier, more open attitude toward inclusion.
- The companion provides one-to-one assistance so that general recreation staff members do not have to spend an inordinate amount of time with one individual. This extra assistance allows the normal rhythms of the program to remain undisturbed.

Because the role of the inclusion companion is so vital to the success of many inclusion situations, Howard County Department of Recreation and Parks has placed a great deal of emphasis on matching a companion to an individual wanting to be included. If a volunteer who has the appropriate background for a particular placement is not available, then a qualified companion is hired. This entire process is offered only on a limited basis and needs to be expanded.

Providing support through an inclusion companion must not, however, foster dependency and, consequently, greater "handicapism." As much as possible, a companion serves as a "behind the scenes" person "making it happen" for the individual with a disability without taking away the experience of independent participation and involvement.

Laura Wetherald compiled *A Mainstreaming Companion Handbook* while she worked at Montgomery County Department of Recreation. The handbook explains all of the policies and procedures of the mainstreaming process and gives special attention to the role of the companion. The handbook also includes a job description, discipline techniques, and ways to promote an accepting environment for the individual being integrated. The handbook was revised to adapt to the Howard County Recreation and Parks model.

Training

Training is a very important aspect of the entire inclusion initiative because it is only through the full support of all individuals involved that successful inclusion can be attained. Extensive and timely training can provide an understanding of the basic philosophy of inclusion, the procedures to be followed, and sensitivity to the needs of each major disability group. Training is a tangible resource that provides general information and clarification. However, the inclusion initiative also must be a continuous process of growth, and each individual desiring to be included presents unique needs and accommodation requirements. Two types or levels of training are available:

1. General Workshops—Offer general objectives orientation:

    -   Rationale for inclusion leisure services
    -   Benefits of inclusion leisure services
    -   Methods for achieving successful inclusion
    -   Characteristics of people with disabilities
    -   Evaluating general recreation programs for inclusion "readiness"

2. Specific Workshops—Offer specific detailed training and preparation:

    -   Discussion of the disability of a specific individual
    -   Explanation of the role and supervision of the inclusion companion
    -   Development of sensitivity awareness in participants without disabilities

The key to successful training is flexibility. The therapeutic recreation specialist meets the needs of each specific group by planning a training program in which real learning can occur.

CONCLUDING REMARKS

The comprehensive services provided by the Howard County Department of Recreation and Parks are designed to meet the individual needs of each person with a disability. Potential program participants are welcomed into the program, and needs are addressed through a thorough planning and implementation system. The three levels of accommodation ensure that participants achieve the highest level of inclusion for their needs. Inclusion companions are a versatile means of overcoming barriers and have proved to be effective for promoting inclusion.

◆ ◆ ◆ ◆ ◆

SUMMARY

In this chapter, educators and practitioners from the United States and Israel shared their experiences with inclusive recreation and the strategies that they used to make their own programs exemplary models of inclusion. Although most of the guest authors described how the strategies presented in this book assisted with the process of inclusion, all of them added unique strategies that worked especially well for them and their communities. The intent of this chapter was to demonstrate that efforts of inclusion are alive and well around the United States and the world and to offer replicable strategies for including individuals with disabilities in community recreation programs. The authors of this edition and the guest authors hope that readers will use these strategies as steppingstones for developing inclusive recreation programs to ensure that inclusive communities will soon be a reality for all people.

The Inclusive Community Leisure Service Process

◆ ◆ ◆ ◆ ◆

Social planning process[a]	"Accessible process"	Process tasks
I. Develop philosophic/ideologic framework	*Guidelines for Decision Making* 1. Right to engage in recreation 2. Freedom of choice 3. Allows for individual differences 4. Access to quality leisure environments 5. Consistent, nondiscriminatory service delivery	*Accessibility Checklist* — a. physically accessible — b. age appropriate — c. inclusive (when appropriate) — d. addresses needs and preferences — e. affordable — f. convenient
II. Identify Needs	A. Gather Information: 1. Leisure Attitudes, Values	A.1.1 Examine attitude research in professional literature 1.2 Talk with potential consumers of services, with and without disabilities
	2. Demographic data	2.1 Contact advocacy agencies and schools to ascertain "who, what, where" 2.2 Visit neighborhood to observe environmental and residential modifications signaling "disabled live here" 2.3 Informally interview area residents 2.4 Consult census tables
	3. Available resources	3.1 Consult accessibility survey 3.2 Identify staff skilled in therapeutic recreation 3.3 Note existing programs by other agencies (e.g., community education, schools) 3.4 Determine if existing leisure materials are adaptable by people of varying abilities 3.5 Determine budget allocations for recreation program services
	4. Leisure behavior	4.1 Examine existing studies conducted by leisure researchers, advocacy groups

218

- 4.2 Co-sponsor survey with advocacy agency, parent groups, and/or special education classrooms in schools to determine current leisure involvement by people with disabilities

B. Identify Needs
  1. Conduct preference assessments with constituents of service area
  - B.1.1 Administer formal needs/preference assessment (mail out survey) of neighborhood residents with disabilities and their parents/care providers
  - 1.2 Conduct informal needs/preference assessment (interview) with same groups as in B.1.1
  - 1.3 Contact advocacy groups to determine the general needs of special population group

C. Identify Programs
  1. "Brainstorm" creative ideas considering A & B, above
  2. Choose alternatives
  - C.1.1 Consider accessibility issues related to A.3.1 and A.3.4
  - 2.1 Base decisions on determined needs and preferences in B
  - 2.2 Coordinate program selections and time with advocacy or special recreation groups to avoid duplication or conflicts

D. Publicize Programs/Recruitment
  1. Develop/implement marketing plan
  - D.1.1 Contact advocacy agencies, parent groups, schools regarding program offerings
  - 1.2 Include nondiscrimination statements on all written and verbal advertising and promotion
  - 1.3 Utilize photographs of participants with disabilities alongside participants without disabilities (must obtain photography release)
  - 1.4 Portray participants with disabilities positively: as role models for *everyone*, not just for other people with disabilities
  - 1.5 Gain access to cable TV networks

III. Plan Program Intervention

2. Develop/distribute program brochure

   2.1 Eliminate all references to "special," "adaptive," or "handicapped" programming

   2.2 Distribute program offerings via brochures door to door and through neighborhood/community media, advocacy agency newsletter, community bulletin boards, computer clubs, and school classrooms

E. Conduct Registration
  1. Participant completes and submits form and pays fee, if appropriate

   E.1.1 Include response area for people who may have special considerations on standardized registration forms; include contact number for further information

   1.2 Establish consistent protocol for registering participants (e.g., mail, telephone, on-site, combination)

   1.3 (Refer to RIIP, Chapter 5, for complete detailing of Process Tasks)

   1.4 Determine appropriate adaptations and modifications

IV. Implement Programs/Interventions

F. Implement Programs
  1. Conduct organized programs

   F.1.1 Implement program modifications and adaptations specified in RIIP, Parts 2 and 3

V. Evaluate Programs/Interventions

G. Evaluate Programs
  1. Specify type and method of evaluation
  2. Conduct ongoing (Formative) and final (Summative) evaluations of program

   G.1.1 Collect data on interactions between people with and without disabilities, social behaviors, acquisition of skills, etc.

   2.1 Collect qualitative (natural observation) as well as quantitative data

H. Summarize Findings and Report
  1. Write narrative of evaluation data
  2. Present summary findings to administrative personnel; include

   H.1.1 Analyze data and graphics and summarize findings

   2.1 Present findings to "significant others" (parents/care providers) critique of program design and implementation

3. Consider presentation to professional peers at workshops and conferences

  2.2 Critique modifications/adaptations chosen to facilitate accessibility such as grouping arrangements, volunteer advocates, equipment/material/setting modifications, or behavioral approaches

  3.1 Present findings to appropriate advocacy agencies, parent groups, schools

  3.2 Collaborate with other personnel to report significant findings to allied health professional groups

VI. Feedback, Modification

I. Provide Appropriate Feedback

1. Provide constructive criticism to affected people throughout all phases of programming

  I.1.1 Provide reinforcement to volunteer advocates, instructors, and participants without disabilities throughout program implementation phase

2. Make necessary modifications as needed

  2.1 Develop and evaluate adaptations as needed to ensure successful experience for participant with disabilities

J. Determine Future Programs/Interventions

1. Make decisions based on evaluation information and feedback

  J.1.1 Be proactive versus reactive

  1.2 Make appropriate modifications in leisure service delivery to people with disabilities

2. Modify program philosophy or orientation as needs of constituency change

  2.1 Participate actively on a Community Leisure Advisory Board that provides support for people with disabilities in leisure service delivery

  2.2 Advocate on behalf of participants with disabilities

  2.3 Provide technical assistance to advocacy agencies, parents, schools

3. Modify programs, interventions, other service delivery

  3.1 Modify and upgrade staff training program

Source: Edginton, Compton, and Hanson (1980).

Leisure
Interest Survey

◆ ◆ ◆ ◆ ◆

LEISURE INTEREST SURVEY

Sample

Date _____

Name _____ Age _____ Male _____ Female _____

Address _____

Home phone _____ Business phone _____

Marital status _____ Children's ages _____

PLEASE MARK AN "X" NEXT TO THE ACTIVITIES THAT BEST DESCRIBE YOUR COMMUNITY LEISURE INTERESTS.

Activity	Currently do	Interested in
Team sports		
Bowling	___	___
Softball	___	___
Basketball	___	___
Soccer	___	___
T-Ball	___	___
Football	___	___
Hockey	___	___
Other: (Specify) _____	___	___
_____		
Music		
Singing	___	___
Playing instruments	___	___
Attending concerts	___	___
Other: (Specify) _____	___	___
_____		
Dance		
Folk	___	___
Modern	___	___
Square	___	___
Aerobic	___	___
Tap	___	___
Ballet	___	___
Jazz	___	___
Other: (Specify) _____	___	___
_____		

Individual sports

Gymnastics	——	——
Jogging/Running	——	——
Tennis	——	——
Archery	——	——
Swimming	——	——
Golf	——	——
Badminton	——	——
Horseback riding	——	——
Horseshoes	——	——
Fishing	——	——
Bike riding	——	——
Walking	——	——
Other: (Specify) _____	——	——
_____		

Arts and crafts

Painting	——	——
Knitting	——	——
Crocheting	——	——
Latch hook	——	——
Ceramics	——	——
Other: (Specify) _____	——	——
_____		

Table games

Cards	——	——
Checkers	——	——
Chess	——	——
Dominoes	——	——
Scrabble	——	——
Puzzles	——	——
Billiards	——	——
Table tennis	——	——
Other: (Specify) _____	——	——
_____		

Outdoor leisure/social

Hiking	——	——
Gardening	——	——
Camping	——	——
Barbecues/Picnics	——	——
Skiing	——	——
Canoeing	——	——
Other: (Specify) _____	——	——
_____		

Mini day trips

Historical	——	——
Cultural	——	——
Sporting events	——	——
Shopping/Restaurant	——	——
Other: (Specify) _____	——	——
_____		

Social clubs

Scouts	——	——
Photography	——	——
Travel	——	——
Gourmet cooking	——	——
Card playing	——	——
Other: (Specify) _____	——	——
_____		

My leisure experiences usually are:

—— Physical —— Individual —— Structured —— Active —— Planned —— Expensive
—— Mental —— Social —— Nonstructured —— Passive —— Long-term
—— Spontaneous —— Inexpensive

With whom do you usually engage in leisure experiences (actual names can be used)?

—— Alone —— A friend/s —— Family member/s

During what time of day do you participate in leisure activities?

—— Morning —— Afternoon —— Evening

Are any of the following problems that might prevent you from participating in leisure activities?

—— Financial difficulties —— Lack of transportation —— Facility not accessible —— No one to participate with —— Geographic location —— Disability/Lack skill —— No motivation
—— Child care problems —— Other: (Specify) _____

Please check any special needs or considerations that may affect your participation.

—— Physical
—— Mental
—— Social
—— Other: (Specify) _____
_____

Would you be interested in serving as a member of a Community Leisure Advisory Board on recreation for people with disabilities? —— Yes —— No

Would you attend an open organizational meeting to assist us in planning leisure services for people in your community? —— Yes —— No

Effective Networking in Community Leisure Services

Roles and Responsibilities of Key Players and Networking Referral List

◆ ◆ ◆ ◆ ◆

KEY PLAYERS: COMMUNITY RECREATION PROFESSIONALS

Refers to people employed by the municipal park and recreation agency or other organizations (e.g., special recreation agencies; in some cases, community education) that serve the principal role in providing community leisure services funded by local government(s). People in administrative or leadership positions usually are professionally prepared (i.e., minimum 4-year degree) to manage organized, comprehensive municipal park and recreation programs. Other recreation staff may be nondegreed, part time, or volunteer. Community Therapeutic Recreation Specialists have specific responsibilities related to providing leisure services to people with disabilities but not unlike those responsibilities held by other community recreation professionals.

Examples

Municipal Park and Recreation Staff (e.g., Recreation Worker, Recreator, Director, Instructor, Leader); Community Recreator; Community Therapeutic Recreation Specialist; Community Leisure Facilitator; Leisure Coach; Community Leisure Planner

Responsibilities

The primary responsibilities of the community recreation professional within the networking and community leisure service delivery processes are as facilitator and enabler. That is, the recreation professional has the skills, knowledge, and experience to coordinate activities (e.g., information gathering, needs identification, program selection) that result in accessible community leisure services for people with disabilities. No "special" background or training is needed to assume these roles; only a willingness and motivation to provide high quality leisure services to a group of individuals who traditionally have been denied access to appropriate opportunities to engage in recreational experiences. The community recreation professional also should note that these roles and responsibilities extend beyond any given program season into a year-round effort. Developing a Community Leisure Advisory Board, therefore, should be a high priority to increase the probability that accessible leisure services will have permanence.

KEY PLAYERS: SCHOOL/DAY PROGRAM PERSONNEL

Individuals responsible for the education and training of people with and without disabilities in a variety of curriculum areas including leisure/recreation. In the leisure domain, these instructors might focus on shaping attitudes, developing leisure skills, and providing opportunities for practicing skills. This learning usually takes place on-site at the school or day center, although adjacent parks, community centers, and other natural leisure environments are used frequently.

Examples

Teachers, Administrators, Community Educators, Special Education Teachers, Adapted Physical Educators, Day Program Personnel, Sheltered Workshop Staff, Developmental Learning Center Personnel

Responsibilities

A. Gather Information
1. Identify potential participants from student population.
2. Provide access/link to parents via student's communication book, school newsletters, parent–teacher meetings.
3. Supply recreation professionals and instructors with demographic information.
4. Provide demographic data on student (e.g., age, disability type, family/home status).
5. Identify potential volunteer advocates (e.g., peers without disabilities from other classrooms).

B. Identify Needs
1. Report findings from school-based assessments.
2. Identify leisure-related needs that are part of student's IEP or IHP.

C. Select Programs
1. Identify areas of skill training, leisure education in classroom.
2. Establish link with park and recreation setting in which school-based programs could be implemented.

D. Publicize Programs/Conduct Recruitment
1. Place program brochure on school bulletin boards.
2. Disseminate information to parents/care providers via students.

E. Conduct Registration
1. Assist in completing Part I of the Recreation Inventory for Inclusive Participation.
2. Provide additional information on special needs of participants and other considerations related to disability.
3. Assist with soliciting volunteer advocates and their training in the schools.
4. Assist with identifying appropriate program modifications.

F. Provide Appropriate Feedback
1. Determine consistency of behavioral approaches (i.e., all behavioral changes being detected at school as a result of community leisure participation).
2. Determine generalizability of leisure skills to school and other natural settings.
3. Provide social reinforcement to students participating in community leisure programs.

G. Determine Future Efforts
1. Participate on Community Leisure Advisory Board.
2. Strengthen ties among school, home, and community through parent–teacher–student organizations.
3. Incorporate leisure-related goals and objectives into IEP or IHP.
4. Conduct attitude assessment/sensitivity training for students without disabilities.

KEY PLAYERS: PARENTS/CARE PROVIDERS (REAL OR SURROGATE)

Individuals who, through their biological, foster, or paraprofessional relationships, have responsibility for the care of people with disabilities within residential settings. These people often assume a position of authority as guardians of the health and welfare of their children or residents, including making decisions regarding community leisure participation of these people.

Examples
Parents, Foster Parents, Guardians, Direct Care Workers, Child Care Workers, House Parents, Living Unit Staff

Responsibilities
A. Gather Information
    1. Identify potential consumers; provide demographic data.
    2. Identify potential volunteer advocates (e.g., self, sibling, friend, neighbor).
    3. Describe leisure behaviors and participation patterns of family member/client.
    4. Identify current and subsequent nonschool environments (e.g., shopping malls, parks, community center) that person with disability will want access to.
    5. Provide information on the availability of leisure materials in the home.
    6. Identify community leisure environments that person with disability currently has access to.
    7. Provide information on the amount of time person with disability is able to spend in leisure activity.
    8. Provide financial, transportation assistance.
    9. Accumulate leisure resource file that notes accessibility, barriers, experiences, activities, etc.
B. Identify Needs
    1. Communicate preferences and expectations.
    2. Assist consumer to communicate needs and preferences.
    3. Be a liaison between other parents/care providers.
C. Select Programs
    1. Identify programs and materials and activities that are chronologically age appropriate, functional.
D. Publicize Programs/Conduct Recruitment
    1. Disseminate program information to other parents/care providers, advocacy agencies, community bulletin boards.
E. Conduct Registration
    1. Provide registration and orientation assistance to consumer, if necessary.
    2. Assist with completing the Recreation Inventory for Inclusive Participation and identifying special needs.
    3. Assist in identifying appropriate program modifications and adaptations.
    4. Assist with soliciting and training volunteer advocates.
    5. Identify appropriate behavioral methods.
F. Provide Appropriate Feedback
    1. Report opportunities for maintenance and generalization of skills to home and other community environments.
    2. Provide positive social reinforcement to program staff.
    3. Provide constructive criticism on program development and implementation.
G. Determine Future Efforts
    1. Provide to consumer leisure-related support skills (e.g., opportunities to practice skills, family/staff training).

2. Participate on Community Leisure Advisory Board.
3. Advocate for inclusive community leisure services.
4. Ensure that leisure is an integral part of son's/daughter's or client's IEP/IHP.
5. Motivate and encourage consumer to continue participation in future programs.

KEY PLAYERS: ALLIED HEALTH PROFESSIONALS

Individuals who provide therapeutic services to people with disabilities usually in residential or clinical settings (e.g., Rehabilitation Hospitals, Intermediate Care Facilities for the Mentally Retarded). These services are provided by trained or licensed professionals who typically are endorsed by the medical community. Forms of services range from specific concentration on motor, language, or recreational skills development to the coordination of all services for an individual.

Examples

Communication Disorders Specialist (Speech Therapist), Certified Therapeutic Recreation Specialist, Physical Therapist, Occupational Therapist, Case Manager, Social Worker, Music Therapist, Vocational Rehabilitation Counselor, Psychologist, Activity Coordinator, Physician, Nurse

Responsibilities

A. Gather Information
   1. Identify potential participants.
   2. Provide transportation to community leisure settings/programs.
   3. Accumulate leisure resource file.
   4. Provide consultation services including teaching techniques/curriculum for leisure skill development, adaptations/modifications.
   5. Provide information on positioning/handling techniques.
B. Identify Needs
   1. Conduct and share leisure, social skills assessment information.
C. Publicize Programs/Conduct Recruitment
   1. Disseminate program information to clients.
D. Conduct Registration
   1. Assist with completing various sections of the Recreation Inventory for Inclusive Participation.
   2. Assist with identifying appropriate program modifications.
   3. Assist with soliciting and training volunteer advocates.
E. Provide Appropriate Feedback
   1. Determine maintenance/generalization of leisure skills to other environments.
F. Determine Future Efforts
   1. Provide leisure skills training in non–clinically based environments.
   2. Include leisure-related goals and objectives in IHP.
   3. Provide leisure-related support skills.
   4. Provide referral services.
   5. Participate on Community Leisure Advisory Board.
   6. Assist with in-service training of staff, parents, consumers, volunteers, and others.

KEY PLAYERS: CONSUMERS

Individual residents of a community for whom park and recreation services are organized and administered. The range of individuals who will use these services may be characterized as young, teen, adult, elderly, handicapped, "special," female or male. For the purposes of this matrix, *consumers* will imply those individuals with physical and/or mental disabilities who generally have been denied full access to the range of leisure services provided by municipal park and recreation agencies for any of a variety of reasons.

Examples

"Special Populations," "People with Disabilities," "Mentally Handicapped," "Physically Disabled," "Handicapped," "Challenged"

Responsibilities

A. Gather Information
   1. Provide demographic data (e.g., age, address, residential setting, location).
   2. Relate past participation and current skills and abilities.
   3. Identify possible volunteer advocates (e.g., friend, group home staff, sibling).
B. Identify Needs
   1. State leisure needs and preferences.
   2. Identify obstacles (e.g., lack of transportation, funds, skills).
C. Select Programs
   1. Share ideas on preferred programs, activities, materials.
D. Publicize Programs/Conduct Recruitment
   1. Share program brochures with advocacy agencies, family, friends, neighbors, roommates.
   2. Encourage others to participate.
E. Conduct Registration
   1. Register for preferred programs.
   2. Assist with completing the Recreation Inventory for Inclusive Participation, including identifying special needs.
   3. Identify intact strengths relative to skills needed for participation.
   4. Assist in identifying appropriate program modifications and adaptations.
   5. Assist with soliciting volunteer advocates.
F. Provide Appropriate Feedback
   1. Give constructive feedback to instructors, recreation staff on program modifications, adaptations.
   2. Describe how skills learned in community recreation setting are used in other settings.
G. Determine Future Efforts
   1. Be a self-advocate regarding need and desire to gain access to community leisure services.
   2. Continue participation in future programs.
   3. Participate on Community Leisure Advisory Board.

KEY PLAYERS: ADVOCACY GROUPS

Public or private, usually nonprofit agencies and their representatives, that have as their organizational mission a concern for the health and welfare of a particular constituency. Although not the primary service function of the agency, leisure/recreation services are one of a number of aspects considered in the context of the overall continuum of services to the constituency.

Examples

The Arc; Community Advisory Council on Persons with Disabilities; Multiple Sclerosis Society; Society for the Blind; Society for Children and Adults with Autism; Developmental Disabilities Planning Council, Volunteer Advocates.

Responsibilities

A. Gather Information
   1. Identify potential consumers for inclusive leisure services.
   2. Be a liaison with other advocacy agencies, parent/care provider groups.
   3. Identify programs, services of a similar nature, offered by advocacy groups.
   4. Identify possible volunteer advocates.
B. Identify Needs
   1. Give indication of general leisure/recreation, social needs of people with disabilities.
   2. Identify limitations of advocacy agency to provide community leisure services stressing need to collaborate with municipal park and recreation agency.
C. Select Programs
   1. Coordinate programs, including activities, times, settings, to avoid duplicating leisure services and to ensure that leisure needs of people with disabilities are addressed.
D. Publicize Programs/Conduct Recruitment
   1. Disseminate information to consumers, parents/care providers.
   2. Publish programs in agency newsletter.
   3. Develop speakers' bureau to heighten public awareness regarding availability/accessibility of community recreation programs.
E. Conduct Registration
   1. Assist in identifying appropriate program modifications.
   2. Assist with soliciting volunteer advocates and their training and adaptations.
F. Implement Program
   1. Provide volunteer advocacy to people with disabilities.
G. Provide Appropriate Feedback
   1. Provide constructive criticism on collaborative role.
   2. Be liaison among consumer, parent/care providers, and recreation staff.
H. Determine Future Efforts
   1. Assist in developing and implementing staff, parent, consumer, and volunteer in-service and preservice education.
   2. Provide referral service for consumers wanting to be involved in leisure programs.
   3. Participate on Community Leisure Advisory Board.
   4. Author articles on inclusion for publication in agency newsletter.

KEY PLAYERS: QUASI-PUBLIC RECREATION SERVICES

Organizations basically dependent on voluntary financial support and serving a distinctive clientele. Financial support may come through endowments, donations, member fees, grants, United Way funds, or voluntary contributions of time, materials, facilities, and personnel. These organizations generally are nonprofit and have the health and welfare of their constituency in mind. Clientele include youth, people with disabilities, religious groups, and fraternal or patriotic societies. Public recreation organizations may contract with quasi-public services for use of facilities, materials, setting, or volunteers.

Examples

YMCA; YWCA; Boy Scouts; Girl Scouts; 4-H Club; Catholic Youth Organization; Boy's Club of America; Kiwanis International; Lions Club; American Lung Association; Recreation Clubs.

Responsibilities

A. Gather Information
    1. Identify resources (e.g., financial, transportation, volunteers).
    2. Identify accessible programs and activities available to people with disabilities.
B. Identify Needs
    1. Provide rationale and support for activity participation by people without disabilities and assist with relating needs to people with disabilities.
C. Select Programs
    1. Identify programs complementary to municipal park and recreation programs.
    2. Discuss methods to collaborate on programs, settings.
    3. Co-responsibility with park and recreation for activity offerings that serve as "steppingstones" to quasi-public recreation programs.
D. Publicize Programs/Conduct Recruitment
    1. Post program brochures on bulletin boards.
    2. Referral for people with disabilities to community leisure programs.
E. Conduct Registration
    1. Assist with soliciting volunteer advocates (could be community service project).
F. Implement Program
    1. If facilities, settings physically accessible, permit programs to take place there.
    2. Assist in programs held at quasi-public settings.
G. Evaluation
    1. Assist in programs held at quasi-public settings.
H. Provide Appropriate Feedback
    1. Provide constructive feedback in program planning and implementation.
 I. Determine Future Efforts
    1. Participate on Community Leisure Advisory Board.
    2. Provide volunteer referral services.

KEY PLAYERS: PRIVATE RECREATION SERVICES

Organizations and agencies that exist to provide a direct service for their membership. They are "member-centered" and respond to the unique interests of their membership. This group may be represented by commercial recreation organizations (e.g., video parlors, amusement parks), clubs, and recreation associations and by industries and businesses that sponsor activities on behalf of their employees. Private recreation services are supported by member fees, profits, or business capital rather than by public monies. Public recreation organizations may contract with private services to use facilities, materials, settings, and so forth.

Examples

Sports and health clubs, country clubs, swim and tennis clubs, employee softball and bowling leagues, amusement parks, bowling alleys, skating rinks, restaurants, aerobic workout studios.

Responsibilities

A. Gather Information
    1. Offer to share facilities, environments, materials.
    2. Provide financial support through grants, endowments to people with disabilities.
    3. Share information on programs, activities.

B. Select Programs
    1. Coordinate leisure services in order to make various programs in private recreation settings inclusive.

C. Publicize Programs/Conduct Recruitment
    1. Disseminate program information via bulletin boards, newsletters.

D. Conduct Registration
    1. Assist with soliciting volunteer advocates (could be company service project).

E. Implement Program
    1. If facilities, settings physically accessible, permit programs to take place there.
    2. Assist with implementing those programs held in private recreation settings.

F. Evaluation
    1. Assist with evaluating those programs held in private recreation settings.

G. Provide Appropriate Feedback
    1. Provide feedback on programs held in private recreation settings.
    2. Be liaison between municipal park and recreation organization and business community.

H. Determine Future Efforts
    1. Participate on Community Leisure Advisory Board.
    2. Provide charitable contributions or assist in fund-raising to support inclusive community leisure services.

KEY PLAYERS: PROFESSIONAL AND EDUCATIONAL ASSOCIATIONS/TECHNICAL RESOURCES

Agencies and individuals not specifically organized as providers of leisure services but able to give consultation and/or technical resources in support of the delivery of leisure services within community settings.

Examples

Recreation, Park, and Leisure Studies Departments in universities; publicly or privately funded research institutes; leisure consultants; professional associations (e.g., National Recreation and Park Association, National Therapeutic Recreation Society, The Association for Persons with Severe Handicaps); metropolitan councils.

Responsibilities

A. Gather Information
    1. Conduct formal research, data gathering, evaluation.
    2. Compile and share demographic information.
    3. Serve as a consultant to leisure service agency.
    4. Share mailing lists of agencies (e.g., group homes) serving members of special populations.
B. Identify Needs
    1. Present findings of research on recreation opportunities for people with disabilities.
    2. Train university students in Therapeutic Recreation to conduct preference assessments for people with disabilities.
C. Select Programs
    1. Make recommendations on appropriate and inclusive program offerings.
D. Publicize Programs/Conduct Recruitment
    1. Advertise programs in educational settings and in agency newsletters (e.g., school newspaper, quarterly newsletter).
    2. Assist in outreach/networking among all groups.
E. Conduct Registration
    1. Provide recommendations on program modifications.
F. Implement Program
    1. Assist with activity and/or task analysis of leisure activities and skills.
    2. Provide volunteer advocates (e.g., student interns).
G. Evaluation
    1. Serve as independent observer at program.
    2. Provide student interns to assist.
    3. Analyze evaluative data concerning participant outcomes.
    4. Assist in validating data collection procedures and interobserver reliability.
H. Program Summary and Report
    1. Report findings at workshops, conferences, and in journals and other written media.
    2. Share evaluative data with community recreation professionals.
I. Provide Appropriate Feedback
    1. Provide constructive feedback on inclusion approaches.
    2. Solicit feedback from practitioners for future research and program evaluation.

J. Determine Future Efforts
1. Serve as central coordinating body and facilitator for Community Leisure Advisory Board.
2. Conduct longitudinal research on effects of inclusive programs.
3. Develop new, improved integration technology.
4. Develop curriculum to educate/train community recreation professionals.

NETWORKING REFERRAL LIST

Directions: 1. Make 9 copies of this form (i.e., one page per category) plus multiple copies of this or a similarly formatted page.
2. Designate a category for each sheet (see list immediately below).
3. When a contact is made, fill in appropriate information.
4. Put additional contacts on second and subsequent pages.

Category: ____ Community recreation professional
____ Parents/care providers
____ Consumers
____ Advocacy groups
____ School/Day program personnel
____ Allied health professionals
____ Private recreation services
____ Quasi-public recreation services
____ Professional & educational associations/Technical resources

Name: _____   Title: _____
Agency: _____   Telephone: (w) _____
Address: _____   (h) _____
_____

Name: _____   Title: _____
Agency: _____   Telephone: (w) _____
Address: _____   (h) _____
_____

Name: _____   Title: _____
Agency: _____   Telephone: (w) _____
Address: _____   (h) _____
_____

Name: _____   Title: _____
Agency: _____   Telephone: (w) _____
Address: _____   (h) _____
_____

Name: _____   Title: _____
Agency: _____   Telephone: (w) _____
Address: _____   (h) _____
_____

Name: _____   Title: _____
Agency: _____   Telephone: (w) _____
Address: _____   (h) _____
_____

Name: _____   Title: _____
Agency: _____   Telephone: (w) _____
Address: _____   (h) _____
_____

Building
Access Survey

From Minnesota State Council on Disability. (1992, September). *Building Access Survey.*
St. Paul: Author.

Introduction

Why This Workbook?

The purpose of this Workbook is to help you make your facility accessible to individuals with disabilities. Making your facilities accessible is also staying in compliance with the law by President Bush in July 1990. The ADA is designed to extend civil rights protection to persons with disabilities. The law is divided into four major Titles that prohibit discrimination against any person with a disability in employment, state and local government services, public transportation, public accommodations, and telecommunications.

Title I: Employment

Employers may not discriminate against a person with a disability in hiring or promotion if the person is otherwise qualified for the job. Employers must provide "reasonable accommodation" to persons with disabilities, including such steps as job restructuring and modification of equipment.

Information on the Title I provisions can be obtained from:
The Equal Employment Opportunity Commission, 1801 L. Street N.W., Washington, D.C. 20507. Phone 1-800-USA-EEOC (voice) or 1-800-800-3302 (TDD).

Title II: Public Services and Transportation

Subtitle A prohibits state and local governments from discriminating against persons with disabilities. Subtitle B provides for accessibility to public transit buses, rail lines, and bus and train stations.

Information on the public transportation provisions can be obtained from:
The U.S. Department of Transportation, 400 Seventh Street

S.W., Washington, D.C. 20590. Phone (202) 366-9305 (voice) or (202) 755-7687 (TDD).

Title III: Public Accommodations

Persons with disabilities are to be provided accommodations and access equal to, or similar to, that available to the general public. The final rules implementing Title III of the Americans with Disabilities Act were published in the Federal Register of July 26, 1991. To obtain a copy, call the U.S. Department of Justice at (202) 514-0301.

Questions on the final rules can be directed to:
The Office of the Americans with Disabilities Act, Civil Rights Division, U.S. Department of Justice, P.O. Box 66118, Washington, D.C. 20035-6118. Phone (202) 514-0301 (voice) or (202) 514-0383 (TDD).

Technical information on the ADA accessibility provisions can be obtained from:
The U.S. Architectural And Transportation Barriers Compliance Board, 1111 18th Street N.W., Suite 501 Washington D.C. 20036. Phone 1-800-USA-ABLE (voice or TDD).

Title IV: Telecommunications

Companies offering telephone service to the general public must offer telephone relay service to persons who use telecommunications devices for the deaf (TDDs) or similar devices.

Information on the Title IV provisions can be obtained from:
The Federal Communications Commission, 1919 M Street N.W., Washington, D.C. 20554. Phone: (202) 634-1837 (voice) or (202) 632-1836 (TDD).

Who Will Benefit?

Everyone benefits from a barrier-free environment. In Minnesota alone there are over 600,000 individuals who have some type of disability. At your facility, this group might include the teacher who is blind, the mother who has multiple sclerosis, a client who uses a wheelchair, a vendor that uses crutches or an older visitor who has an issue with fatigue. Keep in mind that disability can affect each of us at any time, either directly or through friends and family. Imagine what might happen to your job and your ability to support yourself and your family if you became disabled and an architectural barrier prevented you from returning to work.

What's In This Workbook?

This workbook presents a step-by-step process to help you identify how best to make your facility accessible.

- A Planning section to help you determine how many survey forms you will need for each area of the building.

- Survey Forms to be used as a checklist as you walk through the building or facility. Please note: the survey forms have been designed to reflect the most restrictive accessibility requirements of either the Minnesota State Building Code or the Americans with Disabilities Act Accessibility Guidelines as they existed at the time of the development of this survey tool. Contact your local building official or the Minnesota State Council on Disability if you have concerns regarding current requirements.

The Planning Section

The Planning section has been designed to make this surveying task more manageable. It will help you prepare for surveying the facility. You can determine ahead of time how much work is involved and whether you will need other staff to help you. Specifically, the planning section allows for you to decide - before you leave your office – how many Survey Forms you will need to copy and take with you.

For each building that you evaluate you will be looking at four different aspects of the building and the land around it. Each aspect has several sub-components.

SITE:	Parking
	Disability Transfer Zone
	Walkway
	Steps
ENTRANCE:	Lift
	Steps
	Doorways
BUILDING:	Elevator
	Lift
	Corridor
	Stairs
	Ramp
SPACES:	Toilet Rooms
	Bathing Facilities
	Special Spaces such as auditoriums, cafeterias, libraries, etc.

Planning Analysis

What needs to be accessible at my facility?

This section will help you analyze the four critical areas of your building/facility: Site, Entrance, Building, and Spaces.

Read the entire Planning section carefully to determine what parts of your facility must be accessible. At the same time, note (on the Planning Summary Sheet) what Survey Forms you will need for completing the field survey portion of the process. *If you have more than one building at your facility, you will need to plan for each one individually.*

Planning Analysis – Step-By-Step

1. **Identify team members.** These individuals will provide guidance and assistance during the planning, surveying and reviewing steps. The team might include the facility manager, chief administrator, maintenance supervisor, 504 Coordinator or Equal Opportunity officer, financial staff, and persons with disabilities.

2. **Fill in the Planning Summary Sheet.** For each building to be surveyed, read through the entire Planning section and mark on the Planning Summary Sheet the total number of Survey Forms that will be needed. If you have more than two buildings at your facility, use additional Planning Summary Sheets.

3. **Copy the Survey Form.** Add the columns horizontally on the Planning Summary Sheet to arrive at the total number of forms that should be photocopied. Be sure to copy an extra set of forms to have handy when survey-ing (in the event an unexpected barrier is encountered). Collate and staple the appropriate forms on a building-

by-building basis. For each Survey Form, fill out each and every question. It is very important that each particular issue is addressed and that an answer is provided. *If not applicable, then note this by writing in "N/A".* This will indicate that the question was not overlooked or missed. A comment section is provided at the end of each sur-vey form. Use this area for notes and to clarify special sit-uations which may occur.

Site

Site accessibility involves arriving at the site, parking a vehi-cle or being dropped off, and getting to a building or out-door recreation area. It also includes the ability to move from one building to another when there is more than one building at a facility.

People with mobility issues who arrive by vehicle need to be able to enter buildings on their own - independently - with-out assistance from others. Direct and safe walkways from these areas as well as from the street and transportation stops are essential for individuals with mobility or sight impairments.

Parking Survey Form

For each building at your facility, <u>determine the closest parking to the accessible entrance.</u> Count the total number of parking spaces available and use the table to determine how many accessible parking spaces are required. You may find that your facility has a greater need for accessible parking space than the code requires.

Fill in the PLANNING SUMMARY SHEET with the number of SITE: PARKING Survey Forms you will need for this building.

Entrance

An accessible entry is the keystone to making a building usable by people with disabilities. As many entrances as possible should be accessible, especially the entrance used most often by non-disabled people. Asking individuals with disabilities to use basement or back doors not used by others not only discriminates against them but also puts them at a disadvantage by depriving them of services provided in a front lobby: signage, reception, and waiting areas. It is important that once someone is inside the entrance that they be able to easily gain direct access to elevators and corridors that lead to other parts of the building.

The entrance includes all elements – doorways, steps, or lift – that get you from an accessible walkway to just inside the building through front doors and vestibule to a main corridor or lobby.

Fifty percent of primary public entrances to a building are required to be accessible. As many employee and service entrances as possible should also be accessible. For example, in large buildings such as hospitals there may be an emergency entrance, a visitor entrance, and an entrance for staff use located close to where they park their cars. In this instance, all three entrances should be accessible. It is often the case that parking lots are located at the back of buildings. If the main entrance is located on a public street but a long walk from the back of the building, both entrances should be made accessible.

Some criteria for determining which entrances should be accessible include:

- It is referred to as the "main entrance" to the building. (If you asked for directions to this building, you would be directed to this entrance.)

Disability Transfer Zone Survey Form

If there is a disability transfer zone near the accessible entrance for this building, you will need to use the SITE: DISABILITY TRANSFER ZONE Survey Form to evaluate the transfer zone. Use one Survey Form for each transfer zone.

Fill in the PLANNING SUMMARY SHEET with the number of SITE: DISABILITY TRANSFER ZONE Survey Forms you will need for this building.

Walkway Survey Form

For each building you will need to determine the most direct, accessible walkway from the parking lot, transfer area, and transportation stops to the accessible entrance. For each identified walkway complete one SITE: WALKWAY Survey Form.

For facilities with many buildings, identify the most direct, accessible walkway between the buildings. For each identified walkway between buildings you will need to complete one SITE: WALKWAY Survey Form.

Fill in the PLANNING SUMMARY SHEET with the number of SITE: WALKWAY Survey Forms you will need for this building.

Steps Survey Form

If your site has any changes in level there may be a number of locations other than at building entrances where steps have been constructed. For each set of site steps, complete the SITE: STEPS Survey Form.

Fill in the PLANNING SUMMARY SHEET with the number of SITE: STEPS Survey Forms you will need for this building.

243

- It provides the most direct access to main corridors and/or elevators as well as major public function spaces at the entry level such as an auditorium or cafeteria.

- It is an entrance that people use when they enter the building from visitor or staff parking areas.

Identify the ENTRANCES that should be accessible for this building.

For each entrance you have identified, you will need to complete all applicable ENTRANCE Survey Forms – LIFT, STEPS, and DOOR.

Steps Survey Form

For each entrance you have identified with steps, you will need to complete one ENTRANCE: STEPS Survey Form.

Fill in the PLANNING SUMMARY SHEET with the number of BUILDING: STEPS Survey Forms you will need for this building.

Doorway Survey Form

For each entrance you have identified, you will need to complete one ENTRANCE: DOORWAY Survey Form.

Fill in the PLANNING SUMMARY SHEET with the number of BUILDING: DOORWAY Survey Forms you will need for this building.

Lift Survey Form

For each entrance you have identified with a lift, you will need to complete one ENTRANCE: LIFT Survey Form.

Fill in the PLANNING SUMMARY SHEET with the number of ENTRANCE: LIFT Survey Forms you will need for this building.

Building

The key components to getting around in the building are elevators, corridors, stairs, and ramps that can be used safely by people with disabilities. People often think that accessibility is only a problem for someone using a wheelchair. Individuals with low or no vision find it difficult to use buildings with poor signage, obstructions in the hallways, and elevators without audible signals. People with leg braces or prosthesis find poorly designed stairs difficult, if not impossible, to use. It is important to remember that even in elevator buildings some stairways are major connections between floors and therefore need to be accessible. Fire egress stairs, on the other hand, if restricted to emergency use are unlikely to be a critical factor in getting around within the building.

There are four key components to getting around within the building. ELEVATORS, CORRIDORS, STAIRS, and RAMPS. Some of these items already exist in the building and need to be surveyed to determine whether they conform to the code. Others, such as elevators, may not exist at all. In buildings where there are no elevators or where corridors change level, planning decisions must be made to determine whether a modification is needed to allow users to travel beyond the floor they enter on.

Elevator Survey Form

In multistory buildings with elevators, count the number of elevator banks (a cluster of elevators around a common lobby) in this building. (Do not include the freight elevator.) You need to select one BUILDING: ELEVATOR Survey Form for each elevator bank. Use it to survey one elevator.

Fill in the PLANNING SUMMARY SHEET with the number of BUILDING: ELEVATOR Survey Forms you will need for this building.

Corridor Survey Form

Decide which floors of this building are regularly used by staff, clients, or visitors. Determine which of these floors have similar corridor layouts. (A similar layout means that the corridors could be laid one over the other and they would match – but the rooms do not have to be identical on each floor.) You will need to survey only one corridor from each group of similar layouts. The following chart may help you in counting the number of BUILDING: CORRIDOR Survey Forms you will need.

Floors _____,_____,_____,_____,_____,
are similar (use one Survey Form)
Floors _____,_____,_____,_____,_____,
are similar (use one Survey Form)
Floors _____,_____,_____,_____,_____,
are similar (use one Survey Form)

Fill in the PLANNING SUMMARY SHEET with the total number of BUILDING: CORRIDOR Survey Forms you will need for this building.

Stairs Survey Form

Count the number of stairways in this building. Include stairs that connect only two or three floors as well as exit stairwells that serve every floor of the building. Also use this form for any steps (less than a full flight of stairs) that you find along a corridor. You will need one BUILDING: STAIRS Survey Form for every stairway or set of steps.

Fill in the PLANNING SUMMARY SHEET with the total number of BUILDING: STAIRS Survey Forms you will need for this building.

Ramp Survey Form

In buildings with interior ramps, use the BUILDING: RAMP Survey Form for each ramp.

In buildings where two floor levels are connected by a few steps, such as lobbies and mezzanines, evaluate the potential need for a ramp (or a lift).

Fill in the PLANNING SUMMARY SHEET with the total number of BUILDING: RAMP Survey Forms you will need for this building.

Spaces

Once you have made it possible for people to get around the facility easily, you need to determine what spaces should be accessible. Even if there are only a few people with disabilities currently using a building, there will eventually be more. Remember, individuals with disabilities are not only visitors and clients, but they are also employees and management personnel.

Rooms like toilet rooms will be found in all buildings. Other spaces are more specialized and occur less frequently but must be accessible because of their public use. Examples of special spaces include break rooms (with kitchens), auditoriums, libraries, cafeterias and conference rooms.

Sometimes included in these spaces are elements such as telephones and drinking fountains. These elements must also meet accessibility requirements. There are Survey Forms to be completed for each of these elements and if for example, there is a bank of public telephones in the library and also a bank of phones in the break room, both banks must be surveyed.

245

Planning Summary Sheet

Facility: _____

Completed by: _____

Total number of buildings: _____

Completion date: _____

This form is used to identify the specific number of survey forms you will need to package for each building at your facility. Fill it out as you become acquainted with the layout of each building being surveyed. After it is completed, photocopy the total number of each Survey Form that you will need to take into the field with you and then collate the forms on a building-by-building basis. (If more than 2 buildings, use additional Planning Summary Sheets.)

List The Number Of Survey Forms Needed Below

	Building 1	Building 2
Site		
Parking	_____	_____
Disability Transfer Zone	_____	_____
Walkways	_____	_____
Steps	_____	_____
Entrance		
Lift	_____	_____
Steps	_____	_____
Doorway	_____	_____

Building

	Building 1	Building 2
Elevator	_____	_____
Lift	_____	_____
Corridor	_____	_____
Stairs	_____	_____
Ramp	_____	_____

Spaces

	Building 1	Building 2
Toilet Room Male	_____	_____
Female	_____	_____
Unisex	_____	_____
Total	_____	_____

	Building 1	Building 2
Bathtub Male	_____	_____
Female	_____	_____
Unisex	_____	_____
Total	_____	_____
Shower Male	_____	_____
Female	_____	_____
Unisex	_____	_____
Total	_____	_____
Break Room	_____	_____
Auditorium	_____	_____
Assembly Areas other than Auditoriums	_____	_____
Library	_____	_____
Cafeteria	_____	_____
Telephone	_____	_____
Drinking Fountain	_____	_____
Total Survey Forms	_____	_____

247

Building Access Survey

Date Of Survey _____

Building _____

Street Address _____

City/State _____

Building Contact Name _____

Building Contact Phone _____

Surveyor's Name _____ Phone _____

Surveyor's Position _____

248

Survey Forms

Site: Parking Survey Form

Parking Space Table

Total Parking Spaces	Accessible Spaces Required	"Van Accessible" Spaces Required
1 to 25	1	1
26 to 50	2	1
51 to 75	3	1
76 to 100	4	1
101 to 150	5	1
151 to 200	6	1
201 to 300	7	1
301 to 400	8	1
401 to 500	9	2
501 To 1000	2% Of Total	1 In Every 8
1001 And Over	20 Plus 1 For Each Additional 100	Accessible Spaces

Table 1

Site: Parking Survey Form (Continued)

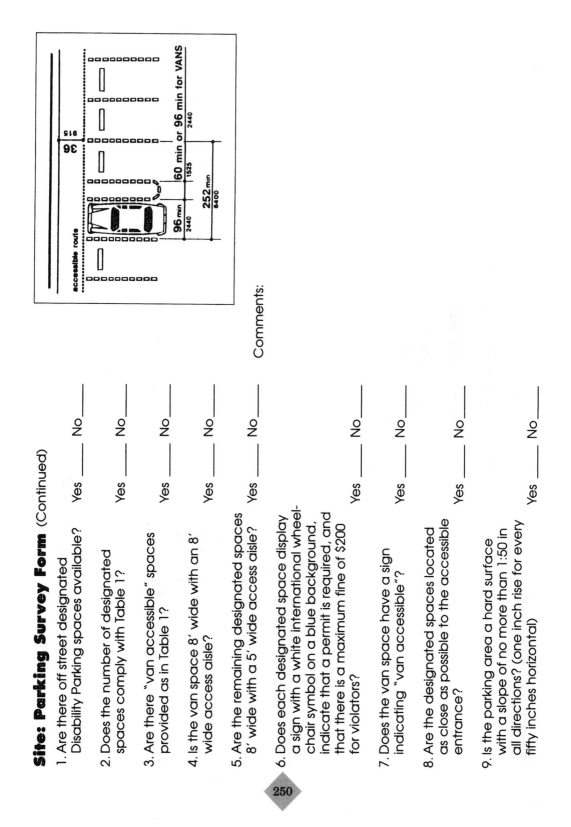

1. Are there off street designated Disability Parking spaces available? Yes _____ No _____

2. Does the number of designated spaces comply with Table 1? Yes _____ No _____

3. Are there "van accessible" spaces provided as in Table 1? Yes _____ No _____

4. Is the van space 8' wide with an 8' wide access aisle? Yes _____ No _____

5. Are the remaining designated spaces 8' wide with a 5' wide access aisle? Yes _____ No _____

6. Does each designated space display a sign with a white international wheelchair symbol on a blue background, indicate that a permit is required, and that there is a maximum fine of $200 for violators? Yes _____ No _____

7. Does the van space have a sign indicating "van accessible"? Yes _____ No _____

8. Are the designated spaces located as close as possible to the accessible entrance? Yes _____ No _____

9. Is the parking area a hard surface with a slope of no more than 1:50 in all directions? (one inch rise for every fifty inches horizontal) Yes _____ No _____

Comments:

250

Site: Disability Transfer Zone Survey Form

1. Is there a disability transfer zone provided?

Yes _____ No _____

2. Does the disability transfer zone provide an access aisle 5' wide by 20' long?

Yes _____ No _____

3. Does the disability transfer zone provide a vertical clearance of at least 114"?

Yes _____ No _____

4. Is there a sign indicating "disability transfer zone"?

Yes _____ No _____

5. Is there a curb-cut provided where necessary?

Yes _____ No _____

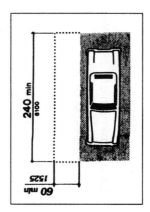

Comments:

251

Site: Walkway Survey Form
(Exterior ramps are considered walkways)

Comments:

1. Is the walkway at least 4' wide?   Yes _____ No _____

2. Is the walkway sloped a maximum of
   1:20 in the direction of travel?   Yes _____ No _____

3. Is the cross slope a maximum of 1:50?   Yes _____ No _____

4. Are there abrupt changes in level
   exceeding 1/2"?   Yes _____ No _____

5. Are curb-cuts provided along the
   accessible route where necessary?   Yes _____ No _____
   (i.e. along the accessible route from parking, transfer or sidewalk)

6. Do curb-cuts measure a minimum
   of 36" in width excluding flared edges?   Yes _____ No _____

7. Is the slope of the curb-cut no
   greater than 1:12?   Yes _____ No _____

flared side

1
10

If X is less than 48 in,
then the slope of the flared side
shall not exceed 1:12.

252

Site: Steps Survey Form

1. Are riser heights and tread widths uniform throughout the entire stair run? Yes ——— No ———

2. Are risers closed with a maximum nosing of 1"? Yes ——— No ———

3. Are there continuous handrails on both sides of the stairway? Yes ——— No ———

4. Do handrails extend 12" horizontally beyond the top riser? Yes ——— No ———

5. Do bottom handrails continue on slope a distance equal to the width of one tread past the bottom riser and horizontally for 12" beyond that point? Yes ——— No ———

6. Do end of handrails return to wall, floor or post? Yes ——— No ———

Comments:

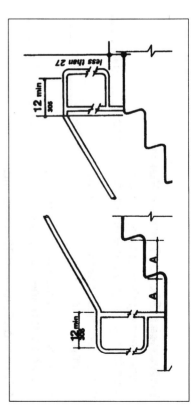

Entrance: Steps Survey Form

1. Are riser heights and tread widths uniform throughout the entire stair run? Yes _____ No _____

2. Are risers closed with a maximum nosing of 1"? Yes _____ No _____

3. Are there continuous handrails on both sides of the stairway? Yes _____ No _____

4. Do handrails extend 12" horizontally beyond the top riser? Yes _____ No _____

5. Do bottom handrails continue on slope a distance equal to the width of one tread past the bottom riser and horizontally for 12" beyond that point? Yes _____ No _____

6. Do end of handrails return to wall, floor or post? Yes _____ No _____

Comments:

Entrance: Lift Survey Form

1. Does the lift have a maximum vertical travel of 12'? Yes _____ No _____

2. Does the lift provide independent entry, operation and exit such that a person can operate the lift without assistance? Yes _____ No _____

Comments:

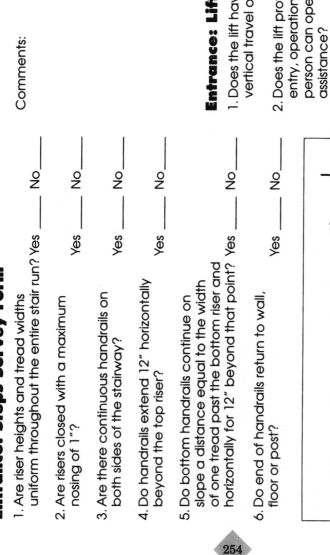

Entrance: Doorways Survey Form

1. With door in open position, is there a 32" clear space from the face of the door to the latch side door stop?

    Yes_____ No_____

2. If doorway has two independently operated door leaves, does at least one leaf provide the 32" clear space?

    Yes_____ No_____

3. If there are two sets of doors, as in a vestibule, is there a minimum width between the doors of 4' plus the width of the in-swinging door?

    Yes_____ No_____

4. Is the threshold no more than 1/2" in height?

    Yes_____ No_____

5. Is the door hardware operable by a single effort with one hand not requiring tight grasping or twisting of the wrist?

    Yes_____ No_____

6. Is the door hardware either a lever handle or loop-style type?

    Yes_____ No_____

7. Is the door hardware mounted no more than 42" above the floor?

    Yes_____ No_____

8. Is the force for pushing or pulling open the door no more than 8.5 lbs. (Fire doors excluded)

    Yes_____ No_____

9. Is there a minimum of 18" clear space on the latch side from the pull side of the door?

    Yes_____ No_____

10. Is there a minimum of 12" clear space on the latch side from the push side of the door?

    Yes_____ No_____

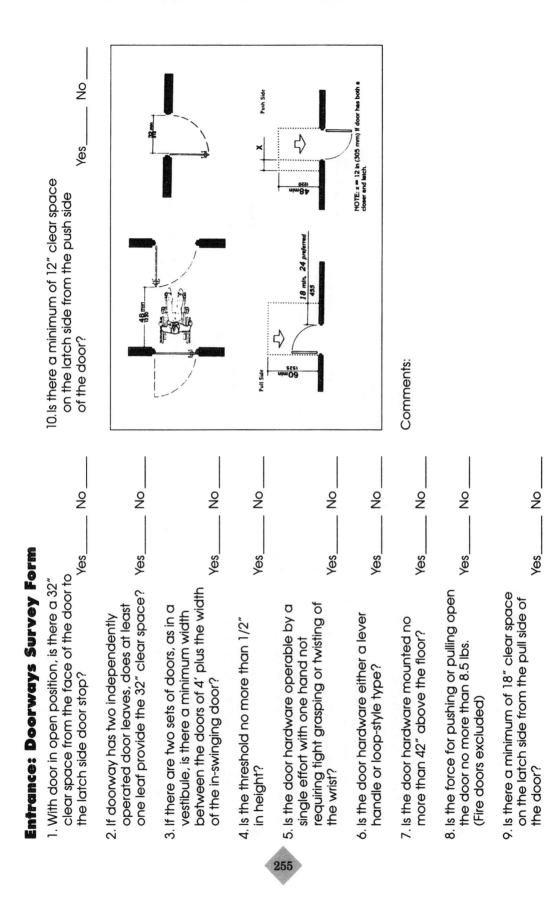

Comments:

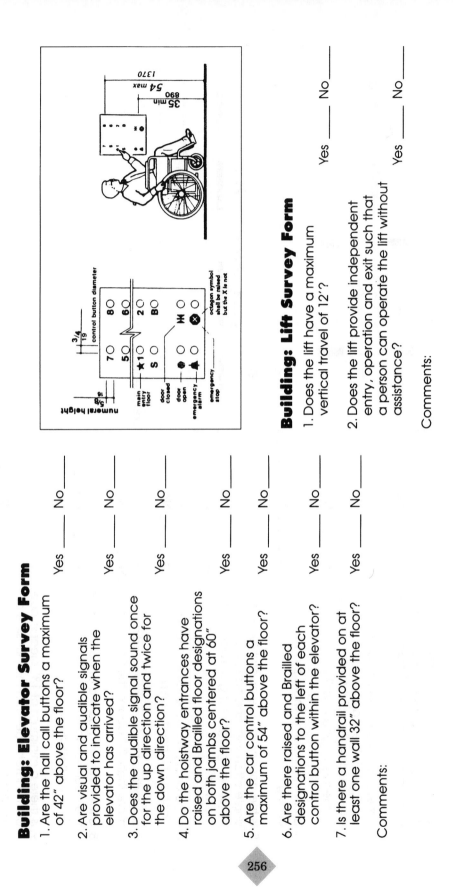

Building: Elevator Survey Form

1. Are the hall call buttons a maximum of 42" above the floor?

Yes _____ No _____

2. Are visual and audible signals provided to indicate when the elevator has arrived?

Yes _____ No _____

3. Does the audible signal sound once for the up direction and twice for the down direction?

Yes _____ No _____

4. Do the hoistway entrances have raised and Brailled floor designations on both jambs centered at 60" above the floor?

Yes _____ No _____

5. Are the car control buttons a maximum of 54" above the floor?

Yes _____ No _____

6. Are there raised and Brailled designations to the left of each control button within the elevator?

Yes _____ No _____

7. Is there a handrail provided on at least one wall 32" above the floor?

Yes _____ No _____

Comments:

Building: Lift Survey Form

1. Does the lift have a maximum vertical travel of 12'?

Yes _____ No _____

2. Does the lift provide independent entry, operation and exit such that a person can operate the lift without assistance?

Yes _____ No _____

Comments:

256

Building: Corridor Survey Form

1. Are all corridors serving an occupant load of 10 or more a minimum of 44" wide?　　Yes _____ No _____

2. Are all corridors serving an occupant load of less than 10, a minimum of 36" wide?　　Yes _____ No _____

3. If the corridor is less than 5' wide, are there passing spaces at least 5' x 5' located at intervals not exceeding 200'?　　Yes _____ No _____
   (Corridor intersections are considered passing spaces)

4. Do all doorways along the corridor provide a 32" clear opening from the face of the open door to the latch side door stop?　　Yes _____ No _____
   (Doors not requiring full user passage, such as shallow closets, may have a clear opening not less than 20".)

5. Is the door hardware either a lever handle or loop-style type which does not require tight grasping or twisting to operate?　　Yes _____ No _____

6. Is the the force for pushing or pulling open the door no more than 5 lbs.?　　Yes _____ No _____

7. Are signs designating permanent rooms and spaces mounted 60" above the floor on the latch side of the door?　　Yes _____ No _____

8. Do signs in Question 7 above have raised and Brailled characters?　　Yes _____ No _____

257

9. If there are counters along the corridor, is there a section a minimum of 36" wide a maximum of 36" above the floor?　　Yes _____ No _____

10. If alarms are required by code or otherwise provided, are both audible and visual alarms provided?　　Yes _____ No _____

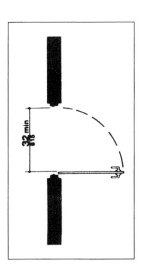

32 min

Comments:

Building: Stair Survey Form

1. Are riser heights and tread widths uniform throughout the entire stair run? Yes _____ No _____

2. Are risers closed with a maximum nosing of 1"? Yes _____ No _____

3. Are there continuous handrails on both sides of the stairway? Yes _____ No _____

4. Do handrails extend 12" horizontally beyond the top riser? Yes _____ No _____

5. Do bottom handrails continue on slope a distance equal to the width of one tread past the bottom riser and horizontally for 12" beyond that point? Yes _____ No _____

6. Do end of handrails return to wall, floor or post? Yes _____ No _____

Comments:

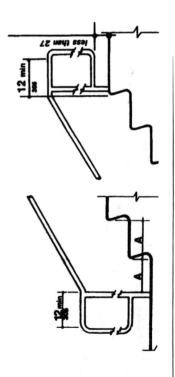

258

Building: Ramp Survey Form

1. Is the ramp a minimum of 36" wide? (measured between handrails)

Yes _____ No _____

2. Is the slope a maximum of 1:12? (1 inch rise for every 12 inches of run)

Yes _____ No _____

3. Is there a 6' long landing, measured in the direction of the ramp, at the bottom of the ramp?

Yes _____ No _____

4. Is there a 5' long landing, measured in the direction of the ramp, at the top of the ramp?

Yes _____ No _____

5. If the total rise exceeds 30", is there a 5' intermediate landing located no more than 30" above the bottom of the ramp?

Yes _____ No _____

6. If total rise is 6" or greater, are there handrails provided on both sides of the ramp?

Yes _____ No _____

7. Do end of handrails return to wall, floor or post?

Yes _____ No _____

Comments:

34-38
865·965

36 min
915

vertical guard rail

259

Spaces: Toilet Room Survey Form

_____ Male _____ Female _____ Unisex

_____ Floor or Building

1. Does the entry door provide a 32" clear opening from the face of the open door to the latch side door stop? Yes _____ No _____

2. If there are two sets of entry doors opening in the same direction, is there a minimum of 4' plus the width of the in-swinging door separating the two sets of doors? Yes _____ No _____

3. Is a standard toilet stall provided which measures a minimum of 5' in width? Yes _____ No _____

4. Does the standard stall have a minimum of 36" clear space from the front of the toilet bowl to the stall wall or door? Yes _____ No _____

5. Is the stall door hardware easy to operate requiring no tight grasping or twisting? Yes _____ No _____

6. If there are 6 or more toilet stalls, is there an alternate stall measuring 36" wide with a minimum of 36" from the tip of the toilet to the closed stall door provided in addition to the standard stall? Yes _____ No _____

7. Is the height of the toilet seat between 17" and 19" above the floor? Yes _____ No _____

8. Are both horizontal and vertical grab bars provided as shown in diagrams? Yes _____ No _____

9. Is the toilet paper dispenser mounted below the horizontal grab bar? Yes _____ No _____

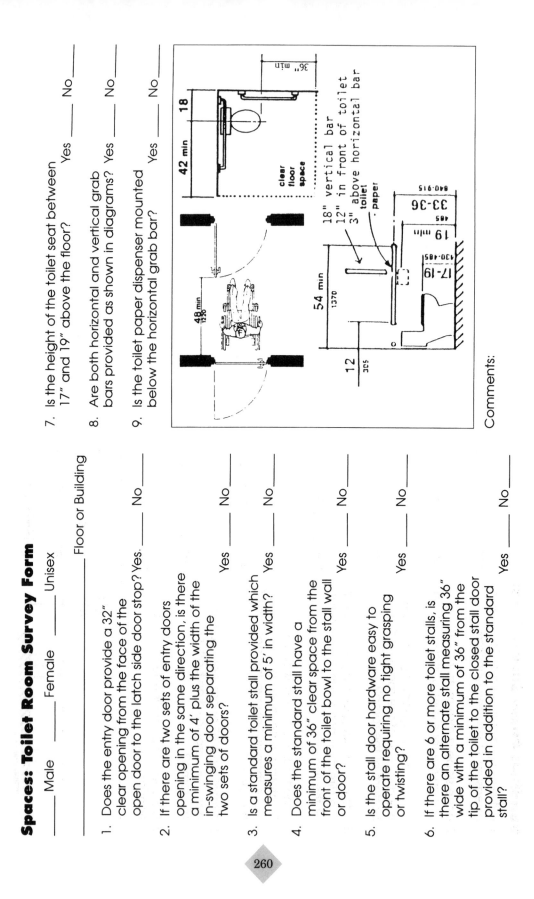

Comments:

Spaces: Toilet Room Survey Form (Continued)

____ Male ____ Female ____ Unisex

_____ Floor or Building

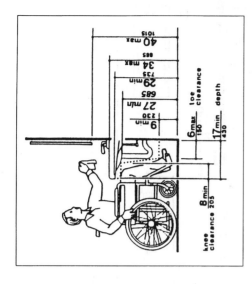

10. Is the rim of the sink a maximum height
    of 34" above the floor?   Yes ____ No ____

11. Is there a minimum of 29" of knee
    clearance from the floor to the
    bottom of the apron or counter?   Yes ____ No ____

12. Do the faucets have lever handles
    or are they electronically controlled? Yes ____ No ____

13. Is the plumbing insulated or otherwise
    covered so that there are no sharp
    or abrasive edges exposed?   Yes ____ No ____

14. Is the mirror mounted no higher than
    40" to the bottom edge?   Yes ____ No ____

15. Is there at least one of each type of
    accessory, i.e. soap dispenser, towel
    dispenser, etc., mounted such that the
    operating mechanism is no more
    than 40" above the floor?   Yes ____ No ____

Comments:

261

Spaces: Bathtub Survey Form

_____ Male _____ Female _____ Unisex

Floor or Building _____

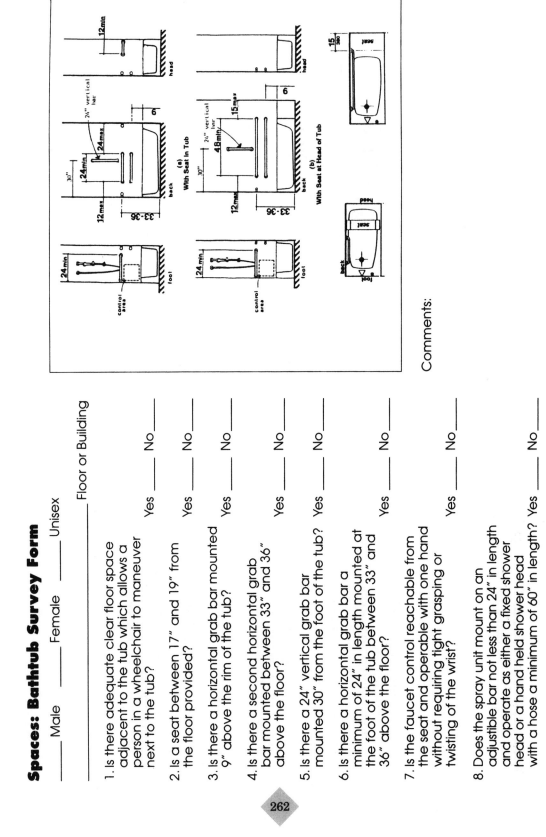

1. Is there adequate clear floor space adjacent to the tub which allows a person in a wheelchair to maneuver next to the tub?

Yes _____ No _____

2. Is a seat between 17" and 19" from the floor provided?

Yes _____ No _____

3. Is there a horizontal grab bar mounted 9" above the rim of the tub?

Yes _____ No _____

4. Is there a second horizontal grab bar mounted between 33" and 36" above the floor?

Yes _____ No _____

5. Is there a 24" vertical grab bar mounted 30" from the foot of the tub?

Yes _____ No _____

6. Is there a horizontal grab bar a minimum of 24" in length mounted at the foot of the tub between 33" and 36" above the floor?

Yes _____ No _____

7. Is the faucet control reachable from the seat and operable with one hand without requiring tight grasping or twisting of the wrist?

Yes _____ No _____

8. Does the spray unit mount on an adjustible bar not less than 24" in length and operate as either a fixed shower head or a hand held shower head with a hose a minimum of 60" in length?

Yes _____ No _____

Comments:

Spaces: Shower Survey Form

_____ Male _____ Female _____ Unisex

_____
Floor or Building

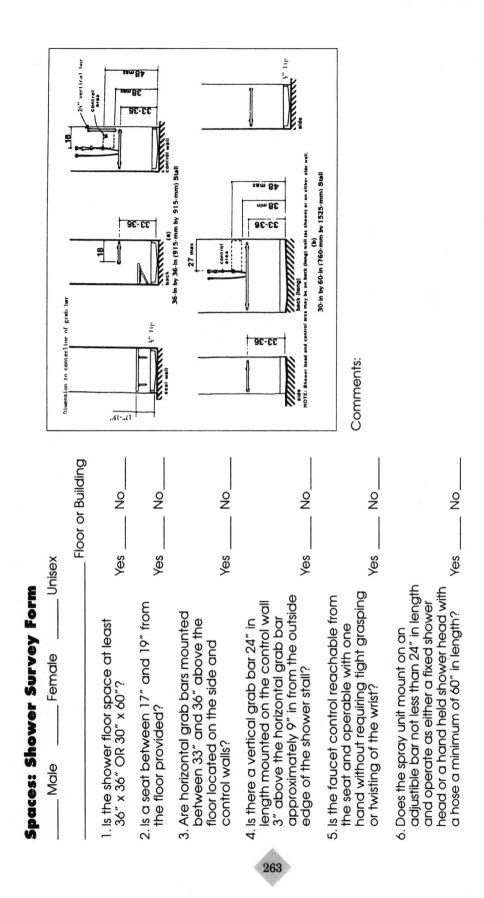

1. Is the shower floor space at least 36" x 36" OR 30" x 60"?

Yes _____ No _____

2. Is a seat between 17" and 19" from the floor provided?

Yes _____ No _____

3. Are horizontal grab bars mounted between 33" and 36" above the floor located on the side and control walls?

Yes _____ No _____

4. Is there a vertical grab bar 24" in length mounted on the control wall 3" above the horizontal grab bar approximately 9" in from the outside edge of the shower stall?

Yes _____ No _____

5. Is the faucet control reachable from the seat and operable with one hand without requiring tight grasping or twisting of the wrist?

Yes _____ No _____

6. Does the spray unit mount on an adjustable bar not less than 24" in length and operate as either a fixed shower head or a hand held shower head with a hose a minimum of 60" in length?

Yes _____ No _____

Comments:

263

Spaces: Break Room Survey Form

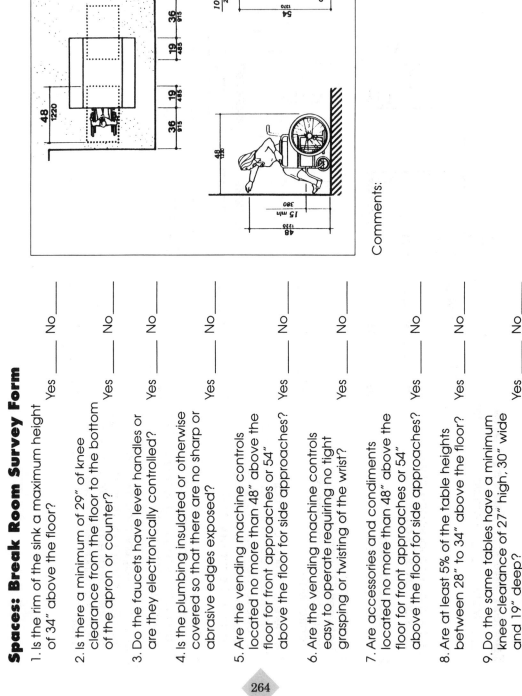

1. Is the rim of the sink a maximum height of 34" above the floor?

   Yes _____ No _____

2. Is there a minimum of 29" of knee clearance from the floor to the bottom of the apron or counter?

   Yes _____ No _____

3. Do the faucets have lever handles or are they electronically controlled?

   Yes _____ No _____

4. Is the plumbing insulated or otherwise covered so that there are no sharp or abrasive edges exposed?

   Yes _____ No _____

5. Are the vending machine controls located no more than 48" above the floor for front approaches or 54" above the floor for side approaches?

   Yes _____ No _____

6. Are the vending machine controls easy to operate requiring no tight grasping or twisting of the wrist?

   Yes _____ No _____

7. Are accessories and condiments located no more than 48" above the floor for front approaches or 54" above the floor for side approaches?

   Yes _____ No _____

8. Are at least 5% of the table heights between 28" to 34" above the floor?

   Yes _____ No _____

9. Do the same tables have a minimum knee clearance of 27" high, 30" wide and 19" deep?

   Yes _____ No _____

Comments:

264

Spaces: Auditorium Survey Form

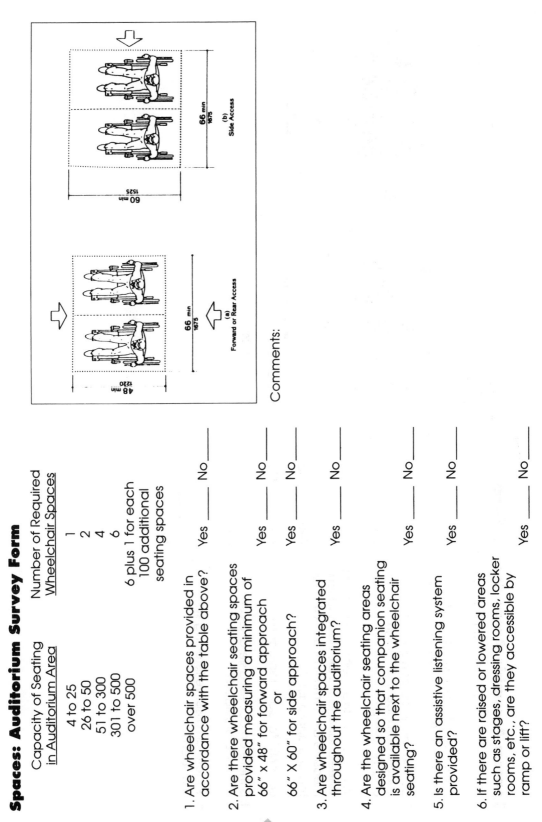

Capacity of Seating in Auditorium Area	Number of Required Wheelchair Spaces
4 to 25	1
26 to 50	2
51 to 300	4
301 to 500	6
over 500	6 plus 1 for each 100 additional seating spaces

1. Are wheelchair spaces provided in accordance with the table above? Yes _____ No _____

2. Are there wheelchair seating spaces provided measuring a minimum of 66" x 48" for forward approach

   or

   66" X 60" for side approach? Yes _____ No _____

3. Are wheelchair spaces integrated throughout the auditorium? Yes _____ No _____

4. Are the wheelchair seating areas designed so that companion seating is available next to the wheelchair seating? Yes _____ No _____

5. Is there an assistive listening system provided? Yes _____ No _____

6. If there are raised or lowered areas such as stages, dressing rooms, locker rooms, etc., are they accessible by ramp or lift? Yes _____ No _____

Comments:

265

Spaces: Assembly Areas Survey Form

(Other than Auditoriums)

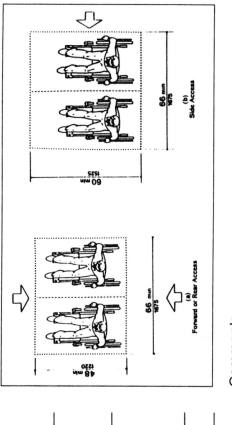

1. Are at least 5% of the table tops between 28" to 34" above the floor?   Yes _____ No _____

2. Do the same tables have a minimum knee clearance of 27" high, 30" wide and 19" deep?   Yes _____ No _____

3. In areas with fixed seating, are there wheelchair spaces provided which measure a minimum of 66" x 48" for forward approach?   Yes _____ No _____

   or

   66" x 60" for side approach?   Yes _____ No _____

4. Is there an access aisle at least 44" wide provided?   Yes _____ No _____

5. Is there an assistive listening system provided?   Yes _____ No _____

Comments:

Spaces: Library Survey Form

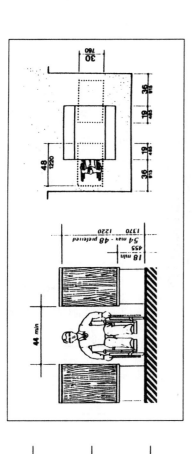

1. Are at least 5% of the table heights between 28" to 34" above the floor? Yes _____ No_____

2. Do the same tables have a minimum knee clearance of 27" high, 30" wide and 19" deep? Yes _____ No_____

3. Are a minimum of 5% of each type of fixed seating, or carrels in compliance with questions 1 and 2 above? Yes _____ No_____

4. At the check-out aisle, is there at least one section with a minimum counter area 36" wide that is no more than 36" above the floor? Yes _____ No_____

5. Is there a minimum clear space of 44" between book racks, card catalogs, magazine displays, etc.? Yes _____ No_____

6. Are card catalog and magazine display reach ranges no more than 48" above the floor for front approaches or 54" above the floor for side approaches? Yes _____ No_____
(Maximum of 48" preferred)

Comments:

267

Spaces: Cafeteria Survey Form

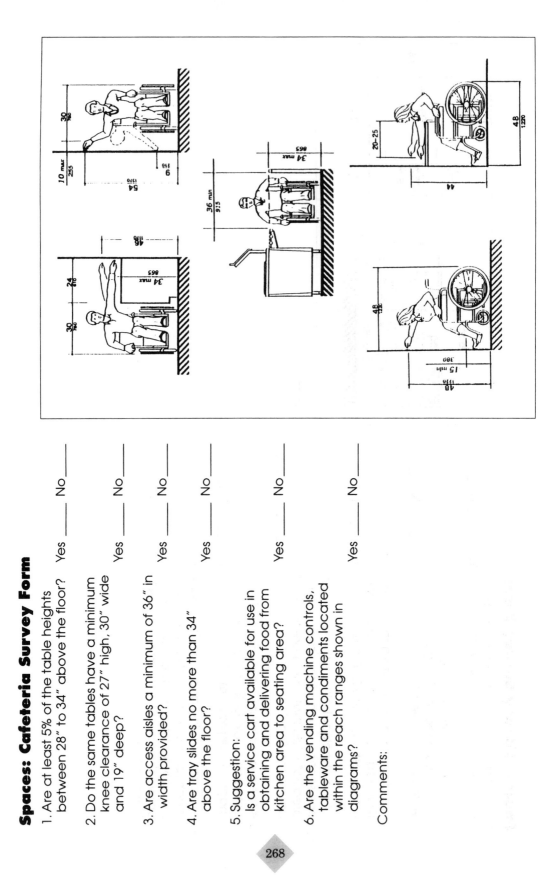

1. Are at least 5% of the table heights between 28" to 34" above the floor?

Yes _____ No _____

2. Do the same tables have a minimum knee clearance of 27" high, 30" wide and 19" deep?

Yes _____ No _____

3. Are access aisles a minimum of 36" in width provided?

Yes _____ No _____

4. Are tray slides no more than 34" above the floor?

Yes _____ No _____

5. Suggestion:
Is a service cart available for use in obtaining and delivering food from kitchen area to seating area?

Yes _____ No _____

6. Are the vending machine controls, tableware and condiments located within the reach ranges shown in diagrams?

Yes _____ No _____

Comments:

268

Spaces: Telephone Survey Form

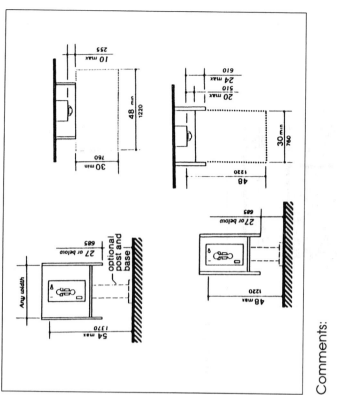

1. Does at least one phone per bank have a clear floor space of at least 30" x 48" adjacent to the telephone?　　　Yes ——— No ———

2. Are the operating controls located no more than 48" above the floor for front approaches or 54" above the floor for side approaches?　　　Yes ——— No ———

3. Do the telephones provide a volume control feature?　　　Yes ——— No ———

4. Are the telephone controls pushbutton type?　　　Yes ——— No ———

5. Is the cord from the telephone to the handset at least 29" long?　　　Yes ——— No ———

6. If there are 3 or more pay telephones in a bank of phones, does at least one of the phones have a text telephone (TDD) permanently installed?　　　Yes ——— No ———

or

Does at least one of the phones have a shelf and outlet with a portable text telephone (TDD) available?　　　Yes ——— No ———

Comments:

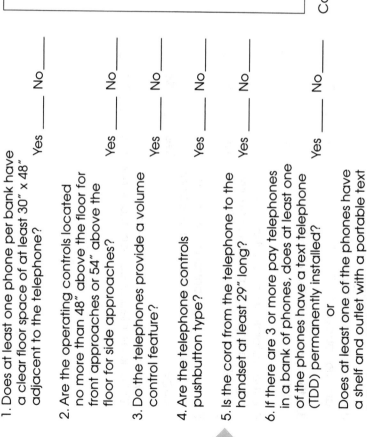

269

Spaces: Drinking Fountain Survey Form

Note: At least 50% of the drinking fountains per floor must comply with the following requirements.

1. Is there a clear floor space of at least 30" x 48" adjacent to the drinking fountain?

   Yes _____ No _____

2. Is the spout mounted between 33" and 36" above the floor?

   Yes _____ No _____

3. Is the spout mounted at the front of the unit?

   Yes _____ No _____

4. Is the water flow at least 4 inches high in a trajectory parallel or nearly parallel to the front of the unit?

   Yes _____ No _____

5. Is the operating control mounted at the front or on the side near the front edge?

   Yes _____ No _____

6. If wall mounted, is there at least 27" of knee clearance from the floor?

   Yes _____ No _____

Comments:

Directory of National Organizations and Associations Serving People with Disabilities

◆ ◆ ◆ ◆ ◆

◆ Organizations ◆

AbleData
8455 Colesville Road, Suite 935
Silver Spring, MD 20910

Ablenet, Inc.
1081 Tenth Avenue, S.E.
Minneapolis, MN 55414

American Foundation for the Blind, Inc.
15 W. 16th Street
New York, NY 10011

Autism Society of America
7910 Woodmont Avenue, Suite 650
Bethesda, MD 20814

Brain Injury Association, Inc.
1776 Massachusetts Avenue, N.W.
Suite 100
Washington, DC 20036-1904

Council for Exceptional Children
1920 Association Drive
Reston, VA 22091

Epilepsy Foundation of America
4351 Garden City Drive, Suite 406
Landover, MD 20785-2267

Information Center for Individuals with Disabilities
20 Providence Street, Room 329
Boston, MA 02116

Learning Disabilities Association of America
4156 Library Road
Pittsburgh, PA 15234

Muscular Dystrophy Association, Inc.
810 Seventh Avenue
New York, NY 10019

National Amputation Foundation
12–45 150th Street
Whitestone, NY 11357

National Association for Mental Health
10 Columbus Circle
New York, NY 10019

National Association of Developmental Disabilities Councils
1234 Massachusetts Avenue, N.W.
Suite 103
Washington, DC 20005

National Center for Youth with Disabilities
P.O. Box 1492
Washington, DC 20013

National Down Syndrome Society
666 Broadway, Suite 810
New York, NY 10012

National Easter Seal Society
2023 W. Ogden Avenue
Chicago, IL 60612

National Federation of the Blind
1800 Johnson Street
Baltimore, MD 21230

National Information Center on Deafness
Gallaudet College
800 Florida Avenue, N.E.
Washington, DC 20002-3695

National Multiple Sclerosis Society
733 3rd Avenue
New York, NY 10017

The National Parent Network on Disabilities
1600 Prince Street, Suite 115
Alexandria, VA 22314

National Spinal Cord Injury Association
600 W. Cummings Park, Suite 2000
Woburn, MA 01801

The Arc
(a national organization on mental retardation)
500 E. Border Street, Suite 300
Arlington, TX 76010

The Association for Persons with Severe Handicaps
29 W. Susquehanna Avenue, Suite 210
Baltimore, MD 21204

United Cerebral Palsy Associations
1522 K Street, N.W., Suite 1112
Washington, DC 20005

U.S. Architectural and Transportation Barriers Compliance Board
1111 18th Street, N.W., Suite 501
Washington, DC 20036-3894

◆ Sports and Recreation Associations ◆

American Alliance for Health, Physical Education, Recreation, and Dance (AAHPERD)
1900 Association Drive
Reston, VA 22091

American Blind Bowling Association
150 N. Bellaire Avenue
Louisville, KY 40206

American Therapeutic Recreation Association
P.O. Box 15215
Hattiesburg, MS 39404

Disabled Outdoorsmen
5223 S. Lorel Avenue
Chicago, IL 60638

Disabled Sports, USA
451 Hungerford Drive, Suite 100
Rockville, MD 20850

International Committee of the Silent Sports
Gallaudet College
800 Florida Avenue and 7th Street, N.E.
Washington, DC 20002

International Wheelchair Road Racers Club, Inc.
165 78th Avenue, N.E.
St. Petersburg, FL 33702

National Amputee Skiing Association
3738 Walnut Avenue
Carmichael, CA 95608

National Council-Boy Scouts of America
Scouting for the Handicapped
1325 Walnut Hill Lane
Irving, TX 75038-3096

National Foundation of Wheelchair Tennis
941 Calle Amanecer, Suite B
San Clemente, CA 92672

National Recreation & Park Association
2775 S. Quincy Street, Suite 300
Arlington, VA 22206-2204

National Sports Center for the Disabled
P.O. Box 36
Winter Park, CO 80482

National Therapeutic Recreation Society
2775 S. Quincy Street, Suite 300
Arlington, VA 22206-2204

National Wheelchair Athletic Association
3617 Betty Drive, Suite S
Colorado Springs, CO 80907

National Wheelchair Softball Association
P.O. Box 737
Sioux Falls, SD 57101

Northeast Passage
P.O. Box 127
Durham, NH 03824

Office of Special Programs and Populations
National Park Service
U.S. Department of
the Interior
P.O. Box 371127
Washington, DC 20013

Ski for Light, Inc.
1455 W. Lake Street
Minneapolis, MN 55408

United States Association for Blind Athletes
Kiowa and Institute Streets
Colorado Springs, CO 80903

United States Cerebral Palsy Athletic Association
34518 Warren Road, Suite 264
Westland, MI 48185

United States Olympic Committee's Committee on Sport for the Disabled
1750 E. Boulder Avenue
Colorado Springs, CO 80909-5760

Vinland Center
3675 Ihduhapi Road
Loretto, MN 55357

Wilderness Inquiry
1313 Fifth Street, S.E.
P.O. Box 84
Minneapolis, MN 55414-1546

Recreation Inventory for Inclusive Participation and Recreation Evaluation Forms

◆ ◆ ◆ ◆ ◆

RECREATION INVENTORY FOR INCLUSIVE PARTICIPATION (RIIP)
PART I: (A) APPROPRIATENESS OF RECREATION ACTIVITY/SETTING

When an activity or setting is being examined for recreation involvement, several key areas should be addressed prior to implementing the program. These areas relate to the *appropriateness* of the activity or setting to an individual's needs, preferences, and skill level.

With such a wide variety of leisure-related activities and settings available to individuals with disabilities, the information gained from the following questions will assist the person with a disability, his or her care providers, and the recreation staff in determining the appropriateness of the activity and setting for participation. In situations in which a decision between two or more activities must be made, this information may assist in determining the next ideal activity to meet the individual's needs and skill level.

Record the participant's name, activity, setting, and date, and check the appropriate responses to the following seven questions. If the responses to the questions are affirmative (i.e., yes), then proceed to the next step of the RIIP (Part II: Activity/Discrepancy Analysis). If the responses to these questions fail to show positive results, then an alternative recreation activity or setting should be selected for analysis and potential participation.

Name of Participant: _____ Date: _____

Activity/Skill: _____

Community Leisure Setting: _____

Parent/Professional Filling Out Form: _____

1. Is the activity or setting selected appropriate for people without disabilities of the same chronological age?
   ____ yes ____ no

2. Does the individual demonstrate a preference for this activity, or could he/she benefit (i.e., individual has related goals/objectives stated in program plan, IEP, IHP) from participating in this particular activity or setting?
   ____ yes ____ no

3. Can the individual financially afford/receive financial assistance to gain access to this specific activity/setting?
   ____ yes ____ no

4. If materials or equipment are necessary for participating in the activity or setting, does the individual own or have access to the necessary materials/equipment (e.g., borrow from recreation center, family, friend)?
   ____ yes ____ no

5. If necessary, are material and/or procedural adaptations available for the individual with physical disabilities?
   ____ yes ____ no

6. Does the individual have access to some form of transportation to get to the leisure setting?
   ____ yes ____ no

7. If physical accessibility is a special consideration for participating, does the setting provide easy access (e.g., handicapped parking, curb cuts, accessible restrooms, ramp to entrance)?
   ____ yes ____ no

RECREATION INVENTORY FOR INCLUSIVE PARTICIPATION (RIIP)
PART I: (B) GENERAL PROGRAM AND PARTICIPANT INFORMATION

General Information

Recreation Program Experience: _____
Directions: Check or write in the requested information on the following items. If necessary, use space on back.

1. Dates: from _____ to _____
   Days/times:
   Number of sessions:

2. Registration required: ____ yes ____ no
   Procedure: ____ in person ____ mail ____ phone
   Deadline date:

3. Guardian permission required:
   ____ yes ____ no Comment:

4. Fee charged or money required: ____ yes ____ no
   Amount: $ ____ Payment procedure:
   Are memberships available for free or reduced entrance fee?
   ____ yes ____ no Cost: ____ Good for how long?

5. Transportation provided: ____ yes ____ no
   If yes, is it handicapped accessible (e.g., wheelchair lift)?
   ____ yes ____ no
   Other comments:

6. Comment on type of dress worn:

7. List required equipment and materials:
   a. Facility owned:
   b. Participant owned:

8. Special rules related to this activity (e.g., appropriate dress):

Participant Information

Name: _____ Date: _____
Directions: Refer to item in left column. Check correct response for participant. Add comments when appropriate.

1. ____ Can participate
   ____ Any conflicts (i.e., arrive late, leave early)? Comment:

2. ____ Registration not required
   ____ Can register independently
   ____ Needs assistance; Comment:

3. ____ Permission not needed
   ____ Permission granted (consent form attached)

4. ____ Participant can afford financial costs.
   ____ Other arrangements; Comment:

5. Participant's transportation choice(s):
   ____ Walk ____ Drive ____ Bus ____ Bike
   ____ Dropped off ____ Other:
   Assistance needed: ____ yes ____ no

6. ____ Participant has appropriate attire.
   ____ Other; Comment:

7. ____ Equipment/materials are supplied
   ____ Participant has equipment
   ____ Equipment/materials need to be purchased
   ____ Other; Comment:

8. ____ Participant can meet requirement
   ____ Other; Comment:

RECREATION INVENTORY FOR INCLUSIVE PARTICIPATION (RIIP)
PART II: ACTIVITY/DISCREPANCY ANALYSIS

Leisure Skill Inventory

Activity/Skill: _____

Leisure Setting: _____

Directions: Below, give a step-by-step breakdown of those *basic* and *vital* skills a person without disabilities would need in order to participate in the activity. Include all components (e.g., breaks, using restrooms, drinking fountain, telephone).

Inventory for Participant with Disability

Name: _____

Directions: Read the step(s) in left column. If participants can perform the step, mark a plus (+) in the center column. If the participant cannot perform the step, mark a minus (−) in the center column. If the participant's performance is marked (−), identify a teaching procedure or adaptation/modification for that step in the right column. Upon completion, go to Part III: Specific Activity Requirements.

STEPS (Activity Analysis):	+	−	Teaching Procedure, Adaptation/Modification, Strategy for Partial Participation
1.			1.
2.			2.
3.			3.
4.			4.
5.			5.
6.			6.

(continued)

(continued)

7.

8.

9.

10.

11.

12.

13.

14.

15.

16.

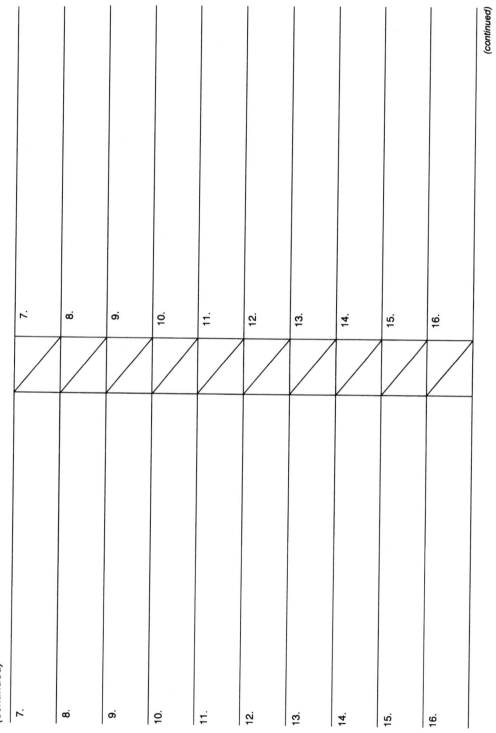

(continued)

(continued)

STEPS (Activity Analysis):	+ / −	Teaching Procedure, Adaptation/Modification, Strategy for Partial Participation
17.		17.
18.		18.
19.		19.
20.		20.
21.		21.
22.		22.
23.		23.
24.		24.
25.		25.

(If needed, use additional space on back.)

RECREATION INVENTORY FOR INCLUSIVE PARTICIPATION (RIIP)
PART III: SPECIFIC ACTIVITY REQUIREMENTS

Name: _____ Date: _____

Question: After completing and reviewing the ACTIVITY/DISCREPANCY ANALYSIS, if particular responses would be difficult for the participant to perform, would special material/procedural adaptations or teaching procedures be readily available to enable at least partial participation?

_____ yes _____ no

If *yes*, participate in the program.

If *no,* please check the area(s) of concern listed below. This allows for an in-depth analysis of the specific requirements needed for this activity in the identified area of concern (e.g., physical, cognitive/academic, xsocial/emotional).

____ Physical Skill Requirements: Refer to RIIP PART IV (A).

____ Cognitive/Academic Skill Requirements: Refer to RIIP PART IV (B).

____ Social/Emotional Skill Requirements: Refer to RIIP PART IV (C).

RECREATION INVENTORY FOR INCLUSIVE PARTICIPATION (RIIP)

PART IV: FURTHER ACTIVITY CONSIDERATIONS—(C) SOCIAL/EMOTIONAL CONSIDERATIONS

Activity: _____   Name: _____   Date: _____

Directions: Check, circle, or write in the correct information.

Directions: Refer to information in left column. Answer yes or no as to whether the participant can participate at the level requested. If the answer is "no," comment on the assistance that is required.*

---

1. a. This activity occurs: ____ alone ____ with 2 ____ in small group (3–8) ____ in large group (8 or more)
   b. This activity is structured:
   ____ class structure ____ no structure ____ combination
   c. Comment on the type and amount of supervision:
   _____

1. a.	____ yes ____ no
	Comments:
b.	____ yes ____ no
c.	____ yes ____ no
	Comments:

---

2. This activity involves: ____ females ____ males
   Age range: ____ preschool (under 5)
   ____ children (5–12) ____ teens (13–19)
   ____ adults (20–64) ____ senior citizens (65 +)

2.	____ yes ____ no
	Comments:

---

3. a. Check the social interactions listed below that pertain to this activity.
   ____ Share materials ____ Take turns ____ Compete
   ____ Communicate with other participants
   ____ Have physical contact with other participants
   b. Noise level: ____ quiet. ____ medium ____ loud ____ mixed

3. a.	____ yes ____ no
	Comments:
b.	____ yes ____ no
	Comments:

---

4. List words or common phrases associated with or used during this activity (e.g., nice shot).
   _____
   _____
   _____

4.	____ yes ____ no
	Comments:

---

*If social/emotional considerations have been met, proceed as planned. If not, an alternative activity or setting should be considered for investigation and potential participation.

SKILL ACQUISITION EVALUATION

A. Name: _____ D. Program: _____ Date: _____

B. Goal Statement: _____

C. Verbal Cue: _____

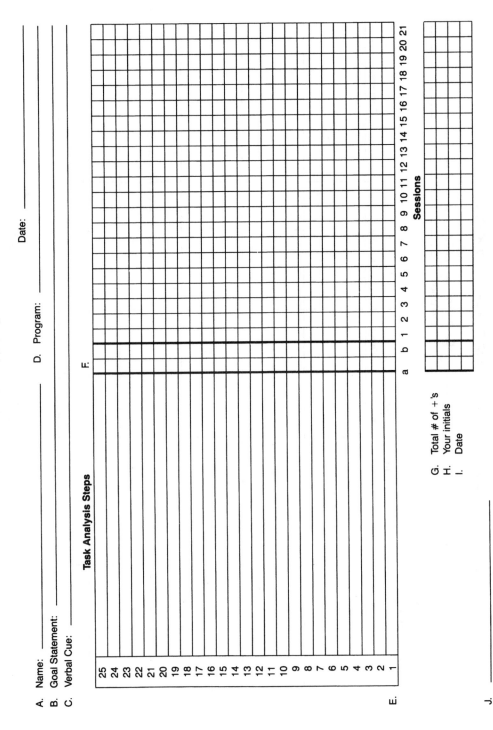

E. Task Analysis Steps

F.

G. Total # of +'s

H. Your initials

I. Date

J. _____ Skill

SOCIAL INTERACTION EVALUATION FOR ONE PARTICIPANT

A. Program Title: _____

B. Program Goal: _____

C. Name: _____

Evaluator: _____

D. Date: _____

E. Level of Interaction

Time (preset)	None	Staff	Part. w/dis.	Part. w/o dis.	Other	Activity	Comments

F.

G.

H. Totals

A					
I					

Key

A = Appropriate Social Interaction
I = Inappropriate Social Interaction

284

SOCIAL INTERACTION EVALUATION FOR TWO OR MORE PARTICIPANTS

A. Program Title: _____

B. Program Goal: _____

D. Date: _____

E. Times to Observe: 1. _____ 2. _____ 3. _____

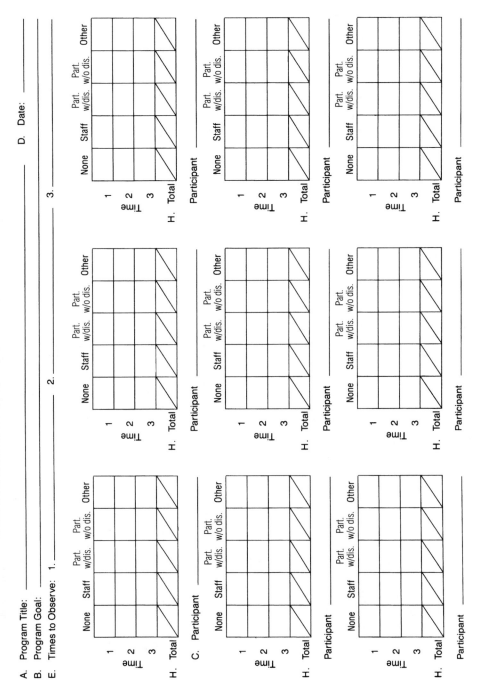

C. Participant _____

285

SOCIAL INTERACTION EVALUATION SUMMARY SHEET

A. Program Title: _____

B. Program Instructor: _____

C. Other Staff: _____

D. Duration of Program: _____   Date: _____

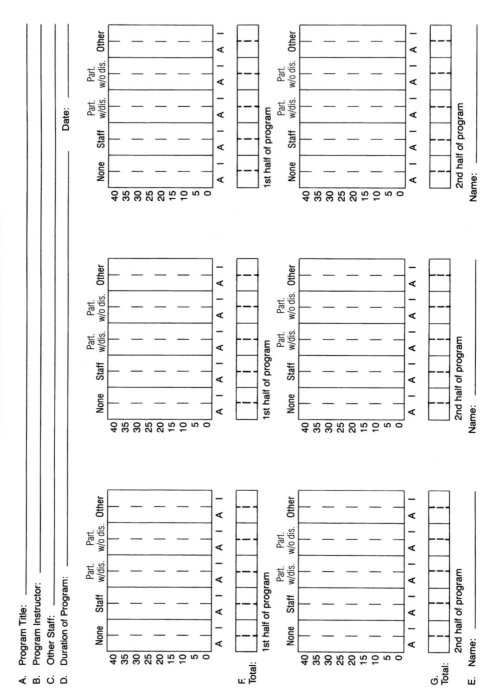

F. Total:

G. Total:

E. Name:

SOCIOMETRY EVALUATION INFORMATION FORM

A. Program Title: _____

B. Program Goal: _____

C. Date of Evaluation: _____

D.

Participant	Symbol	G. 1	2	3	4	5	6	7	8	9	10	11	12	13	14	15	16	17	18	19	20
1																					
2																					
3																					
4																					
5																					
6																					
7																					
8																					
9																					
10																					
11																					
12																					
13																					
14																					
15																					
16																					
17																					
18																					
19																					
20																					

TOTAL:

E. Question(s) Asked: _____

Symbol: ○ = participant without a disability; △ = participant with a disability.

SOCIOGRAM EVALUATION GRAPHING FORM

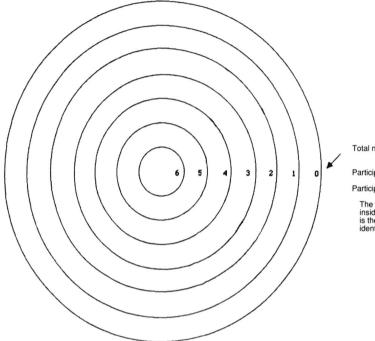

Total number of interactions

Participant without a disability ◯

Participant with a disability △

The number
inside each symbol
is the participant's
identification number.

PEER ACCEPTANCE SURVEY

Name: _____

1. I don't have any friends who have mental retardation or a disability.
   Agree_____   Disagree_____   Undecided_____

2. If my sister or brother had mental retardation, I wouldn't talk about it to anyone.
   Agree_____   Disagree_____   Undecided_____

3. I have talked to people who use wheelchairs.
   Agree_____   Disagree_____   Undecided_____

4. If I found out that someone I hang around with has mental retardation, I would still be his/her friend.
   Agree_____   Disagree_____   Undecided_____

5. I have talked with some people with mental retardation at the park.
   Agree_____   Disagree_____   Undecided_____

6. It snows in Minnesota in the winter.
   Agree_____   Disagree_____   Undecided_____

7. There is no reason for me to spend time with anyone who has a disability.
   Agree_____   Disagree_____   Undecided_____

8. I think that a student who is deaf or blind could be in my recreation program.
   Agree_____   Disagree_____   Undecided_____

9. I wouldn't want a person with a disability to be my partner in an activity.
   Agree_____   Disagree_____   Undecided_____

10. I believe that I could become close friends with a person who has a disability.
    Agree_____   Disagree_____   Undecided_____

11. I have helped some people who are in wheelchairs.
    Agree_____   Disagree_____   Undecided_____

12. Minneapolis is a large city in Minnesota.
    Agree_____   Disagree_____   Undecided_____

13. People who have mental retardation should not come to the park for activities.
    Agree_____   Disagree_____   Undecided_____

14. I wish I could become friends with a person with mental retardation.
    Agree_____   Disagree_____   Undecided_____

15. I would not like to be around a person who looked or acted different.
    Agree_____   Disagree_____   Undecided_____

16. If someone told me about a new TV program about disabilities, I would probably watch it.
    Agree_____   Disagree_____   Undecided_____

17. I have never talked with a person who is paralyzed or couldn't walk.
    Agree_____   Disagree_____   Undecided_____

18. I don't say "Hi" to people who have mental retardation.
    Agree_____   Disagree_____   Undecided_____

19. Minnesota has many lakes.
    Agree_____   Disagree_____   Undecided_____

20. I believe students with disabilities should participate with other people in the recreation department's programs.
    Agree_____   Disagree_____   Undecided_____

Finished! Thank you for completing the survey.

(This questionnaire was adapted from Voeltz, L. [1980]. Children's attitudes toward handicapped peers. *American Journal of Mental Deficiency, 84,* 455–464.)

PEER ACCEPTANCE SURVEY ANSWER KEY

1. I don't have any friends who have mental retardation or a disability.
    Agree __0__   Disagree __2__   Undecided __1__
2. If my sister or brother had mental retardation, I wouldn't talk about it to anyone.
    Agree __0__   Disagree __2__   Undecided __1__
3. I have talked to people who use wheelchairs.
    Agree __2__   Disagree __0__   Undecided __1__
4. If I found out that someone I hang around with has mental retardation, I would still be his/her friend.
    Agree __2__   Disagree __0__   Undecided __1__
5. I have talked with some people with mental retardation at the park.
    Agree __2__   Disagree __0__   Undecided __1__
6. It snows in Minnesota in the winter.
    Agree __2__   Disagree __0__   Undecided __0__
7. There is no reason for me to spend time with anyone who has a disability.
    Agree __0__   Disagree __2__   Undecided __1__
8. I think that a student who is deaf or blind could be in my recreation program.
    Agree __2__   Disagree __0__   Undecided __1__
9. I wouldn't want a person with a disability to be my partner in an activity.
    Agree __0__   Disagree __2__   Undecided __1__
10. I believe that I could become close friends with a person who has a disability.
    Agree __2__   Disagree __0__   Undecided __1__
11. I have helped some people who are in wheelchairs.
    Agree __2__   Disagree __0__   Undecided __1__
12. Minneapolis is a large city in Minnesota.
    Agree __2__   Disagree __0__   Undecided __0__
13. People who have mental retardation should not come to the park for activities.
    Agree __0__   Disagree __2__   Undecided __1__
14. I wish I could become friends with a person with mental retardation.
    Agree __2__   Disagree __0__   Undecided __1__
15. I would not like to be around a person who looked or acted different.
    Agree __0__   Disagree __2__   Undecided __1__
16. If someone told me about a new TV program about disabilities, I would probably watch it.
    Agree __2__   Disagree __0__   Undecided __1__
17. I have never talked with a person who is paralyzed or couldn't walk.
    Agree __0__   Disagree __2__   Undecided __1__
18. I don't say "Hi" to people who have mental retardation.
    Agree __0__   Disagree __2__   Undecided __1__
19. Minnesota has many lakes.
    Agree __2__   Disagree __0__   Undecided __0__
20. I believe students with disabilities should participate with other people in the recreation department's programs.
    Agree __2__   Disagree __0__   Undecided __1__

(This questionnaire was adapted from Voeltz, L. [1980]. Children's attitudes toward handicapped peers. *American Journal of Mental Deficiency, 84,* 455–464.)

PEER ACCEPTANCE EVALUATION SUMMARY FORM

A. Name: _____

B. Program Title: _____

C. Program Goal: _____

D. Objective: _____ will increase his/her
    _____(name)_____
    posttest score _____ points above his/her pretest score after attending _____ sessions
    _____(number)_____   _____(number)_____
    of _____ .
      (program)

Total number of points possible = 40.

Date	Pretest Score	Date	Posttest Score	Difference between Pretest and Posttest Score
E.	F.	I.	J.	K. (J. − F.)

G. Number of program sessions _____

L. Number of sessions attended by the participant _____

Activities engaged in by the participant:

Date	Activity	Comment	Initial
H. _____	_____	_____	___
_____	_____	_____	___
_____	_____	_____	___
_____	_____	_____	___
_____	_____	_____	___
_____	_____	_____	___
_____	_____	_____	___
_____	_____	_____	___
_____	_____	_____	___
_____	_____	_____	___
_____	_____	_____	___
_____	_____	_____	___
_____	_____	_____	___
_____	_____	_____	___

SELF-CONCEPT QUESTIONNAIRE

Name: _____

Date: _____

1.	I feel like I can improve how I look.	Never	Seldom	Sometimes	Often	Always
2.	Others think of me as a leader.	Never	Seldom	Sometimes	Often	Always
3.	I make friends easily.	Never	Seldom	Sometimes	Often	Always
4.	I learn how to play games fast.	Never	Seldom	Sometimes	Often	Always
5.	I consider myself smart.	Never	Seldom	Sometimes	Often	Always
6.	Others tease me.	Never	Seldom	Sometimes	Often	Always
7.	I want to be like someone else.	Never	Seldom	Sometimes	Often	Always
8.	I enjoy making decisions.	Never	Seldom	Sometimes	Often	Always
9.	I get picked last in games.	Never	Seldom	Sometimes	Often	Always
10.	I feel good when I learn something new.	Never	Seldom	Sometimes	Often	Always
11.	When I look in the mirror, I like myself.	Never	Seldom	Sometimes	Often	Always
12.	I am a leader when I am with others my own age.	Never	Seldom	Sometimes	Often	Always
13.	I like to play alone.	Never	Seldom	Sometimes	Often	Always
14.	Others consider me smart.	Never	Seldom	Sometimes	Often	Always
15.	Others like playing games with me.	Never	Seldom	Sometimes	Often	Always
16.	Others ask me to be their friend.	Never	Seldom	Sometimes	Often	Always
17.	I feel bad when my team loses.	Never	Seldom	Sometimes	Often	Always
18.	Others tell me what to do.	Never	Seldom	Sometimes	Often	Always
19.	I can make up my own mind.	Never	Seldom	Sometimes	Often	Always
20.	I enjoy playing by myself.	Never	Seldom	Sometimes	Often	Always
21.	I only like to play if I win.	Never	Seldom	Sometimes	Often	Always
22.	I get mad when someone teases me.	Never	Seldom	Sometimes	Often	Always
23.	I get picked first in games.	Never	Seldom	Sometimes	Often	Always
24.	I like to play with others.	Never	Seldom	Sometimes	Often	Always
25.	I feel like I can get things done.	Never	Seldom	Sometimes	Often	Always
26.	I get what I can from others.	Never	Seldom	Sometimes	Often	Always
27.	I feel it's my fault when my team loses.	Never	Seldom	Sometimes	Often	Always
28.	Others enjoy being with me.	Never	Seldom	Sometimes	Often	Always
29.	I can choose what to do during my free time.	Never	Seldom	Sometimes	Often	Always
30.	Others like to be around me.	Never	Seldom	Sometimes	Often	Always

Finished! Thank you for completing the survey.

SELF-CONCEPT QUESTIONNAIRE ANSWER KEY

		1	2	3	4	5
1.	I feel like I can improve how I look.	Never	Seldom	Sometimes	Often	Always
2.	Others think of me as a leader.	Never	Seldom	Sometimes	Often	Always
3.	I make friends easily.	Never	Seldom	Sometimes	Often	Always
4.	I learn how to play games fast.	Never	Seldom	Sometimes	Often	Always
5.	I consider myself smart.	Never	Seldom	Sometimes	Often	Always
6.	Others tease me.	Never (1)	Seldom (5)	Sometimes (4)	Often (3)	Always (1)
7.	I want to be like someone else.	Never (4)	Seldom (5)	Sometimes (3)	Often (2)	Always (1)
8.	I enjoy making decisions.	Never (1)	Seldom (2)	Sometimes (3)	Often (4)	Always (5)
9.	I get picked last in games.	Never (1)	Seldom (3)	Sometimes (4)	Often (5)	Always (1)
10.	I feel good when I learn something new.	Never (1)	Seldom (2)	Sometimes (3)	Often (4)	Always (5)
11.	When I look in the mirror, I like myself.	Never (1)	Seldom (2)	Sometimes (3)	Often (4)	Always (5)
12.	I am a leader when I am with others my own age.	Never (1)	Seldom (3)	Sometimes (4)	Often (5)	Always (1)
13.	I like to play alone.	Never (1)	Seldom (4)	Sometimes (5)	Often (3)	Always (1)
14.	Others consider me smart.	Never (1)	Seldom (2)	Sometimes (3)	Often (4)	Always (5)
15.	Others like playing games with me.	Never (1)	Seldom (2)	Sometimes (3)	Often (4)	Always (5)
16.	Others ask me to be their friend.	Never (1)	Seldom (3)	Sometimes (4)	Often (5)	Always (1)
17.	I feel bad when my team loses.	Never (1)	Seldom (3)	Sometimes (4)	Often (5)	Always (1)
18.	Others tell me what to do.	Never (1)	Seldom (3)	Sometimes (4)	Often (5)	Always (1)
19.	I can make up my own mind.	Never (1)	Seldom (2)	Sometimes (3)	Often (4)	Always (5)
20.	I enjoy playing by myself.	Never (1)	Seldom (4)	Sometimes (5)	Often (3)	Always (1)
21.	I only like to play if I win.	Never (5)	Seldom (4)	Sometimes (3)	Often (2)	Always (1)
22.	I get mad when someone teases me.	Never (5)	Seldom (4)	Sometimes (3)	Often (2)	Always (1)
23.	I get picked first in games.	Never (1)	Seldom (3)	Sometimes (4)	Often (5)	Always (1)
24.	I like to play with others.	Never (1)	Seldom (3)	Sometimes (4)	Often (5)	Always (1)
25.	I feel like I can get things done.	Never (1)	Seldom (2)	Sometimes (3)	Often (4)	Always (5)
26.	I get what I can from others.	Never (1)	Seldom (3)	Sometimes (4)	Often (5)	Always (1)
27.	I feel it's my fault when my team loses.	Never (1)	Seldom (5)	Sometimes (4)	Often (3)	Always (1)
28.	Others enjoy being with me.	Never (1)	Seldom (2)	Sometimes (3)	Often (4)	Always (5)
29.	I can choose what to do during my free time.	Never (1)	Seldom (2)	Sometimes (3)	Often (4)	Always (5)
30.	Others like to be around me.	Never (1)	Seldom (2)	Sometimes (3)	Often (4)	Always (5)

SELF-CONCEPT EVALUATION SUMMARY FORM

A. Name: _____

B. Program Title: _____

C. Program Goal: _____

D. Objective: _____ will increase his/her
   _____(name)
   posttest score _____ points above his/her pretest score after attending _____ sessions
                  (number)   (number)
   of _____ .
      (program)

Total number of points possible = 150.

Date	Pretest Score	Date	Posttest Score	Difference between Pretest and Posttest Score
E.	F.	I.	J.	K. (J. − F.)

G. Number of program sessions _____

L. Number of sessions attended by the participant _____

Activities engaged in by the participant:

Date	Activity	Comment	Initial
H. _____	_____	_____	___
_____	_____	_____	___
_____	_____	_____	___
_____	_____	_____	___
_____	_____	_____	___
_____	_____	_____	___
_____	_____	_____	___
_____	_____	_____	___
_____	_____	_____	___
_____	_____	_____	___
_____	_____	_____	___
_____	_____	_____	___
_____	_____	_____	___
_____	_____	_____	___

NUMERICAL EVALUATION INFORMATION FORM

A. Program Title: _____

B. Program Site: _____

C. Program Goal: _____

D. Program Information (include cost, meeting times, duration, day held, age of participants, etc.):

_____

_____

_____

	E. Number of participants without disabilities	F. Number of participants with disabilities	G. Program date	H. Comment
Session				
1	_____	_____	_____	_____
2	_____	_____	_____	_____
3	_____	_____	_____	_____
4	_____	_____	_____	_____
5	_____	_____	_____	_____
6	_____	_____	_____	_____
7	_____	_____	_____	_____
8	_____	_____	_____	_____
9	_____	_____	_____	_____
10	_____	_____	_____	_____

I. Total number of participants without disabilities

J. Total number of participants with disabilities

K. Total number of participants (with and without disabilities)

_____

_____

_____

L. Number of sessions conducted

M. Average number of participants per session

N. Number of participants registered

_____

_____

_____

Volunteer
Advocacy Forms

VOLUNTEER ADVOCACY FORMS
Application for Volunteer Advocacy

Name _____ Date _____

Address _____

City/Zip _____

Home Phone _____ Business Phone _____

Birth Date _____ Age _____ Gender _____ Marital Status _____

Education _____

Employer _____

Special Skills/Interests _____

Have you taken Community Education/Community Recreation classes before?

Yes ____ No ____

Have you ever worked/volunteered with people with mental or physical disabilities?

Yes ____ No ____

How did you hear about this program?

_____ Local Newspaper(s). Specify: _____

_____ Radio Station. Specify: _____

_____ The Arc Newsletter
_____ United Way Voluntary Action Center
_____ Other. Specify: _____

Please specify what age/gender you would prefer to participate with in recreation.

____ Child ____ Teen ____ Adult ____ Older Adult ____ Male ____ Female

Do you have your own transportation? Yes ____ No ____

Would you be willing to transport the participant to class? Yes ____ No ____

How much time per week, on the average, would you be able to spend with a participant who has disabilities?

_____

Please list two personal and one work-related reference (name and day phone number).

1.

2.

3.

Please state the city/county locations you would be willing to travel to: _____

_____

Please indicate your areas of interest:

____ Sports/Fitness   ____ Health   ____ Other. Specify: _____
____ Arts/Crafts/Hobbies   ____ Aquatics   _____
____ Finance/Budget Management ____ Cooking   _____

Volunteer Advocate Call Sheet

Name _____

Address _____

Date called _____   Date material sent _____

Date material received in office _____

Date of personal interview _____

Date assignment given _____   Date of in-service training _____

Volunteer Advocate–Participant Match

Participant Name _____ Phone _____

Volunteer Name _____ Phone _____

Date of final confirmation _____ Date session begins _____

Date session ends _____ Session Title _____

Location of session _____

District _____ Is volunteer transporting student? Yes ___ No ___

Additional Comments:

Volunteer Advocate Program Evaluation Form
(Sample Form)

Directions:

To be filled out by volunteer advocate. Return to community recreation professional.

1. Do you feel you received adequate orientation? If not, what do you suggest?

2. Was the program leader helpful to you?

3. In what ways was the experience beneficial to you?

4. Did you feel overworked during the program? If so, in what ways?

5. Did you enjoy the work? Explain.

6. Would you volunteer again?

7. Additional comments:

**Volunteer Advocate Evaluation Form
(Sample Form)**

Directions:

To be completed by community recreation professional or program leader.

1. Did the volunteer attend the scheduled training program?

2. Did the volunteer attend all program days as arranged? If not, why?

3. Did the volunteer offer any suggestions to improve the program? If yes, what were they?

4. How much supervision did the volunteer require?

5. Would you ask the volunteer back? If not, explain.

6. Additional comments:

Annotated
Bibliography

*with Linda A. Heyne
and Leo H. McAvoy*

Bedini, L.A., Bullock, C.C., & Driscoll, L.B. (1993). The effects of leisure education on factors contributing to the successful transition of students with mental retardation from school to adult life. *Therapeutic Recreation Journal, 27(2),* 70–82.

The purpose of the study was to determine the effectiveness of a leisure education program taught in a public school system on factors contributing to the successful transition (i.e., independent functioning within the community, especially in relation to leisure pursuits) of students with mental retardation from secondary schools to adult life. Since there were no leisure education programs in the public schools in North Carolina, project staff conceptualized, developed, and implemented the *Wake Leisure Education Program*, which addressed perceived leisure-related needs of students with mental retardation in transition. The 38 participants, ages 17–22, included high school students in special education classes in eight schools. Students participated in individualized instruction for 1 academic year, which included two sessions per week conducted in small groups or within a classroom until students were ready to apply the planning process to community settings. Data were collected from several sources, and the collection process employed three different methods: 1) surveys of students, parents, and teachers; 2) case studies; and 3) progress notes that were recorded after each session for each student. The results of the study suggest that a leisure education curriculum applied in the public school system for students with mental retardation has potential for increasing leisure wellness and contributing to successful transition from school to adult life. The results of this study also suggest improvement in initiation skills, decision making, and independent planning.

Braddock, D., & Fujiura, G. (1991). Politics, public policy, and the development of community mental retardation services in the United States. *American Journal on Mental Retardation, 95,* 369–387.

This article addresses factors that shape public policy and influence federal funding for community services for individuals with mental retardation. Public policy factors include the state's size, wealth, degree of federal assistance, political culture, and interest group activity. A shift in federal funding from large congregate facilities to smaller, community-based facilities is described. The authors note that transformation in community services has just begun and many needs remain unmet. They conclude that to develop greater community services, it is necessary to consider political context and advocacy.

Brasile, F.M. (1990). Wheelchair sports: A new perspective on integration. *Adapted Physical Activity Quarterly, 7,* 3–11.

This article addresses segregated and reverse-integrated wheelchair sports programs. The author notes that segregated programs often have focused on disability rather than on ability, but segregated programs can be positive if they assist in human growth and development. The author suggests that segregated sports should not be compared with sports for people without disabilities but should be viewed as unique opportunities in their own right. The author maintains that one method of integration is to encourage participation by individuals without disabilities in previously segregated programs. In this way, the focus can be transferred from disability to ability. By allowing reverse integration, myths will be eliminated, social self-esteem will be promoted, and norm-referenced performance standards will be generated.

Dattilo, J. (1991). Recreation and leisure: A review of the literature and recommendations for future directions. In L.H. Meyer, C.A. Peck, & L. Brown (Eds.), *Critical issues in the lives of people with severe disabilities* (pp. 171–193). Baltimore: Paul H. Brookes Publishing Co.

This chapter provides a review of the literature that addresses leisure for people with developmental disabilities as it relates to The Association for Persons with Severe Handicaps (TASH) *Deinstitutionalization Policy* resolution, the *Gramm-Rudman Resolution*, and the *Policy Statement for Cessation of Capital Investment in Segregated Settings*. Five critical issues are addressed: 1) the implications of TASH resolutions on leisure service delivery, 2) current status of leisure services for people with significant disabilities, 3) research that supports the principles espoused by the TASH resolutions and provides a rationale for leisure education, 4) protocols for developing leisure assessments, and 5) recommendations for research priorities. This chapter discusses how recent research efforts have addressed TASH resolutions, particularly as they relate to the following five specific goal areas: 1) competence demonstrated through choice/decision making, 2) an awareness of chronologically age-appropriate community-based leisure behavior, 3) the demonstration of social interaction skills, 4) an understanding of available leisure resources, and 5) the acquisition of leisure participation skills.

Dattilo, J., & Schleien, S. (1994). Understanding leisure services for individuals with mental retardation. *Mental Retardation, 32*(1), 53–59.

This article was developed to further the understanding of the complex process of leisure service delivery for people with mental retardation. Limitations of leisure services for individuals who challenge service delivery systems and the right for all people to experience leisure are discussed. Suggestions are made for developing programs involving social integration with peers without disabilities. Also, ideas about facilitating active participation, developing age-appropriate behaviors, and encouraging self-determined participation are espoused. Finally, the authors discuss the committed involvement of and communication among consumers, family members, leisure service providers, and educators that are necessary to provide comprehensive and inclusive services.

Green, F., & Schleien, S. (1991). Understanding friendship and recreation: A theoretical sampling. *Therapeutic Recreation Journal, 25*(4), 29–40.

The purpose of this study was to determine how friendship is perceived by adults with mental retardation. The subjects included 11 adults with mental retardation, ages 25–38 years, who lived in an intermediate care facility. The participants were interviewed and observed over a 5-month period. Maps of social relationships (e.g., friends, best friends, significant others, service providers, acquaintances) were constructed for each of the participants. The results indicated that the participants perceived staff and family to be obligatory friends and could not distinguish between friends and service providers. Participants seldom developed reciprocal relationships with peers without disabilities. The participants did not meet or make new friends during recreation, but the authors suggest that recreation may serve as a medium to developing friendships. Social skill limitations exhibited in segregated programs (e.g., absence of common courtesy, reluctance to interact with peers, engagement in parallel play) are noted. The authors conclude that friendship development should be a priority for service providers, including instruction in social and friendship skills.

Hamre-Nietupski, S., Hendrickson, J., Nietupski, J., & Sasso, G. (1993). Perceptions of teachers of students with moderate, severe, or profound disabilities on facilitating friendships with nondisabled peers. *Education and Training in Mental Retardation, 28,* 111–127.

This investigation examines the perceptions of teachers of students with significant disabilities about facilitating friendships between students with and without disabilities. One hundred and fifty-eight special education teachers working with students with significant disabilities responded to the survey. The teachers consisted of a volunteer cohort of individuals who spent part or all of their instructional time during the school year with students with moderate, severe, or profound disabilities. Two methods of recruiting teachers were employed. Results of the survey indicated that teachers of students with moderate, severe, and profound disabilities clearly believed that friendships with peers without disabilities are possible, can be facilitated, should be facilitated, and are beneficial to students with and without disabilities and that they have a lead role to play in facilitating friendships. It is recommended that future research build upon these findings and enhance teachers' abilities to facilitate mutually rewarding friendships.

Hanline, M.F. (1993). Inclusion of preschoolers with profound disabilities: An analysis of children's interactions. *Journal of The Association for Persons with Severe Handicaps, 18,* 28–35.

The purpose of the study was to explore the nature of peer social interactions in a preschool program that included children with profound disabilities. Three children with disabilities and three children without disabilities participated in the study. The program took place at the educational research center for child development located on the campus of Florida State University. A developmentally appropriate play-based curriculum was implemented. Interactions between children with and without disabilities were encouraged within the context of ongoing play activities by positioning the children with disabilities to promote participation in activities, prompting and reinforcing appropriate social interactions, modeling appropriate interaction behavior, interpreting the behavior of the children with disabilities as meaningful, and answering questions of children without disabilities about the children with disabilities. Positive and negative social behaviors that served to initiate an interaction, terminate an interaction, or respond to the behavior of another child within an ongoing interaction were recorded. Results showed that the children with profound disabilities had many opportunities to participate in peer social interactions and that the children with and without disabilities were mutually responsive to each other. It was recommended that, in the future, particular attention be paid to encouraging the initiation of interactions and to increasing understanding of the idiosyncratic behaviors of children with profound disabilities by the children without disabilities.

Havens, M.D. (1992). *Bridges to accessibility: A primer for including persons with disabilities in adventure curricula.* **Dubuque, IA: Kendall/ Hunt.**

The book illustrates the attitudes and technical skills necessary to make integration a reality in community-based adventure programs. The book starts with a brief history of accessible adventure programs and a rationale for integration. It gives practical descriptions of common disabling conditions (mental and physical) with practical implications for adventure leaders. The author addresses the issue of adventure leader attitudes toward disabilities and integration, with a recommended training process to sensitize staff and other participants to the realities and capabilities of people with disabilities. The book includes a well-described accessible adventure curriculum with specific recommendations on how to make a typical set of adventure activities and events accessible and integrated, including best professional practices. There are a number of practical solutions to challenges and problems of integrating adventure programs, a number of case studies and scenarios, and generous use of pictures to illustrate equipment and program adaptations. A resource section lists publications, videotapes, and organizations one can turn to for assistance, as well as accessibility surveys, safety considerations, and a staff training curriculum.

Heyne, L.A., & Schleien, S.J. (1994). Leisure and recreation programming to enhance quality of life. In E. Cipani & F. Spooner (Eds.), *Curricular and instructional approaches for persons with severe disabilities* **(pp. 213–240). Needham, MA: Allyn & Bacon.**

This chapter provides an overview of how inclusionary leisure and recreation programming, as a curricular component, can enhance the quality of life of individuals with disabilities. Information is presented on the purposes of therapeutic recreation, historical and legislative background related to recreation services for people with disabilities, barriers to participation in community recreation programs, and strategies for including individuals with disabilities in community recreation. Inclusionary strategies that are described include 1) assessing individual needs and preferences; 2) selecting recreation activities for instruction based on programming principles such as functionality, chronological age–appropriateness, individualization, and the promotion of collateral skills; 3) use of environmental inventories and task analyses; 4) behavioral teaching methods; and 5) program evaluation. Curricula that promote inclusionary community recreation are recommended, and a model inclusive recreation program is described.

Hutchison, P., & McGill, J. (1992). *Leisure, integration and community.* **Concord, Ontario, Canada: Leisurability Publications.**

This is the first Canadian text in the field of leisure and people with disabilities. It is intended to be used as a college and university text and as a resource for those facilitating integrated leisure opportunities and services in community settings. The authors believe the text also is relevant for those working in community health care, parents, advocates, and volunteers. The authors provide a philosophical framework for creating change that is necessary for people with disabilities to have full leisure lifestyles and be participating members of their communities. The book gives a full description of life experiences of people with disabilities in Canada; describes the process of devaluation that can affect people with disabilities; and outlines steps to be taken in integration, empowerment, and community building. The authors propose a number of strategies to make integration a reality and relate a number of success stories to illustrate procedures and impacts of programs.

Jolly, A.C., Test, D.W., & Spooner, F. (1993). Using badges to increase initiations of children with severe disabilities in a play setting. *Journal of The Association for Persons with Severe Handicaps, 18,* **46–51.**

The purpose of the study was to extend the literature on student-initiated approaches to teaching play skills by empowering students with significant disabilities to choose and initiate preferred activities within a free-play setting. Participants included two nonverbal males with severe and profound mental retardation and three students without disabilities from a fourth-grade classroom. The study took place in the self-contained classroom of the participants with disabilities and was divided into zones in which different activities took place. Materials used in the study were selected from an age-appropriate wish list of toys generated by two fourth graders without disabilities not involved in the study and were judged by the classroom teacher as toys that would promote reciprocal social interaction. Data were collected on the number of play organizers (i.e., showing or pointing to a badge to indicate choice of a play activity) provided by the students with disabilities, the number of shares (i.e., student offering or giving an object to another child, or two or more children using a common object in mutual play). Results of the study indicated that teaching students with significant disabilities to use badges as play organizers increased their ability to successfully initiate play activities and interact with their peers without disabilities.

McAvoy, L., Schatz, E., Stutz, M., Schleien, S., & Lais, G. (1989). Integrated wilderness adventure: Effects on personal and lifestyle traits of persons with and without disabilities. *Therapeutic Recreation Journal, 23*(3), 50–64.

The purpose of this study was to determine the effects of a wilderness adventure program on personal and lifestyle traits of 180 individuals with and without disabilities, ages 20–70 years. Participants took part in canoe trips through Wilderness Inquiry, an organization in Minneapolis, Minnesota, which provided integrated wilderness adventure programming. Trait anxiety levels were measured via a standardized self-evaluation questionnaire administered before and after the activity. Qualitative structured interviews presented 50 questions about participants' lifestyles; feelings about integration and wilderness experiences; and attitudes toward individuals with and without disabilities, new situations, and tolerance of others. Results demonstrated positive changes in attitudes toward people with disabilities, confidence levels, risk-taking, self-esteem, goal-setting abilities, tolerance of stress, and ability to approach new situations. The authors conclude that wilderness adventure participation can lead to positive attitude and lifestyle changes for individuals with and without disabilities.

McAvoy, L., & Schleien, S. (1988). Effects of integrated interpretive programs on persons with and without disabilities. In L.A. Beck (Ed.), *Research in interpretation: Proceedings of the 1988 National Association of Interpretation Research Symposium* (pp. 13–26). San Diego: Institute for Leisure Behavior, San Diego State University.

This study explored the effects of an integrated interpretive program on individuals with disabilities. Participants included 68 children and youths with and without disabilities, ages 8–15 years. The program occurred at nature interpretative facilities in Minnesota. Integration strategies included recreation skill instruction, cooperative learning groupings, "Special Friends" training, and use of trainer advocates. Effects of integration were measured by behavioral observation of social interactions using partial interval time sampling procedures, nondisabled peer acceptance surveys, and staff interviews. Cognitive skills were measured by surveys of information learned and staff interviews. Acquisition of the skill of snowshoeing was measured by task analytic assessments and staff interviews. Results indicated significant increases in the level of appropriate social interactions between the children with disabilities and their peers without disabilities. Peer acceptance levels and mastery of snowshoeing also increased significantly. The authors conclude that people with disabilities can successfully acquire outdoor leisure skills.

McDonnell, J., Hardman, M.L., Hightower, J., Keifer-O'Donnell, R., & Drew, C. (1993). Impact of community-based instruction on the development of adaptive behavior of secondary-level students with mental retardation. *American Journal on Mental Retardation*, 97, 575–584.

This study investigated the effects of community-based leisure instruction on the adaptive behavior of 34 high school students with moderate to profound mental retardation, ages 15–22 years. Three research questions were asked: 1) Do students with mental retardation make significant gains in adaptive behavior as a result of participation in a program emphasizing community-based leisure instruction? 2) Which individual student characteristics are predictive of the amount of community-based instruction provided? and 3) Is the amount of community-based instruction or student characteristics a stronger predictor of gains made by students in independent behavior? Students participated in five secondary-level programs using the Utah Community-Based Transition Model. Peer tutors without disabilities provided training to the participants with disabilities on targeted leisure activities. Results indicated that participants with disabilities made significant gains on three subscales of independent behavior (social and communication, personal living, community living) as a result of community-based leisure instruction. Intelligence (IQ), student mobility, and the presence of inappropriate behaviors were not significant predictors of the amount of instruction students received; the amount of instruction students received was a more powerful predictor of student gains on two subscales of independent behavior (social and communication, community living) than were individual student characteristics; and the amount of instruction students received was directly related to the development of leisure skills.

Rynders, J.E., Schleien, S.J., Meyer, L.H., Vandercook, T.L., Mustonen, T., Colond, J.S., & Olson, K. (1993). Improving integration outcomes for children with and without severe disabilities through cooperatively structured recreation activities: A synthesis of research. *The Journal of Special Education*, 26(4), 386–407.

This article provides a synthesis of research that illustrates how cooperative learning strategies have been utilized to facilitate the social inclusion of children with significant disabilities in recreation settings (e.g., art, bowling, theater, camp). The intent of the article is to assist program leaders to plan, direct, and sustain inclusionary recreation programming. Five questions related to experimental findings in studies that employed cooperative learning strategies are discussed: 1) How can recreation activities be structured to maximize their cooperative aspects? 2) What types of recreation activities are particularly conducive to promoting cooperative interactions? 3) What peer-participant characteristics should one look for in promoting cooperative recreational groupings? 4) Once recreation activities have been selected, how should participants with and without disabilities be prepared for successful cooperation in these activities? and 5) What can be done to keep cooperation growing and prospering? This article proposes that through cooperative learning strategies in inclusionary recreation settings, participants with and without disabilities both can benefit. Participants with disabilities benefit by being included in typical community activities; participants without disabilities benefit through personal growth and a deeper enjoyment of life.

Rynders, J., Schleien, S., & Mustonen, T. (1990). Integrating children with severe disabilities for intensified outdoor education: Focus on feasibility. *Mental Retardation, 28*(1), 7–14.

This study investigated the feasibility of integrating children with and without disabilities during a 2-week camping experience. The campers included three children with severe disabilities, ages 9–11 years, and eight children without disabilities, ages 10–13 years. The program occurred at Wilder Forest, an environmental education site in Minnesota. The children without disabilities received training on how to be a "Special Friend," and the children both with and without disabilities took turns assisting the children with disabilities during cooperative activities. Observations of initiated social interaction and appropriate behaviors were recorded. In addition, the attitudes of the children without disabilities toward the children with disabilities were recorded daily on a five-item questionnaire. Frequency of appropriate behaviors and type, frequency, and direction of social interaction were recorded during 45-second observation intervals. Acquisition of camping skills also was recorded using a task analytic procedure. A substantial increase in the number of steps performed independently on two camping skills (swimming, clearing the table) were demonstrated by the campers with disabilities. The campers without disabilities increased the amount of social interactions toward the campers with disabilities. Friendship ratings by the children without disabilities toward the children with disabilities improved as well.

Sable, J. (1992). Collaborating to create an integrated camping program: Design and evaluation. *Therapeutic Recreation Journal, 26*(3), 38–48.

This article describes in detail an integrated residential camping program that grew out of a commitment of three collaborating organizations (Easter Seals, the University of New Hampshire's Leisure Management and Tourism Department, and the Daniel Webster Boy Scout Council of New Hampshire) to close a traditionally segregated camping program and offer a camping experience guided by a philosophy of inclusion. The residential summer camp served 200 campers per week, ages 10–16, 10% of whom had disabilities. Programmatic aspects such as individualized adaptations, staff training, sleeping arrangements, friendship development between campers with and without disabilities, the use of the Boy Scout badge system within the program design, and the role of the certified therapeutic recreation specialist are described. Evaluation methods included a Leisure Interest/Participation Inventory, a Social Interaction Evaluation, an Integration Assessment, an assessment of campers' attitudes toward people with disabilities, and a parent questionnaire. Descriptive and anecdotal evaluation information is provided. The article concludes by presenting a resource list of additional integrated camping models.

Schleien, S.J., Cameron, J., Rynders, J., & Slick, C. (1988). Acquisition and generalization of leisure skills from school to the home and community by learners with severe multihandicaps. *Therapeutic Recreation Journal, 22*(3), 53–71.

This study investigates the acquisition of leisure skills within a school setting and the generalization of those skills to home and community environments. Participants include a girl, age 5, and a boy, age 8, with significant multiple disabilities.

Systematic training procedures include task analysis, error correction, behavior-specific positive reinforcement, "special friends" training, and parent training. Parental involvement is crucial in the study to ensure that the learned skills would generalize to the home environment. The children demonstrated acquisition of the skills within the school setting and generalization of the skills in the home environment. The authors suggest that networking is essential to developing independent leisure lifestyles by children with disabilities and to facilitate successful community integration.

Schleien, S., Green, F., & Heyne, L. (1993). Integrated community recreation. In M. Snell (Ed.), *Instruction of students with severe disabilities* (4th ed., pp. 526–555). New York: Macmillan.
This chapter presents an overview of integrated community recreation programming within a text that addresses the curricular needs of students with significant disabilities. The authors offer a rationale for integrated recreation opportunities and a description of how therapeutic recreation services can support those opportunities. Three approaches to integrated recreation programming are described: 1) integration of generic recreation programs, 2) reverse mainstreaming, and 3) zero exclusion. Best professional practices in community recreation integration are presented, including individual needs/preference assessments, activity selection guidelines, collateral skill development, environmental analyses, adaptations, ability awareness orientations, friendship training, cooperative grouping arrangements, behavioral teaching methods, and program evaluation. To illustrate how these best professional practices work in a real-life setting, a description of an exemplary zero-exclusion integration program is provided. The chapter closes with a discussion of friendship development between individuals with and without disabilities and recommendations for planning integrated community recreation services.

Schleien, S.J., Heyne, L.A., & Berken, S.B. (1988). Integrating physical education to teach appropriate play skills to learners with autism: A pilot study. *Adapted Physical Activity Quarterly, 5,* 182–192.
The study describes the effects of a collaborative, sociomotor therapeutic recreation and adapted physical education curriculum on the social play and motor development of 12 students with autism, ages 4–12, who participated in an integrated general physical education setting. The students, who attended a Minneapolis public school, participated in a 9-week integrated physical education class that met twice weekly. Six of the students with autism participated in the classroom using the collaborative therapeutic recreation–adapted physical education curriculum. The remaining six students were taught using a traditional curriculum. Through the collaborative curriculum, students participated in activities at five levels of play: 1) isolate, 2) parallel, 3) cooperative/competitive dyad, 4) cooperative/competitive group, and 5) team play. Special-friends training was provided to the participants without disabilities. Specialized instruction in a variety of lifelong recreational activities was implemented with a focus on teaching social and motor skills. Instructional techniques such as adaptations, social reinforcement, and small-group activities were utilized to facilitate learning. Significant reductions in inappropriate play behaviors occurred for the students with disabilities who participated in the activities at the parallel and cooperative/competitive dyad social levels of play.

Schleien, S., Heyne, L., Rynders, J., & McAvoy, L. (1990). Equity and excellence: Serving all children in community recreation. *Journal of Physical Education, Recreation, and Dance, 61*(8), 45–48.

This article examines programmatic aspects that inhibit or contribute to successful integrated recreation participation by children with disabilities. A survey is described that identifies barriers to participation by children with disabilities in integrated recreation programs and solutions to those barriers. Recommended integration strategies include using trainer advocates, contingent social reinforcement, companionship training for peers without disabilities, and cooperatively structured activities. The benefits of these methods include friendship development between children with and without disabilities and positive attitude changes by participants without disabilities toward participants with disabilities. Two model integrated programs are featured: Kidspace at the Minnesota Museum of Art and the Special Needs Program at the Jewish Community Center of the Greater St. Paul Area. A model is presented to illustrate how policy makers, administrators, staff, participants, and families can work collaboratively to support successful integrated experiences for children with and without disabilities.

Schleien, S., Light, C., McAvoy, L., & Baldwin, C. (1989). Best professional practices: Serving persons with severe multiple disabilities. *Therapeutic Recreation Journal, 23*(3), 27–40.

This article proposes the following rationale for recreation participation by people with severe disabilities: promoting physical health and conditioning, enhancing social relationships, and developing new skills. "Severe multiple disability" is defined as that which limits daily activities so that more innovative, extensive, and intensive programming is required. "Best professional practices" in integrated recreation are described as needs/preference assessments, skill selection guidelines, task analysis, behavioral techniques such as shaping and chaining, choice training, adaptations, concern for maintenance and generalization of skills learned, and networking. Roles and responsibilities of therapeutic recreation specialists and other key players in the integration process are provided.

Schleien, S.J., McAvoy, L.H., Lais, G.J., & Rynders, J.E. (1993). *Integrated outdoor education and adventure programs.* **Champaign, IL: Sagamore.**

This text focuses on preparing individuals and environments for successful, integrated experiences in a number of outdoor program settings, including outdoor education centers, interpretive facilities, environmental education and school settings, camps, adventure program facilities, and adventure travel programs. The book describes administrative and programmatic guidelines for simplifying the creation, implementation, and evaluation of successful inclusive services for people with and without disabilities. It is a practical "how to" guide presenting a framework and rationale for integration. This book includes strategies for funding, safety, accessibility, and staffing; screening procedures to match participants with activities; program and equipment adaptation strategies; six complete curriculum lesson plans; accessibility survey instruments; examples of participant medical and assumption risk forms; lists of resource agencies and organizations; and systems change strategies to promote integration efforts in outdoor programs. The book is intended for college courses and for practitioners in outdoor education and adventure programs and facilities.

Schleien, S.J., & Meyer, L.H. (1988). Community-based recreation programs for persons with severe developmental disabilities. In M.D. Powers (Ed.), *Expanding systems of service delivery for persons with developmental disabilities* **(pp. 93–112). Baltimore: Paul H. Brookes Publishing Co.**

This chapter summarizes the features of various recreation programs and identifies the availability of a range of options for participation by individuals with developmental disabilities. It is proposed that these newly expanded recreation options can generate added benefits to individuals with developmental disabilities who choose them. The ability to use leisure time appropriately is cited as an important factor in living successfully in the community. Suggestions for successful participation in recreation within the community are provided. That is, the setting should be in the least restrictive environment, natural proportions should be considered, and the appropriate natural environment should be utilized. Staff should be adequately trained, and specialized staff should interact both formally and informally with all other staff. An environmental analysis should be completed, and various methods of instruction should be employed including task analysis, cue hierarchy, reinforcement, role playing, modeling, and graduated assistance. In addition, friendship models to foster leisure skill development and cooperatively structured activities should be employed. Activities should be age appropriate and integrated, transportation and financial assistance should be available if needed, and participants without disabilities should be prepared for the program. In addition, ongoing evaluation should be completed to ensure that each individual's needs are met.

Schleien, S.J., Meyer, L.H., Heyne, L.A., & Brandt, B.B. (1995). *Lifelong leisure skills and lifestyles for persons with developmental disabilities.* **Baltimore: Paul H. Brookes Publishing Co.**

Although recreation seems like a natural part of life, it actually involves a range of skills that need to be learned, refined, and generalized in order for a person to enjoy a variety of activities. This progressive second edition, based on the critically acclaimed *Longitudinal Leisure Skills for Severely Handicapped Learners: The Ho'onanea Curriculum Component* (Wuerch & Voeltz, 1982), offers a wealth of practical strategies—all extensively field tested and data based—for helping individuals with developmental disabilities learn leisure skills. The heart of this book lies in its step-by-step descriptions of 10 popular activities, including aerobics, pottery, and hand-held video games. Using sample charts, reproducible forms, simple diagrams, and concise explanations, this practical resource shows parents, recreation professionals, teachers, and leisure educators how to set instructional objectives; select age-appropriate activities; promote skill acquisition and generalization; incorporate leisure education into ongoing activities; adapt activities to fit varying cognitive, social, and physical abilities; encourage independent choice making; involve families in the development of leisure skills; and promote community recreation participation. Parents, teachers, recreation professionals, and anyone who values the inclusion and empowerment of individuals with disabilities can look to this guide to learn effective methods for teaching people with disabilities essential lifelong leisure skills.

Schleien, S., Ray, M., & Johnson, D. (1989). An architectural accessibility survey of community recreation centers. *Journal of Park and Recreation Administration*, 7(3), 10–22.

This article studies the architectural accessibility of community recreation centers and how participation by individuals with disabilities is limited when facilities are not accessible. A Building Access Survey was administered to 42 community park and recreation centers within the Minneapolis (Minnesota) Park and Recreation Board. The survey, developed in 1984 by the Minnesota State Council for the Handicapped, addressed parking, exterior paths, entrances, interior, sanitation facilities, bathing facilities, and kitchen facilities. Surveys were completed by recreation center directors and two university students on site. Results of the survey showed that the greatest code variance occurred in sanitation facilities, followed by interiors, kitchen facilities, entrances, and bathing facilities. The authors conclude that city planners, agency supervisors, and recreation center directors must identify accessibility as a priority and coordinate their actions to alleviate barriers. Surveying facilities and communicating with individuals with disabilities will ensure that accessibility is a priority during budgeting decisions.

Schleien, S., Rynders, J., & Mustonen, T. (1988). Art and integration: What can we create? *Therapeutic Recreation Journal*, 22(4), 18–29.

This study describes a 3-year investigation that examined the effects of cooperative learning groups, strategies to promote friendship development between children with and without disabilities, and staff training in instructional procedures (e.g., prompting, reinforcing). The participants, children with and without disabilities who attended elementary and middle schools, were placed in age-matched cooperative groups with natural proportions. Staff received training in art education and behavioral teaching methods (e.g., partial participation, use of adaptive equipment, providing one-to-one assistance). Staff taught the peers without disabilities sign language, showed them how to involve the children with disabilities in activities, and provided disability awareness information. The results of the first year showed that the attitudes of the children without disabilities toward the children with disabilities positively and significantly changed, the children with disabilities engaged more frequently in appropriate behavior, and the amount of social interaction between the children with and without disabilities increased. During the second year, the frequency of social interactions increased. By the end of the third year, cooperative behaviors increased, and three of the students with disabilities acquired functional art skills. The authors suggested that additional benefits of the integrated art program included exposure to art, improvement of self-concept, and an opportunity to participate in integrated groups.

Schleien, S., Rynders, J., Mustonen, T., & Fox, A. (1990). Effects of social play activities on the play behavior of children with autism. *Journal of Leisure Research*, 22, 317–328.

This study compares the effects of different levels of social play (e.g., dyadic, isolate, cooperative, team play) on the behavior of children with autism in integrated play settings. Participants included children with autism, ages 5–12 years, and their same-age peers without disabilities. The program occurred in the elementary school gymnasium. The children participated in three baseline sessions to determine their levels of appropriate play. After baseline, the adapted physical education instructor conducted activities at the various levels of play. The duration of appropriate play behaviors during 15-second intervals was recorded. Results indicated that the isolate play condition generally produced the lowest amount of appropriate play, as compared with the other three play conditions. The authors maintain that carefully structured integrated play activities that are cooperative in nature elicit significantly higher levels of appropriate play activity in children with autism.

Seidler, T.L., Turner, E.T., & Horine, L. (1993). Promoting active lifestyles through facilities and equipment—A look at children, seniors, and people with disabilities. *Journal of Physical Education, Recreation and Dance, 64*(1), 39–42.

This article provides an overview of special facility and equipment needs of three subgroups: children, older adults, and people with disabilities. The Americans with Disabilities Act (ADA), which requires recreation or sports service providers to offer "reasonable accommodation" to any participant regardless of disability, is discussed. The following guidelines are offered: Sports and recreation facilities should not just be accessible but also should be inviting and user friendly. When planning a new physical education, health, or recreation facility, one or more people with disabilities should be included on the planning committee. Talk to people with disabilities who use the facility to obtain their input about what works and what does not work. Sports participants who have physical or mental limitations should use the same sports and recreation equipment as the general population uses. If this is not possible, adaptations should be provided (e.g., modify rules, use specialized equipment). The primary goal in designing facilities or selecting equipment is to provide equal access for all participants.

References

Abery, B., Dahl, L.A., & Shelberg, G. (1993). *IMPACT*: Feature issue on self-determination, *6*(4).

Abery, B.H., & Fahnestock, M. (1994). Enhancing the social inclusion of persons with developmental disabilities. In M.F. Hayden & B.H. Abery (Eds.), *Challenges for a service system in transition: Ensuring quality community experiences for persons with developmental disabilities* (pp. 83–119). Baltimore: Paul H. Brookes Publishing Co.

Adkins, J., & Matson, L. (1980). Teaching institutionalized mentally retarded adults socially appropriate leisure skills. *Mental Retardation, 18*(5), 249–252.

Allen, W.T. (1989). *Read my lips: It's my choice.* St. Paul, MN: Governor's Planning Council on Developmental Disabilities.

Amado, A.N. (Ed.). (1993). *Friendships and community connections between people with and without developmental disabilities.* Baltimore: Paul H. Brookes Publishing Co.

Amado, A.N., Conklin, F., & Wells, J. (1990). *Friends: A manual for connecting persons with disabilities and community members.* St. Paul, MN: Human Services Research and Development Center.

American Heritage dictionary of the English language (3rd ed.). (1994). Boston: Houghton Mifflin.

Americans with Disabilities Act of 1990, PL 101-336, 42 U.S.C. § 12101 *et seq.*

Architectural Barriers Act of 1968, PL 90-480, 42 U.S.C. § 4151–4156.

Architectural and Transportation Barriers Compliance Board (ATBCB). (1992). *Americans with Disabilities Act accessibility guidelines for: Buildings and facilities (ADAAG).* Washington, DC: Author.

Arndt, K., Rudrud, E., & Sorenson, M.E. (1994). *We can do it! A curriculum for teaching self-determination.* St. Paul: Minnesota Department of Education.

Arsenault, C.C. (1990). *Let's get together: A handbook for building relationships between individuals with developmental disabilities and their community.* Boulder, CO: Developmental Disabilities Center.

Association for Retarded Citizens of North Dakota v. Olson, 561F.Supp.473 (D.ND1982).

Austin, D.R., Peterson, J.A., Peccarelli, L.M., Binkley, A., & Laker, M. (1977). *Therapeutic recreation in Indiana: Health through recreation.* Bloomington: Department of Recreation and Park Administration, Indiana University.

Austin, D.R., & Powell, L.G. (1981). What you need to know to serve special populations. *Parks & Recreation, 16*(7), 40–42.

Baker, M.J., & Salon, R.S. (1986). Setting free the captives: The power of community integration in liberating institutionalized adults from the bonds of their past. *Journal of The Association for Persons with Severe Handicaps, 11*, 176–181.

Bandura, A. (1977). *Social learning theory.* Englewood Cliffs, NJ: Prentice Hall.

Bates, P., & Renzaglia, A. (1982). Language instruction with a profoundly retarded adolescent: The use of a table game in the acquisition of verbal labeling skills. *Education and Treatment of Children, 5*(1), 13–22.

Bedini, L. (1991). Modern day "freaks"?: The exploitation of people with disabilities. *Therapeutic Recreation Journal, 25*(4), 61–70.

Bedini, L.A., & McCann, C.A. (1992). Tearing down the shameful wall of exclusion. *Parks & Recreation, 27*(4), 40–44.

Belmore, K., & Brown, L. (1976). A job skill inventory strategy for use in a public school vocational training program for severely handicapped potential workers. In L. Brown, N. Certo, K. Belmore, & T. Crowner (Eds.), *Papers and programs related to public school services for secondary age severely handicapped students* (Vol. VI, Part 1). Madison, WI: Madison Metropolitan School District. (Revised and republished: In N. Haring & D. Bricker [Eds.]. [1977]. *Teaching the severely handicapped* [Vol. III]. Columbus, OH: Special Press).

Bender, M., & Valletutti, P.J. (1976). *Teaching the moderately and severely handicapped: Curriculum objectives, strategies and activities* (Vol. 2). Baltimore: University Park Press.

Beveridge, M., Spencer, J., & Miller, P. (1978). Language and social behavior in severely educationally subnormal children. *British Journal of Social and Clinical Psychology, 17*(1), 75–83.

Birenbaum, A., & Re, M.A. (1979). Resettling mentally retarded adults in the community—Almost 4 years later. *American Journal of Mental Deficiency, 83,* 323–329.

Blacher, J. (Ed.). (1984). *Severely handicapped young children and their families: Research in review.* New York: Academic Press.

Bohlig, M. (1991). Recreational programming for women. *NIRSA Journal, 16*(1), 8–10.

Bork, K. (1989, December). Easy access with Trail Partners. *Parks and Recreation,*

Bowerman, J., & Mitchell, M. (1995). *A Rockford park district survival guide to recing your life.* Rockford, IL: Extended Services Department, Rockford Park District.

Brademus, D.J. (1991). Status of insurance liability in public leisure service agencies for eight Midwestern states. *Journal of Park and Recreation Administration, 9*(3), 1–14.

Bright, A.D. (1994). Information campaigns that enlighten and influence the public. *Parks & Recreation, 29*(8), 48–54.

Brinker, R.P. (1985). Interactions between severely mentally retarded students and other students in integrated and segregated public school settings. *American Journal of Mental Deficiency, 89,* 587–594.

Browder, D. (1991). *Assessment of individuals with severe disabilities: An applied behavior approach to life skills assessment* (2nd ed.). Baltimore: Paul H. Brookes Publishing Co.

Bullock, C.C., Mahon, M.J., & Welch, L.K. (1992). Easter Seals' progressive mainstreaming model: Options and choices in camping and leisure services for children and adults with disabilities. *Therapeutic Recreation Journal, 26*(4), 61–70.

Burkhour, C.K. (1992). *Inclusive recreation: Planning recreation opportunities for people of all abilities.* Lansing, MI: Department of Natural Resources.

Busser, J.A. (1993). Leisure programming: The state of the art. *Journal of Physical Education, Recreation, and Dance, 64*(8), 25, 33.

Cameron, J. (1989). *The effect of integration strategies and careprovider training on a child with autism attending an integrated day camp.* Unpublished master's thesis, University of Minnesota, Minneapolis.

Cangemi, P., Williams, W., & Gaskell, P. (1992). Going to the source for accessibility assessment. *Parks & Recreation, 27*(10), 66–69.

Carlson, N. (1990). *Arnie and the new kid.* New York: Viking.

Carney, I., Clobuciar, G., Corley, E., Wilcox, B., Bigler, J., Fleisher, L., Pany, D., & Turner, P. (1977). Social interaction in severely handicapped students: Training basic social skills and social acceptability. In *The severely and profoundly handicapped child.* Springfield: Illinois State Board of Education and Specialized Educational Services.

Chubb, M., & Chubb, H. (1981). *One third of our time?* New York: John Wiley & Sons.

Clegg, J.A., & Standen, J. (1991). Friendships among adults who have developmental disabilities. *American Journal on Mental Retardation, 95,* 663–671.

Cnaan, R.A., Adler, I., & Ramot, A. (1986). Public reaction to establishment of community residential facilities for mentally retarded persons in Israel. *American Journal of Mental Deficiency, 90,* 677–685.

Cole, D., Vandercook, T., & Rynders, J. (1988). Comparison of two peer interaction programs: Children with and without severe disabilities. *American Educational Research Journal, 25,* 415–439.

Cooperative Research in Education Act of 1954, PL 83-531, 20 U.S.C. § 1851 *et seq.*

Council of Better Business Bureaus' Foundation. (1992). *Access equals opportunity: Fun and fitness centers.* Arlington, VA: Author.

Crapps, J.M., Langone, J., & Swaim, S. (1985). Quantity and quality of participation in community environments by mentally retarded adults. *Education and Training of the Mentally Retarded, 20,* 123–129.

Crawford, D., Jackson, E., & Godbey, G. (1991). A hierarchical model of leisure constraints. *Leisure Sciences, 13,* 309–320.

Cullen, B., & Pratt, T. (1992). Measuring and reporting student progress. In S. Stainback & W. Stainback (Eds.), *Curriculum considerations in inclusive classrooms: Facilitating learning for all students* (pp. 175–196). Baltimore: Paul H. Brookes Publishing Co.

Cummings, L.E., & Busser, J.A. (1994). Forecasting in recreation and park management: Need, substance, and reasonableness. *Journal of Park and Recreation Administration, 12*(1), 35–50.

Curran, D. (1983). *Traits of a healthy family.* Minneapolis, MN: Winston.

Dark, S., & Wright, J. (1988). *Leisure/recreation curriculum for secondary aged students with disabilities.* Gretna, LA: Jefferson Parish Schools.

Dattilo, J. (1991). Mental retardation. In D.R. Austin & M.E. Crawford (Eds.), *Therapeutic recreation: An introduction* (pp. 163–188). Englewood Cliffs, NJ: Prentice Hall.

Dattilo, J. (1994). *Inclusive leisure services: Responding to the rights of people with disabilities.* State College, PA: Venture.

Dattilo, J., & Murphy, W.D. (1991). *Leisure education program planning: A systematic approach.* State College, PA: Venture.

Dattilo, J., & Smith, R.W. (1990). Communicating positive attitudes toward people with disabilities through sensitive terminology. *Therapeutic Recreation Journal, 24*(1), 8–17.

Descartes, R. (1964). Meditations I-II. In D.J. Bronstein, Y.H. Krikorian, & P.P. Wiener (Eds.), *Basic problems of philosophy* (3rd ed., pp. 24–34). Englewood Cliffs, NJ: Prentice Hall.

Deutsch, M. (1949). A theory of cooperation and competition. *Human Relations, 2,* 129–152.

Deutsch, M. (1962). Cooperation and trust: Some theoretical notes. In M.R. Jones (Ed.), *Nebraska symposium on motivation* (pp. 275–319). Lincoln: University of Nebraska Press.

Donder, D., & Nietupski, J. (1981). Nonhandicapped adolescents teaching playground skills to their mentally handicapped peers: Toward a less restrictive middle school environment. *Education and Training of the Mentally Retarded, 16,* 270–276.

Driskell, D., & Wohlford, S. (Eds.). (1993). *Universal access to outdoor recreation: A design guide.* Berkeley, CA: PLAE, Inc.

Duck, S. (1991). *Understanding relationships.* New York: Guilford Press.

Edginton, C.R., Compton, D.M., & Hanson, C.J. (1980). *Recreation and leisure programming: A guide for the professional.* Philadelphia: Saunders College.

Edginton, C.R., Compton, D.M., Ritchie, A.J., & Vederman, R.K. (1975). The status of services for special populations in park and recreation departments in the state of Iowa. *Therapeutic Recreation Journal, 9*(3), 109–116.

Edginton, C.R., & Ford, P.M. (1985). *Leadership in recreation and leisure service organizations.* New York: John Wiley & Sons.

Education for All Handicapped Children Act of 1975, PL 94-142, 20 U.S.C. § 1401 *et seq.*

Education of the Handicapped Act Amendments of 1983, PL 98-199, 20 U.S.C. § 101 *et seq.*

Education of the Handicapped Act Amendments of 1986, PL 99-457, 20 U.S.C. § 1400 *et seq.*

Elementary and Secondary Education Act of 1965, PL 89-10, 79 U.S.C. § 27 *et seq.*

Elementary and Secondary Education Act of 1994, PL 103-382, 20 U.S.C. § 6301 *et seq.*

Fenrick, N., & Petersen, T.K. (1984). Developing positive changes in attitudes towards moderately/severely handicapped students through a peer tutoring program. *Education and Training of the Mentally Retarded, 19,* 83–90.

Finding funding for assistive technology. (1993, March). *Exceptional Parent,* 18–24, 28.

Flavell, J. (1973). Reduction of stereotypies by reinforcement of toy play. *Mental Retardation, 11*(4), 21–23.

Fletcher, D. (1990, May). *Ensuring enjoyment in integrated community recreation and leisure activities.* Paper delivered at the National Conference of the American Association on Mental Retardation, Atlanta.

Forest, M. (Ed.). (1987). *More education/integration.* Downsview, Ontario, Canada: G. Allan Roeher Institute.

Furman, W. (1984). Issues in the assessment of social skills of normal and handicapped children. In T. Field, J.L. Roopnarine, & M. Segal (Eds.), *Friendships in normal and handicapped children* (pp. 3–30). Norwood, NJ: Ablex.

Germ, P.A. (1993). *Evaluation of "best professional practices" in integrated community leisure services in Minnesota.* Unpublished master's thesis, University of Minnesota, Minneapolis.

Gibbons, F.X. (1985). A social-psychological perspective on developmental disabilities. *Journal of Social and Clinical Psychology, 3,* 391–404.

Glidden, L.M. (1993). What we do not know about families with children who have developmental disabilities: Questionnaire on resources and stress as a case study. *American Journal on Mental Retardation, 97*(5), 481–495.

Godbey, G. (1991). Redefining public parks and recreation. *Parks & Recreation, 26*(10), 56–61, 74–75.

Godbey, G., Graefe, A., & James, S. (1993). Reality and perception: Where do we fit in? *Parks & Recreation, 28*(1), 76–83, 110–111.

Gold, D., & McGill, J. (1988). *The pursuit of leisure: Enriching lives with people who have a disability.* Downsview, Ontario, Canada: G. Allan Roeher Institute.

Gold, S.M. (1994). Behavioral approach to risk management. *Parks & Recreation, 29*(11), 34–36.

Green, F.P. (1992). *A study of the impact of community recreation skill acquisition on the social lives of adults with mental retardation.* Unpublished doctoral dissertation, University of Minnesota, Minneapolis.

Green, F.P., & Schleien, S. (1991). Understanding friendship and recreation: A theoretical sampling. *Therapeutic Recreation Journal, 25*(4), 29–40.

Green, F.P., Schleien, S.J., Mactavish, J., & Benepe, S. (1995). Nondisabled adults' perceptions of relationships in the early stages of arranged partnerships with peers with mental retardation. *Education and Training in Mental Retardation and Developmental Disabilities, 30,* 91–108.

Hall, L. (1994). A descriptive assessment of social relationships in integrated classrooms. *Journal of The Association for Persons with Severe Handicaps, 19,* 302–313.

Hartsoe, C.E. (1985). From playgrounds to public policy. *Parks & Recreation, 20*(8), 46–49, 68–69.

Hawkins, B.A. (1991). An exploration of adaptive skills and leisure activity of older adults with mental retardation. *Therapeutic Recreation Journal, 25*(4), 9–28.

Hawkins, B.A. (1993). An exploratory analysis of leisure and life satisfaction of aging adults with mental retardation. *Therapeutic Recreation Journal, 26,* 98–109.

Hayden, M., Lakin, K.C., Hill, B., Bruininks, R., & Copher, J. (1992). Social and leisure integration of people with mental retardation in foster homes and small group homes. *Education and Training in Mental Retardation, 27,* 187–199.

Henderson, K.A., & Bedini, L.A. (1991). A continuum of action: Using volunteers in therapeutic recreation. *Journal of Physical Education, Recreation, and Dance, 62*(4), 49–51.

Herchmer, B. (1994). Policy . . . A four letter word? A question of planning and community development. *Journal of Leisurability, 21*(3), 32–34.

Heyne, L., Schleien, S., & McAvoy, L. (1993). *Making friends: Using recreation activities to promote friendships between children with and without disabilities.* Minneapolis: School of Kinesiology and Leisure Studies, College of Education, University of Minnesota.

Hill, B.K., & Bruininks, R.H. (1981). *Family, leisure, and social activities of mentally retarded people in residential facilities.* Minneapolis: Developmental Disabilities Project on Residential Services and Community Adjustment, University of Minnesota.

Hill, J.W., Perkins, B., & Thompson, B. (Eds.). (1992). *The Open Doors recreation project: Full inclusion of persons with disabilities in community recreation opportunities.* Chesterfield, VA: Chesterfield Community Services Board.

Hill, M.S. (1988). Marital stability and spouses' shared time. *Journal of Family Issues, 9,* 427–451.

Holman, T.B., & Jacquart, M. (1988). Leisure activity patterns and marital satisfaction: A further test. *Journal of Marriage and the Family, 50,* 69–78.

House, J.S., Umberson, D., & Landis, K.R. (1988). Structures and processes of social support. *Annual Review of Sociology, 14,* 293–318.

Howe, C.Z. (1993). The evaluation of leisure programs: Applying qualitative methods. *Journal of Physical Education, Recreation, and Dance, 64*(8), 43–46.

Howes, C. (1984). Social interactions and patterns of friendships in normal and emotionally disturbed children. In T. Field, J.L. Roopnarine, & M. Segal (Eds.), *Friendships in normal and handicapped children* (pp. 163–185), Norwood, NJ: Ablex.

Hultsman, J., & Colley, J.A. (1995). Park and recreation management for the 21st century. *Journal of Park and Recreation Administration, 13*(2), 1–10.

Humphrey, F. (1986). The future of leisure services: Will we be architects or reactors? *Parks & Recreation, 21*(5), 38–42, 63.

Hutchison, P., & Lord, J. (1979). *Recreation integration: Issues and alternatives in leisure services and community involvement.* Ottawa, Ontario, Canada: Leisurability Publications.

Hutchison, P., & McGill, J. (1992). *Leisure, integration and community.* Concord, Ontario, Canada: Leisurability Publications.

Individuals with Disabilities Education Act (IDEA) of 1990, PL 101-476, 20 U.S.C. § 1400 *et seq.*

Johnson, D., & Johnson, R. (1989). *Cooperation and competition: Theory and research.* Edina, MN: Interaction Book Company.

Kaiser, R.A., & Mertes, J.D. (1991). Safety in the design of recreation facilities: The intersection of legal and design standards. *Journal of Park and Recreation Administration, 9*(2), 34–47.

Kappel, B., Nagel, S., & Wieck, C. (1990). *The heart of community is inclusion.* St. Paul: State of Minnesota, State Planning Agency, The Governor's Planning Council on Developmental Disabilities.

Kelly, J.R. (1974). Socialization toward leisure: A developmental approach. *Journal of Leisure Research, 6,* 181–193.

Kelly, J. (Ed.). (1982). *Leisure.* Englewood Cliffs, NJ: Prentice Hall.

Kennedy, C.H., Horner, R.H., & Newton, J.S. (1989). Social contacts of adults with severe disabilities living in the community: A descriptive analysis of relationship patterns. *Journal of The Association for Persons with Severe Handicaps, 14,* 190–196.

Kennedy, D., Smith, R., & Austin, D. (1991). *Special recreation: Opportunities for persons with disabilities* (2nd ed.). Dubuque, IA: William C. Brown.

Krueger, R. (1988). *Focus groups: A practical guide for applied research.* Newbury Park, CA: Sage Publications.

Kunstler, R. (1985). Emerging special populations and how they can be helped. *Adapted Physical Activity Quarterly, 2*(3), 177–181.

Kutner, L. (1990, October 1). Friendship ranks above popularity. *Minneapolis Star Tribune,* p. E-1.

Lakin, K.C., & Bruininks, R.H. (Eds.). (1985). *Strategies for achieving community integration of developmentally disabled citizens.* Baltimore: Paul H. Brookes Publishing Co.

Lancaster, K. (1976). Municipal services. *Parks & Recreation, 18,* 18–27.

Landesman, S., & Vietze, P. (Eds.). (1987). *Living environments and mental retardation.* Washington, DC: American Association on Mental Retardation.

Levin, J., & Enselein, K. (1990). *Fun for everyone: A guide to adapted leisure activities for children with disabilities.* Minneapolis, MN: Ablenet.

Lewin, K. (1935). *A dynamic theory of personality.* New York: McGraw-Hill.

LIFE Project Staff. (1991). *The parent training guide to recreation.* Chapel Hill: University of North Carolina, Center for Recreation and Disability Studies.

LIFE Project Staff. (1992). *Leisure is for everyone: Support manual.* Chapel Hill: University of North Carolina, Center for Recreation and Disability Studies.

Little, S.L. (1993). Leisure program design and evaluation. *Journal of Physical Education, Recreation, and Dance, 64*(8), 29, 33.

Lord, J. (1983). Reflections on a decade of integration. *Journal of Leisurability, 10*(4), 4–11.

Lynch, L. (1977). *The broken heart: The medical consequences of loneliness.* New York: Basic Books.

MacAndrew, C., & Edgerton, R.B. (1966). On the possibility of friendship. *American Journal of Mental Deficiency, 70,* 612–621.

Mactavish, J. (1994). *Recreation in families that include children with developmental disabilities: Nature, benefits, and constraints.* Unpublished doctoral dissertation, University of Minnesota, Minneapolis.

Mactavish, J. (1995). Why is a family focus imperative to inclusive recreation? In S.J. Schleien, J. Rynders, L. Heyne, & C. Tabourne (Eds.), *Powerful partnerships: Parents and professionals building inclusive recreation programs together* (pp. 8–13). Minneapolis: Institute on Community Integration, University of Minnesota.

Mahon, M.J. (1994). The use of self-control techniques to facilitate self-determination skills during leisure in adolescents and young adults with mild and moderate mental retardation. *Therapeutic Recreation Journal, 28*(2), 58–72.

McCarville, R.E., & Smale, B.J.A. (1993). Perceived constraints to leisure participation within five activity domains. *Journal of Park and Recreation Administration, 11*(2), 40–59.

McEvoy, M., Nordquist, V., Twardosz, S., Heckaman, K., Wehby, J., & Denny, K. (1988). Promoting autistic children's peer interaction in an integrated early childhood setting using affection activities. *Journal of Applied Behavior Analysis, 21*, 193–200.

McGill, J. (1984). Training for integration: Are blindfolds really enough? *Journal of Leisurability, 11*(2), 12–15.

McKinney, W.R., & Lowrey, G.A., Jr. (1987). *Staff training and development for park, recreation, and leisure service organizations.* Alexandria, VA: National Recreation and Parks Association.

McLean, D.D. (1993). Partnering: Extending resources and building networks. *Parks & Recreation, 28*(12), 48–51.

Mental Retardation Facilities and Community Mental Health Centers Construction Act of 1963, PL 88-164, 42 U.S.C. § 2670 *et seq.*

Meyer, H.D., & Brightbill, C.K. (1964). *Community recreation: A guide to its organization* (3rd ed.). Englewood Cliffs, NJ: Prentice Hall.

Meyer, L.H., & Kishi, G.S. (1985). School integration strategies. In K.C. Lakin & R.H. Bruininks (Eds.), *Strategies for achieving community integration of developmentally disabled citizens* (pp. 231–252). Baltimore: Paul H. Brookes Publishing Co.

Minnesota State Council on Disability. (1992). *Building access survey* (rev.). St. Paul: Author.

Mobley, T.A., & Toalson, R.F. (1992). The 21st century: Part I. *Parks & Recreation, 27*(9), 100–105.

Moon, M.S. (Ed.). (1994). *Making school and community recreation fun for everyone: Places and ways to integrate.* Baltimore: Paul H. Brookes Publishing Co.

Moon, M.S., Hart, D., Komissar, C., & Friedlander, R. (1995). Making sports and recreation activities accessible. In K.F. Flippo, K.J. Inge, & J.M. Barcus (Eds.), *Assistive technology: A resource for school, work, and community* (pp. 187–198). Baltimore: Paul H. Brookes Publishing Co.

Moreno, J.L. (1934). *Who shall survive?* Washington, DC: Nervous and Mental Disease.

Mount, B., & Zwernik, K. (1988). *It's never too early, it's never too late: A booklet about personal futures planning.* St. Paul, MN: Metropolitan Council.

Murray, F. (1982). Teaching through social conflict. *Contemporary Educational Psychology, 7*, 257–271.

Newcomer, B., & Morrison, T.I. (1974). Play therapy with institutionalized mentally retarded children. *American Journal of Mental Deficiency, 78*(6), 727–733.

Nevin, R.S., & McCubbin, H.I. (1979, August). *Parental coping with physical handicaps: Social policy implications.* Paper presented at the National Council for Family Relation, Boston.

Nietupski, J., Hamre-Nietupski, S., & Ayres, B. (1984). Review of task analytic leisure skill training efforts: Practitioner implications and future research needs. *Journal of The Association for Persons with Severe Handicaps, 9*(2), 88–97.

Nirje, B. (1969). The normalization principle and its human management implications. In R. Kugel & W. Wolfensberger (Eds.), *Changing patterns in residential services for the mentally retarded* (pp. 179–195). Washington, DC: President's Committee on Mental Retardation.

O'Brien, J., Forest, M., Snow, J., & Hasbury, D. (1989). *Action for inclusion: How to improve schools by welcoming children with special needs into regular classrooms.* Toronto, Ontario, Canada: Frontier College.

Ohio Developmental Disabilities Planning Council (1995). [Community recreation and people with disabilities current status survey—1995]. Unpublished raw data.

Orthner, D.K., & Mancini, J.A. (1980). Leisure behavior and group dynamics: The case of the family. In S.E. Iso-Ahola (Ed.), *Social psychological perspectives on leisure and recreation* (pp. 307–328). Springfield, IL: Charles C Thomas.

Orthner, D.K., & Mancini, J.A. (1990). Leisure impacts on family interaction and cohesion. *Journal of Leisure Research, 22*(2), 125–137.

Palisi, B.J. (1984). Marriage companionship and marriage well-being: A comparison of metropolitan areas in three countries. *Journal of Comparative Family Studies, 15*, 43–56.

Patton, M.Q. (1990). *Qualitative evaluation and research methods*. Newbury Park, CA: Sage Publications.

Peck, C., Donaldson, J., & Pezzoli, M. (1990). Some benefits nonhandicapped adolescents perceive for themselves from their social relationships with peers who have severe handicaps. *Journal of The Association for Persons with Severe Handicaps, 15*, 241–249.

Pedlar, A. (1990). Normalization and integration: A look at the Swedish experience. *Mental Retardation, 28*, 275–282.

Pedlar, A., Gilbert, A., & Gove, L. (1994). The role of action research in facilitating integrated recreation for older adults. *Therapeutic Recreation Journal, 28*(2), 99–106.

Perrin, B., & Nirje, B. (1985). Setting the record straight: A critique of some frequent misconceptions of the normalization principle. *Australia and New Zealand Journal of Developmental Disabilities, 11*(2), 69–74.

PL 85-926, 20 U.S.C. § 611 *et seq.*

Putnam, J.W., Werder, J.K., & Schleien, S.J. (1985). Leisure and recreation services for handicapped persons. In K.C. Lakin & R.H. Bruininks (Eds.), *Strategies for achieving community integration of developmentally disabled citizens* (pp. 253–274). Baltimore: Paul H. Brookes Publishing Co.

Pogrebin, L.C. (1987). *Among friends*. New York: McGraw-Hill.

Ray, M.T. (1991). *SCOLA leisure activity fun guide*. St. Paul, MN: Arc Ramsey County.

Ray, M.T. (1994). *Teaching the possibilities: Recreation and leisure: A resource guide for transition planning*. St. Paul: Minnesota Department of Education.

Ray, M.T., Schleien, S.J., Larson, A., Rutten, T., & Slick, C. (1986). Integrating persons with disabilities into community leisure environments. *Journal of Expanding Horizons in Therapeutic Recreation, 1*, 45–55.

Rehabilitation Act of 1973, PL 93-112, 29 U.S.C. § 701 *et seq.*

Reid, M., Clunies-Ross, L., Goacher, B., & Vile, C. (1981). Mixed ability teaching: Problems and possibilities. *Educational Research, 24*(1), 3–10.

Repp, A.C. (1983). *Teaching the mentally retarded*. Englewood Cliffs, NJ: Prentice Hall.

Reynolds, R. (1981). A guideline to leisure skills programming for handicapped individuals. In P. Wehman & S. Schleien (Eds.), *Leisure programs for handicapped persons: Adaptations, techniques, and curriculum* (pp. 1–13). Austin, TX: PRO-ED.

Reynolds, R. (1995). A look toward the future in service delivery. In S. Schleien, L. Meyer, L. Heyne, & B. Brandt (Eds.), *Lifelong leisure skills and lifestyles for persons with developmental disabilities* (pp. 219–229). Baltimore: Paul H. Brookes Publishing Co.

Rosenbaum, J. (1980). Social implications of educational groupings. In D. Berliner (Ed.), *Review of research in education* (Vol. 8, pp. 361–401). Washington, DC: American Educational Research Association.

Ross, C.D. (1983). Leisure in the deinstitutionalization process: A vehicle for change. *Journal of Leisurability, 10*(1), 13–19.

Rossman, J.R. (1988). Development of leisure programming theory. *Journal of Park and Recreation Administration, 6*(4), 1–13.

Rossman, J.R. (1995). *Recreation programming: Designing leisure experiences* (2nd ed.). Champaign, IL: Sagamore.

Roth, R., & Smith, T.E.C. (1983). A statewide assessment of attitudes toward the handicapped and community living programs. *Education and Training of the Mentally Retarded, 18*, 164–168.

Rubenstein, J. (1984). Friendship development in normal children: A commentary. In T. Field, J. Roopnarine, & M. Segal (Eds.), *Friendships in normal and handicapped children* (pp. 125–135). Norwood, NJ: Ablex.

Rubin, L.B. (1985). *Just friends: The role of friendship in our lives*. New York: Harper and Row.

Russell, R.V. (1982). *Planning programs in recreation*. St. Louis: C.V. Mosby.

Rynders, J., & Horrobin, J. (1995). *Down syndrome, birth to adulthood: Giving families an EDGE*. Denver: Love.

Rynders, J.E., Johnson, R.T., Johnson, D.W., & Schmidt, B. (1980). Producing positive interaction among Down syndrome and nonhandicapped teenagers through cooperative goal structuring. *American Journal of Mental Deficiency, 85*, 268–273.

Rynders, J.E., & Schleien, S.J. (1988). Recreation: A promising vehicle for promoting the community integration of young adults with Down syndrome. In C. Tingley (Ed.), *Down syndrome: A resource handbook* (pp. 182–198). Boston: Little, Brown.

Rynders, J., & Schleien, S. (1991). *Together successfully: Creating recreational and educational programs that integrate people with and without disabilities.* Arlington, TX: Association for Retarded Citizens—United States, National 4-H, and the Institute on Community Integration, University of Minnesota.

Rynders, J., Schleien, S., Meyer, L., Vandercook, T., Mustonen, T., Coland, J., & Olson, K. (1993). Improving interaction outcomes for children with and without disabilities through cooperatively structured, recreation activities: A synthesis of research. *Journal of Special Education, 26*(4), 386–407.

Rynders, J., Schleien, S., & Mustonen, T. (1990). Integrating children with severe disabilities for intensified outdoor education: Focus on feasibility. *Mental Retardation, 28*(1), 7–14.

Sailor, W., & Guess, D. (1983). *Severely handicapped students: An instructional design.* Boston: Houghton Mifflin.

Sapon-Shevin, M. (1992). Celebrating diversity, creating community: Curriculum that honors and builds on differences. In S. Stainback & W. Stainback (Eds.), *Curriculum considerations in inclusive classrooms: Facilitating learning for all students* (pp. 19–36). Baltimore: Paul H. Brookes Publishing Co.

Schleien, S., Cameron, J., Rynders, J., & Slick, C. (1988). Acquisition and generalization of leisure skills from school to the home and community by learners with severe multihandicaps. *Therapeutic Recreation Journal, 22*(3), 53–71.

Schleien, S., Fahnestock, M., Green, R., & Rynders, J. (1990). Building positive social networks through environmental interventions in integrated recreation programs. *Therapeutic Recreation Journal, 24*(4), 42–52.

Schleien, S.J., Germ, P., & McAvoy, L. (in press). Inclusive community leisure services: Promising professional practices and barriers encountered. *Therapeutic Recreation Journal.*

Schleien, S.J., & Green, F.P. (1992). Three approaches for integrating persons with disabilities into community recreation. *Journal of Park and Recreation Administration, 10*(2), 51–66.

Schleien, S., Green, F., & Heyne, L. (1993). Integrated community recreation. In M. Snell (Ed.), *Instruction of students with severe disabilities* (4th ed., pp. 526–555). Columbus, OH: Charles E. Merrill.

Schleien, S., Heyne, L., & Dattilo, J. (1995). Teaching severely handicapped children: Social skills development through leisure skills programming. In G. Cartledge & J. Milburn (Eds.), *Teaching social skills to children: Innovative approaches* (3rd ed., pp. 262–290). Needham, MA: Allyn & Bacon.

Schleien, S., Heyne, L., Rynders, J., & McAvoy, L. (1990, October). Equity and excellence: Serving all children in community recreation. *Journal of Physical Education, Recreation, and Dance,* 45–48.

Schleien, S., Hornfeldt, D., & McAvoy, L. (1994). Integration and environmental outdoor education: The impact of integrating students with severe disabilities on the academic performance of peers without disabilities. *Therapeutic Recreation Journal, 28*(1), 25–34.

Schleien, S.J., Kiernan, J., & Wehman, P. (1981). Evaluation of an age-appropriate leisure skills program for moderately retarded adults. *Education and Training of the Mentally Retarded, 16*(1), 13–19.

Schleien, S.J., & McAvoy, L.H. (1989). *Learning together: Integrating persons of varying abilities into outdoor education centers.* Minneapolis: University of Minnesota.

Schleien, S., McAvoy, L., Lais, G., & Rynders, J. (1993). *Integrated outdoor education and adventure programs.* Champaign, IL: Sagamore.

Schleien, S., Meyer, L., Heyne, L., & Brandt, B. (1995). *Lifelong leisure skills and lifestyles for persons with developmental disabilities.* Baltimore: Paul H. Brookes Publishing Co.

Schleien, S.J., Porter, J., & Wehman, P. (1979). An assessment of the leisure skill needs of developmentally disabled individuals. *Therapeutic Recreation Journal, 13*(3), 16–21.

Schleien, S.J., & Ray, M.T. (1988). *Community recreation and persons with disabilities: Strategies for integration.* Baltimore: Paul H. Brookes Publishing Co.

Schleien, S., Rynders, J., Heyne, L., & Tabourne, C. (Eds). (1995). *Powerful partnerships: Parents and professionals building inclusive recreation programs together.* Minneapolis: Institute on Community Integration and the University of Minnesota.

Schleien, S.J., Rynders, J.E., Mustonen, T., & Fox, A. (1990). Effects of social play activities on the play behavior of children with autism. *Journal of Leisure Research, 22,* 317–328.

Schleien, S.J., & Werder, J.K. (1985). Perceived responsibilities of special recreation services in Minnesota. *Therapeutic Recreation Journal, 19*(3), 51–62.

Schloss, P.J., Smith, M.A., & Kiehl, W. (1986). Rec. club: A community centered approach to recreational development for adults with mild to moderate mental retardation. *Education and Training of the Mentally Retarded, 21*, 282–288.

Sessoms, H.D. (1984). *Leisure services* (6th ed.). Englewood Cliffs, NJ: Prentice Hall.

Sherrill, C., Rainbolt, W., & Ervin, S. (1984). Physical recreation of blind adults: Present practices and childhood memories. *Journal of Visual Impairment and Blindness, 78*(8), 367–368.

Shores, R., Hester, E., & Strain, P.S. (1976). The effects of amount and type of teacher–child interaction during free play. *Psychology in the Schools, 13*, 171–175.

Skinner, B.F. (1968). *The technology of teaching*. New York: Meredith.

Smith, R.W. (1985). Barriers are more than architectural. *Parks & Recreation, 20*(10), 58–62.

Snell, M. (Ed.). (1993). *Instruction of students with severe disabilities* (4th ed.). Columbus, OH: Charles E. Merrill.

Social Security Act of 1935, PL 74-271, 42 U.S.C. § 301 *et seq.*

Spangler, K., & O'Sullivan, E. (Eds.). (1995). Active living: Healthy lifestyles [Special issue]. *Parks & Recreation, 30*(10).

Sparrow, W.A., & Mayne, S.C. (1990). Recreation patterns of adults with intellectual disabilities. *Therapeutic Recreation Journal, 24*(3), 45–49.

Stainback, S., & Stainback, W. (1985). *Integration of students with severe handicaps into regular schools*. Reston, VA: Council for Exceptional Children.

Stainback, W., & Stainback, S. (1987). Facilitating friendships. *Education and Training in Mental Retardation, 22*(1), 18–25.

Stainback, S., Stainback, W., & Jackson, H. (1992). Toward inclusive classrooms. In S. Stainback & W. Stainback (Eds.), *Curriculum considerations in inclusive classrooms: Facilitating learning for all students* (pp. 3–17). Baltimore: Paul H. Brookes Publishing Co.

Stensrud, C. (1993). *A training manual for Americans with Disabilities Act compliance in parks and recreation settings*. State College, PA: Venture.

Stinnett, N., Sanders, G., DeFrain, J., & Parkhurst, A. (1982). A nationwide study of families who perceive themselves as strong. *Family Perspective, 16*, 15–22.

Strain, P.S., Cook, T., & Apolloni, T. (1976). The role of peers in modifying classmates' social behavior: A review. *Journal of Special Education, 10*(4), 351–356.

Stumbo, N.J. (1995). Social skills instruction through commercially available resources. *Therapeutic Recreation Journal, 29*(1), 30–55.

Swanson, J., & Rivard, S. (1995). *Access to opportunities: How to include people of all abilities in community programs*. Loretto, MN: Vinland National Center.

Technology-Related Assistance for Individuals with Disabilities Act of 1988, PL 100-407, 29 U.S.C. § 2201 *et seq.*

Technology-Related Assistance for Individuals with Disabilities Act Amendments of 1994, PL 103-218, 29 U.S.C. § 2201 *et seq.*

Tindall, B.S. (1995). Beyond "fun and games." *Parks & Recreation, 30*(3), 86–93.

Toalson, R.F., & Mobley, T.A. (1993). The 21st century: Part II. *Parks & Recreation, 28*(5), 56–61.

Turnbull, A.P., & Turnbull, H.R. (1990). *Families, professionals, and exceptionality: A special partnership*. Columbus, OH: Charles E. Merrill.

U.S. Department of Justice, Civil Rights Division. (1991). *28 CFR Part 35, Nondiscrimination on the basis of disability in state and local government services; Final rule*. Washington, DC: Government Printing Office.

Vandercook, T., Tetlie, R., Montie, J., Downing, J., Levin, J., Glanville, M., Solberg, B., Branham, S., Ellson, L., & McNear, D. (1994). *Lessons for inclusion: Including everyone, liking myself, making and keeping friends, cooperating with others*. Toronto, Ontario, Canada: Inclusion Press.

Vandercook, T., York, J., & Forest, M. (1989). The McGill action planning system (MAPS): A strategy for building a vision. *Journal of The Association for Persons with Severe Handicaps, 14*, 205–215.

Vandercook, T., York, J., & MacDonald, C. (1991, Fall). Inclusive education (K–12). *Impact, 4*(3), 1, 20.

Voeltz, L.M. (1980). Children's attitudes toward handicapped peers. *American Journal of Mental Deficiency, 84*, 455–464.

Voeltz, L.M. (1982). Effects of structured interactions with severely handicapped peers on children's attitudes. *American Journal of Mental Deficiency, 86*, 380–390.

Voeltz, L.M., & Wuerch, B.B. (1981). Monitoring multiple behavioral effects of leisure activities training upon severely handicapped adolescents. In L.M. Voeltz, J.A. Apttel, & B.B. Wuerch (Eds.), *Leisure activities training for severely handicapped students: Instructional and educational strategies*. Honolulu: University of Hawaii, Department of Special Education.

Voeltz, L.M., Wuerch, B.B., & Wilcox, B. (1982). Leisure and recreation: Preparation for independence, integration, and self-fulfillment. In B. Wilcox & G.T. Bellamy, *Design of high school programs for severely handicapped students* (pp. 175–209). Baltimore: Paul H. Brookes Publishing Co.

Wehman, P., Renzaglia, A., & Bates, P. (1985). *Functional living skills for moderately and severely handicapped individuals*. Austin, TX: PRO-ED.

Wehman, P., & Schleien, S.J. (1980). Assessment and selection of leisure skills for severely handicapped individuals. *Education and Training of the Mentally Retarded, 15*(1), 50–57.

Wehman, P., & Schleien, S.J. (1981). *Leisure programs for handicapped persons: Adaptations, techniques, and curriculum*. Austin, TX: PRO-ED.

Wehman, P., Schleien, S.J., & Kiernan, J. (1980). Age appropriate recreation programs for severely handicapped youth and adults. *Journal of The Association for the Severely Handicapped, 5*, 395–407.

Wells, J., & Wells, M. (1995). *Teaching the possibilities: Community participation—Resource guide for transition planning*. St. Paul: Minnesota Department of Education.

Wessel, J. (1976). *I Can program*. Northbrook, IL: Hubbard Scientific.

West, P.C. (1982). Organizational stigma in metropolitan park and recreation agencies. *Therapeutic Recreation Journal, 16*(4), 35–41.

West, P.C. (1984). Social stigma and community recreation participation by the mentally and physically handicapped. *Therapeutic Recreation Journal, 18*(1), 40–49.

Wetherald, L., & Peters, J. (1986). *Mainstreaming: A total perspective*. Silver Spring, MD: Montgomery County Department of Recreation, Therapeutics Section.

Wheeler, M.A.T., Lynch, J.M., & Thom, C.D. (1984, May). *Barriers to leisure: Identification and program implications*. Paper presented at the meeting of the American Association on Mental Deficiency, Minneapolis, MN.

Whyte, D.N.B. (1992). Key trends and issues impacting local governments' recreation and park administration in the 1990s: A focus for strategic management and research. *Journal of Park and Recreation Administration, 10*(3), 89–106.

Wilhite, B., & Kleiber, D.A. (1992). The effects of Special Olympics participation on community integration. *Therapeutic Recreation Journal, 26*(4), 9–20.

Wilkenson, P.F. (1984). Providing integrated play environments for disabled children: A design or attitude problem? *Journal of Leisurability, 11*(3), 9–14.

Williams, B. (1979). The status of recreation for individuals with handicaps in Oregon park and recreation agencies. *Therapeutic Recreation Journal, 13*(2), 44–49.

Wolfensberger, W. (1972). *The principle of normalization in human services*. Toronto, Ontario, Canada: National Institute on Mental Retardation.

Wolfensberger, W. (1975). *The origin and nature of our institutional models*. Syracuse, NY: Human Policy Press.

Wolfensberger, W. (1983). Social role valorization: A proposed new term for the principle of normalization. *Mental Retardation, 21*, 234–239.

Wolfensberger, W. (1995). An "if this, then that" formulation of decisions related to social role valorization as a better way of interpreting it to people. *Mental Retardation, 33*, 163–169.

York, J. (1993, Spring/Summer). *What's working in inclusive education*. Minneapolis: University of Minnesota, Institute on Community Integration.

Young, J.T. (1986). A cognitive-behavioral approach to friendship disorders. In V. Derlaga & B. Winstead (Eds.), *Friendship and social interaction* (pp. 247–276). New York: Springer-Verlag.

Index

◆ ◆ ◆ ◆ ◆

Page numbers followed by "f" indicate figures; those followed by "t" indicate tables.